The Complete
WORD BOOK

Other books by Mary A. De Vries

The Practical Writer's Guide
Guide to Better Business Writing
The Prentice Hall Complete Secretarial Letter Book
The New American Handbook of Letter Writing
The New American Dictionary of Abbreviations

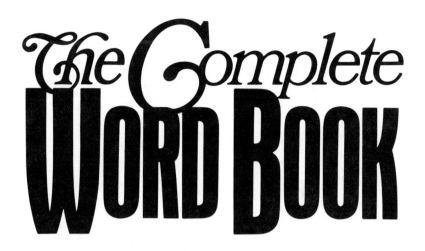

The Complete WORD BOOK

THE PRACTICAL GUIDE TO ANYTHING AND EVERYTHING YOU NEED TO KNOW ABOUT WORDS AND HOW TO USE THEM

MARY A. DE VRIES

PRENTICE HALL
Englewood Cliffs, New Jersey 07632

Prentice-Hall International (UK) Limited, *London*
Prentice-Hall of Australia Pty. Limited, *Sydney*
Prentice-Hall of Canada, Inc., *Toronto*
Prentice-Hall Hispanoamericana, S.A., *Mexico*
Prentice-Hall of India Private Limited, *New Delhi*
Prentice-Hall of Japan, Inc., *Tokyo*
Simon & Schuster Asia Pte. Ltd., *Singapore*
Editora Prentice-Hall do Brasil, Ltda., *Rio de Janeiro*

10 9 8 7 6 5 4 3 2 1

Library of Congress Cataloging-in-Publication Data

De Vries, Mary Ann.
  The complete word book : the practical guide to anything and
everything you need to know about words and how to use them / Mary
A. De Vries.
    p. cm.
  Includes index.
  ISBN 0-13-161902-0 (h). — ISBN 0-13-161894-6 (p)
  1. English language—Usage. 2. Vocabulary. I. Title.
PE1460.D44 1991
428—dc20   90-44372
                                                               CIP

ISBN   0-13-161902-0

ISBN   0-13-161894-6 (pbk)

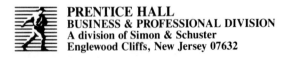
PRENTICE HALL
BUSINESS & PROFESSIONAL DIVISION
A division of Simon & Schuster
Englewood Cliffs, New Jersey 07632

Printed in the United States of America

How to Use
This Book

Unless you are a masochist, you won't enjoy it when the words you choose make you sound dull, arrogant, insensitive, immature, vague, abrupt, antagonistic, uneducated, negative, old-fashioned, or anything else that is equally unimpressive. But that's what happens to many of us when we fail to understand and profit from the power of words. *The Complete Word Book* will help you avoid these and other embarrassing mistakes. Not only does it provide an extensive compilation of helpful and harmful words, it is also a practical guide to the crucial matter of word choice. Indeed, it's like having many books—grammar, writing, spelling, style, word use/abuse dictionaries, and much more—all in one.

The Complete Word Book categorizes and lists all sorts of words (positive, negative, trite, slang, and many more) for quick and easy reference. Because most entries in its sixty-five chapters are arranged alphabetically, you can immediately draw on the word lists for every imaginable purpose. Whether you want to write a thank-you letter, to apply for a new job, to make a speech, to write a report, or to do anything else that requires words, you will find here an abundance of the "right" words to use as well as the "wrong" ones to avoid.

To get the greatest benefit possible from this book, first consider your weak points in spoken and written language.

Do you have trouble with spelling (chapters 41–48)?
Grammar (Chapters 24–34)?
Capitalization (Chapter 35)?
What about word choice; for example, do you say *infer* when you mean *imply* (Chapter 23)?

Do your messages sound tired and passive (Chapters 11, 15, 32)?
Is your tone negative (Chapter 7)?
Do you tend to repeat words and phrases too often (Chapter 12)?
Are you unintentionally using discriminatory language (Chapter 6)?
Do you sometimes use the wrong preposition (Chapter 28)?

Turn to the chapters pertaining to each problem on your list. There you'll find numerous lists and examples, as well as definitions and rules, that will help you make the right choice every time.

Because of the way the book is organized—with lists and examples—you will be able to select the word you need simply and quickly. For instance:

Assume that you are writing a letter to a client in which you want to sound vigorous and positive. Select words from the various chapters in Part I, "Words That Work," especially Chapter 5, "Action Words for Productive Messages." At the same time, edit out of your letter words from Part II, "Words to Avoid," especially Chapter 7, "Negative Words and Phrases," and Chapter 10, "Vague Words."

Follow this procedure with other written and spoken material such as business messages, speeches, reports, and various types of nonfiction or fiction.

The Complete Word Book contains sixty-seven chapters organized in twelve easy-to-use parts:

     I. Words That Work
    II. Words to Avoid
   III. New and Unusual Forms of Words
    VI. Words That Are Not What They Seem
     V. The Grammar of Words
    VI. The Style of Words
   VII. Spelling and Word Division
  VIII. Abbreviated Forms of Words
    IX. Foreign Words and Phrases
     X. Famous Words
    XI. Reference Potpourri
   XII. Glossary of Linguistics

In *The Complete Word Book* you will find familiar topics such as words that *please* . . . words that *antagonize* . . . words that add *variety* . . . words that are *discriminatory* . . . words that are too *general* . . . words that are *cliches* . . . words that are easily *confused.* You'll also find less familiar subjects, such as *oxymorons, slang, homophones,* and *neologisms.* Also included are numerous chapters with practical tips about the grammar, spelling, and style of words as well as eight chapters concerning abbreviated forms of words and seven chapters dealing with the proper use of foreign words and phrases. Chapter 65 has a large collection of quotable famous words to draw on for use in speeches and various written material. The reference section that follows consists of a medley of words and terms ranging from the names of the principal languages of the world to the Latin terms for North American mammals. The book concludes with a glossary of terms pertaining to language and word usage.

The Complete Word Book is intended for anyone whose speech consists of more than a grunt and whose written messages are more demanding than a grocery list. It is for people who simply enjoy words as well as those who realize that they must use words more carefully and judiciously to improve their social or professional status. *The Complete Word Book* is a practical guide to everything you need to know about words and how to use them properly and effectively.

Mary A. De Vries

Contents

How to Use This Book v

PART I. WORDS THAT WORK

Chapter 1. Words That Please 2
Chapter 2. The Use of Synonyms for Variety 6
Chapter 3. Transitional Words and Phrases 9
Chapter 4. The Use of Words for Emphasis 11
Chapter 5. Action Words for Productive Messages 13

PART II. WORDS TO AVOID

Chapter 6. Discriminatory Language 18
Chapter 7. Negative Words and Phrases 23
Chapter 8. Overused Intensifiers 26
Chapter 9. Jargon and Buzzwords 28
Chapter 10. Vague Words 31
Chapter 11. Trite Expressions 33
Chapter 12. Redundant Words and Phrases 37
Chapter 13. Euphemisms 43
Chapter 14. Pompous Expressions 45

Chapter 15. Cliches 48
Chapter 16. Words and Phrases That Antagonize 51

PART III.   NEW AND UNUSUAL FORMS OF WORDS

Chapter 17. A Dictionary of Neologisms 54
Chapter 18. A Dictionary of Contemporary Slang 58
Chapter 19. Oxymorons 61

PART IV.   WORDS THAT ARE NOT WHAT THEY SEEM

Chapter 20. Homophones: Words That Sound the Same but Have Different Meanings 64
Chapter 21. Homographs: Words That Look Alike but Have Different Meanings 70
Chapter 22. Misplaced Words That Change Your Meaning 74
Chapter 23. A Dictionary of Misused Words 76

PART V.   THE GRAMMAR OF WORDS

Chapter 24. The Eight Parts of Speech 92
Chapter 25. Plural Nouns That Need a Singular Verb 98
Chapter 26. Adjectives That Cannot Be Compared 100
Chapter 27. Common English Prepositions 101
Chapter 28. Commonly Misused Prepositions 103
Chapter 29. Common Conjunctions 105
Chapter 30. The Six Verb Tenses 107
Chapter 31. Common Irregular Verbs 110
Chapter 32. Assertive versus Passive Verbs 114
Chapter 33. Essential Grammatical Terms 116
Chapter 34. Idiomatic Expressions 121

PART VI. THE STYLE OF WORDS

Chapter 35.   Capitalization Style   126
Chapter 36.   The Use of Diacritical Marks   144
Chapter 37.   Words That Should Be in Italics   145
Chapter 38.   Words That Should Be in Quotation Marks   148
Chapter 39.   When to Use Words for Numbers   151
Chapter 40.   When to Use Words for Symbols   153

PART VII. SPELLING AND WORD DIVISION

Chapter 41.   Guide to Spelling   156
Chapter 42.   Commonly Misspelled Words   162
Chapter 43.   Guide to Prefixes   171
Chapter 44.   Common Prefixes   172
Chapter 45.   Guide to Suffixes   176
Chapter 46.   Common Suffixes   185
Chapter 47.   Guide to Writing Compounds   189
Chapter 48.   Common Compounds   194
Chapter 49.   Guide to Word Division   198

PART VIII. ABBREVIATED FORMS OF WORDS

Chapter 50.   Guide to Abbreviating   204
Chapter 51.   General Forms   209
Chapter 52.   Technical Forms   239
Chapter 53.   Organizations   267
Chapter 54.   Academic Degrees   298
Chapter 55.   States   303
Chapter 56.   Countries   305
Chapter 57.   Signs and Symbols   310

PART IX. FOREIGN WORDS AND TERMS

Chapter 58. Greek and Latin Roots and English
                Derivatives   316
Chapter 59. A Dictionary of Foreign Terms   318
Chapter 60. Overused Foreign Terms   324
Chapter 61. Familiar Foreign Words That Do Not Need
                Accents   326
Chapter 62. Alphabets of Familiar Foreign Languages   328
Chapter 63. Currencies of the World   364
Chapter 64. Nouns and Adjectives Denoting Nationality   369

PART X. FAMOUS WORDS

Chapter 65. Quotable Words for All Occasions   376

PART XI. REFERENCE POTPOURRI

Chapter 66. Special Names, Words, and Terms   434

PART XII. GLOSSARY OF LINGUISTICS

Chapter 67. Glossary of Linguistics   482
                Index   485

The Complete
WORD BOOK

Skill in expression consists in nothing else than steadily choosing the fittest among all possible words, idioms, and constructions.

—Excerpt from *Modern American Usage* by WILLIAM FOLLETT. Copyright © 1966 by Hill and Wang. Reprinted by permission of Hill and Wang, a division of Farrar, Straus and Giroux, Inc.

Part I

WORDS THAT WORK

1 Words That Please

2 The Use of Synonyms for Variety

3 Transitional Words and Phrases

4 The Use of Words for Emphasis

5 Action Words for Productive Messages

1

Words That Please

Certain words that we hear or read make us feel good. Perhaps they increase our self-esteem; perhaps they motivate us to do something we need or want to do; perhaps they alleviate stress or a feeling of apprehension about something we must face; or perhaps they simply help to promote happy feelings, a sense of excitement, or general well-being and confidence. Such words and expressions are positive by definition or in the context in which they are used. The following list contains examples of words you can use to make others feel better and to make your comments sound more positive. For words that have the opposite impact, see Chapter 7.

able	assure	compatible
absolutely	bargain	compliment(ary)
accommodate	basic	concur
admirable	beautiful	confident
admire	benefit	congratulate
advantage	boundless	congratulation
agree(able)	brilliant	conscientious
aid	capable	cooperate
alleviate	care(free)(ful)	cooperation
amicable	caring	cooperative
anticipate	certain	courteous
appreciate	cheerful	courtesy
appreciation	clear(ly)	creative
approval	commendable	declare
approve	common	dedicate
assist	compassion(ate)	dedication

definite
delight(ful)
demonstrate
depend(able)
desirable
desire
determine(d)
develop(ment)
direct
distinct
eager
easy
effective
efficient
elate(d)
energetic
enhance(ment)
enjoy
enrich(ed)
enthuse
enthusiasm
enthusiastic
establish
excellent
exceptional
excite(ment)
exciting
explore
express
extraordinary
facilitate
faithful
favor(able)
feasible
fervent
fine
first
flair
fluent
foremost
fortify

fortitude
fortunate
forward
free
freedom
fresh
friend(ly)
fulfill
future
genuine
generous
glamor(ous)
glorious
goal
good
grateful
great
greet(ings)
growth
guarantee
handle
handsome
happily
happy
harmonious
help(ful)
hero(ine)
high
honest(y)
honorable
hope(ful)
humorous
idea
ideal
imaginative
impetus
important
improve(ment)
incentive
increase
infallible

infinite
influence
ingenious
initiative
integrity
intelligence
intelligent
invaluable
invincible
joy(ful)(ous)
jubilant
kind(ness)
lasting
legitimate
liberal
liberate
liberty
lifelong
like(able)
live(ly)
longevity
love(ly)
loyal(ty)
luck(y)
lucrative
lustrous
luxurious
luxury
magical
magnetic
magnificence
magnificent
magnitude
majestic
majesty
major
manage(able)
markedly
marvel(ous)
massive
masterful

matchless
mellow
merit(orious)
might
miracle
modern
momentous
motivation
moving
multiply
mutual
natural
necessary
negotiate
negotiation
notable
numerous
nurture
nutrient
objective
oblige
obtain
offer
often
onward
open door
opportune
opportunity
optimism
orderly
original
palatable
palatial
particular
patronage
payment
peaceful
perfect(ly)
permanent
perpetual
persevere

persistence
personality
pertinent
play
pleasant
please
pleasure
plentiful
plenty
plus
popular(ity)
positive
prestige
pretty
produce
productive
proficient
progress(ive)
promise
prompt(ly)
propitious
prove
quick(ly)
reasonable
recommend
regular(ity)
repay
respect(ful)
responsible
rest(ful)
revenue
revitalize
revive
reward
right
safe(ty)
salutary
salute
sanction
sane
satisfaction

satisfactory
satisfy
scientific
secure
security
sensitive
service
shield
shine
significant
smile
smooth
solid
soothing
sparkling
special
spectacular
splendid
spontaneous
standard
staunch
steady
strength
stupendous
substantiate
subtle
success(ful)
superb
superior(ity)
superlative
support(ive)
supreme
sure(ly)
surmount(able)
surpass
sustain(ing)
sweet
sympathetic
sympathy
tempt(ing)
terrific

thank(s)	total	undoubtedly
thank you	tranquil(ity)	unforgettable
therapeutic	transform	unique
therapy	tremendous	unlimited
thorough	trust(worthy)	well
timely	uncommon	well-being
together(ness)	understand(able)(ing)	wonder(ful)

2

The Use of Synonyms for Variety

Business and social writers often search for just the right word to express an idea, or they may want to find substitutes for a word to avoid boring repetition of the same expression. The following list of synonyms includes selected examples of words that can be substituted in letters, reports, and other material to make your writing more interesting and varied. Some writers, however, may want to repeat the same word for emphasis (see Chapter 4). Using obscure synonyms merely for the sake of diversity suggests affectation and can be counterproductive, but, when chosen wisely, they can add spice to your writing and conversation.

abandon: leave, quit, discontinue
ability: capacity, capability, qualification, talent, knowledge
about: concerning, regarding, around, approximately
absolute: entire, complete, unconditional, unqualified
accept: receive, acquire, gain, agree
account: description, detail, report, statement, bill
accountable: answerable, responsible, amenable
accurate: correct, exact, precise, right, conclusive, reliable, dependable
achieve: do, accomplish, fulfill, effect, succeed
add: increase, extend, augment, amplify
adjust: arrange, regulate, adapt, accommodate
administer: dispense, execute, conduct, control, discharge, regulate, provide, manage
advise: counsel, direct, inform, tell, apprise, warn, instruct, suggest
agent: operator, actor, promoter, representative, instrument

aid: help, advance, encourage, assist, support, back

alleviate: mitigate, lessen, assuage, abate, relieve

allow: assent, authorize, empower, warrant, permit, let, grant, consent

announce: tell, reveal, report, state, declare, notify, communicate

apology: excuse, defense, acknowledgment, confession

arrange: adjust, classify, group, make, set, sort

business: occupation, calling, profession, work, trade, commerce, job, employment

cease: stop, quit, terminate, finish, conclude

chief: principal, leading, prime, first, main

comply: conform, concur, agree, consent

corroborate: strengthen, confirm, approve, support, affirm

decision: conclusion, opinion, resolution, result

demand: ask, request, require, want, implore

direction: way, goal, aim, end, bearing

doubt: question, mistrust, disbelieve, hesitate

efficient: competent, suitable, able, effective

error: blunder, mistake, fault, oversight, slip, indiscretion

expense: cost, price, expenditure, payment, amount, disbursement

fast: quick, rapid, swift, accelerated, brisk

forecast: prognosis, forethought, foresight, prediction, conjecture

foundation: base, basis, ground, origin

fundamental: basic, essential, principal, chief, primary

generate: make, produce, yield, cause, originate

good: honest, true, just, moral, fine, honorable, real, reputable, reliable, appropriate

habit: custom, practice, tendency, manner, method, style

illustration: example, comparison, case, instance, specimen

inclination: leaning, disposition, tendency, proneness

indicate: show, tell, point out, reveal, specify, signify

infinite: unlimited, immeasurable, eternal, countless, endless, perpetual

justice: fairness, impartiality, equity, lawfulness, truth, honor, right

large: big, vast, immense, extensive, enormous

long: lengthy, extended, lasting, continued, prolonged

make: do, form, construct, produce, establish, generate, accomplish

merit: worth, goodness, excellence, reward, value, credit

model: prototype, standard, example, form, design, pattern, copy, illustration

mutual: reciprocal, joint, common, similar, like, analogous

necessary: essential, expedient, required, urgent, imperative, binding

negligent: careless, thoughtless, remiss, neglectful, perfunctory

notify: declare, announce, inform, tell, express, communicate, convey, proclaim, reveal, report

objective: object, goal, aim, purpose, end

oppose: resist, check, combat, obstruct, contradict, rebuff, protest

pay: compensation, salary, reward, payment, remuneration, fee, wages, earnings

persuade: coax, prevail upon, entice, urge, convince, prompt, induce

plan: arrangement, scheme, design, map, project, view, undertaking, proposition, course of action, program

portion: division, share, part, fraction, parcel, subdivision, section, piece, slice

produce: bear, yield, give, make, breed, bring about, manufacture, create

promote: advance, encourage, organize, further, push, foster

quote: cite, repeat, note, illustrate, paraphrase, excerpt, extract, explain, confirm, detail

rational: wise, sensible, reasonable, intelligent, analytical, discerning, thoughtful, clear-headed

regulate: arrange, organize, direct, supervise, control, systematize

report: story, statement, account, description, announcement, communication

rule: sway, regulation, direction, order, canon, precept, guide, formula

satisfy: pay, repay, settle, accommodate, remedy, gratify, fulfill

simple: plain, easy, common, humble, elementary

stimulate: stir, rouse, provoke, kindle

support: maintain, uphold, sustain, keep, preserve, assist, advance

temporary: transitory, short, brief, passing, momentary

therefore: accordingly, consequently, since, hence

tool: instrument, mechanism, apparatus, utensil, implement, machine

true: real, accurate, trustworthy, honorable, actual, sincere, genuine, factual

urgent: pressing, compelling, necessary, imperative, grave

valid: sound, substantial, powerful, real, authentic, well-founded, effective

worthless: valueless, useless, unproductive, profitless

zenith: top, pinnacle, summit, apex

3

Transitional Words and Phrases

Words and phrases such as *therefore, in fact,* and *for instance* can be used to make one sentence or one paragraph flow smoothly into another. Without this type of transition, the material might sound abrupt or choppy: "Chemical sensitivity may cause a variety of ailments. Without adequate tests, *however,* the source of any affliction can be difficult to pinpoint." If you eliminate the word *however,* the transition from the first to the second sentence will be somewhat abrupt.

The following list contains examples of transitional words and phrases that can be used to move a reader clearly and smoothly from idea to idea. But be wary of overuse; too many *therefores* and *howevers* can be distracting and counterproductive.

accordingly	because	for example
after all	besides	for instance
afterwards	but	for this purpose
again	by reason	for this reason
also	clearly	furthermore
although	consequently	hence
and yet	doubtless	however
anyhow	equally important	immediately
and then	eventually	in addition
as a result	evidently	in any case
at any rate	finally	in any event
at last	first (second, etc.)	inasmuch as
at length	for	in brief
at the same time	forasmuch as	in comparison

in conclusion	nevertheless	since
in contrast	next	soon
in fact	no doubt	still
in like manner	notwithstanding	that is
in other words	obviously	then
in short	on account of	thence
in sum(mary)	on the contrary	therefore
in the meantime	on the other hand	thereupon
later	on the whole	thus
likewise	otherwise	to be sure
meanwhile	perhaps	to(ward) this end
moreover	possibly	whence
namely	rather	wherefore
naturally	similarly	yet

4

The Use of Words for Emphasis

You can emphasize the points you want to make in various ways. Using italics, provided they are not overused, is one way (words underlined in manuscript copy are set in italics in printed copy). Using an active verb (I *said*) instead of a passive verb (it *was said*) is another way. Repeating key words can be effective, but be careful to avoid the appearance of unintentional, careless repetition. Being concise and direct (avoiding wordiness) will also help to make your points clearer and more forceful. In addition, choosing and advantageously positioning words in a sentence, as well as using proper punctuation, are all necessary ingredients for achieving the desired degree of emphasis. Sometimes including a compound personal pronoun will add emphasis too. Finally, placing an adverb before rather than after the verb in a sentence can add emphasis.

Italics: In this job an *error* is synonymous with a *catastrophe.*
Active voice: Read all of the instructions before starting work (*not* All of the instructions should be read before starting work).
Repetition: The seasons come and go, fashions come and go, businesses come and go, but humankind's quest to survive prevails.
Concise, direct statements: The fine for illegal parking has been increased to $20 per vehicle per violation.
Correct word choice and position: The fossil-fuel crisis will be discussed at the next Board of Realtors meeting (*not* At the next Board of Realtors meeting, fossil fuels will be discussed.)
Punctuation: Property taxes—indeed, all local taxes—are bound to increase this year.

Compound personal pronoun: I wrote the play myself (*not* I wrote the
   play).
Position of adverb: We recently bought a new car (*not* We bought a new
   car recently).

5

Action Words for Productive Messages

If you have ever studied a persuasive sales letter or an appealing proposal or an effective response, you know that word choice is an all-important ingredient when the writer wants the message to effect a certain result, that is, to be productive. Use the following list when you want your message to have an impact on the recipient. (Note that you can change the tense as needed: *arrange/arranged, construct/constructed, launch/launched,* and so on.) See also Chapter 32 in Part V, "Assertive versus Passive Verbs."

accept	assist	convert
accommodate	begin	cooperate
accompany	believe	coordinate
accelerate	benefit	correlate
achieve	budget	correspondence
acquire	build	create
act	clarity	deal
administer	command	debate
advise	compare	decide
affect	compel	delegate
allot	compete	deliver
analyze	complete	demonstrate
appear	compose	depend
appreciate	conceive	describe
approve	conduct	design
aspire	construct	detail
arrange	consume	determine
assemble	control	develop

devise	head	mediate
discover	help	merit
discuss	hire	monitor
display	honor	motivate
distribute	hope	negotiate
direct	hurry	nominate
double	imagine	normalize
earn	implement	obtain
educate	improve	officiate
effect	improvise	operate
eliminate	increase	order
emphasize	indict	organize
enact	induce	orient
encourage	influence	originate
endorse	initiate	overcome
energize	innovate	participate
engineer	inspire	pay
enhance	install	perceive
enthuse	instruct	perfect
establish	insure	perform
evaluate	integrate	persuade
exceed	intensify	pilot
excel	intercede	pinpoint
exhibit	interpret	pioneer
expand	invent	place
expedite	judge	plan
experience	justify	please
explain	key	possess
facilitate	keynote	practice
form	know	praise
finalize	last	prepare
finance	launch	preside
formalize	lead	procure
formulate	license	produce
found	like	profess
fulfill	locate	progress
gauge	maintain	promote
generate	manage	prompt
govern	manufacture	propel
graduate	market	propose
handle	master	prove

provide
pursue
realize
reason
recede
receive
recognize
recommend
reconcile
reduce
refer
regulate
reign
reinforce
relate
relieve
reorganize
repeat
report
research
revamp
review
revise
route

satisfy
save
schedule
secure
seem
seize
sense
serve
service
show
simplify
solve
spark
stabilize
stimulate
streamline
structure
study
substantiate
succeed
supersede
supervise
support
suppress

surprise
teach
tend
think
tie
tolerate
train
transfer
transform
treble
try
turn
understand
unify
use
vacate
value
verify
vitiate
win
wrestle
write

The ill and unfit choice of words wonderfully obstructs the understanding

—FRANCIS BACON
Advancement of Learning

Part II

WORDS TO AVOID

6 Discriminatory Language

7 Negative Words and Phrases

8 Overused Intensifiers

9 Jargon and Buzzwords

10 Vague Words

11 Trite Expressions

12 Redundant Words and Phrases

13 Euphemisms

14 Pompous Expressions

15 Cliches

16 Words and Phrases That Antagonize

6

Discriminatory Language

Most people don't realize it when they are using discriminatory language. The employer who refers to the *men* and the *girls* (instead of *men* and *women*) on his staff usually speaks out of ignorance. Someone who refers to a *black scientist* scheduled to give a lecture when there is no reason to call attention to the person's race usually speaks with an unconscious bias. A person who mentions that his next-door neighbor is *crippled* (instead of *disabled* or *handicapped*) probably speaks with unintentional insensitivity.

The distinction that was formerly made between masculine and feminine forms has largely disappeared in contemporary English. Although writers and speakers still designate gender in family members (*mother, father, brother, sister, uncle, aunt*), in titles (*he, she, Mr., Mrs., Miss, Ms.*), and the like, it is now considered old-fashioned and sexist to use feminine word endings such as *-ess (deaconess), -ette (majorette), -enne (equestrienne),* and *-rix (testatrix).*

The fact that discriminatory language may be unintentional does not excuse it, and everyone should make an effort to avoid it. The following list contains examples of common forms of discriminatory language and suggests substitutes for the offensive words. These substitutes are appropriate for most situations and general usage, but there may be exceptions. If a school's *official* degree title is listed as "*bachelor* of arts," for example, you should use that wording in reference to the degree in that school; otherwise, in general references to this degree level, you could change the wording to "*baccalaureate* degree."

adman/advertising man/adwoman/advertising woman: ad(vertising) agent, ad(vertising) writer, advertising representative, advertiser

administratrix: administrator
adulteress: adulterer
advance man: advance agent
adventuress: adventurer
airman: aviator, flier, pilot
alderman: alderperson, member of the town board, town board
  member
altar boy: altar child, altar youngster, altar youth
alumna(e)/alumni/alumnus: former student, graduate
ambassadress: ambassador
anchorman/anchorwoman: anchor, anchorperson
assemblyman: assembly member
authoress: author
average man: average person
aviatrix: aviator, pilot
bachelor: single person
bachelor's degree: baccalaureate degree
bandmaster: band conductor, band leader
barmaid/barman: bartender
beachboy: beach attendant
bellboy: bell captain, bellhop
black worker/black scientist/black teacher/etc.: worker, scientist, teacher, etc.
bondsman/bondswoman: bonder, bondsperson, guarantor, surety
brotherly love/sisterly love: human love
busboy/busgirl: busperson
businessman/businesswoman: businessperson, executive, manager
cameraman/camerawoman: camera operator, photographer,
  videographer
cattleman: cattle owner, cattle rancher
chairman/chairwoman: chair, chairperson, moderator, presiding
  officer
checkout boy/checkout girl: checker
choirmaster: choir director
churchman/churchwoman: a church member
cleaning lady/cleaning man: cleaner, domestic worker, janitor
comedienne: comedian, humorist
congressman/congresswoman: member of Congress, representative, senator
craftsman/craftswoman: crafter, craftsperson, handcrafter
crewman: crew member

crippled: disabled, handicapped

deaf and dumb: speech and hearing handicapped, speech and hearing
  impaired

delivery boy/delivery girl/delivery man/delivery woman:
  delivery person

directress: director

disadvantaged minority: Asian, black, Mexican-American, etc.,
  heritage

divorce/divorcee: single

editress: editor

everyman: average person

executrix: executor

fatherland/motherland: homeland

fiance/fiancee: betrothed

fit: seizure

foreman: manager, supervisor

founding father: founder

gentleman/gentlewoman: aristocrat, courteous person,
  gentleperson

Girl Friday/Man Friday: aide, right arm

handyman: handyperson, odd-jobber

he/him/his: he or she, him or her, his or hers (*or rewrite to use* they)

head master/head mistress: director, head, principal

heiress: heir

heroine: hero

hostess: host

househusband/housewife: homemaker

husband/wife: spouse

insane: emotionally or mentally disabled

insurance man/insurance woman: insurance agent

Jack-of-all-trades: handyperson, person of all trades

Jewess: Jew

lady: aristocrat, courteous person, gentleperson

ladylike: courteous, proper, well bred

landlady/landlord: landowner, manager, property owner

maid: domestic, servant

mailman: mail carrier, postal carrier

manageress: manager

manhood/womanhood: adulthood

man-hour: hour, person-hour, work-hour

mankind: civilization, humankind, people, society

manmade: artificial, constructed, handmade, machine made, synthetic

manpower: personnel, work force

manservant: servant

masseur/masseuse: massager, physiotherapist

master/mistress: head, leader, owner, ruler, superior, teacher

masterful: authoritative, excellent, skillful

master of ceremonies/mistress of ceremonies: host

master plan: model plan, prototype

mayoress: mayor

men and girls: men and women

middleman: intermediary, jobber, middleperson, wholesaler

millionairess: millionaire

Miss/Mrs.: Ms.

Mother Nature: nature

Negress: black, Negro

newsman/newswoman: editor, newscaster, reporter, news writer

office boy/office girl: office employee, office helper, office worker

ombudsman: ombudsperson

pageboy/pagegirl: page

paperboy/papergirl: paper carrier

patrolman/patrolwoman: patrol officer, police officer

policeman/policewoman: police officer

postmaster/postmistress: head of the Post Office, postal chief, postal director

priestess: priest

proprietress: proprietor

retarded/semiretarded: learning disabled, slow learner

rewrite man: rewriter

saleslady/salesman: sales clerk, salesperson

schoolmarm/schoolmaster: educator, principal, teacher

seaman: sailor

serviceman/servicewoman: member of the armed services; repairer, service representative

she/her/hers: she or he, her or him, hers or his (*or rewrite to use* they)

spokesman/spokeswoman: representative, spokesperson

starlet: actor, aspiring star

statesman/stateswoman: statesperson

steward/stewardess: flight attendant

tailoress: tailor

testatrix: testator

toastmaster/toastmistress: toastperson, presider
waitress: waiter
weathergirl/weatherman: weathercaster, weather reporter
widow/widower: surviving spouse
wives/husbands: spouses
workman: worker
workmen's compensation: worker's compensation

7

Negative Words and Phrases

Some words have unflattering, pessimistic, or negative connotations in certain contexts; they may make you sound unsure or weak. They may even create feelings of irritation, anger, rebellion, apprehension, or dissatisfaction in the listener or reader.

Although sometimes a negative word such as *pessimistic* is more precise than another word or term, often a milder, less critical word such as *doubtful* is preferred. In such cases, substitute a synonym that fits the context of your material. The following list contains examples of words that, depending on the context, could have an adverse impact on a listener or reader and should be avoided or used judiciously if your intent is to create a favorable impression and a positive response.

For a list of loaded words and expressions, see Chapter 16. For a list of positive expressions, see Chapter 1.

abandon(ed)	affected	apology
abhor(ed)	afraid	argue(d)
abolish(ed)	alarm	aversion
abominable	alibi	bad
abrasive	allege(d)	banal
abscond(ed)	altercation	bankrupt
absurd	ambiguous	beware
abuse(d)	anger(ed)	bias(ed)
accident	anguish(ed)	blame
acrimony	antagonize(d)	bleak
admonish(ed)	anxiety	calamity
adversity	apathy	callous

cancel(ed)	fail(ure)	in vain
careless	fall	invalid
censure(d)	false	irritate(d)
chaos	fatal	liable
cheap	fault	long winded
claim(ed)	fear(ed)	lose
clash(ed)	fiasco	ludicrous
collapse(d)	flagrant	meager
collusion	flat	meddle(d)
commonplace	flimsy	mediocre
complain(ed)	forsake	menial
complaint	foul	misfortune
contaminate(d)	gloss over	misinform(ed)
contempt	gratuitous	misrepresent(ed)
control(led)	grave	muddle(d)
crisis	grief	mundane
crocked	hamper(ed)	naive
cruel	hapless	negate(d)
damage(d)	harass(ed)	neglect(ed)
deadlock(ed)	hardship	negligence
deceive(d)	hate(d)	nullify
deception	hazy	oblique
decline(d)	hinder(ed)	obscure(d)
defeat(ed)	hurt(ful)	obstinate
defy, defied	idiot	opinionate(d)
demand(ed)	ignoble	overbearing
deny, denied	ignorant	oversight
deplore(d)	illiterate	partisan
desert(ed)	imitation	pessimist(ic)
despise(d)	immature	plausible
destroy(ed)	impass	pernicious
disadvantage(d)	impede(d)	precipitate(d)
disaster	implicate(d)	prejudice(d)
discredit(ed)	impossible	premature
dismal	improvident	pretentious
dispute(d)	inadequate	quibble(d)
dominate(d)	incompetent	radical
dread(ed)	indulge	recalcitrant
evict(ed)	insidious	repulsive
exaggerate(d)	insist(ed)	rude
extravagant	insolvent	ruin

ruthless
sarcastic
senseless
shameful
shirk
shortsighted
shrink
sketchy
slack
slow
split hairs
squander(ed)
stagnant
standstill

stereotype
straggling
stubborn
stunt(ed)
stupid
superficial
superfluous
taint(ed)
tamper(ed)
tardy
timid
tolerable
troublesome
ugly

unfair
unfortunate
unnerve(d)
unsuccessful
untimely
useless
usurp
verbiage
victim
wanton
waste(ful)
weak(ness)
worry
wrong(ful)

8

Overused Intensifiers

A word that intensifies or emphasizes another word that it modifies is called an *intensifier*, for example, *rather* good, *really* pretty, *quite* interesting. Intensifiers often occupy the same position in a sentence that the word *very* would occupy: "He called *very* (*rather, quite, really,* and so on) often."

When the intensifier modifies an adjective (*very* good movie), it functions like an adverb. But some adjectives ending in *-self* such as *himself* or *yourself* are intensifiers too: "You *yourself* have experienced the same thing." Although intensifiers can serve a necessary and legitimate function, those used as adverbs are often overused and unnecessary. In such cases they simply contribute to wordiness. The following intensifiers tend to clutter our language unnecessarily and can usually be deleted without affecting our meaning. For example, "It is cold today" is as clear as the needlessly wordy "It is *rather* cold today."

best	really
more	somewhat
most	such
pretty	too
quite	very
rather	

The following are common adjectival intensifiers. Although these intensifiers are sometimes useful when special emphasis is desired, they should be used sparingly. For example, in most contexts "I am going to the concert too" is as clear as the needlessly wordy "I *myself* am going to the concert too."

herself   ourself
himself   ourselves
itself   themselves
myself   thyself
oneself   yourself
one's self   yourselves

9

Jargon and Buzzwords

Jargon (*saleswise, functional, prioritize, cash in on,* etc.) is a specialized form of slang, or shorthand, that usually pertains to one or more trades or professions. Although specialized terminology may be useful or even essential at work and although members of a particular trade or profession often find that it is easier to communicate by using their own technical language, to others outside the workplace, the jargon frequently is a pretentious, often less precise or unfamiliar, substitute for the actual concrete term it replaces. *Shop talk* (such as *alibi copy,* meaning *duplicate of the original copy*) is a particularly specialized form of jargon and should never be used with outsiders. *Gobbledygook* (such as *facilitize,* meaning *make easier*) is a particularly vague, abstract form of jargon and should be avoided in all situations. A *buzzword* (such as *optimize,* meaning *enhance, improve,* or *increase*) is an important-sounding word or phrase, often with less clarity of meaning, that people use in the belief that it will impress others. A careful, skilled writer or speaker will use a more concrete and more accurate term.

The following words and phrases are examples of jargon and buzzwords that should be avoided unless the term is essential to express a particular attitude or meaning or is limited to accepted shorthand within a particular office or work setting. Some terms such as *interface,* meaning the connection of machines, are acceptable in their technical context but are misused in other contexts. *Interface,* for instance, should not be used to mean a meeting of people. Some terms such as *enhance* or *projection* are not jargon but are valid terms when used in a proper context. However, writers or speakers may overuse them or use them in inappropriate situations so that they begin to sound like business jargon. In such cases there often is another, less pretentious term that could be used to avoid this.

See also Chapter 14, "Pompous Expressions," and Chapter 18, "A Dictionary of Contemporary Slang."

advance planning: planning
at liberty: unemployed
ballpark figure: estimate
bottom line: cost or price of something
bounce around: think about and discuss something
budgetwise: in terms of or in regard to the budget
causative factor: cause
contact: call, write to, speak to, etc.
deplane: get off the plane
downsize: reduction in size
expertise: special knowledge or ability
finalize: end, finish
frame of reference: viewpoint, theory
gameplan: plan, approach
graveyard shift: in business, from midnight until early morning
hardware: equipment
hype: to build up something by exaggerating its importance or appeal
inaugurate: begin
infrastructure: underlying foundation or basic framework
input: ideas, comments
interface: cooperate, interact, meet
interpersonal: human, personal
justify: in printing, to make the lines in both sides of a column equal
kick an idea around: discuss an idea
know the ropes: know the procedure
logistical: relating to symbolic logic
Mickey Mouse: petty, unnecessary
moot point: debatable point
the nature of: *omit*
no strings attached: no obligation or conditions
off the record: confidentially
off line: computer that is not controlled by a central machine
on line: computer system where central processor controls the operation
operative: defining, determining, important
optimize: enhance, improve, increase

optimum: most
paradigm: archetype, model, outline, pattern
parameter: boundary, constraint, guideline
phase: part, stage
prioritize: list in order of priority
prior to: before
responsive: responding, sensitive
rollback: return to lower prices
rollover: reinvestment
scenario: estimate, event, outline, possibility, situation
smart money: predictions of one who knows best
stonewall: present an inflexible front
systematize: to arrange according to a plan, to order
think tank: an organization or group that conducts interdisciplinary research
time frame: length of time
update: bring up to date
user friendly: relatively easy to use
viable: capable of working or developing
whole ball of wax: everything
workup: routine diagnostic procedures

10

Vague Words

The only way to be certain that people understand your message is to use specific concrete words and phrases. Vague, abstract terms are more likely to annoy and confuse than to impress anyone. Sometimes, however, a general word may be necessary when the specific term is unknown. In those cases, it may be necessary to add a qualifying phrase to explain the general word. Perhaps, for instance, you want to refer to a book of quotations but don't know the title. The word *book* is so general that it needs the qualifier *of quotations.* But in most cases, a specific word or phrase is known, and then there is no excuse for using vague, abstract terms such as the examples shown here.

activity: exercise, fund raising, word processing
animals: cats, dogs, squirrels
book: book of poems, the book *Ode to Spring*
building: clubhouse, courthouse, high school
color: blue, green, orange
concerns: interests, questions, worries
design: drawing, plan, scheme, sketch
distribute: hand out, mail, scatter
emotion: anger, joy, shock
enlighten: acquaint, educate, persuade
flowers: marigolds, petunias, tulips
food: eggs, ham, pizza, steak
good: accurate, enjoyable, honest, valuable
great: large, magnanimous, wide
happy: buoyant, cheerful, excited

hot: burning, eager, passionate
impeccable: accurate, neat, spotless
increase: augment, raise, widen
journey: bus tour, ocean voyage, wandering
juvenile: young boy, twelve-year-old girl
keen: eager, piercing, witty
kind: affectionate, charitable, humane, soft-hearted
liquor: peach brandy, Rhine wine, Scotch whiskey
laborious: backbreaking, irksome, tiresome
meat: beef, fish, pork, poultry
misfortune: bankruptcy, car accident, head injury
neat: attractive, clean, orderly, tidy
nice: attractive, colorful, funny, interesting, polite
obligation: debt, duty, promise, responsibility
operations: manufacture, editorial production, work
pay: allowance, fee, honorarium, salary
properties: assets, characteristics, features
quell: defeat, calm, overthrow, silence
quest: adventure, expedition, pursuit, search
raw: crude, inexperienced, unprepared
regard: consider, notice, observe, value
saying: aphorism, epigram, proverb, quotation
system: method, plan, scheme
tools: hammer, pliers, screwdriver
tree: ash tree, maple tree, oak tree
ugly: deformed, homely, quarrelsome, unpleasant
unfit: incapable, inappropriate, unhealthy
vehicle: bicycle, car, motorcycle, truck
vulgar: common, obscene, rude
went: drove, ran, walked
work: filing, typing, writing
youth: boy, girl

11

Trite Expressions

Trite expressions, including cliches and hackneyed language, are expressions that are overused to the point of exhaustion. *Few and far between* is a good example. Some of the trite expressions such as *beg to advise* are stilted and excessively formal today, even though they were once fashionable in correspondence and other writing. Others, such as *I have before me,* are stuffy and awkward ways of saying something such as *thank you for* or *I received.* Modern social and business writers have abandoned such stiff, verbose language.

The following list contains examples of trite expressions that should be avoided in both written and spoken language. See also the list of redundant expressions, pompous words, and cliches in Chapters 12, 14, and 15 and the dictionary of contemporary slang in Chapter 18.

absence makes the heart grow
  fonder
acid test
acknowledge receipt of
add insult to injury
age before beauty
all in all
all that glitters is not gold
all things being equal
all work and no play
and oblige
apple of one's eye
ascertain

as luck would have it
as per
at all times
at one fell swoop
at an early date
at this time
at your convenience
bark up the wrong tree
bated breath
beat a hasty retreat
beg to acknowledge
beg to advise
beg to state

best foot forward
best-laid plans of mice and men
better late than never
beyond the pale
bitter end
blood is thicker than water
blow one's horn
blushing bride
bolt from the blue
bone to pick
born with a silver spoon
brave as a lion
breathe a sigh of relief
bright and early
bright future
bring home the bacon
budding genius
busy as a beaver
busy as a bee
butterflies in my stomach
caught red-handed
checkered career
cherchez la femme
chip off the old block
clear as mud
cock-and-bull story
cold as ice
cold feet
cold sweat
consummate the project
contents carefully noted
cool as a cucumber
conspicuous by his absence
cradle of the deep
cut a long story short
dead as a doornail
dead giveaway
depths of despair
die is cast
dog days
doomed to disappointment

down my alley
draw the line
drown one's sorrows
drunk as a skunk
duck out of water
dull thud
duly
each and every
ear to the ground
eat, drink, and be merry
enclosed please find
encounter difficulty
enlighten
esteemed favor
et tu, Brute
exception proves the rule
eyes of the world
face the music
fair sex
far cry
fast and loose
fat's in the fire
favor with a selection
feather in his cap
feel his oats
few and far between
few well-chosen words
fight like a tiger
fill the bill
filthy lucre
fine and dandy
first and foremost
fish out of water
flash in the pan
flat as a pancake
flesh and blood
fly off the handle
fond farewell
fool and his money are soon parted
fools rush in where angels fear to
    tread

free as the air
fresh as a daisy
garden variety
gentle as a lamb
get one's number
get the sack
get the upper hand
get up on the wrong side of the bed
get what I mean?
gild the lily
God's country
good time was had by all
grain of salt
grand and glorious
graphic account
green as grass
green with envy
Grim Reaper
grin like a Cheshire cat
hale and hearty
hand-to-mouth
hapless victim
happy as a lark
happy pair
hard row to hoe
haul over the coals
have before me
head over heels
heart of gold
hereto
herewith
high on the hog
hungry as a bear
if truth be told
ignorance is bliss
in re
inspiring sight
interesting to note
intestinal fortitude
in the event that
in the final analysis

in the long run
irons in the fire
irony of fate
it goes without saying
it is requested that
it stands to reason
jig is up
land-office business
last but not least
last straw
law unto himself
lean and hungry look
lean over backward
leave in the lurch
left-handed compliment
let one's hair down
let the cat out of the bag
like a newborn babe
limp as a rag
little did I think
lock, stock, and barrel
mad dash
make a clean breast of it
make ends meet
make hay while the sun shines
make no bones about it
make things hum
mantle of snow
master of all he surveys
method to this madness
mind your *p*'s and *q*'s
miss the boat
moot question
more easily said than done
more than meets the eye
Mother Nature
motley crew
naked truth
necessary evil
needs no introduction
never a dull moment

nip in the bud
not to be sneezed at
number is up
of a high order
on the ball
open-and-shut case
opportunity knocks but twice
our Miss (Jones, etc.)
out of sight, out of mind
over a barrel
pay the piper
penny for your thoughts
per annum
pillar of society
play fast and loose
play second fiddle
play up to
point with pride
pretty as a picture
pretty penny
pull your leg
pull the wool over his eyes
pull up stakes
pure as the driven snow
put a bug in one's ear
put on the dog
rack one's brains
raining cats and dogs
read the riot act
recent date
red as a beet
rendered a selection
ring true
rub the wrong way
sadder but wiser
save for a rainy day
seal one's fate

self-made man
sell like hot cakes
set up shop
seventh heaven
sick and tired
sight to behold
sing like a bird
sow wild oats
start the ball rolling
steal one's thunder
stick in one's craw
stir up a hornet's nest
strong as an ox
stubborn as a mule
stuffed shirt
take it easy
take pleasure in
thanking you in advance
that is to say
throw the book at
time hangs heavy
tired as a dog
tit for tat
too funny for words
too many irons in the fire
truth to tell
turn over a new leaf
under separate cover
valued order
view with alarm
wee small hours
wet to the skin
wide-open spaces
wish to state
without further ado
you can say that again
your guess is as good as mine

12

Redundant Words and Phrases

Redundant means superfluous, or exceeding what is normal or necessary. Some writers believe that if using a few words is good, using many words must be better. Sometimes this is true. Advertising messages often contain intentional repetition to imprint their messages on the readers' or the viewers' minds. Some famous historical figures, both writers and speakers, also have used repetition effectively. Careless wordiness, however, is rarely effective. Expressions such as *final conclusion* (for *conclusion*) or *help and assist* (for either *help* or *assist* but not both) are not used by careful writers and speakers. The following list contains such superfluous expressions and the preferred short form.

absolutely essential: essential
a certain person: a person
accounted for by: due to *or* caused by
add the point that: add that
advance warning: warning
advise and inform: advise *or* inform
a great deal of: much
a great many: many
all of the: all
along the line of: like *or* in
a majority of: most
an example of this is the fact that: for example
another aspect of the situation to be considered is: as for
a number of: about
appraise and determine: determine *or* appraise

are engaged in: are *or* are in
are of the opinion that: think that
arrange to send: send
as regards: for *or* about
as related to: for *or* about
as to: about
at a later date: later
at a meeting held in: at a meeting in
at a time when: when
at the hour of: at
at the present writing: now
based on the fact that: because
be in possession of: have
be of the opinion that: believe
bright and shiny: bright *or* shiny
by means of this: by this
chemotherapeutic agent: drug
chief protagonist: protagonist
close proximity to: close, proximity, *or* near to
collect together: collect
color of blue: blue
completely unanimous: unanimous
complete monopoly: monopoly
concerning the nature of: about
conditions that exist in: conditions in
cooperate together: cooperate
deeds and actions: deeds *or* actions
demand and insist: demand *or* insist
depreciate in value: depreciate
depressed socioeconomic area: slum
due to the fact that: because
during the course of: during
during the time that: while
during the year of: during
each and every: each *or* every
eliminate completely: eliminate
except in a small number of cases: usually
exhibit a tendency to: tend to
few in number: few
final conclusion: conclusion *or* end
first and foremost: first *or* foremost

first began: began
for the purpose of: for *or* to
for the reason that: because
from the point of view of: for or to
future plans: plans
future prospect: prospect
green in color: green
had occasion to be: was
have an input into: contribute to
help and assist: help *or* assist
hopes and aspirations: hopes *or* aspirations
i.e.: *avoid*
if at all possible: if possible
immediately and at once: immediately
in about three days' time: in about three days
in advance of: before
inasmuch as: because
in both of them: in both *or* in them
in case: if
in case of: if
in close proximity: near
in favor of: for *or* to
in light of the fact that: because
in many cases: often
in many instances: often
in order to: to
in rare cases: rarely
in reference to: about
in regard to: about
in relation with: with
inside of: inside
in spite of the fact that: although
in terms of: in *or* for
in the case of: regarding
in the case that: if *or* when
in the city of: in
in the course of: during
in the event that: if
in the field of: in
in the first place: first
in the majority of instances: usually

in the matter of: about
in the nature of: like
in the neighborhood of: about
in the normal course of our procedure: normally
in the not-too-distant future: soon
in the opinion of this writer: in my opinion *or* I believe
in the vicinity of: near
in view of the fact that: therefore
involve the necessity of: require
is defined as: is
is dependent on: depends on
is indicative of: indicates
it is clear that: therefore *or* clearly
it is observed that: *omit*
it is often the case that: often *or* frequently
it is our conclusion in light of investigation: we conclude that
it should be noted that the: the
it stands to reason: *omit*
it was noted that if: if
it would not be unreasonable to assume: I assume
large in number: many
large in size: large
leaving out of consideration: disregarding
making an examination of: examine
many in number: many
marketing representative: salesperson
may possibly: may
mental attitude: attitude
month of January: January
mutual compromise: compromise
not of a high order of accuracy: inaccurate
notwithstanding the fact that: although
obligation and responsibility: obligation *or* responsibility
of considerable magnitude: big, large, *or* great
of very minor importance: unimportant
on account of the conditions described: because of the conditions
on account of the fact that: because
on a few occasions: occasionally
one or another reason: some reason
on the grounds that: because
on the order of: about

out of: of
outside of: outside
owing to the fact that: since *or* because
perform an analysis of: analyze
perhaps it may be that you: perhaps *or* it may be that *or* you may
personal friend: friend
positive growth: growth
prior to: before
proceed to investigate: investigate
prompt and speedy: prompt, quick, *or* speedy
put in an appearance: appeared
refer to as: call
refuse and decline: refuse *or* decline
relative to this: about this
renovate like new: renovate
resultant effect: effect
right and proper: right *or* proper
round in shape: round
short minute: minute *or* moment
sincere and good wishes: sincere *or* good wishes
small in size: small
small in number: few
solid facts: facts
someone or other: someone
some reason or another: some reason
spell out in detail: spell out *or* detail
subsequent to: after
successful triumph: triumph
take into consideration: consider
taking this factor into consideration, it is apparent that: there-
    fore *or* therefore it seems
temporary reprieve: reprieve
that is: *avoid*
the bulk of: most
the color of yellow: yellow
the data show that we can: we can
the existence of: *avoid*
the fact that he had arrived: his arrival
the foregoing: the, this, that, these, *or* those
the fullest possible: most, completely, *or* fully
the only difference being that: except

the question as to whether: whether
there are not very many: few are
the sum of five dollars: five dollars
the year of 19XX: 19XX
tire and fatigue: tire
to be sure: *avoid*
to summarize the above: in sum *or* in summary
true facts: facts
uniform and invariable: uniform
unjust and unfair: unjust *or* unfair
variously different: different
within the realm of possibility: possible *or* possibly
with reference to: about
with the exception of: except
with the result that: so that
with this in mind, it is clear that: therefore *or* clearly

13

Euphemisms

Euphemisms are agreeable or inoffensive substitutes for expressions that might offend someone or suggest something unpleasant. Whether or not an expression is offensive depends on the audience. One person might think that the word *belly* is crude and would prefer *abdomen;* another person might prefer *belly.* Although the justification for using euphemisms such as those shown below is based on a sensitivity toward the feelings of others, the use of such substitutes is sometimes carried to the point of silliness (e.g., *preowned* car). In most cases, use the actual term rather than the euphemism unless doing so would offend the reader or listener.

abdomen: belly
amenity center: public toilet
archivist: library clerk, museum clerk
au naturel: naked
capital punishment: death penalty
casket: coffin
comfort station: public toilet
confrontation: fight, heated argument
custodial engineer: janitor
deceased: dead, the person who is dead
demise: death
dentures: false teeth
disadvantaged: poor
erotica: pornography
exceptional child: retarded child, disabled child, handicapped child
expecting: pregnant

experienced tires: recaps, retreads
explosive device: nuclear bomb etc.
food-preparation center: kitchen
furlough: in business, layoff from work
gay: homosexual
hairpiece: toupee, wig
halitosis: bad breath
homemaker: housewife
indigent: poor
indisposed: ill, nauseated, sick
interment: burial
intoxicated: drunk
john: customer of a prostitute, a toilet
kickback: bribe
love child: illegitimate child
lay to rest: bury
marketing representative: salesperson
minority: Asian, black, Hispanic, etc.
mortality rate: death rate
motion: discomfort, nausea
not doing well: dying
passed away: died
patron: customer
paying guest: boarder
police action: war
powder room: toilet
preowned car: secondhand car, used car
prevaricate: lie
private parts: genitals
reconditioned auto: secondhand car, used car
remains: corpse
restroom: public toilet
rotund: fat
sanitary engineer: garbage collector
scent: smell
security coordinator: bodyguard
senior citizens: old people
social disease: gonorrhea, syphilis
stretch the truth: lie
take under advisement: defer action, shelve
tissue: toilet paper
underprivileged: destitute, poor
unmentionables: underwear

14

Pompous Expressions

Pretentious language is not fashionable in contemporary society. Someone who uses *obfuscate* for *confuse* or *chef d'oeuvre* for *masterpiece* is considered pompous by today's standards. The rule of modern writers is: never use a long or complex word when a short or simple word will do. This does not mean that a word such as *feedback* is off limits. In the right context (computer operations), the word may be not only proper but preferable to something else. But to describe a letter from an associate as *feedback* is a misuse of the word. Also, basic English words (*genuine*) are preferred over Latin expressions (*bona fide*). The following list contains words that usually sound pretentious in general writing. Use the alternatives in most cases.

abate, abatement: cut down, decrease, drop
aggregation: total
approximately: about
ascertain: find out
assistance: aid, help
attempting: trying
behest: request
bona fide: genuine
chef d'oeuvre: masterpiece
chemotherapeutic agent: drug
cognizant: aware
commence: begin, start
commendation: praise
commercialization: commerce
concerning: about

construct: make
consummate: complete
customary channels: usual way
delineate: describe, draw
depressed socioeconomic area: slum
dialogue: conversation
disseminate: circulate, send out
domicile: home
effected, effectuated: make, did
endeavoring: trying
enlighten: tell
equivalent: equal
facilitate: ease, help
feedback: comments
forward: send
functionalization: use
germane: relevant
hiatus: gap, interval
impair: damage, hurt, weaken
inaugurate: begin, start
initiate: begin, start
in toto: altogether, in all
input: advice
inquire: ask
instantaneously: now, quickly
instrumentalities: means, ways
interface with: meet with
involving: about
ipso facto: by the very nature of the case
lethal: deadly, fatal
marketing representative: salesperson
milieu: surroundings, environment
modus operandi: method
multitudinous: many
nadir: low point
obfuscate: confuse
obviate: prevent, do away with
palpable: clear, obvious, visible
per annum: a year, each year
per diem: a day, each day
per se: as such

peruse: read
procedural practices: what to do and how do it
procure: get
promulgate: circulate, send out
raison d'être: reason for
remuneration: pay
render: offer
sine qua non: essential
succumbed: died
terminate: end
transmit: send
utilize, utilization: use
vicissitude: change
wherewithal: means

15

Cliches

Cliches are trite expressions (Chapter 11) that are worn out and often vague and wordy. Usually, there is a much more precise and fresh way to make your point. People who rely on cliches to express themselves often sound unimaginative and boring. Some cliches, however, have gained a legitimate status in certain contexts. The term *A-1,* for instance, is a rating label used by many organizations. A few cliches are acceptable language in certain professions, such as *arm's length* in labor relations and *vested interest* in the legal field. But, generally, avoid tired words and phrases such as those shown in the following list. For additional examples of trite expressions, see Chapter 11. See also the dictionary of contemporary slang in Chapter 18.

A-ok
A-1
ace in the hole
ace up his sleeve
actions speak louder than words
ants in his pants
arm's length
as the crow flies
babe in the woods
back-seat driver
back to square one
back to the drawing board
baptism by fire
barking up the wrong tree

bats in the belfry
bear the brunt
beat a dead horse
beat a hasty retreat
beat around the bush
beauty is in the eye of the beholder
beauty is only skin deep
beggars can't be choosers
beg the question
birds of a feather flock together
bite the dust
black sheep
blessing in disguise
blow off steam

born yesterday
bosom buddy
both feet on the ground
bright-eyed and bushy-tailed
brink of disaster
bull in a china shop
burn the candle at both ends
bury the hatchet
business as usual
by the grapevine
by the same token
call a spade a spade
can't see beyond the end of his nose
cardinal sin
cast the first stone
cat's meow
change of heart
checkered career
chew the fat
chip off the old block
clean slate
climb the wall
coast is clear
come off it
come up smelling like roses
conventional wisdom
cool it
crazy as a coot
cream of the crop
cry over spilled milk
cut the mustard
dark horse
days are numbered
deep six
diamond in the rough
dog eat dog
dose of his own medicine
down and out
drop in the bucket
eat your heart out
evil eye

fair shake
false alarm
feel the punch
finishing touch
food for thought
foregone conclusion
for what it's worth
full steam ahead
get to the bottom of it
gild the lily
go bananas
go off half-cocked
hand over fist
handwriting on the wall
hell to pay
hold the fort
if worse comes to worse
in hot water
ivory tower
keep your fingers crossed
lame duck
let sleeping dogs lie
live and let live
long shot
many are called but few are chosen
milk of human kindness
mind your own business
more or less
movers and shakers
needless to say
net result
now and then
no way
on the ball
one fell swoop
on the tip of my tongue
open and shut case
out of the frying pan, into the fire
pay through the nose
piece of cake
plain as day

play with fire

possession is nine-tenths of the law

pure and simple

rags to riches

rank and file

red-letter day

rule of thumb

safe and sound

see red

ships that pass in the night

short and sweet

signed, sealed, and delivered

smell a rat

sooner or later

stem the tide

take it or leave it

thick as thieves

time is ripe

tip of the iceberg

turn the other cheek

unwritten law

vested interest

vicious circle

water over the dam

water under the bridge

wave of the future

whole ball of wax

wreak havoc

you can't win 'em all

16

Words and Phrases
That Antagonize

Some words, when used in a particular context, may irritate or anger people. These words are commonly referred to as "loaded." When you write to a customer, for example, and state, "You *claim* that you sent us your check on April 4," the reader is likely to feel threatened or insulted because it suggests that you don't believe the customer is telling the truth. It would be less provocative to state, "Thank you for letting us know that you sent us your check on April 4. I'm sorry to report, however, that it did not reach us."

Many of the examples given below are fine in the proper context: "*Apparently* the storm damage is more extensive than we realized." But in other contexts the word might create the wrong impression. "*Apparently* you haven't read my letter." Tone and intent, therefore, are all-important. They can change even the most innocent word into an attack weapon.

The following words and phrases should be avoided in any context that might offend a reader or listener. For examples of other types of negative words to avoid (such as those that create feelings of fear or distrust), see Chapter 7.

abominable	banal	claim(ed)
absurd	beware	Communist
abuse(d)	big mouth	contempt
antagonize(d)	blame(d)	contend(ed)
apparently	butt out	cruel
appeased	cancel(ed)	damage(d)
argue(d)	capitalist	deceive(d)
assume(d)	careless(ness)	defy, defied
bad	cheap	demagogue

demand(ed)
dense
deny, denied
deplore(d)
deprive(d)
destroy(ed)
dictator
dominate(d)
drunk
dumb
extravagant
fail(ure)
false(ly)
fault
fiasco
filthy lucre
flagrant
flimsy
get off my back
hamper(ed)
harass(ed)
hate(d)
hogwash
hurt
idiot

ignorant
inadequate
insist(ed)
invalid
liable
liar
lie(d)
ludicrous
meddle(d)
mediocre
misinform(ed)
misrepresent(ed)
mundane
must
naive
negligence
obligated
obstinate
obstruction(ist)
opinionated
overbearing
partisan
perhaps
pessimist
predatory

prejudice(d)
pretentious
rude
ruthless
sarcastic
senseless
shameful
shortsighted
slow
squander(ed)
stubborn
stupid
superficial
ugly
unsuccessful
useless
waste(ful)
weak
wrong
you claim
you misrepresented
you must
your carelessness

No living language stands still, however much we might wish at times that it would.

—*Webster's Ninth New Collegiate Dictionary*
(Springfield, Mass.: Merriam-Webster, 1990), p. 24.

PART III

NEW AND UNUSUAL FORMS OF WORDS

17 A Dictionary of Neologisms

18 A Dictionary of Contemporary Slang

19 Oxymorons

17

A Dictionary of Neologisms

Neologisms are relatively new words, expressions, or usages. For our purposes, most of those illustrated have come into use since the 1960s. Sometimes critics disapprove of neologisms simply because they are new but, more often, because they are slang expressions. However, if they remain in use long enough, such words may become an accepted part of standard English.

In deciding whether or not to use a new word in your writing or speaking, think about your audience. Will you be understood, will you offend, is the situation formal or informal? Neologisms can add to the variety of your language when used in the right context but can detract from what you have to say when used inappropriately.

The following are examples of words and expressions that are relatively new and, in most cases, still in use, although sometimes on the fringe of accepted English. Some, however, are already so much a part of the English language that people do not realize the words have been in use for only a few decades or less.

access: retrieve data from computer storage
acid: the hallucinogen LSD
add-on: equipment that can be added to a basic machine
agribusiness: the production, processing, and distribution of farm products
bit: binary digit
black power: mobilization of political and economic power of blacks
bread: money
bug off: leave someone alone or stop annoying someone

busted: arrested

cameo: in movies or television, a brief appearance by a noted performer

can: toilet

chicken: afraid

computer hacker: one who breaks into or disturbs other people's computer data

computer virus: uninvited program that disrupts activity

discotheque (French): nightclub for dancing

disk: magnetic medium for storing information electronically

downscale/downsize: make smaller

drop out: someone who abandons school, work, or some other activity or life-style

econometrics: application of statistical methods to economic problems

E-mail: electronic mail transmission

exit: to abandon a computer program or operation

fax: facsimile machine or transmission

fix: drug injection

FORTRAN: computer program—*For*mula *Tran*slation

freeze-dry: to dry food in a frozen state for preservation

fuzz: police

get it all together: trying to improve oneself to function successfully

Ginnie Mae: Government National Mortgage Association

glastnost (Russian): openness in communication and operations

grass: marijuana

groovy: wonderful

hangup: mental block

high five: raised hand as a greeting

high rise: multistory building

hippie: member of 1960s counterculture

hooked: addicted

ice: bribes

iffy: doubtful

in: currently popular

input: data fed into a machine

insider trading: illegal use of one's inside knowledge of stock market activity for profit

jog: run a slow trot

joint: marijuana cigarette

jumper: actual or potential suicide victim

junkie: drug addict

latchkey child: one who is left at home unsupervised

liftoff: launch of a rocket

local-area network (LAN): interconnected machines, usually wired together

looker: one who looks at properties without serious interest in buying

make my day: challenge to someone to go ahead with something so you can enjoy stopping the person

mainline: inject drugs into a blood vessel

Medicare: government-sponsored medical program for the elderly

moon: to show bare buttocks, usually at a window

nerd: tedious, boring person

New Age movement: spiritual and mystical development of 1960s counterculture

nuke: to destroy with nuclear weapons

OD: overdose of narcotics

off line: a computer not under the control of a central machine

oink: police officer

on line: a system whereby a central computer controls everything

overkill: excess of something beyond what is needed

pig: police officer

po'd: angry

pot: marijuana

power trip: obvious display of personal power

preppie: student in or graduate of a preparatory school

RAM: random-access memory in computer

rat race: stressful situation in ordinary world

recall: notifying consumers to return a product to a dealer for repair or replacement

scuba diver: one who swims under water using scuba gear

scrolling: moving information up or down on a computer screen

software: program of instructions for computer

splashdown: landing of manned spacecraft in the ocean

swing both ways: bisexual

swinger: sexually promiscuous person

Teflon: nonstick material used to coat utensils

Third World: underdeveloped, or developing, countries

trip: drug reaction

turn on: become excited or aroused

uptight: anxious

user: one who uses narcotics

user friendly: a machine or program that is easy to learn or use

word processing: preparing textual material on a computer; a type of computer program

whistleblower: one who reveals wrongdoing

yuppie: twenty- to thirty-year-old affluent, urban professional

zap: sudden energy

18

A Dictionary of
Contemporary Slang

Slang is informal and sometimes crude language developed by adapting existing words or coining new words, usually without regard for scholastic standards. Slang is frequently peculiar to certain age groups or social classes. Although it is widespread and regularly intermixed with standard English, careful writers and speakers avoid it in all business and formal social situations.

The listing given here provides some familiar examples selected from the innumerable words and phrases that qualify as contemporary slang.

ace: someone who has unusual skills or abilities
across the board: an equal adjustment for everyone in a certain group
ask for it: provoke
ax: dismiss
back out: cancel or renege
bad-mouth: denigrate
blackball: deny someone something
bogus: phony
call the shots: be in charge
ceiling: upper limit
clout: power
creep: disgusting person
deadbeat: moocher
deep six: discard
dog: unappealing person
dummy up: keep quiet
eat one's words: retract a statement

eat your heart out: be envious of
egghead: intellectual
ex: former wife, boyfriend, etc.
eyeball: look at
fag: male homosexual
fallout: result of something
fancy footwork: skillful evasion
flip out: behave irrationally
garbage: nonsense
get away with murder: go unpunished or unharmed after doing
   something questionable
glad-hand: be especially warm and friendly
gutsy: brave
ham: one who overacts
hangout: place to pass the time
has-been: someone who was once successful but no longer is
hit the fan: cause trouble
ID: identification
in hock: in debt
in the soup: in trouble
itchy: restless or eager
jeans: denim trousers
Jim Crow: black person
jive: tease
junk: useless and worthless things
kaput: broken or inoperative
keep tabs on: keep informed about
kinky: bizarre
know-how: skill
laid-back: relaxed
lay on the line: be candid
like a bandit: successfully
lower the boom: punish
macho: aggressively and blatantly masculine
main man: best friend
make the rounds: circulate
muck around: tinker or tamper
narc(o): narcotics agent
nickel and dime: make a lot of charges in small amounts
noncom: noncommissioned officer
nuts and bolts: fundamentals or basics

off the wall: outrageous
old hat: out of style
once-over: scrutiny
over the hill: middle age and older
pack in: give up
pad: bed or room
payola: graft or extortion
quick fix: hasty repair
quiz: brief examination
rabbi: influential sponsor
rattle the cage: stir into action
red faced: embarrassed
run of the mill: ordinary
sack: discharge, bed
scam: swindle
schmaltzy: corny
screwed up: confused
tab: bill or check
ten-four: signal that message was received
throw money at: spend excessive amounts to solve a problem
two-bit: cheap and tacky
up: happy and optimistic
upper: stimulant narcotic
up the ante: raise the price
vanilla: white woman
vet: veteran, veterinarian
vibes/vibration: what is sensed from someone or something
vino: wine
waffle: be evasive
wangle: get or arrange by being clever
wild card: unpredictable; outside of the normal rules
world class: outstanding
X-rated: obscene
yatata: idle chatter
yen: craving
yucky: disgusting
zinger: a sharp quip
zonk out: lose consciousness

19

Oxymorons

An *oxymoron* is a term consisting of two or more contradictory words or parts. Some, such as *bittersweet,* have become part of our language. As a rule, however, such terms are rarely used in ordinary social or business situations. But literary writers (poets, short story writers, novelists, and so on) use oxymorons for special effect. Oxymorons can be created for any type of passage simply by coupling contradictory words that will effectively describe an unusual emotion or setting or will create a desired mood. Try using a dictionary of synonyms and antonyms, combining a word from the synonym listing with a word from the associated antonym listing. The following are examples of this type of incongruity.

agreeably disagreeable	foul purity
beautiful ugliness	gentle savage
bittersweet	icy flame
boldly fearful	loud silence
bountiful poverty	loving hatred
cheerful morbidity	modest extravagance
cruel kindness	modestly arrogant
different uniformity	normally abnormal
disgustingly attractive	painful joy
earnest neglect	peacefully hostile
expectant surprise	proudly humble
falsely true	pure obscenity
flattering rudeness	raging calm
foolish wisdom	rudely courteous

stupidly clever   uneasy comfort
tactfully harsh   wretched nobility
tearful laughter   zealously frigid

[T]he meaning we convey by an exact word ordinarily is bound to be clearer than the meaning we convey by an inexact word.

—JAMES J. KILPATRICK
The Writer's Art
(Fairway, Kans.: Andrews, McMeel & Parker, 1984), p. 15.

Part IV

WORDS THAT ARE NOT WHAT THEY SEEM

20 Homophones: Words That Sound the Same but Have Different Meanings

21 Homographs: Words That Look Alike but Have Different Meanings

22 Misplaced Words That Change Your Meaning

23 A Dictionary of Misused Words

Homphones: Words That Sound the Same but Have Different Meanings

Misspellings often occur in correspondence and other written material because some words sound the same but have different meanings and different spellings. The noun *compliment,* for example, refers to an expression of flattery, whereas the noun *complement* means something that completes or supplements something else. The following list contains examples of words with different meanings that cause problems because of their similarity in pronunciation. See also problems with homographs in Chapter 21 and the list of easily confused words in Chapter 23.

acclamation: loud, enthusiastic expression of approval, praise, or ascent
acclimation: physiological adjustment to environmental change
affect: influence
effect: result; to accomplish

aid: help
aide: assistant

air: atmosphere
err: to make a mistake
heir: one who inherits something

aisle: passageway between seats
isle: small island

allude: refer indirectly
elude: evade

allusion: indirect reference
illusion: something misleading

altar: a place of worship, ritual, or sacrifice
alter: to change

amend: to improve
emend: to correct text

ante: poker stake
anti: against

arc: part of a curve
ark: a boat or ship

area: portion of space
aria: a melody or tune

ascent: climb; upward slope
assent: concur

assay: examination of characteristics
essay: short literary composition

axes: cutting tool
axis (pl. axes): straight reference line

basal: fundamental
basil: plant

bite: to seize with teeth
byte: binary digits

born: brought forth by; deriving from
borne: endured or tolerated

calendar: tubular register of days
calender: to press; a machine for calendering

capital: stock of accumulated goods
capitol: building in which state legislative body meets
Capitol: building in which U.S. Congress meets

canvas: woven cloth; to cover with canvas
canvass: personally solicit votes or opinion; discuss

cent: monetary unit
scent: odor
sent: past tense of *send*

cite: mention or quote
sight: something that is seen
site: location

complement: something that supplements, completes; the act of complementing

compliment: to offer praise or commendation

comptroller: public official who audits and approves expenditures

controller: someone or something that controls

council: deliberative body

counsel: advice, deliberation; lawyer or consultant

curser: one who curses

cursor: something moved over a surface such as a video display screen

depravation: corruption

deprivation: being deprived of something; removal from office

descent: moving downward

dissent: differ in opinion

die: expire

dye: to color; coloring matter

eave: roof overhang

eve: evening

elicit: draw forth or bring out

illicit: unlawful

epic: greater or more than usual; heroic

epoch: memorable event or date; event marking a new beginning

exercise: bringing into play; carrying out terms or duties; bodily activity

exorcise: expel by adjuration

fir: evergreen tree

fur: hair on mammals; dressed pelt

flu: influenza

flue: enclosed passageway or channel for directing a current

florescence: state or period of flourishing

fluorescence: emission of or property of emitting electromagnetic radiation

forward: in advance of something; moving ahead

foreword: prefatory comments

fort: fortified place

forte: strong point; loudly

gaff: spear or hook; gimmick

gaffe: social or diplomatic blunder

gel: jelly; gelatin
jell: take shape or become cohesive

gild: cover with gold
guild: association of persons with like interests

gorilla: anthropoid ape
guerilla: someone who practices irregular warfare

hangar: place for aircraft storage and repair
hanger: device on which to hang things

heroin: narcotic
heroine: principal female character in literary or dramatic work

hoar: frost
whore: female prostitute

immanent: inherent
imminent: ready to take place

indiscreet: imprudent
indiscrete: not separated

intercession: mediation
intersession: period between terms or meetings

laches: negligence; undue delay
latches: fastening devices

leach: pass out or through by percolation
leech: carnivorous or blood-sucking worm

magnate: someone of distinction
magnet: something that attracts

millenary: group of 1,000 things
millinery: women's apparel for the head

moral: ethical; conforming to that which is right
morel: edible fungus

naval: relating to ships or shipping
navel: central depression in the abdomen where the umbilical cord
  was attached

overdo: do too much
overdue: past due

palate: roof of mouth
palette: board on which to mix paints
pallet: straw mattress; portable platform

parlay: increase the value
parley: discussion

pimento: allspice

pimiento: sweet pepper

pollan: white fish

pollen: microspores in seed plant

principal: chief; most important

principle: fundamental law or doctrine

rack: framework or stand; acute suffering

wrack: to ruin; wreckage

raise: lift up

raze: destroy

retch: try to vomit

wretch: miserable person

saccharin: crystalline compound used as artificial sweetener

saccharine: overly sweet or sentimental

sailer: ship

sailor: crew member on ship

sisal: strong white fiber

sisel: ground squirrel

shear: cut or clip

sheer: thin or transparent; unqualified; steep

sleight: deceitful craftiness; skill

slight: slim or delicate; meager

straight: without curves, bends, and so on

strait: narrow passageway connecting bodies of water; juncture; difficulty

tach: tachometer

tack: nail

tartar: substance from juice of grapes; incrustation on teeth

tarter: sharper in taste

taught: instructed

taut: pulled tight

terrain: geographical area

terrane: area where particular rocks are evident

tic: twitch of muscles

tick: blood-sucking arachnid

triptik: roadmaps

triptych: three pictures side by side

unwanted: not wanted
unwonted: unusual

vail: to let fall or lower, often as a show of respect
vale: valley
veil: cloth covering; something that obscures

veracious: truthful
voracious: ravenous

viscous: sticky
viscus: body organ

wain: farm vehicle
wane: dwindle

waive: voluntarily relinquish
wave: hand motion; liquid swell; successive curves

whirl: rotate rapidly
whorl: part of weaving or spinning machinery; swirled shape

xenia: effect of genes introduced by male nucleus on structures other than embryo
zinnia: tropical American herb with showy flower head

21

Homographs: Words That Look Alike but Have Different Meanings

Whereas *homophones* (Chapter 20) are words that sound the same but have different meanings, *homographs* look the same but sound different and have different meanings. Pronunciation symbols in the list below are consistent with *Webster's Third International Dictionary*.

agape (ə-'gāp): wide open
agape (ä-'gä-,pā): love feast

agnostic (ag' nästick): someone who doubts the existence of a god
agnostic (ag:nōstik): someone who cannot recognize familiar objects by seeing, hearing, or touching

allege (ə'lej): to declare without full proof
allege (a'lezh): thinned part of a wall

allonge (a'lōⁿzh): paper attached to a document for additional endorsements
allonge (:a,lōⁿ:zhā): ballet movement

ape ('āp): monkey; to mimic
ape ('ä,pā): herbaceous aroid cultivated as ornamental plant

assemble (ə'sembəl): bring together
assemble (àsäⁿblā): ballet movement

August ('ȯgəst): eighth month in the Gregorian calendar
august ('ȯ:gəst): grand; majestic dignity

aye ('ī): affirmative vote; yes
aye ('ā): forever

barrage ('bärij):   artificial dam in river or watercourse
barrage (bə'rä|zh):   a screen of artillery fire; massive outpouring
bass ('bas):   fish
bass ('bās):   deep tone; lowest voice or instrument
bow ('baů):   bend; forward part of a ship
bow ('bō):   weapon; curve or arch
buffet ('bəfət):   blow or slap
buffet (:bə:fā):   counter for refreshments
chap ('chap):   man or boy; crack or split
chap ('chäp):   jaw or fleshy covering of jaw
charge ('chärj):   entrust; accuse; rush
chargé ('shär:zhā):   chargé d'affaires
chose ('chōz):   past participle of choose
chose ('shōz):   piece of personal property
conduct ('kän,dəkt):   mode or standard of personal behavior
conduct (kən'dəkt):   lead; execute; manage
console (kən'sōl):   comfort
console ('kän,sōl):   cabinet or panel
contract ('kän·,trakt):   agreement
contract (kən'trakt):   catch; condense
cure ('kyůər):   curacy; parish; healing
curé (kyə'rā):   parish priest
desert ('dəzər|t):   barren or arid region
desert (dė'zər|t):   reward or punishment deserved or earned
diffuse (dė'fyüs):   widespread
diffuse (dė'fyüz):   allow to spread freely
dive ('dīv):   plunge head first; fall
dive ('dēvə):   plural of diva; prima donnas
entrance ('en·trəns):   place to enter
entrance (ən·'trans):   put into a trance
forte ('fȯr|d·,ā):   loudly
forte ('fōər|t):   one's strong point
gene ('zhen):   embarrassment
gene ('jēn):   element of germ plasm
gill ('jil):   measurement unit
gill ('gil):   organ for obtaining oxygen from water

grave ('grāv): tomb
grave ('grä,vā): slowly and solemnly

halo ('hā,lō): circle of light
halo ('ha,lō): containing halogen

incense ('in,sens): material producing a fragrant odor when burned
incense ('in:sens): to inflame or arouse

intimate ('intə,māt): announce
intimate ('intə,mėt): innermost; familiar

jus ('jəs): law
jus ('zhü): gravy

lame ('lām): physically disabled
lamé ('la:mā): brocaded clothing fabric

lien ('lēən): a charge on real or personal property to satisfy a debt
lien ('līən): spleen

lira ('lirə): Italian monetary unit
lira ('lērə): musical instrument

math ('math): mathematics
math ('məth): Hindu monastery

minute ('minət): unit of time
minute ('mī:nüt): very small

mow ('maů): stack of hay
mow ('mō): cut down

nadir ('nādər): lowest point
nadir ('nä,diər): Malayan fishing boat

object ('äbjikt): something tangible or visible
object (əb'jekt): oppose

pace ('pās): rate of movement
pace ('pāsē): with all due respect

pique ('pēk): offense
pique ('pē:kā): clothing fabric; inlaid

present ('prezᵊnt): donation or gift; now
present (prĕ'zent): introduce; to give

project ('prä,jekt): undertaking; plan
project (prə'jekt): devise; throw or cast forward

raven ('rāvən): large black bird
raven ('ravėn): devour eagerly

refuse (rə'fyüz): decline
refuse ('re,fyüs): rubbish

resume (rə'züm): begin again
résumé (:re|z|ə:mā): condensed statement

rose ('rōz): plant or flower
rose ('rō:zā): table wine

sake ('sāk): end; purpose; for the good of something or someone
sake ('säkē): Japanese beverage

sow ('saù): female hog
sow ('sō): plant; set in motion

subject ('səbjəkt): vassal; citizen; theme
subject (səb'jekt): subjugate; exposure

tear ('tiər): fluid in eyes
tear ('ta|ər): divide or split

vale ('vāl): low-lying tract
vale ('v|ä,lā): salutation on leaving

wind ('wind): air movement
wind ('wīnd): encircle or coil

wound ('wünd): injury
wound ('waund): past participle of wind; encircled

22

Misplaced Words That Change Your Meaning

Words that appear in the wrong place in a sentence not only can change the meaning but, as some of the examples below illustrate, also can sound silly. Even in a sentence that sounds normal, a misplaced word can give readers an impression very different from the one you intended. Sometimes this happens because a single-word modifier is in the wrong place; sometimes an entire phrase is misplaced or dangling. The modifier then appears to refer to or modify the wrong word. The examples that follow show how meaning changes by moving around words and phrases within a sentence.

She *almost* froze in fear every time she heard a siren.
She froze in fear *almost* every time she heard a siren.

She bought a vase for her mother *with a round bottom*.
She bought a vase *with a round bottom* for her mother.

You said that he fell *on the telephone* yesterday.
You said *on the telephone* that he fell yesterday.

I told my associate *only* what I had read.
I told *only* my associate what I had read.

He bought a car from his uncle *in mint condition*.
He bought a car *in mint condition* from his uncle.

He saw the fig tree *having a pizza*.
Having a pizza, he saw the fig tree.

WANTED: Man to wash dishes and *three waitresses*.
WANTED: *Three waitresses* and man to wash dishes.

We *really* care about what happens.
We care about what *really* happens.

He saw the supplies *getting into his car.*
Getting into his car, he saw the supplies.

SALE: All wine to anyone over twenty-one *in a one-liter jug.*
SALE: All wine *in a one-liter jug* to anyone over twenty-one.

He *truly* looks miserable.
He looks *truly* miserable.

You agreed to call me *on Friday.*
You agreed *on Friday* to call me.

The old woman called to the cat *holding a pan of milk.*
The old woman *holding a pan of milk* called to the cat.

They are *just* walking to the store.
They are walking *just* to the store.

She *even* plays the piano.
She plays *even* the piano.

The hostess served punch to her guests *in the good crystal.*
The hostess served punch *in the good crystal* to her guests.

I said that I would write to him *every day.*
I said *every day* that I would write to him.

Ellen sent the painting to her agent *in a large crate.*
Ellen sent the painting *in a large crate* to her agent.

The children saw a large bird *drinking sodas.*
The children *drinking sodas* saw a large bird.

Alice married her boyfriend after dating for six years *on a boat.*
Alice married her boyfriend *on a boat* after dating for six years.

WANTED: Babysitter to take care of two-year-old child *who does not smoke.*
WANTED: Babysitter *who does not smoke* to take care of two-year-old child.

23

A Dictionary of Misused Words

Choosing the correct word is not always an easy task. Are you *anxious* or *eager* about an impending assignment? Are you *delaying* or *postponing* a meeting? Are you *dissatisfied* or *unsatisfied* with your child's grades? The following examples of commonly misused words are adapted from *A Guide to Better Business Writing,* by Mary A. De Vries (New Century Publishers, 1981). Some of the words and expressions may have additional meanings not described here, and occasionally authorities disagree on matters of word usage. Consult any modern dictionary for additional detail.

a while/awhile

A while, a noun phrase, refers to a period or interval. (If you can wait for *a while,* the copier will be fixed by noon.)

Awhile, an adverb, means "for a short time." (The manager wanted to work *awhile* before leaving the office.) Do not use *for* with *awhile* since *for* is implied.

accidentally/accidently

Accidentally means "by chance; without design." (He hit the post *accidentally.*)

Accidently is a mispronounced and misspelled version of *accidentally.*

acknowledge/admit

Acknowledge means "to concede; to grant; to say that something is true." (The manager *acknowledged* the problem.)

Admit also means "to concede or to say that something is true" (she *admitted* her mistake) but is used more often to suggest the involvement of force or pressure.

adapt/adept/adopt

Adapt means "to change something for one's own purpose; to adjust." (I *adapted* the meter to our console.)

Adept means "proficient, skilled." (She is *adept* in foreign languages.)

Adopt means "to accept something without changing it." (They *adopted* the resolutions.)

adverse/averse

Adverse means "opposed; strongly disinclined." (The company had an *adverse* reaction to the union's action.)

Averse means "reluctant; having a distaste for." (She is *averse* to romantic involvements at work.)

affect/effect

Affect, a verb, means "to influence." (How will this policy *affect* our schedule?)

Effect, as a noun, means "a result." (What *effect* did the speech have on the audience?) As a verb, it means "to bring about." (The new policy will *effect* better customer relations.)

aid/assist/help

Aid means "to provide relief or assistance" and suggests incapacity or helplessness on the part of the recipient. (The government provided *aid* to flood victims.)

Assist means "to support or aid" and suggests a secondary role. (Her staff will *assist* in the presentation.)

Help means "to assist; to promote; to relieve; to benefit," and suggests steps toward some end. (He *helped* them move the machine.)

aim/intend

Aim refers to a matter of positioning (take aim) or means "to try." (I *aim* to meet our goal.)

Intend means "to plan on; to design." (The task force *intends* to complete its work this week.)

all right/alright

All right means "safe; acceptable; yes." (The schematic looks *all right* to me.)

Alright is a misspelling of *all right.*

all together/altogether

All together refers to everyone in the same place. (The staff was *all together* for the Christmas party.)

Altogether means "wholly; completely; all told." (*Altogether,* we accomplished a great deal.) *Completely* is preferred by some authorities in reference to *wholly.*

alter/change

Alter means "to make different without changing into something else." (She *altered* the curtains before hanging them.)

Change also means "to make different" but is not restricted in the sense that *alter* is. (He *changed* into a tuxedo for dinner.)

although/though

Although means "regardless; even though." It is preferred over *though* at the beginning of a sentence. (*Although* the plan failed, we learned a lot from the experience.)

Though means the same thing but is used more to link words and phrases in the middle of a sentence. (It is true, *though,* that the index is too high.)

amend/emend

Amend means "to improve; to make right." (The directors want to *amend* the bylaws.)

Emend means "to correct; to alter." (The editor will no doubt *emend* the introduction.)

among/between

Among refers to the relationship of more than two things. (The exchange of opinions *among* the participants was hostile.)

Between refers to the relationship of two things or more than two things if each one is individually related to the others. (The exchange of opinions *between* Smith and Wright was hostile.)

anxious/eager

Anxious refers to uneasiness or worry. (I am *anxious* to know the outcome of the surgery.)

Eager suggests earnest desire or anticipation. (I am *eager* to start my new job.)

apt/liable/likely

Apt means "fit" (*apt* in journalism) or "inclined to do something" (*apt* to come early).

Liable means "obligated by law; responsible." (The company is *liable* if an accident occurs on the property.)

Likely means "probable." (An economic slowdown is *likely.*)

as/since

As is a less effective conjunction than *since,* but it has other uses in the English language: preposition, adverb, and pronoun.

Since (or *because, when*) is more effective and is preferred. (*Since* this issue is late, we will have to reschedule the next issue.)

as . . . as/so . . . as

As . . . as is preferred for positive expressions. (The next conference will be *as* successful *as* the last one.)

So . . . as is often preferred, but not essential, for negative expressions. (The revised proposal is not *so* good *as* the original version.)

as if/as though/like

As if is less formal than *as though.* (She hesitated to begin the project *as if* she were afraid it would fail.)

As though is used in the same sense, and like *as if,* it is followed by a verb in the subjunctive mood. (He angrily rejected the proposal *as though* it were a personal affront.)

Like is widely used and misused in informal conversation (*like* I said), but authorities still recommend that it be used as a preposition and with a noun or pronoun that is *not* followed by a verb. (The president acts *like* a dictator.)

assure/ensure/insure

Assure means "to guarantee." It is used only in reference to persons. (I can *assure* you that we intend to complete the job on schedule.)

Ensure, a less common variation of *insure,* means "to make certain." (This long-range policy will *ensure* our continuing success.)

Insure, the preferred spelling of *ensure,* also means "to make certain; to guard against risk or loss." (The new network will *insure* better communications.)

balance/remainder

Balance refers to "a degree of equality" (we want to *balance* the budget) or to "bookkeeping" (please double-check the *balance* in our account).

Remainder should be used in all other instances to mean "what is left over." (Five hundred of the one thousand brochures were mailed this morning, and the *remainder* are almost ready for mailing now.)

barely/hardly/scarcely

Barely means "meagerly; narrowly." (He could *barely* fit into the small foreign car.)

Hardly means "with difficulty." (She could *hardly* control the car in the driving rain.)

Scarcely means "by a narrow margin" and suggests something hard to believe. (He could *scarcely* believe his application was rejected.)

Do not use a negative with any of these terms since each already has a negative quality (not *not barely, not hardly,* or *not scarcely*).

because/due to/owing to

Because should be used with nonlinking verbs. (They were exhausted *because* of overwork.)

Due to means "caused by" and may be followed by a linking verb. (Their exhaustion was *due to* overwork.) *Due to* is often used by careless business writers as a wordy substitute for *since* or *because.*

Owing to is primarily a compound preposition. (The play succeeded *owing to* the expert direction.)

candid/frank

Candid means "open; straightforward." (Her remarks were *candid.*)

Frank means the same thing but suggests an outspoken, possibly less tactful remark. (The two opponents had a *frank* exchange of views.)

censor/censure

Censor means to "examine for possible deletions." (The editor *censors* all manuscripts.)

Censure means "to condemn; to blame." (The committee *censured* the derogatory report.)

close/near

Close means "very near" (*close* race) or "intimate" (*close* friend).

Near means "closely related" (*near* neighbors) or "narrow margin" (a *near* victory).

common/mutual

Common refers to the sharing of something. (They have a *common* purpose.)

Mutual refers to something directed by one or more persons to one or more other persons. (The two competitors had a *mutual* respect for each other.)

comparatively/relatively

Comparatively refers to a degree of comparison (the winter was *comparatively* mild) but is often misused when no comparison with another factor is intended.

Relatively refers to the state of something in relation to something else. (The drug is *relatively* fast acting.) *Relatively* is used improperly and unnecessarily by many business writers.

compare/contrast

Compare means "to examine for difference or similarity, mostly similarity." *Compare* is followed by *with* when specifics are examined. (She *compared* her record *with* his.) But in a general reference, *compare* is followed by *to.* (*Compared to* yesterday, today is tranquil.)

Contrast means "to show only differences." The noun form of *contrast* is followed by *to.* (The new typewriters have correcting features in *contrast to* the old models.) But the verb *contrast* is usually followed by *with.* (His present position *contrasts* markedly *with* his old one.)

complement/compliment

Complement means "to complete." (The new study *complements* the previous report.)

Compliment means "to flatter or praise." (His employer *complimented* him on his achievement.)

complementary/supplementary

Complementary means "completing to make up the whole." (The printing and binding operations are *complementary.*)

Supplementary means "added to something." (The catastrophic insurance is *supplementary* to his basic policy.)

compose/comprise

Compose means "to make up by combining." (Seven rooms *compose* the suite. *Or:* The suite is *composed* of seven rooms.) A general rule is that the parts (seven rooms) compose the whole (the suite).

Comprise means "to include." (The company *comprises* two hundred employees.) A general rule is that the whole (the company) *comprises* the parts (the employees).

consistently/constantly

Consistently means "with uniformity or regularity; steady continuity." (He *consistently* pursued the same theme in all of his speeches.)

Constantly means "with steadfast resolution; faithfulness" (he has been a *constant* ally) or "without interruption" (the machines ran *constantly*).

continual/continuous

Continual means "always going on; repeated over and over," and often implies a steady or rapid succession. (The company is *continually* seeking part-time help.)

Continuous means "connected; unbroken; going on without interruption." (The company is in *continuous* operation, day and night.)

convince/persuade

Convince means "to lead someone to understand, agree, or believe." (She *convinced* her employer that funding was inadequate.)

Persuade means "to win someone over." (I *persuaded* him to take the day off.)

currently/presently

Currently means "the time now passing; belonging to the present time." (The company is *currently* being formed.)

Presently means "shortly or before long." (She will arrive *presently.*)

customary/usual

Customary means "according to usual practices." (It is *customary* in this office to stagger the lunch breaks.)

Usual means "something common, normal, or ordinary." (He left for work at the *usual* time.)

deduction/induction

Deduction refers to reasoning by moving from the general to the particular. (All computers accept some form of symbolic data; therefore, the XL100 should accept symbolic input.)

Induction refers to reasoning by moving from the particular to the general. (Having read thousands of business letters, most of which have one or more grammatical errors, I believe that most business people need further education in basic English composition.)

defer/delay/postpone

Defer means "to put off something until later." (He *deferred* his decision until next week.)

Delay means to set aside; to detain; to stop." (Let's *delay* further work on that project.)

Postpone means "to put off something until later, with full intention of undertaking it at a specific time." (The director *postponed* the meeting until Wednesday, October 6.)

different from/different than/different to

Different from is preferred by careful business writers. (My objective is *different from* yours.)

Different than is sometimes used when followed by a clause. (The results were *different than* he had expected they would be.)

Different to is a form of British usage.

differentiate/distinguish

Differentiate means "to show in detail a difference in." (You can *differentiate* among the paper samples by weight and grain.)

Distinguish also means "to show the difference in" but is used to point out general differences that separate one category from another. (You can easily *distinguish* radios from television sets.)

disinterested/uninterested

Disinterested means "objective, free from selfish motive; unbiased." (The researchers remained *disinterested* while making their survey.)

Uninterested means "indifferent, not interested." (He was *uninterested* in the new office decor.)

disorganized/unorganized

Disorganized means "lack of an orderly system; lack of coherence." (A *disorganized* person would never succeed in this position.)

Unorganized means "not characterized by an orderly whole." (The disgruntled workers were *unorganized.*)

disregardless/irregardless

Disregardless is used improperly for *regardless.*

Irregardless is also used improperly for *regardless.* In both cases, the prefixes *dis-* and *ir-* are unnecessary. (*Regardless* of the outcome, I am going ahead with our plan.)

dissatisfied/unsatisfied

Dissatisfied means "unhappy; upset; displeased." (She is *dissatisfied* with her new position.)

Unsatisfied means "not content, not pleased; wanting something more or better to be done." (The supervisor was *unsatisfied* with the quality of the work.)

doubt if/doubt that/doubt whether

Doubt if should be avoided in business writing.

Doubt that is the preferred expression in negative or interrogative sentences when little doubt exists. (I *doubt that* we can meet the deadline.)

Doubt whether is usually limited to situations involving strong uncertainty. (I *doubt whether* anything will come of it.)

each other/one another

Each other is used when referring to two persons or objects. (The two attorneys consulted *each other* before taking action.)

One another is used when referring to three or more persons or objects. (The six candidates were debating with *one another* off camera as well as on camera.)

effective/effectual/efficient

Effective means "producing the desired result" and applies to either agents or their action. The emphasis is on the production of the desired effect. (The publicity was *effective.*)

Effectual means "able to produce a desired result" and usually applies to the action. The emphasis is on the thing that was able to produce the desired effect. (Her efforts were *effectual* in gaining the necessary support.)

Efficient means "capable of producing the desired result" and applies to agents, their action, or the instrument used. The emphasis is on the capability of producing the desired effect. (They run an *efficient* organization.)

emigrate/immigrate

Emigrate means "to move from one place to another." (Feldman *emigrated from* Israel last year.)

Immigrate means "to enter a country to establish permanent residence." (O'Connell *immigrated to* the United States this spring.)

endless/innumerable

Endless means "boundless; interminable." (The sky is *endless.*)

Innumerable means "countless; too many to count." (The duties of a secretary are *innumerable.*)

envisage/envision

Envisage means "to confront; to view in a particular way." (I *envisage* a four-story structure with one executive dining room and two employee cafeterias.)

Envision means "to foresee; to picture." (I *envision* an exciting career with many adventures.)

essential/necessary

Essential means "basic; indispensable; necessary" and suggests a sense or urgency. (It is *essential* that we meet our deadline.)

Necessary also means "indispensable" but usually sounds less urgent than *essential.* (Your presence is *necessary* to show our support.)

essentially/substantially

Essentially is used most often to mean "basically." (The new copier is *essentially* the same as the old one.) The word *essential* implies something indispensable. (Insurance is *essential.*)

Substantially is used in the same way to mean "basically," but the word *substantial* suggests a significant size or quantity. (The company showed a *substantial* net gain.)

farther/further
Farther refers to physical distance or spatial measurement.(Salespersons travel *farther* today, thanks to readily available air service.)
Further refers to quantity or degree. (This roll of film will go *further* than I expected.) It also means "to promote." (He hopes to *further* his career.) Some business writers have stopped using both *farther* and *further* and are using only one of them (usually *further*) for all situations.

fashion/manner/mode
Fashion usually means "a particular style at a particular time." (Her suit is the latest *fashion*.)
Manner describes "behavior; social conduct." (The director's *manners* were exemplary.)
Mode means "a particular form of something." (His *mode* of governing is straightforward and open.)

feasible/possible
Feasible means "capable of being done." (The suggestion sounds *feasible* to me.)
Possible means "within realistic limits; likely to occur." (An economic upturn next quarter is possible.)

frequent/recurring
Frequent means "habitual; persistent; occurring at short intervals." (He is a *frequent* customer.)
Recurring means "occurring again and again; occurring repeatedly." (Her *recurring* headaches suggest a serious problem.)

handle/manage
Handle means "to control or manage; to deal with," and is preferred over *manage* when physical action is involved. (He *handled* the controls like an expert.)
Manage also means "to control or handle; to deal with," and is preferred over *handle* when nonphysical action is involved. (She *managed* the office efficiently.)

happen/occur/transpire
Happen means "to occur by chance." (He *happened* to be in the neighborhood.)
Occur means "to take place, often unexpectedly," and usually refers to a specific event. (The computer breakdown *occurred* before closing.)
Transpire means "to pass off; to excrete as a vapor." (The leaves *transpired*.) Figuratively, it means "to become apparent." (The state of the company became clear as events *transpired*.)

if/whether

If is used to introduce one condition and often suggests doubt. (I'll meet you at the airport *if* the weather permits.)

Whether is used to introduce more than one condition. (Her client asked *whether* she should sue or accept the settlement.)

imagine/suppose

Imagine means "to form a mental image of something." (I like to *imagine* myself surfing in Hawaii.)

Suppose means "to assume or suspect something." (I *suppose* you have a contract already drawn up.)

imply/infer

Imply means "to suggest by inference or association." (The report *implies* that research was inadequate.)

Infer means "to reach a conclusion from facts or circumstances." (The manager *inferred* from the report that research was inadequate.)

impracticable/impractical/unpractical

Impracticable means "not capable of being used or accomplished." (The plan is *impracticable.*)

Impractical means "not capable of dealing sensibly or practically with something." (Her approach is *impractical.*)

Unpractical is an obsolete term for *impractical.*

ineffective/ineffectual

Ineffective means "not producing the intended effect; not effective," and often suggests incompetence in some particular area. (He is *ineffective* as a salesperson.)

Ineffectual also means "not producing the intended effect; not effective," and often suggests a general lack of competence. (He is *ineffectual.*)

know/realize

Know means "to perceive; to understand." (I *know* a better route.)

Realize means "to accomplish; to grasp fully," and implies a more thorough understanding than *know.* (I *realize* the implications of our action.)

lack/need/want

Lack, as a noun, means "deficient or absent." (The program suffers from a *lack* of money.)

Need, as a noun, refers to "a lack of something desirable or useful" and often is used in an emotional context. (The *need* was for security.)

Want, as a noun, refers to "a lack of something needed or desired." (My *wants* seem to increase with age.)

As verbs, *lack* suggests a deficiency; *need,* a necessity; and *want,* a desire.

lawful/legal

Lawful means "to be in harmony with some form of law; rightful, ethical." (The directors considered the *lawful* implications of the amendment.)

Legal means "founded on the law; established by law." (The lottery is *legal* in New Hampshire.)

meticulous/scrupulous

Meticulous refers to extreme care in attending to details. (Her work is *meticulous.*)

Scrupulous refers to high principles and conscientious regard." (He is *scrupulous* in his dealings with minorities.)

one's self/oneself

One's self is used less often than *oneself,* except when the emphasis is on the *self.* (Psychologists say *one's self* is an amazing entity to be explored endlessly.)

Oneself is the preferred spelling in most general usage. (One has to discipline *oneself* in any type of work.)

part/portion/share

Part means "a subdivision of the whole." (This is one *part* of the proposal.)

Portion means a part or share of something usually intended for a specific purpose." (This *portion* of the program is reserved for questions and answers.)

Share means "the part or portion of something belonging to or given by someone." (His *share* of the estate is being held in trust.)

persons/people

Persons is often preferred in references to a few individuals or when specific individuals are being discussed. (The president and the treasurer were the only *persons* there from the board.)

People is often preferred in references to large groups or indefinite numbers. (The *people* from Eastern cultures sometimes find it difficult to adjust to Western ways.)

practical/practicable

Practical means "sensible; useful; realistic." (He used a *practical* approach to the problem.)

Practicable means "usable; feasible." (It simply is not *practicable* to complete the project in two weeks.)

presumably/supposedly

Presumably means "taken for granted; reasonably assume to be true." (*Presumably,* he is correct since he ran all of the required tests.)

Supposedly means "believed, sometimes mistakenly, to be true; imagined to be true." (The order to halt production *supposedly* came from someone in the executive offices.)

principal/principle

Principal, as a noun, means "chief participant or head" (the *principal* of the school) or "a sum of money." (The mortgage payment included the *principal* and interest.) As an adjective, it means "most important or consequential" (the *principal* reason).

Principle, a noun, refers to "a rule, doctrine, or assumption" (the *principle* of universal sovereignty).

proved/proven

Proved is the past tense of *prove.* (They *proved* their contention.)

Proven is an adjective (the *proven* method) and a past participle. (The volunteers have *proven* their loyalty.)

Proved is preferred. (The volunteers have *proved* their loyalty.)

purposefully/purposely

Purposefully means "with determination; with a purpose." (She *purposefully* planned her campaign to avoid the holidays.)

Purposely means "intentionally; deliberately." (He *purposely* avoided the subject.)

reaction/reply/response

Reaction means "a response to stimuli." (The injection caused a violent *reaction.*) It should not be used to mean "attitude, viewpoint, feeling, or response."

Reply means "a response in words." (She sent her *reply* by messenger.)

Response is "a reply; an answer." (The client's *response* was positive.)

shall/will

Shall, traditionally, is used in the first person to express future time. (I *shall* be happy to go.) Some authorities believe *shall* sounds stuffy and snobbish and prefer to use *will.*

Will, traditionally, is used in the second and third persons to express future time. (He *will* be happy to go.) Contemporary usage shows an increasing preference for *will* in all instances. (I *will,* you *will,* he or she *will,* they *will.*)

strain/stress

Strain, as a verb, means "to misuse; to filter; to stretch beyond belief; to overexert." (He *strained* his muscles.) As a noun, it means "excessive exertion or tension." (No *strain* on his heart was evident.)

Stress, as a verb, means "to accent; to emphasize." (He *stressed* the danger involved.) As a noun, it means "pressure; tension." (She suffered great *stress* during the competition.)

systematize/systemize

Systematize is the more familiar expression meaning "to arrange systematically; to put in order." (The committee needs to *systematize* its work.)

Systemize, although used less often, means the same as *systematize.*

that/which

That refers to persons, animals, or things and should be used in restrictive clauses when the clause introduced by *that* is essential to explain the preceding information. (The group *that* won last year came in first again.) The clause "that won last year" provides essential information about the group. It should not be set off with commas.

Which refers to animals and things and should be used in nonrestrictive clauses when the clause introduced by *which* is not essential for the reader to understand the meaning of the other information in the sentence. (The robin, which flies south in the winter, has a colorful orange breast.) The clause "which flies south in the winter" is not essential for the reader to understand that the robin has an orange breast. It should be set off with commas.

varied/various

Varied means "diverse; with numerous forms." (The logos on business letterheads are *varied.*)

Various means "dissimilar; separate; different." (The memo was sent to *various* divisions in the company.)

viable/workable

Viable means "capable of existence." (The new company is a *viable* entity.)

Workable means "practicable; feasible; capable of working or succeeding." (The plan seems *workable* to me.)

want/wish

Want suggests a need or longing. (I *want* that promotion.)

Wish is used more often to suggest hope as well as desire. (I *wish* I had more money.)

The major purpose of language is to communicate meaning. All languages accomplish this purpose by combining meaningful units, or words, into meaningful arrangements, or grammatical constructions.

—W. Nelson Francis,
The English Language: An Introduction
(New York: W. W. Norton & Company, 1965), p. 112.

Part V

THE GRAMMAR OF WORDS

24 The Eight Parts of Speech

25 Plural Nouns That Need a Singular Verb

26 Adjectives That Cannot Be Compared

27 Common English Prepositions

28 Commonly Misused Prepositions

29 Common Conjunctions

30 The Six Verb Tenses

31 Common Irregular Verbs

32 Assertive versus Passive Verbs

33 Essential Grammatical Terms

34 Idiomatic Expressions

24

The Eight Parts of Speech

Parts of speech are terms used to describe the grammatical function of certain words in particular contexts. The eight parts of speech are the noun, pronoun, adjective, adverb, verb, preposition, conjunction, and interjection. (See Chapter 33 for a description of other grammatical terms.)

NOUN

A noun is the name of a person, place, thing, idea, action, or quality (see examples below). The initial letter of proper nouns (official names) is always capitalized, whereas common nouns begin with a lowercase letter.

Nouns may be singular (*boy*), collective (*group*), or plural (*houses*); may show possession (*doctor's*); and may be used as the subject of a sentence (*John* is home), as the object of a preposition or verb (wrote the *letter*), or as a predicate noun (She is a capable *worker*).

See also Chapter 25, "Plural Nouns That Need a Singular Verb." Chapter 64 gives a list of nouns denoting nationality.

arena	insult
attitude	Mississippi River
boat	physician
class	population
corporation	Rose Bowl
decision	travel
Ellen Foster	Washington, D.C.
hunger	yeoman's

PRONOUNS

A *pronoun* is a word that takes the place of a noun. There are seven classes of pronouns.

1. A *personal pronoun* is a personal reference used in place of a noun in the first (*I*), second (*you*), or third (*he*) person. Those used as a subject are *I, you, he, she, it/we, you, they*; as an object: *me, you, him, her, it/us, you, them*; as possessives: *mine, yours, his, hers, its/our–ours, your–yours, their-theirs.*

2. A *demonstrative pronoun* points to an antecedent (a noun) directly or demonstratively (*this* house): *this, that/these, those.*

3. An *interrogative pronoun* asks a question: *who, whose, whom, which, what.*

4. A *relative pronoun* relates an antecedent to a dependent or qualifying clause: "It is the *season* (antecedent) *that* (relative pronoun) I like best." The relative pronouns are *who, which, what,* and *that.*

5. An *indefinite pronoun* stands for an object generally or indefinitely. The long list of indefinite pronouns includes *all, another, any, anybody, anyone, anything, both, each, each one, each other, either, everybody, everyone, everything, few, least, many, more, most, much, neither, none, no one, nobody, nothing, one, other, several, some, somebody, someone, something, such.*

6. A *reflexive* or *intensive pronoun* is a compound formed by adding the suffix *-self* to a personal or indefinite pronoun: *myself, yourself, himself, herself, itself/ourselves, yourselves, themselves.*

7. An *adjective pronoun* modifies a noun. It includes these demonstrative pronouns: *this, that/these, those*; these interrogative and relative pronouns: *which, what*; and all indefinite pronouns except *none: another, any, both, each, either, neither, one, other, some, such.*

ADJECTIVE

An *adjective* describes or limits (modifies) a noun or pronoun (see examples below). A *predicate adjective* follows a linking verb but still modifies a noun or pronoun (The train is *late*). A *relative adjective* is a relative pronoun used as an adjective (He is the one *whose* car was stolen). The two main classes of adjectives are descriptive (*cold* day) and limiting (*two* reasons). Adjectives may be in the comparative degree (This mattress is *harder* than the other one) or the superlative degree (This mattress is the *hardest* of all).

See also chapter 26, "Adjectives That Cannot Be Compared," and the list of adjectives that require a particular preposition in Chapter 34. Chapter 64 gives a list of adjectives denoting nationality.

Descriptive:	*beautiful* person
	hungry dog
	warm weather
Limiting:	*double* row
	second person
	weekly newspaper

ADVERB

An *adverb* modifies a verb, adjective, another adverb, and sometimes a noun or pronoun. A *relative adverb,* such as *where, when,* or *why,* refers to an antecedent in the main clause but modifies a word in the subordinate clause (They planned their party for a holiday *when* everyone was in town).

1. Place (*where, here, there, south,* etc.): The car went *south.*
2. Time (*now, then, when, early, soon,* etc.): The class will begin *soon.*
3. Manner (*how, well, ill, otherwise, worse,* etc.): The car ran *poorly.*
4. Cause (*therefore, wherefore, why,* etc.): She didn't specify *why.*
5. Number (*first, second,* etc.): *First,* let's have lunch.
6. Degree (*less, more, too,* etc.): The jacket is *too* small.

VERB

A verb expresses action (*run*) or state of being (*appear*). An *auxiliary verb* helps another verb form or phrase (She *is* driving). An *intransitive verb* has no object (The boy *walked* slowly) whereas a *transitive verb* expresses action or state of being and does have an object (She *studied* the textbook). The properties of verbs are voice, mood, tense, person, and number.

Chapter 32 defines active and passive verbs (voice). The other three properties are described below. See also Chapter 31, "Common Irregular Verbs," and the list of verbs and adjectives that must be followed by a certain preposition in Chapter 34. See Chapter 33 for a definition of an auxiliary verb.

Mood: Verbs have three moods:

1. The *indicative mood* states or questions a fact: *Is* this your car?

2. The *subjunctive mood* expresses an action or a state of being as possible, desired, conditional, doubtful, imagined, or contrary to fact: If I *leave,* I'll be happy. I wish you *were* coming.

3. The *imperative mood* expresses a command, wish, or something similar: *Come* with me.

Person: This property refers to which person (first, second, or third) is expressing the action or state of being.

First person: I *believe* it is true.
Second person: You *believe* it is true.
Third person: She *believes* it is true.

Number: This property refers to whether the verb expresses an action or state of being of one person or more than one.

Singular: I *know,* you *know,* he *knows*
Plural: We *know,* you *know,* they *know*

PREPOSITION

A *preposition* is a word such as *to, of, for, in, with,* or *between* that shows the relationship between its object and an antecedent of the preposition, which may be a noun, pronoun, adjective, verb, adverb, or phrase: They *went* (antecedent) *to* (preposition) the *concert* (object of the preposition).

A *prepositional phrase* consists of the preposition, its object, and any modifiers of the object:

in the store   over the hill
of the new list   with his aunt

Some participles are used like prepositions, including the following examples:

barring   past
concerning   pending
considering   regarding
during   respecting
excepting   saving
notwithstanding   touching

See Chapter 27 for a list of common English prepositions and Chapter 28 for a review of commonly misused prepositions. Chapter 34 has a list of verbs and adjectives that must be followed by a particular preposition.

CONJUNCTION

A *conjunction* connects words, phrases, clauses, or sentences or shows the relationship between sentences. The two main classes of common conjunctions are coordinate and subordinate.

1. *Coordinate,* or *coordinating, conjunctions,* such as *and, or, nor, but,* and *for,* connect two elements of equal rank such as two independent clauses:

> Mr. Ross *and* Ms. Bleeker are here.
> It both is *and* is not true.

2. *Subordinate,* or *subordinating, conjunctions,* such as *after, although, as, because, before, if, since, though, unless, until, when,* and *while,* connect a subordinate and principal element or clause in a sentence.

> He will report *when* he has finished his research.
> The office is closed *because* the manager is out of town.

When conjunctions are used in pairs (*either-or*), they are referred to as *correlative conjunctions.*

> *Either* she *or* I will conduct the course.
> The president is *not only* an author *but also* an artist.

See Chapter 29 for a list of common conjunctions and correlative conjunctions.

INTERJECTION

An *interjection* is a word (such as *oh!*) expressing strong or sudden feeling. It may be part of a sentence or may stand on its own. When another part of speech is used to express intense feeling (*Good!*), it has the force of an interjection.

> *What!* I can't believe it.
> *Oh!* So that's it.
> *Oh,* come on!

In many cases, the emphasis is obvious, and an exclamation point is unnecessary.

Oh, isn't that too much?
Ah, I see what you mean.

25

Plural Nouns That Need a Singular Verb

In the usual form, a plural noun such as *trees* takes a plural verb such as *are*: The *trees are* green. But some nouns that are plural in form are singular in meaning. Such nouns should have a singular verb: *Aeronautics is* part of the curriculum. *Mathematics is* more than numbers. Some plural nouns are singular only in certain contexts. *Politics is* often a matter of public relations. *Measles is* a childhood disease. The following list contains a sampling of nouns that are always plural in form but often singular in meaning; when the meaning is singular, a singular verb is required.

acoustics (*s.* or *pl.*)
aeronautics (*s.*)
analytics (*s.* or *pl.*)
athletics (*s.* or *pl.*)
bellows (*s.* or *pl.*)
civics (*s.* or *pl.*)
dynamics (*s.* or *pl.*)
economics (*s.* or *pl.*)
esthetics (*s.* or *pl.*)
ethics (*s.* or *pl.*)
hydraulics (*s.*)
linguistics (*s.*)
mathematics (*s.*)
measles (*s.* or *pl.*)

metaphysics (*s.*)
mumps (*s.* or *pl.*)
news (*s.*)
optics (*s.* or *pl.*)
phonetics (*s.*)
phonics (*s.*)
physics (*s.* or *pl.*)
pneumatics (*s.*)
poetics (*s.* or *pl.*)
politics (*s.* or *pl.*)
statistics (*s.* or *pl.*)
tactics (*s.* or *pl.*)
whereabouts (*s.* or *pl.*)

Numerical amounts may have a plural form, but when the amount is conceived of as a unit, use a singular verb.

One hundred dollars is a fair price.
Sixty-five miles per hour is the posted speed limit.
Fourteen inches is adequate space.
Twelve pounds is enough to fill the container.
Thirty years is the length of my mortgage.

Collective nouns pertaining to groups also take a singular verb when thought of as a unit.

The *group* is assembling now.
The *committee* is ready to report.
The *board* is meeting tomorrow.
The *staff* is industrious.
The *population* is multiethnic.
The *team* is excited.

See also the discussion of nouns in Chapter 24. Chapter 64 gives a list of nouns and adjectives denoting nationality.

26

Adjectives That Cannot Be Compared

The form of adjectives can normally be changed to compare two or more things. The *comparative* is formed by adding *-er* to the basic adjective (*older*) or by using the word *more* with it (*more* people). The *superlative* is formed by adding *-est* (*largest*) or using *most* (*most* states). But some adjectives cannot be compared. An idea may be *perfect*, but it cannot be *more perfect*, since *perfect* already implies the most or best that it can be. For this reason, do not use *more* or *most* with words such as those listed below.

See also the discussion of adjectives in Chapter 24 and the list of adjectives that must be followed by a particular preposition in Chapter 34. Chapter 64 gives a list of adjectives denoting nationality.

absolute	fatal	possible
basic	final	primary
chief	full	ultimate
comparative	fundamental	unanimous
complete	meaningless	unique
contemporary	mortal	universal
empty	obvious	whole
essential	perfect	worthless

27

Common English Prepositions

The words listed here are the most familiar prepositions in the English language. Writers should remember, however, that some of these words can also be used as other parts of speech. The word *aboard,* for instance, also functions as an adjective and adverb. When any of the following terms are used as prepositions, they function to show the relationship between the object of the preposition and the antecedent of a preposition. The discussion of prepositions in Chapter 24 describes this relationship. See also Chapter 28 for a list of commonly misused prepositions and Chapter 34 for a list of adjectives and verbs that must be followed by a specific preposition.

aboard	bating	during
about	before	ere
above	behind	except(ing)
across	below	for
after	beneath	from
against	beside(s)	in
along	between	inside
alongside	betwixt	into
amid(st)	beyond	like
among(st)	but	mid
around	by	midst
aslant	concerning	near
at	considering	notwithstanding
athwart	despite	of
barring	down	off

on	round	under
onto (*or* on to)	save	underneath
opposite	saving	until (*or* till)
out	since	unto
outside	through	up
over	throughout	upon
past	till	via
pending	to	with
per	touching	within
regarding	toward(s)	without
respecting		

Phrasal prepositions, or *compound prepositions,* consist of two or more words regarded as a single preposition.

according to	from behind	in regard to
ahead of	from beneath	in respect to
alongside of	from between	inside of
along with	from over	in spite of
apart from	from under	instead of
as against	in accordance with	in view of
as between	in addition to	on account of
as compared with	in apposition with	on behalf of
as for	in back of	opposite to
aside from	in behalf of	out of
astern of	in case of	outside of
as to	inclusive of	over
as well as	in comparison to	owing to
away from	in comparison with	regardless of
because of	in compliance with	relating to
by dint of	in consequence of	relative to
by means of	in consideration of	round about
by reason of	in default of	up to
by virtue of	independently of	with a view to
by way of	in front of	without regard to
contrary to	in lieu of	with reference to
due to	in opposition to	with regard to
exclusive of	in place of	with respect to
for the sake of	in preference to	with the intention of
from above	in reference to	with the view of
from among	in regard to	

28

Commonly Misused Prepositions

Since many prepositions have more than one meaning, misuse is not uncommon. Some of the most troublesome prepositions are listed here. For an extensive list of verbs and adjectives that must be followed by certain prepositions, see Chapter 34. See also Chapter 27 for a list of common prepositions and the discussion of prepositions in Chapter 24.

among/between

Among is used with three or more persons or things, and *between* is used for only two.

The road runs *between* Phoenix and Tucson.
The report was circulated *among* the five members of the staff.

by/with

By refers to the person or thing doing something, and *with* concerns the object used to do it. (But use *by* after the word *surrounded* and *disturbed*. Use *with* after the word *infested*.)

The street was ruined *by* the salt.
The street was cleared *with* heavy equipment.
He was surrounded *by* fans.
The house was infested *with* roaches.

during/over

During is used in reference to time or a certain period, and *over* refers to a position above.

The price increased *during* the year.
She drove *over* the pothole.

from/with

From is used to distinguish one person or thing from another, and *with* is used in various references such as in regard to opinion, separation, opposition, or instrumentality.

The downtown area differs *from* the suburbs in many ways.
Your ideas differ considerably *from* hers.
They were threatened *with* a lawsuit.
He disagreed *with* his broker.

in/under

In is preferred in reference to being surrounded by, and *under* is preferred when one means influenced by, controlled by, subject to, or below. *In* also is used as a function word to suggest qualification.

She went *in* the store.
Under the circumstances, I agree.
In many ways you are alike.
The play was performed *under* the canopy.

of/off

Of has many uses such as a reference to origin, cause, or quality. *Off* refers to separation or suspension.

He is a descendant *of* the royal family.
She died *of* complications.
The top comes *off.*
He is *off* his diet.

29

Common Conjunctions

Two lists are given here—first common coordinate and subordinate conjunctions and then correlative conjunctions. The first list includes both *coordinating conjunctions,* which join words or sentences, and *subordinating conjunctions,* which join a subordinate element to another element in a sentence. *Correlative conjunctions* are used in pairs or in a series. Some of the words listed below, however, can function as more than one part of speech. *Since,* for example, can be used as an adverb, preposition, or conjunction. See also the discussion of conjunctions in Chapter 24.

after	except for	or
also	for the purpose of	provided
although	how	provided that
and	however	save
as	if	seeing
as if	in case	since
as long as	inasmuch as	so
as often as	in order that	so that
as soon as	in spite of	so . . . as (that)
as though	in that	still
because	lest	such . . . as (that)
before	neither	than
both	nevertheless	that
but	nor	then
but that	notwithstanding	therefore
either	now that	though
even if	only	till

unless
until
what
whatever
when
whence
whenever
where
whereas
whereat

whereby
wherever
wherefore
wherein
whereof
whereupon
wherever
whether
which

whichever
while
whither
who
whoever
why
with a view to
without
yet

The correlative conjunctions are:

although . . . yet
as . . . as
as . . . so
both . . . and
either . . . or
if . . . then
neither . . . nor

not only . . . but also
now . . . now
now . . . then
so . . . as
though . . . yet
whereas . . . therefore
whether . . . or

30

The Six Verb Tenses

Six verb tenses are used to denote the time that an action is or will be completed. The three basic time divisions in which an action can take place are past, present, and future. In addition, since an act may also be completed, or *perfected,* in time, there are three other tenses—the present perfect, past perfect, and future perfect.

For more about verbs, see the discussion in Chapter 24; see also Chapter 31 on irregular verbs and Chapter 32 on active and passive verbs. For a definition of an auxiliary verb, see Chapter 33.

1. *Present.* Denotes something occurring now—in the present—or is used to express an idea that is generally true. Unlike the *simple progressive (work, think, like,* and so on), the *progressive present* combines a form of the verb *to be* with the present participle of the main verb.

I *take* the test. (simple present)
They *are taking* the test. (progressive present)

2. *Present perfect.* Denotes something completed at the time it is mentioned or continuing into the present. This tense combines the past participle of the main verb with *have* or *has.*

As of now, I *have taken* the test.
As of now, she *has taken* the test.

3. *Past.* Denotes something already completed.

You *took* the test.
They *took* the test.

4. *Past perfect.* Denotes something completed before some specific time in the past. This tense combines the past participle of the main verb with *had.*

By noon, she *had taken* the test.
By noon, we *had taken* the test.

5. *Future.* Denotes something that will happen in the future. This tense adds *shall* or *will* to the main verb. Although formerly *shall* was used in the first person and *will* in the second and third persons to express the simple future, this rule is now primarily observed only in formal usage. *Will* is preferred in all cases in informal usage, especially to express forcefulness.

I *shall take* the test. (formal)
I *will take* the test. (informal)
He *will take* the test. (formal and informal)

6. *Future perfect.* Denotes something that will be completed at a specific time in the future. This tense combines the past participle of the main verb with *shall have* or *will have.*

By noon, I *shall have taken* the test. (formal)
By noon, I *will have taken* the test. (informal)
By noon, she *will have taken* the test. (formal and informal)

The following conjugation shows the use of the six tenses in the indicative mood (active voice), subjunctive mood (active voice), and imperative mood (active voice). (See the descriptions of mood in Chapters 24 and 33.) The example below uses the regular verb *call.* Regular verbs form the past and past participle by adding *-d* or *-ed.*

Indicative Mood (Active Voice)

Present: I call, he calls, we call, you call, they call
Present perfect: I have called, he has called, we have called, you have called, they have called
Past: I called, he called, we called, you called, they called
Past perfect: I had called, he had called, we had called, you had called, they had called
Future declarative: I shall call, he will call, we shall call, you will call, they will call
Future purposive: I will call, he shall call, we will call, you shall call, they shall call

Future perfect declarative: I shall have called, he will have called, we shall have called, you will have called, they will have called

Future perfect purposive: I will have called, he shall have called, we will have called, you shall have called, they shall have called

Subjunctive Mood (Active Voice)

Present: *If:* I call, he call, we call, you call, they call

Present perfect: *If:* I have called, he has called, we have called, you have called, they have called

Past: *If:* I called, he called, we called, you called, they called

Past perfect: *If:* I had called, he had called, we had called, you had called, they had called

Imperative Mood (Active Voice)

Present: Call.

31

Common Irregular Verbs

Whereas regular verbs all form the past and past participle by adding -d or
-ed, irregular verbs form the past and past participle in different ways. This
list includes the most commonly used irregular verbs in the present, past,
and past participle. The present participle of irregular verbs is generally
formed by using an -ing ending (blow, blew, blowing, blown; give, gave, giving, given; and so on). Note that when using the past participle, you should
add have, has, or had.

Present	Past	Past Participle
abide	abode	abode
awake	awaked/awoke	awaked/awoke
arise	arose	arisen
be (am)	was	been
bear	bore	borne
beat	beat	beaten/beat
become	became	become
begin	began	begun
behold	beheld	beheld
bid (offer to buy)	bid	bid
bid (command)	bade	bidden/bid
bind	bound	bound
bite	bit	bitten
bleed	bled	bled
blow	blew	blown
break	broke	broken
breed	bred	bred

bring	brought	brought
broadcast	broadcast/broadcasted	broadcast/broadcasted
build	built	built
burst	burst	burst
buy	bought	bought
cast	cast	cast
catch	caught	caught
choose	chose	chosen
cleave	cleft/clove/cleaved	cleft/cloven
cling	clung	clung
come	came	come
cost	cost	cost
creep	crept	crept
cut	cut	cut
deal	dealt	dealt
do	did	done
draw	drew	drawn
drink	drank	drunk
drive	drove	driven
eat	ate	eaten
fall	fell	fallen
feed	fed	fed
feel	felt	felt
fight	fought	fought
find	found	found
flee	fled	fled
fling	flung	flung
fly	flew	flown
forbid	forbade	forbidden
forget	forgot	forgotten
forsake	forsook	forsaken
freeze	froze	frozen
get	got	got/gotten
give	gave	given
go	went	gone
grind	ground	ground
grow	grew	grown
hang (a picture)	hung	hung
have	had	had
hide	hid	hidden
hit	hit	hit

hold	held	held
hurt	hurt	hurt
keep	kept	kept
know	knew	known
lay (place or put)	laid	laid
lead	led	led
leave	left	left
lend	lent	lent
let	let	let
lie (recline)	lay	lain
lose	lost	lost
make	made	made
mean	meant	meant
meet	met	met
mistake	mistook	mistaken
pay	paid	paid
put	put	put
read	read	read
rid	rid	rid
ride	rode	ridden
ring	rang	rung
rise	rose	risen
run	ran	run
say	said	said
see	saw	seen
seek	sought	sought
sell	sold	sold
send	sent	sent
set	set	set
shake	shook	shaken
shed	shed	shed
shine (give light)	shone	shone
shoot	shot	shot
show	showed	shown/showed
shrink	shrank/shrunk	shrunk/shrunken
shut	shut	shut
sing	sang	sung
sink	sank	sunk
sit	sat	sat
sleep	slept	slept
slide	slid	slid

sling	slung	slung
speak	spoke	spoken
speed	sped	sped
spend	spent	spent
spill	spilt/spilled	spilled
spin	spun	spun
spit	spat	spat
split	split	split
spread	spread	spread
spring	sprang/sprung	sprung
stand	stood	stood
steal	stole	stolen
stick	stuck	stuck
sting	stung	stung
stink	stank	stunk
strike	struck	struck/stricken
string	strung	strung
strive	strove	striven
swear	swore	sworn
sweep	swept	swept
swim	swam	swum
take	took	taken
teach	taught	taught
tear	tore	torn
tell	told	told
think	thought	thought
thrive	throve/thrived	thrived/thriven
throw	threw	thrown
thrust	thrust	thrust
tread	trod	trodden
understand	understood	understood
wake	waked/woke	waked
wear	wore	worn
weave	wove	woven
weep	wept	wept
win	won	won
wind	wound	wound
wring	wrung	wrung
write	wrote	written

32

Assertive versus Passive Verbs

There are two ways of saying things—actively (I *believe*) and passively (it *believed*). Most of the time the active voice (emphasizing the *doer* of an act) is preferred since it gives the impression that one is confident, knowledgeable, and determined. The passive voice (emphasizing the *receiver* of an act) often suggests a timid, uncertain stance. Moreover, the passive voice frequently sounds stuffy (It *is said* that . . .) compared to the straightforward active voice (He *said* that . . .).

The passive voice, however, provides a convenient way to soften the blow when criticism must be rendered: "An error *was made* on page 3" sounds less like a personal attack than "You *made* an error on page 3." Also, in some cases you may want to emphasize the receiver of an action more than the doer; the passive voice is then better: "His new car *was ruined* by water damage" (you want to emphasize the new car more than the water damage).

The following list consists of examples of passive verbs and their active counterpart. For *it* and *he,* you can substitute any desired noun or pronoun (e.g., *it* = *the car* or *the book,* and *he* = *they* or *she*). For more about verbs, see the discussion in Chapter 24 and Chapters 25, 30, and 31. See also Chapter 5 in Part I, "Action Words for Productive Messages."

it *was bought* by/he *bought*
it *was broken* by/he *broke*
it *has been caught* by/he *caught*
it *was cut* by/he *cut*
it *was decided* that/he *decided* that
it *is done* by/he *does*

it *was eaten* by/he *ate*
it *is enjoyed* by/he *enjoys*
it *was feared* that/he *feared* that
it *was forbidden* that/he *forbade* that
it *was grown* by/he *grew*
it *is held* that/he *holds* that
it *is known* that/he *knows* that
it *was left* by/he *left*
it *was lent* by/he *lent*
it *was lost* by/he *lost*
it *was mistaken* by/he *mistook*
it *is piloted* by/he *pilots*
it *has been read* by/he *read*
it *is rung* by/he *rings*
it *was said* that/he *said* that
it *has been seen* that/he *saw* that
it *was sent* by/he *sent*
it *was spread* by/he *spread*
it *was stolen* by/he *stole*
it *is sung* by/he *sings*
it *is taken* by/he *takes*
it *is taught* that/he *teaches* that
it *is thought* that/he *thinks* that
it *was thrown* by/he *threw*
it *is understood* that/he *understands* that
it *is used* by/he *uses*
it *has been washed* by/he *washed*
it *was won* by/he *won*
it *has been written* that/he *wrote* that

33

Essential Grammatical Terms

This list contains important grammatical terms that are essential to a thorough understanding of word usage. The eight parts of speech (noun, pronoun, adjective, adverb, verb, preposition, conjunction, and interjection) and associated terms are defined in Chapter 24. See also Chapters 25–32 and Chapter 34.

Active voice. A verb indicating that the subject of a sentence is performing the action. See Chapter 32.

Adjective. A word that modifies a noun or pronoun. See Chapters 24 and 26.

Adjective pronoun. A pronoun that modifies a noun. See Chapter 24.

Adverb. A word that modifies a verb, adjective, another adverb, and sometimes a noun or pronoun. See Chapter 24.

Antecedent. A noun or pronoun to which another pronoun refers: *Jennifer* (noun) arrived at *her* (pronoun) summer home.

Appositive. A word or words that identify or explain another word or words: Henry Marcus, *president,* resides in Lakeview.

Article. The adjectives *a* and *an* (indefinite articles) and *the* (definite article): He has *a* word processor.

Auxiliary verb. A verb that helps the main verb form a verb phrase: The wind *is* blowing.

Case. See *Nominative case; Objective case; Possessive case.*

Collective noun. A noun denoting a group or collection of objects. See Chapter 24.

Common noun. A noun denoting a class of persons, places, or things. See Chapter 24.

Comparative degree. A word form used to compare two persons or things. See chapter 26.

Comparison. The form of an adjective or adverb used to show the degree of comparison. See Chapters 24 and 26.

Complement. Completes the meaning of a verb: The storm caused the *damage.*

Compound predicate. Consists of two or more connected verbs or verb phrases: She *lectured* and *demonstrated* the equipment.

Compound sentence. Consists of two or more independent clauses: The raise in income was guaranteed, but then the company went bankrupt.

Compound subject. Consists of two or more words joined by *and, or,* or *nor:* The *president* and the *vice-president* disagreed over the action.

Conjunction. A word used to connect other words. See Chapters 24 and 29.

Coordinate conjunction. A conjunction that connects words, phrases, or clauses of equal value or rank. See Chapter 24.

Correlative conjunction. A conjunction used in pairs or a series. See Chapter 29.

Dangling modifier. Something that does not refer to another word or does not modify any other word (see also *Misplaced modifier*): *After hearing* (dangling) *from you, the package was opened. Better: After hearing from you, I opened the package.*

Demonstrative pronoun. A pronoun that points to an antecedent (noun) directly or demonstratively. See Chapter 24.

Dependent (subordinate) clause. Consists of a group of words in a sentence with a subject and predicate that alone does not express a complete thought: The team *that won the game* lost its star player.

Direct object. A noun or noun equivalent that receives a verb's action; it answers the questions *what* or *whom* after the verb: The supervisor attended (*what?*) the *seminar.*

Expletive. An introductory word (e.g., *it, there*) that is in the position of the subject when the actual subject comes after the verb: *There* are many newcomers on the payroll. *Better:* Many newcomers are on the payroll.

Gerund. A verb form that ends in *-ing* and is used as a noun; it may be a subject, a direct object, an object of a preposition, a subjective complement, or an appositive: *Working* is an obsession with him.

Imperative mood. An expression of a command, wish, or something similar. See Chapter 24.

Indefinite pronoun. A pronoun that stands for an object generally or indefinitely. See Chapter 24.

Indicative mood.   An expression that states or questions a fact. See Chapter 24.

Indirect object.   A noun or noun equivalent that usually indicates to whom or for whom something is done; it precedes the direct object in a sentence: Linda Skinner gave her *secretary* (indirect object) a *bonus* (direct object).

Infinitive.   A verb form used as a noun, an objective, or an adverb; it is usually preceded by *to*: They planned to *go* to Europe.

Interjection.   A word that expresses strong or sudden feeling. See Chapter 24.

Interrogative pronoun.   A pronoun that asks a question. See Chapter 24.

Intransitive verb.   A verb that has no object. See Chapter 24.

Irregular verb.   A verb that forms the past and past participle in different ways. See Chapter 31.

Misplaced modifier.   A modifier positioned in a sentence where it seems to modify the wrong word (see also *Dangling modifier*): He *only* (misplaced) read murder mysteries. *Better:* He read *only* murder mysteries.

Modifier.   A word or group of words that restrict or qualify the meaning of another word in a sentence (see also *Dangling modifier* and *Misplaced modifier*): It was a *rainy* day.

Mood.   The form of a verb used to show the attitude of the speaker or writer. See Chapter 24.

Nominative case.   Refers to the case of a subject or a predicate noun (see also *Objective case* and *Possessive case*): The *student* (subject) is also an *athlete* (predicate noun).

Nonrestrictive clause.   A subordinating clause that is not essential to the meaning of the sentence. Therefore, it is usually set off with commas (see also *Restrictive clause*): The new law, *which I find hard to comprehend,* is scheduled to go into effect on January 1.

Noun.   A word that names a person, place, thing, action, idea, or quality. See Chapters 24 and 25.

Objective case.   Refers to the case of a direct object, an indirect object, or the object of a preposition (see also *Nominative case* and *Possessive case*): She brought *him* (indirect object of *brought*) the *report* (direct object of *brought*) to submit to the *manager* (object of *to*).

Participle.   A verb form that is used as an adjective or a predicate adjective: The *expanding* work force is largely female.

Passive voice.   A verb indicating that the subject is receiving an action. See Chapter 32.

Person.   The one speaking, spoken to, or spoken of. See Chapter 24.

Personal pronoun.   A pronoun that indicates whether reference is to the person speaking, spoken to, or spoken of. See Chapter 24.

Phrasal preposition.   Two or more words regarded as a single preposition. See Chapter 27.

Possessive case.   Refers to the case that shows possession (see also *Nominative case* and *Objective case*): The *man's* hat blew away.

Predicate.   That part of a sentence containing the verb and other words that makes a statement about the subject (see also *Subject*): The purchasing agent *is the grandson of the president of the company.*

Predicate adjective.   An adjective that follows a linking verb. See Chapter 24.

Preposition.   A word that shows the relation between its object and an antecedent of the preposition. See Chapters 24, 27, and 28.

Prepositional phrase.   A preposition, its object, and any modifiers of the object. See Chapter 24.

Pronoun.   A word that takes the place of a noun. See Chapter 24.

Proper noun.   A word that names a particular person, place, or thing. See Chapter 24.

Reflexive or intensive pronoun.   A pronoun formed by adding *-self* or *-selves* to a personal or indefinite pronoun. See Chapter 24.

Relative adjective.   A relative pronoun used as an adjective. See Chapter 24.

Relative adverb.   An adverb that refers to an antecedent in the main clause but modifies a word in the subordinate clause. See Chapter 24.

Relative pronoun.   A pronoun that relates an antecedent to a dependent or qualifying clause. See Chapter 24.

Restrictive clause.   A clause that is essential to the sentence's meaning; therefore, it should not be set off with commas (see also *Nonrestrictive clause*): The home *with the eagle on the door* is the one where Marcia lives.

Subject.   A word or group of words in a sentence about which a statement is made (see also *Predicate*): *The shuttle service* was discontinued.

Subjunctive mood.   An expression of an action or state of being as desired, doubtful, or contrary to fact. See Chapter 24.

Subordinate conjunction.   A conjunction that connects a subordinate and principal element or clause in a sentence. See Chapter 24.

Superlative degree.   A form of adjective used to compare more than two persons or things. See Chapter 26.

Tense.   The form of a verb used to show the time of an action or state of being. See Chapter 30.

Transitive verb.   A verb that has an object. See Chapter 24.

Verb.   A word that expresses an action or state of being. See Chapters 24, 30, 31, and 32.

Verbal.   A verb form that is used as another part of speech. See *Gerund, Infinitive,* and *Participle.*

Voice.   The form of a verb indicating whether a subject is the doer or receiver of an action. See Chapter 32.

34

Idiomatic Expressions

Idiomatic expressions are forms of expression that are peculiar to the language and are accepted because of common usage, not because they are consistent with the rules of grammar. Because they aren't always logical, these expressions are sometimes used incorrectly, especially in choice of prepositions. The following list consists of examples of idiomatic usage. See also Chapter 23, "A Dictionary of Misused Words."

absolved by: He was *absolved by* the verdict.

absolved from: He was *absolved from* the obligation.

accompanied by: They were *accompanied by* the director.

accompanied on: They were *accompanied on* the tour by the director.

accord with: She acted in *accord with* company policy.

acquitted of: You are hereby *acquitted of* all charges.

adapted to: The rules can be *adapted to* any association.

adopted by: The film was *adopted by* Marcel Wyatt.

adopted from: The film was *adopted from* a book by Marcell Wyatt.

adverse: They labored under *adverse* conditions.

averse to: We would not be *averse to* that.

agree on: I *agree on* all points.

agree to: We *agree to* the proposed regulation.

agree with: Do you *agree with* me?

aim to prove: I *aim to prove* that you are wrong.

aloud: He said it *aloud.*

angry about: He is *angry about* the demotion.

angry at: She was *angry at* her dog.

angry with: I know you are *angry with* me.

argue about: Let's not *argue about* it.

argue against: One could effectively *argue against* the new law.

argue for: One could effectively *argue for* the new laws.

argue with: Please don't *argue with* me.

as regards: *As regards* your application, we are processing it now.

at home: They are *at home.*

beside: The car is *beside* the house.

besides: *Besides* being annoyed, I'm deeply concerned.

can't help feeling: One *can't help feeling* discouraged.

compared to: *Compared to* Lois, Belinda is an expert typist.

compared with: The increase this year was 30 percent *compared with* 40 percent last year.

communicate about: The exchange students will *communicate about* the technological improvements.

communicate with: The exchange students will *communicate with* one another about the technological improvements.

comply with: We must *comply with* the regulations.

confide in: He should *confide in* her.

confide to: He should *confide to* her that the disease is progressing.

conform to: We will *conform to* your standards.

conform with: We will *conform with* your standards.

conformity with: We will act in *conformity with* your standards.

connected by: The terminals are *connected by* telephone lines.

connected with: He is *connected with* the State Department.

consist in: Honesty *consists in* ethical principles.

consist of: The basic tools *consist of* pencil and paper.

convenient for: Would dinner at seven be *convenient* for you?

convenient to: The airport location is not *convenient to* everyone.

correspond to: Remaining silent does not *correspond to* telling the truth.

correspond with: You should *correspond with* your relatives more often.

described as: It could be *described as* primitive.

described to: The painting was *described to* me as primitive.

despair of: To *despair of* winning the lottery is hardly the end of the world.

died from: He *died from* the toxic chemicals.

died of: He *died of* cancer.

differ about: We *differ about* the value of a lower capital gains tax.

differ/different from: The new films *differ from* the old ones in many ways./The new films are *different from* the old ones in many ways.

differ in: The voters *differ in* their views of deregulation.

differ on: The voters *differ on* the matter of deregulation.

differ with: You may *differ with* me about deregulation, but everyone else agrees.

doubt if: *Avoid.*

doubt that: I (sort of) *doubt that* we can meet the deadline.

doubt whether: I (strongly) *doubt whether* anything will come of it.

enter at: You can *enter at* the side door.

enter for: They decided to *enter for* the state competition.

enter in: *Enter in* the minutes the names of all nominees.

enter into: They plan to *enter into* a formal contract today.

enter on/upon: Today I *enter on/upon* a new career.

free from: He wants to be *free from* his addiction.

free of: Now that the divorce is final, she is finally *free of* him.

graduated from: He *graduated from* college.

identical with: His car is *identical with* hers.

impatient at: She was *impatient at* the delay.

impatient of: He was *impatient of* (intolerant of) her bad manners.

impatient with: They were *impatient with* the waiter's sloppy service.

independent of: The student is now *independent of* his parents.

inquire about: We should *inquire about* her progress.

inquire after: We should *inquire after* her progress.

inquire at: You can *inquire at* the box office.

inquire into: Let's *inquire into* the reasons for her slow progress.

inquire of: You could *inquire of* the head nurse concerning her progress.

in search of: They went *in search of* the treasure.

interest in: I have an *interest in* real estate.

kind of: What *kind of* computer do you have?

lest it become: Let's act now, *lest it become* a problem.

live at: They *live at* the Royal Gardens.

live in: They *live in* a penthouse at the Royal Gardens.

live on: They *live on* an inheritance at the Royal Gardens.

listen at: You can *listen at* the door.

listen to: *Listen to* your friends.

must: We *must* go.

necessity for: The *necessity for* accuracy should be obvious.

necessity of: He pointed out the *necessity of* arriving early.

object to: Do you *object to* the report's language?

oblivious of: He was completely *oblivious of* his surroundings.

overcome by: They were *overcome by* financial difficulties.

overcome with: They were *overcome with* joy.

parallel between: Notice the *parallel between* her religious views and her life-style.

parallel with: The road runs *parallel with* the railroad tracks.

persuaded of: They were *persuaded of* the validity of their views.

persuaded to: They were *persuaded to* give up the fight.

plan to stay: Why don't you *plan to stay?*

preferable to: I think the country is *preferable to* the city.

provided: He will come *provided* you will be there.

superior to: The turbo model is *superior to* the others.

try to: I want to *try to* improve my spelling.

unmindful of: He seems *unmindful of* the heavy traffic.

vary from: Your idea may *vary from* mine.

vary in: The typewriters *vary in* type of keyboard arrangement.

vary with: Your productivity may *vary with* your level of stress.

worthy of: His work is *worthy of* recognition.

Rules and regulations ... must be applied with a certain degree of elasticity. ... They point the way and survey the road, rather than remove the obstacles.

—*The Chicago Manual of Style,* thirteenth edition, revised and expanded.
© 1969, 1982 by the University of Chicago. All rights reserved.

Part VI

THE STYLE OF WORDS

35 Capitalization Style

36 The Use of Diacritical Marks

37 Words That Should Be in Italics

38 Words That Should Be in Quotation Marks

39 When to Use Words for Numbers

40 When to Use Words for Symbols

35

Capitalization Style

Words are capitalized to indicate their significance and importance. Through capitalization, for example, you can distinguish between a *western* direction and a *Western* civilization. Although authorities do not always agree in matters of capitalization, and the preferred style in one office or profession may be very different from that in another, the trend is to use capitalization only for proper nouns (*New York*) and for special situations that require distinction or emphasis (*Big Brother*). Words such as *university* derived from proper nouns (*University of California*) are lowercased (in small letters). Some terms, however, can be used as a proper noun (capitalized) or a common noun (lowercased), and an independent judgment is necessary in such cases (*The Business Network; a business network*). In matters of capitalization, when in doubt, follow the style preferred by your employer or that used in your profession. The following rules and guidelines will help make your decisions easier.

ABBREVIATIONS

Rules and principles of capitalization concerning abbreviations are provided in Chapter 51, "Guide to Abbreviating Words."

ACTS, BILLS, CODES, AND LAWS

Capitalize the full, formal titles of acts, bills, laws, treaties, and the like; also capitalize any title by which something is generally known. But lowercase incomplete names or general references such as *the act*.

Some terms such as *Medicare/medicare* may be capitalized or lower-cased, as preferred.

Capitalize *Constitution* when it refers to the document of a specific country or state, but lowercase general references to *a constitution.*

Capitalize specific amendments, but lowercase general references to *an amendment.*

Declaration of Independence
Monroe Doctrine, the doctrine
Securities Exchange Act, the securities act, the act
Civil Rights Bill, the bill
Social Security/social security
the Reynolds rent-control bill, the rent-control bill, the bill
Code of Criminal Procedure, the code
the building code
the U.S. Constitution, the Constitution (U.S.)
the Ohio Constitution, the constitution (Ohio)
Tenth Amendment, the amendment
Treaty of Versailles, Versailles treaty, the treaty

THE ARTS

Capitalize the important words in titles of plays, hymns, songs, paintings, and so on.

Lowercase movements of a symphony, concerto, or other musical composition. Lowercase words such as *trio, quartet,* and *quintet* when they refer to compositions, but capitalize them when they are used in the name of performers.

In a poem, follow the poet's style in capitalizing or lowercasing the beginning of each line.

Capitalize the principal words in headings and titles of books, articles, lectures, reports, and the like, and lowercase articles, conjunctions, and prepositions. Prepositions of five or more letters may be capitalized, but the trend is to lowercase them. Prepositions of fewer than five letters are usually lowercased. Capitalize articles, prepositions, and conjunctions that immediately follow a marked break in a title, indicated by a colon or dash.

"Amazing Grace" (hymn)
Phantom of the Opera (play)
"Golden Girls" (television show)
"Posies for a Parlour" (short poem)

Rodin's *The Thinker* (sculpture)
Beethoven's Fifth Symphony, Symphony No. 5 in C Minor
William Tell Overture
Winston Trio (performers)
"I bridle in my struggling Muse in vain / That seeks to launch into a no-
    bler strain" (Pope)
Writing Style and Techniques
Operating Your Own Business
Trends in Telemarketing
How to Improve Your Spelling
Desktop Publishing at Home
Rules of Parliamentary Law
Discrimination—Alive and Well?
Word Processing: A Farewell to Typewriters

COMPOUNDS

Authorities differ concerning the capitalization of hyphenated compounds (when in doubt, follow the practice in your profession and use the
style consistently).

Capitalize the parts of a hyphenated word that would be capitalized if the
word were not hyphenated. Capitalize all parts of hyphenated words in titles
and headings, except when the second word modifies the first word or when
the two parts are treated as one word.

Lowercase the second part of compound numeral.

no-par stock
French-speaking countries
Anglo-Saxon history
ex-President Reagan
"Self-taught Writers" (article title)
Anti-intellectual Bias (subheading)
Guide to Nineteenth-Century Politics (book title)
Eighty-fifth Congress

EDUCATION

Capitalize the names of schools and colleges and their actual departments, but lowercase the words *school, college,* and *department* when they
are not part of the formal name.

Capitalize the names of high school, college, or university classes, but lowercase the word when it refers to a member of the class.

Capitalize academic degrees, honors, fellowships, and so on, whether or not they are abbreviated, if the person's full name is given. Lowercase such terms that are not part of an official name or title.

Capitalize the official names of courses.

Robert E. Lee High School, the high school
The George Washington University, the university
Public School No. 2, a public school
Department of Music, the music department
School of Business Administration, the business school
Senior Class, a senior
John Doe, Sc.D.; John Doe, Doctor of Science, the doctor of science
    degree
M.A., master of arts degree
Jennifer Lyons Fellowship, the fellowship
Ph.D., doctor of philosophy degree, the doctorate
History II, the history course
Modern Art 309, the course in modern art
I am studying history, Latin, and English.

FOREIGN NAMES

Articles, prepositions, and conjunctions (such as *du, de, la, le, von, van*) that are a part of foreign names are usually not capitalized unless the name is written without the first name or a title. But since some people with foreign names prefer capitals, writers should follow the person's preference.

E. I. du Pont de Nemours
De Vries, the author
Martin Van Buren (preferred spelling)
Ludwig von Beethoven
Dr. de la Buere

GEOGRAPHY

Capitalize the names of points of a compass when they refer to a section of a country, but lowercase them when they refer to direction or compass points.

Capitalize popular names of specific localities in a country, but lowercase words such as *ghetto* or *fatherland.*

Capitalize regional terms that are part of a precise descriptive title, but lowercase terms that are merely localizing adjectives.

Capitalize the word *coast* only when it refers to popularly recognized regions.

Capitalize major parts of the world or a country, but lowercase adjectives derived from them.

the East, eastern, an east exposure
Corn Belt
West Side
the Loop (Chicago)
Tennessee Valley, the valley
the Continent (Europe), continental Europe, a continent
the ghetto
the Eastern Shore
the South Shore
South Jersey (definite regional term)
northern China (localizing adjective)
southern Nevada (localizing adjective)
East Coast (U.S.), the coast
New England coast, the coast
North Carolina coast, the coast
British Empire, the empire
New World, Old World
Near East, Far East
West Africa, western Africa
Central America
central Europe (general), Central Europe (World War I political division)
North Atlantic, northern Atlantic
Arctic, arctic winter
Tropic of Cancer, the tropics
Orient, oriental
the Union (U.S.)
New England states
the West (U.S. region), western United States
Missouri River, the river

GOVERNMENT AND POLITICS

Capitalize the words *government* and *administration* only when they are part of an official title.

Capitalize the words *federal, national, state,* and so on only when they are part of a title, but lowercase them when they are used as adjectives referring to institutions or activities or as general terms.

Lowercase the word *nationals,* meaning citizens of a country.

Capitalize the full title of governmental departments, boards, committees, commissions, bureaus, and so on, but lowercase words such as *department* or *committee* when they are used alone in place of the full name.

Capitalize the names of domestic and foreign legislative, administrative, and deliberative bodies, but lowercase general or incomplete designations.

Capitalize the word *legislature* only when it is part of the exact name of a specific body.

Capitalize the names of political parties, factions, and alliances but not the word *party.* Lowercase words that are derived from the names of political parties, factions, and alliances.

Her Majesty's Government, the government of Britain, British
    government
the U.S. government, the federal government, the government
the Bush administration, the administration
the Texas government, the government of Texas, the government
the federal courts
Federal Register (publication)
National Labor Relations Board, the board
the National Freedom party, the party
national customs
the nationals in South Africa
Connecticut State, state of Connecticut, the state
Commonwealth of Massachusetts, the commonwealth
New York City, the city of New York, the city
Yavapai County, the county of Yavapai, the county
District of Columbia, the district
Fourth Congressional District, the congressional district
Ward 9, Ninth Ward, the ward
Sixth Precinct, the precinct
Sanitation Department, the department

U.S. Department of Justice, the Justice Department, the department
Bureau of Indian Affairs, the bureau
Council Budget Committee, the Budget Committee, the committee
U.S. Congress, the Congress
U.S. House of Representatives, the House
U.S. Senate, the Senate
Board of Water Control, the board
House of Lords, the House
the House of Commons, the lower house
Parliament (British), parliamentary
Illinois State Senate, the Senate (Illinois), the senate (no particular state)
Delaware General Assembly, the General Assembly (Delaware), the
    assembly (Delaware)
Hartford City Council, the City Council (Hartford), the city council (no
    particular city)
Mississippi Legislature, the legislature
Arkansas General Assembly, Arkansas legislature, the legislature
Republican party, Republicans, the party
the Left, the Right, Left Wing, Right Wing, leftists, rightists (political
    parties)
left wing (CIO)
Socialist party, Socialists (party members), socialists (general
    philosophy)
Communist party, communism, communistic
Democratic party, democratic, democracy

HISTORICAL TERMS

Capitalize eras of history and periods in the history of a language or literature, but lowercase informal adjectives in phrases such as early Victorian
and numerical periods such as twentieth century.

Lowercase very recent designations such as space age.

Capitalize the names of important events, but lowercase the word war unless it is part of the name of a war.

Capitalize the names of important historical documents.

Stone Age
Dark Ages
Middle Ages
Medieval Latin

Christian Era
the Diaspora
the Exile
ancient Greece
antiquity
baroque period
Elizabethan Age
the Renaissance, a renaissance of poetry
colonial period (U.S.)
Roaring Twenties
nineteenth century
World War I, the First World War, the war
Vietnam War, the war in Vietnam, the war
Battle of the Bulge, the battle
Magna Carta
Declaration of Independence, the declaration
Atlantic Charter, the charter
Monroe Doctrine, the doctrine
Missouri Compromise, the compromise

HOLIDAYS, SEASONS, AND FEAST DAYS

Capitalize religious holidays and feast days and secular and specially designated days and weeks. But lowercase descriptive days such as *primary day.*
Lowercase the names of seasons, unless they are personified.

Good Friday
Passover
Christmas Eve
Lent
Yom Kipper
Hanukkah
Thanksgiving day
Memorial Day
Clean-Up Week
inauguration day
spring, summer, autumn, midwinter
Spring, with her arms full of flowers . . .; Winter with his icy fingers . . .

LEGAL TERMS

Capitalize a court's full and official title, but lowercase the word *court* when it is standing alone or used generally. Capitalize references to the Supreme Court of the United States, however, including the word *Court.*

Capitalize titles preceding a proper name, but lowercase words such as *chief justice, associate justice, justice, judge, magistrate,* and *surrogate* when they stand alone.

Capitalize the words *Your Honor* or *His* or *Her Honor* when they refer to the presiding officer or judge, and capitalize the word *Court* when it refers to the presiding officer or judge.

Capitalize the words *bar* and *bench* only when they are used as part of a judicial body.

Capitalize the principal words in a case name, but lowercase the abbreviation *v* or *vs* (versus).

> U.S. Supreme Court, the Supreme Court, the Court
> Court of Appeals of New York, the Court of Appeals (capitalized to distinguish from the U.S. court), the court
> Nevada Supreme Court, the supreme court, the court
> the federal courts
> Judge Wilson's court
> magistrate's court
> traffic court
> night court
> General Sessions
> Associate Justice Mason, the associate justice
> Magistrate Lewis, the magistrate
> Surrogate Steinberg, the surrogate
> If it please *Your Honor* . . .
> In the opinion of the *Court* . . .
> The *Court* sustained the objection.
> Massachusetts Bar Association, the bar
> Court of King's Bench, the bench
> *Jane Doe* v. *City of Trenton,* the *Doe* case

LISTS

Capitalize the first word of each item in a list or outline.

Capitalize the first word in each item of an enumeration if the items are each a complete sentence. Lowercase items that do not form full sentences by themselves, but capitalize them if they are stacked in itemized fashion. Lowercase enumerations that are not introduced or preceded by a colon.

Follow the style preferred in your profession: (1) Spell out numbers one through nine. (2) Spell out numbers one through ninety-nine.

The standard rules apply to the following: (1) fractions, (2) ratios, and (3) proportions.

1. Numbers and fractions
    A. Standard rules
        1. Technical style
        2. Nontechnical style

Define rules for
    1. Sums of money
    2. Time and date
    3. Indefinite amounts

MILITARY SERVICE

Capitalize the official names of branches of the military services, but lowercase words such as *army* and *navy* when they are not part of an official title, when they stand alone, or when they are used collectively in the plural.

Capitalize the titles of various branches or divisions, but lowercase general references such as *army.*

Capitalize certain titles of distinction (listed below) whether the title is standing alone or is followed by a proper name.

Capitalize *Fleet Admiral* and *General of the Army* to avoid ambiguity, but generally lowercase titles when they are standing alone.

United States Army, the army, the armed forces
United States Marines, the marines
United States Navy, the navy
United States Signal Corps, Signal Corps, the corps
National Guard, the guard
Red Army, Russian army, the army
Third Army, the army
Second Division, the division
Company A, the company
Navy Militia, the militia
First Battalion, the battalion
the Chief of Staff

the General of the Army, the general
the Admiral of the Fleet, the admiral
the Adjutant General
the Judge Advocate General
the Paymaster General
Admiral Watts, the admiral
Commander Harmon, the commander
Major Jensen, the major

MONEY

The amount of money is always written out on checks, and each word is capitalized. But amounts are usually not capitalized in general writing.
Spell out amounts of money and capitalize each word in legal documents.

One Hundred Fifty and No/100 (check)
Six Hundred Forty-Seven Dollars ($647) [legal document]
We made a thousand dollars.

NOUNS AND ADJECTIVES

Capitalize the names of particular persons, places, and things (proper nouns), and capitalize common nouns and adjectives that are used in proper names.

Capitalize common nouns and epithets used with, or as substitutes for, proper names, but lowercase words derived from proper nouns that have developed a specialized meaning through use.

Capitalize nouns or abbreviations used with numbers or letters in a title. In general writing, lowercase common references such as *grade* and *article* (*grade 5, article 2*), but capitalize words such as *article* and *section* in formal documents and words such as *room* and *suite* in addresses. Also capitalize particular designations such as *Psalm 22*.

Henry Hudson
New York City
Statue of Liberty
the Canal (Panama)

the First Lady
the Liberty Bell
Peter the Great
anglicize
bohemian
italicize
japan varnish
manila envelopes
roman type, Roman numerals
Division XI
Ward 6
Class A
Precinct 3
grade 8, 8th grade
Sputnik II
World War II

ORGANIZATIONS

Capitalize the full, official names of organizations and institutions, but lowercase a common noun used in the plural with two or more names. Lowercase general references to an organization or institution. But in formal or legal writing, capitalize a general term (the *Corporation*) that stands for a specific organization or institution.

Capitalize trade names and follow the manufacturer's spelling and punctuation.

Prentice Hall, Inc.
Young Women's Christian Association, YWCA, the association
Princeton University, the university
Yale and Harvard universities, the universities
Metropolitan Opera, the opera
Amtrack, the railroad
Independent Order of Odd Fellows, an Odd Fellow, the order
Nashville Chamber of Commerce, the chamber of commerce
the Board of Directors (formal document), the board of directors
    (general)
Melville Transportation Company, the company

Board of Directors of Pendex Corporation, hereinafter called the Corporation, has adopted the following measures.
Coca-Cola, coke
Kleenex, tissue
Q-Tips Cotton Swabs, cotton swabs
Teletype

PEOPLES, RACES, AND TRIBES

Capitalize the names of peoples, races, and tribes, but lowercase terms that refer to color or localized designations.

Aryans
blacks
bush people
Caucasians
Jews
Malays
Negroes
Romans
whites

PERSONAL AND PROFESSIONAL TITLES

Capitalize professional, academic, and military titles or designations preceding names, but lowercase them following names or when they are used instead of names. Lowercase general descriptive titles such as *economist* even before a name.

Capitalize *president* only when it precedes a name. Also, capitalize the titles of cabinet members, heads of departments, and government dignitaries when they are used with names. Always capitalize *Speaker* (of the House of Representatives), even when used alone to avoid ambiguity.

Capitalize titles of state and municipal officials such as *governor, chief executive* (of a state), *lieutenant governor, mayor, borough president, senator, assemblyman, alderman,* or *president* of any municipal body when they are used with proper names. Lowercase these titles when they follow a name or are used as general terms.

Capitalize heads of state and city department such as *police commissioner, city counsel, commissioner of education, attorney general,* and *sheriff,* as well as subordinate titles such as *deputy sheriff* and *assistant attorney general,* when they precede names. Lowercase them when they follow a name or stand alone.

Capitalize business and professional titles when they precede a name, and lowercase them when they follow a name or are used instead of the name of a specific office or official. (In formal or legal writing, titles referring to a specific officer may be lowercase or uppercase.)

Capitalize titles of honor or nobility preceding a name (some British titles are also capitalized when used without a personal name), but lowercase them in all other instances.

Capitalize the words *acting, under,* and *assistant* only when they are part of a capitalized title that precedes a name.

When a common noun precedes a name but is separated from it by a comma, lowercase the noun.

Capitalize all parts of a compound title if any part is capitalized.

In formal lists such as address lists, titles and descriptive designations immediately following a name should be capitalized.

Governor Adams, the governor
District Attorney Schultz, the district attorney
Colonel Parker, Col. Ellen Parker, the colonel
historian Jim Miles, the historian
Mr. Brewer, president of Brewer Consulting, President Brewer, the
   president
Secretary of State Jim Baker, the secretary of state, the secretary
Tom Foley, Speaker of the House (of Representatives)
Governor Hill, the governor
Senator Glenn, the senator
Mayor Duggan, the mayor
Alderperson Ullman, Ms. Ullman, president of the Newton Board of Aldermen, President Ullman
Assistant Attorney General Jamison, the assistant attorney general
Commissioner Ireland, the commissioner
Mrs. Sharon Hart, president of Banner, Inc., President Hart, the
   president
Professor Van Sant, the professor
Dr. Otis, the doctor
Pope John Paul, the pope

Queen Elizabeth, the queen of England
the Duke of Kent
the Princess Royal
His Excellency
Your Grace
Under Secretary of Labor McDonald, the under secretary
The secretary, Miles Shannon, is on the executive committee.
Vice-President Quayle
Congressman-Elect Duvall
Ms. Jeanne Sims, President, Foley Parent-Teacher Association, 907 East
    Sunset Boulevard, Princeton, NJ 08540.

PERSONIFICATION

Capitalize things that are personified (given a human attribute) when
special emphasis is intended, but when in doubt, use lowercase.

Then *Winter* wrapped the hills in his white blanket.
The heavy snows of *winter* subsided.
Thus does *Nature* cry as humans savage her wooden breast.
It's true that *nature* can be violent.

PLANETS

Capitalize the names of planets and imaginative designations of celestial
objects, but capitalize words such as *stars, earth, moon,* and *sun* only when
they are used in connection with other planets that are always capitalized.

Big Dipper
Leo
Mars
Milky Way
Saturn
What is the distance from *Earth* to *Mars?*
The *earth* yields abundant minerals.

QUOTATIONS

Capitalize the first word of an exact quote if it is a complete sentence, but lowercase portions that do not form a complete sentence.

Do not capitalize indirect quotations or the first word of a quotation that is used as a syntactical part of a sentence.

The report stated, "Inflation will likely decline by mid-July."
The report said that "inflation will likely decline by mid-July."
The report said that inflation will probably fall by mid-July.
Was he serious when he said that inflation "will likely" fall by mid-July?
"If the report is correct," he said, "inflation will probably go down by mid-July."
"If the report is correct, inflation will probably go down by mid-July," he said. "But some authorities disagree."

RELIGION

Capitalize the word *church* when it is part of the name of a building.

Capitalize the title of a church dignitary when used before a name, but lowercase it in other instances.

Capitalize names and appellations of God (Lord) and other deities such as Zeus. (In Jewish literature, *the* deity *God* is spelled *G-d*.)

Capitalize the personal pronouns *he, his, him, thee, thou,* and so on when they refer to the deity only in cases where capitalization is necessary to avoid ambiguity, but lowercase the relative pronouns *who* and *whom.*

Capitalize names for the Bible and other sacred books and names of books and versions of the Bible, but do not underscore (italicize) or use quotation marks. Lowercase adjectives such as *biblical.*

Capitalize the names of religious denominations.

St. Paul's Catholic Church, the church
The First Lutheran Church, the church
the Roman Catholic church
the Baptist church
Pope John Paul, the pope
Cardinal Agnew, the cardinal
Deacon Harris, the deacon

Rabbi Goldberg, the rabbi
Father Marcos, the father, the priest
the Reverend Jane Ferris, the reverend
Mother Mary, the mother superior
God
Buddha
Allah
Christian religion
God is merciful, and *he* hears the prayers of all humankind.
the Gospels
Old Testament
Talmud, talmudic
Episcopalians
Gentiles, gentile practices
Mormons
Jesuit Order, the order

RESOLUTIONS

In resolutions, write every letter in the words *WHEREAS* and *RE-SOLVED* in capitals and begin *That* with a capital letter.

RESOLVED That . . .
WHEREAS . . .

SERIES OF QUESTIONS

When a series of questions is included in one sentence, capitalize the first word of each question.

What rules of capitalization apply to historical terms? To scientific terms? To governmental and political terms?

SPORTS

Capitalize colors such as *gold, maroon,* or *crimson* when they designate teams and refer to the associated colors.

Lowercase names of sports and games, unless the names are derived from proper names or are trade names.

Capitalize the names of playing fields and stadiums.

Capitalize words such as *cup, stakes,* and *trophy* only when they are part of a specific title.

The Red Devils lost.
The Blue and Gold are on a winning streak.
Their colors are blue and gold.
bridge
football
going to Jerusalem
Monopoly
Rugby
the Bowl
Madison Square Garden, the Garden (capitalized to avoid ambiguity)
Yankee Stadium, the stadium
Belmont Stakes, the stakes
Davis Cup, the cup
North American Trophy, the trophy

36

The Use of Diacritical Marks

Diacritics, or *diacritical marks,* are the accents on, through, or near letters that distinguish the sound of those accented letters from the same letters without accents. Foreign words often use diacritics (but see Chapter 61, "Familiar Foreign Words That Do Not Need Accents"), and dictionaries frequently use diacritical marks as a guide to pronunciation. The following list gives eight common diacritics with an example of the intended sound.

acute accent	´	(é)	Stress the accented letter as in *résumé.*
grave accent	`	(è)	Make a deep sound with the accented letter, as in *vis-à-vis.*
circumflex	^	(ô)	Make a soft sound with the accented letter, as in *entrepôt.*
tilde	~	(ñ)	Make a nasal *ny* sound with the accented letter as in *mañana.*
macron	–	(ā)	Make a long sound with the accented letter as in *bāke.*
breve	˘	(ŭ)	Make a short sound with the accented letter, as in *răcket.*
diaeresis	··	(oö)	Pronounce the accented vowel separately, as in *coöperate.*
cedilla	¸	(ç)	Make an *s* sound with the accented letter, as in *garçon.*

37

Words That Should Be in Italics

Certain words such as a book title are italicized in printed material to designate their meaning or add emphasis. Words that are meant to be italicized in the final published version of a document should be underlined in the manuscript copy.

The following words are usually italicized; for examples of words and titles that are usually set in roman type and quotes, see Chapter 37, "Words That Should Be in Quotation Marks."

WORDS USED AS WORDS

Words (and certain letters) referred to as words (or letters) or words that are defined are italicized. Also, in mathematical copy, letter symbols are usually italicized.

The word *leftist* is misleading.
Preform means to shape beforehand.
Delete the *e* in *judgement*: *judgment*.
Therefore, $y = 0$, and $x = 3$.

WORDS THAT ARE EMPHASIZED

Although amateur writers overdo it, words can be emphasized by italicizing them. Usually, though, the context in which words are used makes any necessary emphasis clear. In any case, entire sentences should not be italicized. When special terms are employed in a discussion, they may be italicized at first mention, but thereafter they should be set in roman type.

Consider the prospect of *unintentional* loss of data.
This section will discuss the pros and cons of a *living will.*

FOREIGN WORDS

Unfamiliar foreign words are italicized, but familiar foreign words should not be italicized or accented.

Latin abbreviations used in footnotes and bibliographies should not be italicized, although the word *sic,* pointing out a misspelling in quoted material, should be in italics.

It was a typical French *aphorisme.*
We'll begin with an aperitif (familiar term).
See ibid., p. 5.
He wrote that the mob was "desparate [*sic*] to the point of hysteria."

LEGAL CASES

The names of legal cases are usually italicized in nonlegal writing. The abbreviation *v.* or *vs.* (*versus*), however, may be set in either roman or italic.

L. G. McKay v. *State of Alabama*
The *McKay* case
Leonard McKay's case

SHIPS AND OTHER CRAFT

Italicize the official names of ships, submarines, airplanes, spacecraft, and satellites. But do not italicize any abbreviation such as *ss* that precedes a name, and do not italicize designations of class or make.

SS *United States.*
Spirit of St. Louis
Voyager 2

Boeing 727
ICBM

PLANTS AND ANIMALS

The rules for italicizing the names of genus and species vary among the professions of botany, bacteriology, and zoology, and the following examples are intended only as a guide for general use.

Usually, the Latin names of genera, species, and varieties as well as their subgroupings are italicized, whereas roman type is used for the higher-rank phylum, class, order, and family, as well as their subgroupings. Common names are set in roman type.

the *Ficus* species
the family Fringillidae
a golden retriever

TITLES

In both reference notes and in general text, the titles and subtitles of published books, collections, periodicals, newspapers, and pamphlets are set in italics. The word *the* in newspaper and periodical titles is usually omitted in footnotes and set in roman type with a small *t* in text discussion.

The titles of long poems and the titles of plays and motion pictures are italicized. The formal titles of paintings, statues, and other art are also italicized, but descriptive titles are set in roman. The titles of operas, oratorios, motets, tone poems, and other long musical compositions are italicized. But references to a key or musical form are set in roman.

The Complete Word Book (book title)
Time (magazine)
The New York Times (newspaper)
Paradise Lost (long poem)
Cats (play)
Rain Man (motion picture)
Rodin's *The Thinker* (sculpture)
Mona Lisa (descriptive title of painting)
Don Giovanni (opera)
Beethoven's Piano Concerto no. 5, the *Emperor* Concerto (musical
   composition)

38

Words That Should Be in Quotation Marks

Although quotation marks are necessary in certain situations, amateur writers tend to overuse them, and they become distracting and annoying to readers. When used correctly, however, they lend clarity to the text.

In American-style punctuation, periods are placed inside the quotation marks unless single quotes are used to enclose a special term; then the period is placed outside the closing single quote mark. Colons and semicolons are placed outside the quotation mark.

When several paragraphs are quoted from the same source and not set as an extract (blocked and indented from the text), use quotation marks at the beginning of each paragraph but only at the end of the last paragraph. In material set as an extract, quotation marks are not used at the beginnings and ends of paragraphs. Any quoted material, such as dialogue, within the extract, however, must be enclosed in double quotation marks.

EXACT QUOTES

Exact quotes of spoken or written material must be enclosed in quotation marks unless the material is indented as a blocked quotation (*extract*).

"Our lesson today," he said, "will examine the use of 'intuition'."
"'Emphasize biology, not statistics,' is the message in the biology stylebook," wrote the newsletter consultant.

Extract

Use quotation marks to enclose precise quotations. . . , but do not enclose *yes* or *no* except in direct discourse. . . . Do not use quotation marks when the name of a speaker or writer introduces the quoted work, for example:

James: Yes, I did.

This opening paragraph is set flush left because it is not the first sentence in the paragraph from which it is taken. . . . As stated in *Writing Well,* by Dawn Watters, "Use ellipsis points to signify omitted words, sentences, or paragraphs," with three dots signifying words omitted in the middle of a sentence and four dots signifying material omitted at the end of a sentence.

TITLES

Certain titles are set in roman type and enclosed in quotation marks rather than italicized (see also Chapter 37): article and chapter titles, titles of unpublished works, short poems, radio and television programs, and songs and short musical compositions.

"Today's Drug Problem" (article title)
"Winterland" (short poem)
"The Greenhouse Effect on Regional Development in North America"
   (master's thesis)
"Golden Girls" (television program)
"Yesterday" (song)

SPECIAL TERMS

Some professional activities such as theology, philosophy, and linguistics use single quotes for special terms.

The modulation of the voice is 'intonation'. (definition in linguistics)

WORDS USED AS WORDS

Although written words used as words are italicized (see Chapter 37), quotation marks may be used if the spoken language is implied.

When speakers use "you" instead of "one," they are personalizing their comments.

SLANG

Slang words may be enclosed in quotation marks if the term is very unusual or offensive or in some other way must be called to the attention of the reader; do not, however, use quotation marks with commonplace, casual expressions that are clear to the reader.

The high-potency "designer drugs" are extremely dangerous.
The hometown team is hot tonight.

IRONY

Words used in irony may be enclosed in quotation marks if the meaning would otherwise not be clear. In most cases, however, the meaning is obvious, as is the use of *dandy* in the following sentence.

"Oh, isn't that just dandy," he said, surveying the crumpled fender on his car.

SO CALLED

Do not enclose terms following the words *so called* in quotation marks.

This is the so-called summer doldrums.

39

When to Use Words for Numbers

Numbers are usually spelled out as words in nonscientific usage (except in accompanying footnotes and tabular matter), whereas figures are more often used in scientific material.

See also Chapter 40, "When to Use Words for Symbols."

GENERAL RULE

In general nonscientific text, spell out numbers one through ninety-nine and large round numbers, except in paragraphs with large uneven numbers. Also, spell out approximate references such as *a million people.* In scientific material, figures are often used for all numbers above ten. The following examples apply to general, nonscientific writing.

In attendance were *five* engineers and *one hundred* architects.
In attendance were *5* engineers and 101 architects.
The population increased from *two hundred thousand* to *a million.*
The population increased from *two hundred thousand* to *1 million.*
The population increased from *793,642* to *1,832,476.*

BEGINNING OF A SENTENCE

Spell out any word that is the first word in a sentence, whether in nonscientific or scientific usage and whether or not figures are usually called for, as they are in the case of percentages.

Five percent of the profits is reinvested, and *10* percent is assigned to capital accounts.

CENTURIES AND DECADES

Spell out centuries and decades in both general text discussion and in titles of published works.

The book covers *twentieth-century* politics.
He wrote the article "The *Twentieth-Century* Politician."

CLOCK TIME

If the time of day is in even, half, or quarter hours, spell out the numbers in general usage.

The meeting is scheduled for *half-past ten* o'clock in the morning.
The meeting adjourned at *12:35* p.m.

GOVERNMENTAL REFERENCES

Spell out governmental designations such as the *Third Reich.*

The exhibit pertained to the *Tenth* Dynasty.

MONEY

Treat numbers referring to sums of money the same as any other number. See "General Rule."

I think it cost two hundred and fifty dollars.
I think it cost $250.16.

WEIGHTS AND MEASURES

Treat the numbers with weights and measures the same as any other number. See "General Rule."

We traveled *two hundred* kilometers yesterday.
We traveled *207* kilometers yesterday.

40

When to Use Words for Symbols

Although symbols are used freely in scientific text and in business or commercial records and forms, they should be avoided in general, nonscientific usage, and words should be substituted whenever possible.

See also Chapter 39, "When to Use Words for Numbers."

BEGINNING A SENTENCE

The first word in a sentence should always be spelled out.

Fahrenheit (not *F*) has been replaced by *Celsius* measures in many organizations.
Two hundred *dollars* (not $) is a fair price.

CHEMICAL TERMS

Spell out the symbol in general, nonscientific text.

The *mercury* (not *Hg*) content was dangerously high.

MONETARY SYMBOLS

Spell out monetary symbols such as *$* when amounts involve the numbers one through ninety-nine, large round numbers, or approximate numbers. When figures are used for the amount, use a symbol.

forty *pesos,* Mex$473.09
three hundred *Canadian dollars,* Can$384.76
ninety-nine *francs,* F162.39
a thousand *dollars*

PERCENTAGES

Spell out the word *percent* in general, nonscientific usage, except in tabular matter. But use figures instead of words with *percent* unless the amount is the first word in a sentence.

Sixty percent is a good return.
A *60 percent* response is good.

TABULAR MATTER

Use words for symbols in heads and the stub (left column) if space permits. Otherwise, use symbols. Percent, dollar, and other signs and symbols, rather than words, are commonly used throughout the body of a table.

Homes (%)	*Population (%)*
Percentage of Homes	*Percentage of Population*

WEIGHTS AND MEASURES

Use words for the symbols designating a quantity, weight, or measure in general, nonscientific usage, except in tabular matter.

three-by-five-*inch* card
8½-by-11-*inch* paper
thirty *pounds*
a hundred *miles*
eight *cubic centimeters*
98.6 *degrees*

Most spelling difficulties are caused by speech sounds that can be spelled in more than one way.

—Adapted and reprinted by permission from *The Word Book II.*
Copyright © 1983 by Houghton Mifflin Company.

Part VII

SPELLING AND WORD DIVISION

41 Guide to Spelling

42 Commonly Misspelled Words

43 Guide to Prefixes

44 Common Prefixes

45 Guide to Suffixes

46 Common Suffixes

47 Guide to Writing Compounds

48 Common Compounds

49 Guide to Word Division

41

Guide to Spelling

The greatest handicap in spelling is the large number of exceptions to the general rules. But many writers find that even limited rules are better than no rules. If you keep in mind that there are many exceptions, the guidelines in the following sections for forming plurals as well as the guidelines given in Chapters 43, 45, and 47 should help you to increase the accuracy of your spelling. (For rules pertaining to writing the various parts of speech, see Part V.)

SINGULAR NOUNS

Make a singular noun plural by adding *s* or, occasionally, *es*.

car, cars	box, boxes
desk, desks	church, churches
file, files	class, classes
house, houses	fox, foxes
tree, trees	tax, taxes

IRREGULAR NOUNS

With a few nouns, it is necessary to change the spelling to form the plural. In other cases, the singular and plural are spelled the same.

child, children	mouse, mice
foot, feet	ox, oxen
goose, geese	tooth, teeth
man, men	woman, women

athletics, athletics
corp, corps
deer, deer

fish, fish
moose, moose
sheep, sheep

COMPOUND TERMS

With most compound terms, make the most important word plural. Occasionally, both words are equally important, and therefore both are made plural. If no word seems important alone or neither word is a noun, make the last word plural. For more about compounds, *see* Chapters 47 and 48.

adjutants general
ambassadors at large
attorneys general
brigadier generals
lieutenant colonels
notaries public
senators-elect
sergeants major
bills of lading
coats of arms

courthouses
cupfuls (but: two cups full)
forget-me-nots
go-betweens
jack-in-the-pulpits
passers-by
pick-me-ups
trade unions
women doctors

NOUNS ENDING IN CH, S, SH, SS, X, OR Z

Add *es* to form the plural of nouns ending in *ch, s, sh, ss, x,* or *z.*

bias, biases
box, boxes
business, businesses
church, churches
dish, dishes
dress, dresses
fox, foxes
glass, glasses
lens, lenses
process, processes
quartz, quartzes
sketch, sketches
tax, taxes
wish, wishes

NOUNS ENDING IN F, FE, OR FF

Words ending in *f, fe,* or *ff* are made plural in different ways. With some, add *s*; with others, change *f* or *fe* to *ve* and add *s*. Some nouns have two acceptable plural forms.

belief, beliefs
cliff, cliffs
handkerchief, handkerchiefs
proof, proofs
tariff, tariffs
safe, safes
half, halves
knife, knives
life, lives
loaf, loaves
shelf, shelves
wife, wives

NOUNS ENDING IN O

If the final *o* in a word is preceded by a vowel, add *s* to form the plural. If the *o* is preceded by a consonant, add *es* in most cases, *s* in a few cases (and always with musical terms), and *s* or *es* in a few cases.

folio, folios
ratio, ratios
stereo, stereos
studio, studios
hero, heroes
potato, potatoes
tomato, tomatoes
veto, vetoes
auto, autos
dynamo, dynamos
memo, memos
photo, photos
piano, pianos
solo, solos
soprano, sopranos
trio, trios
cargo, cargos, cargoes

ghetto, ghettos, ghettoes
motto, mottos, mottoes
zero, zeros, zeroes

NOUNS ENDING IN Y

Usually, if the final *y* in a word is preceded by a vowel, add *s* to form the plural (but see *soliloquy* and *colloquy* below). If the *y* is preceded by a consonant, change the *y* to *i* and add *es*.

attorney, attorneys
boy, boys
day, days
delay, delays
donkey, donkeys
guy, guys
valley, valleys
baby, babies
berry, berries
century, centuries
colloquy, colloquies
commodity, commodities
copy, copies
country, countries
lady, ladies
liability, liabilities
policy, policies
soliloquy, soliloquies

COMBINATIONS OF *I* AND *E*

The following rhyme is taught in many schools to help students combine *i* and *e* correctly: Use *i* before *e* except after *c* or when sounded like *a* as in *neighbor* and *weigh*; and except *seize* and *seizure* and also *leisure, weird, height,* and *either, forfeit,* and *neither.*

believe	weight
conceive	freight
deceive	either
receive	forfeit
neighbor	height

leisure   seizure
neither   weird
seize

ABBREVIATIONS

Make most abbreviations plural by adding *s.* Some, however, such as metric abbreviations, are considered singular or plural without adding *s*. Others double the letters of the abbreviation, as in *pp.* for *pages.* See Part VIII, "Abbreviated Forms of Words," Chapters 50–57, for numerous examples.

Dr., Drs.
ft., ft.
mgr., mgrs.
mm, mm
mo., mos.
no., nos.
p., pp.
v., vv.
vol., vols.
VW, VWs

FIGURES AND LETTERS

Add an apostrophe with *s* in forming the plural only if *s* alone would be confusing.

a's and *b*'s   Ph.D.'s
p's and *q*'s   YMCAs
3's and 4's   1990s
6's and 7's

POSSESSIVE CASE

Add an apostrophe and *s* to form the possessive of a singular noun that does not end in an *s* sound. If it has an *s* sound, add an apostrophe and *s* if pronouncing the possessive causes a new syllable to be formed. But if that makes the word hard to pronounce, use only an apostrophe. Because so much depends on sound in forming possessives, the way a writer pronounces a word will determine how some are written.

attorney's case
Arizona's desert
Arkansas's White River
boss's promotion
Dallas's skyscrapers
for goodness' sake

Jesus' sermon
Los Angeles' traffic problems
Mary's husband
Phoenix's urban sprawl
witness's testimony

With a plural noun ending in *s*, add an apostrophe alone to form the possessive. If the plural noun does not end in *s*, add an apostrophe and *s* to form
the possessive.

Adamses' house
alumni's fund drive
boys' bicycles
children's playground
companies' policies

men's gymnasium
secretaries' training class
sisters-in-law's friendship
vice-presidents' meeting
witnesses' testimony

42

Commonly Misspelled Words

People who write or process written material sometimes repeatedly misspell the same word. In certain cases the reason is obvious—perhaps the word is unfamiliar or it sounds different from the way it is spelled. Or perhaps it sounds the same as some other word that is spelled differently. (See Chapters 20 and 21 for examples of words that are confusing because they sound the same or look alike.) In other cases, the reason for misspelling a word may be that rules of spelling were never learned or have been forgotten. Or perhaps the numerous exceptions to spelling rules were never mastered. Businesses and business schools believe the following are some of the most frequently misspelled words in the English language.

abhorrence	accuracy	admirable
absence	accustom	advantageous
absurd	achieved	advertisement
accede	achievement	advertising
accept	acknowledgment	advisable
acceptance	acquaintance	advise
accessible	acquainted	adviser
accessory	acquiesce	advisory
accidentally	acquire	affect
accommodate	acquitted	affects
accompanied	across	affidavit
accompanying	adapt	aggravate
accordance	address	agreeable
accrued	adequate	aisle
accumulate	adjustment	allotment

allotted
allowable
allowance
all right
almost
already
altar
alter
altogether
aluminum
alumnus
amateur
ambassador
amendment
among
analogous
analysis
analyze
angel
angle
announce
announcement
annoyance
annual
anticipate
anxiety
anxious
apocalypse
apologize
apparatus
apparel
apparent
appearance
appliance
applicable
applicant
appointment
appraisal
appreciable
appropriate
approximate

archaeology
archipelago
architect
arctic
argument
arrangement
article
ascend
ascertain
assassin
assessment
assignment
assistance
associate
assured
attendance
attention
attorneys
auditor
authorize
auxiliary
available
awkward
baccalaureate
bachelor
bankruptcy
barbarous
bargain
baroque
barren
basis
beggar
beginning
believe
believing
beneficial
beneficiary
benefited
biscuit
bloc (political)
bologna

bookkeeper
bouillon
boundary
boutonniere
brilliant
brochure
bruised
budget
bulletin
buoy
buoyant
bureau
business
businessperson
busy
caddie (golf)
caddy (tea)
cafeteria
calendar
calk
campaign
canceled (cancelled)
cancellation
candidate
cannot
capital
capitol (building)
career
carriage
casualty
catalog(ue)
catechism
catsup
caulk
cellar
cemetery
chancellor
changeable
changing
characteristic
chauffeur

chlorophyll
choice
choose
cigarette
cinnamon
circumstances
client
clientele
clique
coarse
coconut
collar
collateral
colonel
column
coming
commission
commitment
committed
committee
commodity
comparable
comparative
comparatively
comparison
compel
compelled
competent
competitor
complement
compliment
compromise
concede
conceivable
conceive
concern
concurred
conference
confident
confidential
congratulate

concession
connoisseur
conscience
conscientious
conscious
consensus
consequence
consignment
consistent
contemptible
continuous
controlling
controversy
convenience
convenient
cordially
corporation
correspondence
correspondents
council
councilor (council
    member)
counsel
counselor (legal)
courteous
courtesy
coverage
creditor
crescendo
criticism
criticize
cruelty
cryptic
curiosity
current
customer
cyanide
dealt
debater
debtor
deceitful

deceive
decide
decision
deductible
defendant
defense
deference
deferred
deficient
deficit
definite
definitely
delegate
delicatessen
demagogue
dependent
depositor
derivative
descendant
describe
description
desirable
desperate
deteriorate
develop
development
device
devise
dialog(ue)
diaphragm
diarrhea
dictionary
dietitian
difference
different
dilemma
director
disappear
disappoint
disastrous
discipline

discrepancy
disk
disparate
dissatisfied
dissipate
drought
drudgery
dungeon
dying
dyeing
eagerly
ecclesiastical
economical
ecstasy
edible
edition
effect
effects
efficiency
efficient
eighth
eligible
eliminate
embarrass
emergency
eminent
emphasis
emphasize
employee
enclose
encumbrance
endeavor
endorse
endorsement
enemy
enterprise
enthusiasm
envelope
environment
equaled
equipment

equipped
equivalent
especially
essential
esthetic
etiquette
exaggerate
exceed
excel
excellence
excellent
except
excessive
exercise
exhaust
exhibit
exhilarate
existence
expedite
expenditure
expense
experience
explanation
extension
extraordinary
extremely
facilities
familiar
familiarize
fantasy
fascinate
favorable
favorite
feasible
February
fetus
fiery
finally
financial
financially
financier

forbade
forcible
foreign
foremost
forfeit
formally
formerly
fortuitous
forty
forward
fourth
frantically
freight
friend
fulfill
fulfillment
fungus
furthermore
gage
gaily
gallant
galosh
gasoline
gauge
generally
genius
genuine
glamour (glamor)
goddess
good-bye (good-by)
gourmet
government
governor
grammar
grandeur
grateful
grief
grievance
grievous
gruesome
guarantee

guerilla
guidance
guitar
gypsy
hallelujah
handkerchief
handled
harangue
harass
hardware
hazardous
height
heinous
hesitancy
hesitant
hesitate
heterogeneous
heterogenous
hiccup
hindrance
homogeneous
homogenous
hoping
horrible
hosiery
humorous
hundredths
hurriedly
hygienic
hyperbole
hypocrisy
icicle
identical
idiosyncrasy
idyll (idyl)
ignorant
illegible
imaginary
imitation
imitative
immediately

immigration
imminent
imperative
imperiled
impossible
impromptu
inasmuch as
incarcerate
incidentally
inconvenience
incredible
incredulous
incurred
indebtedness
independence
independent
indict
indigestible
indispensable
individual
induce
inducement
inevitable
infinite
influential
initial
innocence
inquiry
installment
instance
intellectual
intelligence
intelligible
intention
intentionally
intercede
interest
interface
interrupted
inventory
investor

irrelevant
irresistible
itemized
itinerary
it's
itself
jeopardize
jeopardy
jewelry
judge
judgment
juggle
justifiable
khaki
kindergarten
kleptomaniac
knapsack
knead
knell
knotty
knowledge
knowledgeable
knuckle
kosher
Ku Klux Klan
laboratory
landlord
larynx
legible
legitimate
leisure
lenient
length
letterhead
liable
liaison
library
license
licorice
lightning
likable

likelihood	modernize	omission
likely	momentous	omit
literature	monolog	omitted
livelihood	morale	operate
llama	mortgage	opinion
loath	murmur	opportunity
loneliness	muscle	optimistic
loose	mustache	ordinary
lose	necessary	organization
lying	negligible	organize
lymph	negotiate	original
magazine	neighborhood	outrageous
maintain	neither	overdue
maintenance	nestle	overrun
management	nevertheless	pageant
manual	niece	paid
manufacturer	niche	pajamas
manuscript	nickel	pamphlet
marital	nil	pantomime
marriage	ninetieth	parallel
Massachusetts	ninety	parliament
material	ninth	partial
materiel	nobody	participant
mathematics	no one	particularly
maximum	noticeable	pastime
meager	notoriety	patronage
medical	nowadays	peculiar
medicine	nuclear	perceive
medieval	nucleus	percent
memorandum	oblige	peremptory
menus	obstacle	periphery
merchandise	occasion	permanent
messenger	occasionally	permissible
mileage	occupant	permitted
miniature	occur	perseverance
minimum	occurred	persistent
miscellaneous	occurrence	personal
mischievous	occurring	personnel
misspell	offense	perspiration
Mississippi	offering	persuade
moccasin	official	phase

physician
physically
picnic
picnicking
piece
planning
pleasant
pleasure
plebiscite
plow
politician
portentous
possess
possession
possibly
practical
practically
practice
prairie
precede
precedence
precision
preferable
preference
preferred
prejudice
preliminary
premium
preparation
presence
prevalent
previous
price list
primitive
principal (adj.)
principle (n.)
privilege
probably
procedure
proceed
prodigy

professor
prominent
promissory
pronunciation
propeller
prophecy
prophesy
prosecute
psyche
psychiatrist
psychology
ptomaine
pumpkin
purchase
pursue
quantity
quay
questionnaire
queue
quiet
quite
quixotic
quiz
quizzes
raccoon
realize
really
reasonable
recede
receipt
receive
recently
recipe
recognize
recognized
recommend
reconnaissance
recurrence
refer
referee
reference

referred
referring
region
registrar
regrettable
reign
reimburse
relieve
religious
remember
reminisce
remittance
renewal
repeat
repetition
representative
respectively
requirement
reservoir
resistance
respectfully
response
responsible
responsibility
restaurant
reticence
rhetoric
rheumatism
rhythm
ridiculous
route
satisfactory
savior (saviour)
scarcely
scenery
scepter
schedule
schism
science
scythe
secession

secretary
securities
seized
sensible
sentinel
separate
sergeant
several
severely
serviceable
shepherd
shipment
shipping
shone
shown
shriek
siege
significant
similar
simile
simultaneous
sincerity
smolder
solemn
soliloquy
somewhat
sophomore
specimen
speech
someone
specialize
stationary
stationery
statistics
strenuous
strictly
studying
suave
submitted
subpoena
subscriber

substantial
succeed
successful
sufficient
suffrage
summarize
superintendent
supersede
supervisor
suppress
surprise
survey
syllable
symmetrical
symmetry
tariff
tendency
temperament
temperature
temporary
theater
their
there
thorough
thousandth
throughout
tied
too
tournament
toward
tragedy
tranquility
transfer
transferred
trauma
treacherous
treasurer
tremendous
tried
truly
twelfth

tying
typical
typing
tyranny
ultimately
unanimous
undoubtedly
unfortunately
universally
unnecessary
until
unusual
urgent
usable
usage
usually
vacancy
vaccination
vacuum
valuable
various
vehicle
vendor
vengeance
vicinity
victory
vigilance
villain
visible
vitiate
volume
voluntary
volunteer
warehouse
weather
Wednesday
weird
whether
wholesale
wholly
who's

whose   yaw   zebra
wintry   yea   zephyr
wiry   yearn   zero
withhold   yeoman   zigzag
worthwhile   yield   zinc
wrestle   yoke   zodiac
writing   yolk   zombie (zombi)
written   your
yacht   you're

43

Guide to Prefixes

A *prefix* is one or more letters or syllables attached to the *beginning* of a base, stem, or root to change its meaning. Most prefixes are attached to a common noun without a hyphen, but a hyphen separates a prefix and a capitalized proper noun (see also other exceptions in discussion below). The following examples illustrate whether a prefix should be written hyphenated or closed. Chapter 44 lists common prefixes and their meanings.

Spelling errors most often occur when the last letter of a prefix is the same as the first letter of the original word to which it is attached. When this occurs, retain both letters.

eminent, *pre*eminent   satisfy, *dis*satisfy
natural, *un*natural   spell, *mis*spell

In most cases, do not put a hyphen between a prefix and the original word. A hyphen is necessary, however, when a prefix is attached to a proper noun and is sometimes preferred for reading clarity when the combination causes the letter *i* to be doubled. It is also common to hyphenate affixes such as *ex-*, *self-*, and *vice-*. The addition is needed to distinguish meaning, as in *reform* (to amend or improve) and *re-form* (to form again) or to avoid confusion with another word, as in *co-respondent* and *correspondent*.

*anti*drug   *non*nuclear   *self*-confident (but: *self*same)
anti-American   *over*confident   *sub*state
*co*operate   *pro*-American   *under*rate
ex-president   *re*enact   *vice*-president
*extra*curricular

44

Common Prefixes

Some prefixes have become commonplace in English-language usage, but they may have Latin or Greek origins. Although the meanings and forms of some prefixes are diverse and complex, the following list illustrates many of the common prefixes that can be added to original word forms without making structural changes. See also Chapter 43 concerning the spelling of prefixes.

a- (on; toward): *a*board
ab- (away; from): *ab*duct
acro- (height; summit): *acro*polis
ad- (to; for): *ad*sorb
after- (after): *after*taste
allo- (divergence): *allo*pathy
ambi- (both; around): *ambi*dextrous
ante- (before): *ante*bellum
anthropo- (man; human): *anthropo*logy
anti- (opposed to): *anti*-Communist
apo- (lack of; defense of): *apo*logy
aqua- (water; liquid): *aqua*plane
audio- (sound; hearing): *audio*visual
auto- (from within; self): *auto*biography
baro- (weight; pressure): *baro*meter
be- (on all sides): *be*set
bene- (well; well-being): *bene*fit
bi- (two): *bi*cycle
bio- (living organism): *bio*logy

by- (out of the way): *by*road
cata- (down): *cata*clinal
centi- (one hundredth): *centi*meter
chrono- (time): *chrono*logy
chryso- (gold; gold color): *chryso*logy
circum- (around): *circum*ference
co- (with; together; jointly): *co*exist
com- (with; together): *com*mingle
con- (with; together): *con*centrate
contra- (against): *contra*band
counter- (contrary): *counter*measure
de- (reversal; removal): *de*compose
deci- (one-tenth): *deci*liter
deka- (ten): *deka*gram
di- (two): *di*chromatic
dia- (across; apart): *dia*meter
dis- (negation; reversal): *dis*approve
duo- (two): *duo*tone
ecto- (outside): *ecto*derm
endo- (inside): *endo*derm
epi- (over; above): *epi*center
equi- (equality): *equi*distant
eu- (good; well): *eu*phemism
ex- (out of; former): *ex*-husband
extra- (outside; except; beyond): *extra*judicial
extro- (outward): *extro*vert
for- (exhaustion): *for*spent
fore- (before in time): *fore*sight
geo- (earth): *geo*logy
hecto- (one hundred): *hecto*meter
hemo- (blood): *hemo*globin
hemi- (half): *hemi*sphere
hyper- (over; above; beyond): *hyper*active
hypo- (beneath; under): *hypo*dermic
il- (not): *il*logical
im- (not): *im*moral
in- (not): *in*discreet
infra- (below; within): *infra*structure
inter- (between; among): *inter*national
intra- (within): *intra*strate
intro- (inside): *intro*jection

ir- (not): *ir*reversible
juxta- (beside): *juxta*pose
kilo- (thousand): *kilo*ton
lacto- (milk): *lacto*protein
litho- (stone): *litho*graphy
macro- (large): *macro*program
mal- (bad; ugly; wrongly): *mal*adjusted
male- (bad; ugly; wrong): *male*volent
micro- (small): *micro*scope
mid- (middle): *mid*century
milli- (one-thousandth): *milli*gram
mini- (miniature): *mini*bus
mis- (wrong): *mis*lead
mono- (single): *mono*syllable
morpho- (shape; structure): *morpho*logy
multi- (many): *multi*faceted
neo- (new; recent): *neo*logism
non- (not): *non*legal
ob- (against): *ob*struct
octo- (eight): *octo*pus
off- (off; unusual): *off*beat
out- (outside): *out*board
over- (above): *over*head
pan- (all): *pan*chromatic
para- (beside): *para*psychology
patho- (disease; suffering): *patho*logy
per- (through; by; away): *per*form
peri- (around): *peri*scope
photo- (light): *photo*graphy
poly- (many): *poly*gamous
post- (after): *post*war
pre- (before): *pre*examine
pseudo- (false): *pseudo*nym
re- (back; again): *re*join
retro- (backward): *retro*spective
semi- (half): *semi*circle
sub- (under; inferior): *sub*terrain
super- (over; above): *super*sede
supra- (above; transcending): *supra*natural
sym- (with): *sym*pathy
syn- (with): *syn*clinal

theo- (god; gods):   *theo*logy
trans- (across):   *trans*national
twi- (two):   *twi*light
ultra- (beyond):   *ultra*conservative
un- (not):   *un*noticed
under- (below):   *under*ground
up- (up):   *up*stairs
zoo- (animal; animals):   *zoo*logy

45

Guide to Suffixes

A *suffix* is one or more letters or syllables attached to the *end* of a base, stem, or root to change its meaning. The spelling of suffixes and verb endings is complicated by the fact that there are numerous exceptions to the extensive list of rules. Nevertheless, the guidelines given below have helped many people improve the accuracy of their spelling. See also guidelines and examples of prefixes in Chapters 43 and 44.

WORDS THAT DOUBLE THE FINAL CONSONANT

Usually, when a one-syllable word ends with one vowel followed by one consonant, you should double the final consonant before adding the word ending *y* or a word ending starting with a vowel.

beg, begg*ar*
drop, dropp*ed*
glad, gladd*en*
ship, shipp*ed*
skin, skinn*y*

Examples of exceptions are

box, box*ed*
bus, bus*es*
dew, dew*y*
pay, pay*ee*

Usually, when a multisyllable word ends with one vowel followed by one consonant and the accent falls on the last syllable, you should double the final consonant before adding a word ending starting with a vowel.

begin, beginn*ing*
control, controll*ing*
forbid, forbidd*en*
infer, inferr*ed*
regret, regrett*able*

Examples of exceptions are

display, display*ed*
enjoy, enjoy*able*
obey, obey*ing*

When the accent is on the first syllable, the final consonant frequently is not doubled (see "Words That Do Not Double the Final Consonant").

offer, offer*ing*
transfer, transfer*able*
travel, travel*ed*

WORDS THAT DO NOT DOUBLE THE FINAL CONSONANT

When a one-syllable word ends with one vowel followed by one consonant, do not double the final consonant before adding a word ending beginning with a consonant.

boy, boy*hood*
glad, glad*ly*
joy, joyful*ly*
ship, ship*ment*

Usually, when a multisyllable word ends with more than one vowel followed by a consonant, you should not double the final consonant before adding a word ending beginning with a vowel.

appeal, appeal*ed*
benefit, benefit*ing*

cancel, cancel*ed*
differ, differ*ent*

Examples of exceptions are

cancel, cancell*ation*
equip, equipp*ing*
quit, quitt*ing*
quiz, quizz*ical*

Usually, when either a single or a multisyllable word ends with more than one consonant, you should not double the final consonant before adding any word ending.

back, back*ward*
hand, hand*ful*
mass, mass*ive*
return, return*ed*
swing, swing*ing*

The following are examples of exceptions when *ll* appears. Notice that one *l* is dropped from the root word when *-ly* is added. A hyphen is inserted to avoid three *l*'s when *less* or *like* is added.

full, full*y*
install, install*ment*
hull, hull-*less*
shell, shell-*like*

WORDS ENDING IN SILENT E

Usually, when a word ends with a silent *e,* you should drop the *e* before adding a word ending starting with a vowel or before adding *y.*

arrive, arriv*al*
desire, desir*ous*
ease, eas*y*
force, forc*ible*
issue, issu*ing*
propose, propos*ition*

salsale, sal*able*
ice, ic*y*

Examples of exceptions are

agree, agree*ing*
cage, cag*ey*
dye, dy*eing*
mile, mil*eage*
see, see*ing*

Usually, when a word ends in a silent *e,* you should retain the *e* before adding a word ending that begins with a consonant unless another vowel precedes the final silent *e.*

argue, argu*ment*
care, care*less*
hope, hope*ful*
manage, manage*ment*
subtle, subtle*ty*
true, tru*ly*

Examples of exceptions are

gentle, gent*ly*
judge, judg*ment*
nine, nin*th*
wise, wis*dom*

WORDS ENDING IN -CE OR -GE

Usually, when a word ends in *-ce* or *-ge,* you should keep the *e* before adding a word ending that starts with *a* or *o* but drop it before adding suffixes beginning with *i.*

change, change*able*
courage, courag*eous*
deduce, deduc*ible*
enforce, enforce*able*
enforce, enforc*ing*

finance, financ*ial*
outrage, outrag*eous*

Examples of exceptions are

age, ag*eism*
mortgage, mortgag*or*
pledge, pledg*or*
singe, sing*eing*

WORDS ENDING IN -IE

Usually, when a word ends in *-ie,* you should change the *-ie* to *y* before adding *-ing.*

die, dy*ing*
lie, ly*ing*
tie, ty*ing*

WORDS ENDING IN Y

Usually, when a word ends in a consonant followed by *y,* you should change the *y* to *i* before all word endings except those starting with *i* or those consisting of *-ship, -like,* and derivations of *lady-* and *baby-.*

accompany, accompani*ment*
easy, eas*ier*
lady, lady*like*
modify, modifi*cation*
fifty, fifti*eth*
ordinary, ordinari*ly*
try, try*ing*

Examples of exceptions are

country, country*wide*
dry, dry*ly*
shy, shy*ly*

Usually, when a word ends in a vowel followed by *y*, you should retain the *y* before adding any word ending.

buy, buy*er*
display, display*ing*
employ, employ*ment*
joy, joy*ful*
survey, survey*or*

Examples of exceptions are

day, dai*ly*
lay, lai*d*
gay, gai*ly*
pay, pai*d*

WORDS ENDING IN -IC

When a word ends in *-ic,* insert a *k* before adding a word ending beginning with *e, i,* or *y.*

colic, colick*y*
frolic, frolick*ed,* frolick*ing*
picnic, picnick*ed,* picnick*ing*
traffic, traffick*er,* traffick*ing*

WORDS ENDING IN -AL

When changing an adjective ending in *-al* to an adverb ending in *-ly,* do not drop any letters from or add any letters to the original word.

accidental, accidental*ly*
practical, practical*ly*
real, real*ly*

WORDS ENDING IN -ATION

When changing a noun ending in *-ation* to an adjective ending in *-able,* substitute *-able* for *-ation* without adding or dropping any other letters.

admir*ation,* admir*able*
applic*ation,* applic*able*
communic*ation,* communic*able*
damn*ation,* damn*able*

WORDS ENDING IN -IBLE

No clear-cut rule exists for using *-able* or *-ible,* but in many words, the letters *ss* precede *-ible.*

access*ible*
permiss*ible*
transmiss*ible*

Also, words ending in *-ible* frequently have a noun form ending in *-ion.* The word ending *-ible* is then substituted for *-ion* without adding or dropping any other letters.

combustion, combust*ible*
destruction, destruct*ible*
digestion, digest*ible*
perception, percept*ible*

When a word stem ends in a soft *c* or *g,* use *-ible* rather than *-able.*

conduce, conduc*ible*
deduce, deduc*ible*
intelligence, intellig*ible*
reduce, reduc*ible*

WORDS ENDING IN -AR

Very few words end in *-ar.* The following are familiar examples.

begg*ar*	doll*ar*
calend*ar*	regul*ar*
coll*ar*	singul*ar*

WORDS ENDING IN -ARY AND -ERY

Whereas several hundred words end in *-ary,* only two end in *-ery.*

cemet*ery*   mission*ary*
contr*ary*   station*ery*
extempor*ary*

WORDS ENDING IN -ANCE, -ANCY, AND -ANT

No clear-cut rules exists for words ending in *-ance, -ancy,* and *-ant.* Often, though, *-ance, -ancy,* or *-ant* is used with words that have a *c* sounding like *k* or a *g* with a hard sound.

assist*ant,* assist*ance*
extravag*ant,* extravag*ance,* extravag*ancy*
signific*ant,* signific*ance,*
relev*ant,* revel*ance,* revel*ancy*

WORDS ENDING IN -ENCE, -ENCY, AND -ENT

No clear-cut rule exists for words ending in *-ence, -ency,* or *-ent.* Often, though, *-ence, -ency,* or *-ent* is used with words that have a *c* sounding like *s* or a *g* sounding like *j.* But when in doubt, consult a dictionary.

depend*ent,* depend*ence,* depend*ency*
exist*ent,* exist*ence*
insist*ent,* insist*ence,* insist*ency*
persist*ent,* persist*ence,* persist*ency*

WORDS ENDING IN -ISE, -IZE, AND -YZE

No rule exists for *-ise, -ize,* and *-yze,* but most words end in *-ize.* Only a few end in *-yze.*

advert*ise*   critic*ize*
anal*yze*   merchand*ise*
apolog*ize*   paral*yze*

WORDS ENDING IN -CEDE, -CEED, AND -SEDE

One word ends in *-sede;* three words, in *-ceed;* the rest from this category end in *-cede.*

con*cede*	pro*ceed*
ex*ceed*	re*cede*
inter*cede*	suc*ceed*
pre*cede*	super*sede*

46

Common Suffixes

Like prefixes, many suffixes are of Greek and Latin origin but are now commonplace in English-language usage. The following list contains familiar examples of suffixes and illustrates how they are attached to root forms. Many suffixes can be added to root words without changes, although as in the case of prefixes, the meanings and forms of some suffixes are diverse and complex.

-able (capable of): manage*able*
-acean (organism): crust*acean*
-aceous (organism): heb*aceous*
-acity (quality or state of): ten*acity*
-age (result): break*age*
-agogue (leader; inciter): dem*agogue*
-an (belonging to): Afric*an*
-ance (state of; action): continu*ance*
-ancy (state of; action): redund*ancy*
-andry (number of husbands): poly*andry*
-ant (causing; being): depend*ant*
-arch (ruler; leadership): mon*arch*
-archy (rule; government): hier*archy*
-arium (place; housing): planet*arium*
-blastic (buds; growth): diplo*blastic*
-cade (procession): motor*cade*
-chore (plant distributed by specific agency): anemo*chore*
-chrome (color): mono*chrome*

-cide (killer): insecti*cide*
-coccus (berry-shaped microorganism): micro*coccus*
-cracy (government): demo*cracy*
-c[u]le (small): cubi*cle*
-cy (state of being): bankrupt*cy*
-don (condition): free*dom*
-ectomy (surgical removal): append*ectomy*
-ed (having): cultur*ed*
-eer (one concerned with): action*eer*
-emia (blood): an*emia*
-en (consisting of): earth*en*
-ence (state of): dependen*cy*
-ent (state of): prevale*nt*
-er (performer of action): writ*er*
-esce (become): coale*sce*
-ese (relating to): Japan*ese*
-est (most): clos*est*
-fer (agency; bearing): coni*fer*
-ferous (bearing): carboni*ferous*
-fuge (driving away from): centri*fuge*
-ful (full of): fear*ful*
-fy (form; make): ampli*fy*
-gamous (marrying): mono*gamous*
-gamy (marriage): poly*gamy*
-genesis (birth): bio*genesis*
-gnosis (knowledge; recognition): dia*gnosis*
-gram (written material): mail*gram*
-graph (written material): mono*graph*
-hood (condition): state*hood*
-ia (disease): hyster*ia*
-ial (pertaining to): manager*ial*
-ian (of; resembling): Californ*ian*
-iasis (pathological or morbid condition): psor*iasis*
-iatric (relating to medical treatment): ger*iatric*
-iatry (relating to medical treatment): pod*iatry*
-ible (capable of): deduc*ible*
-ic(s) (pertaining to): athlet*ic*
-ine (of; resembling): fel*ine*
-ing (to form present participle): look*ing*
-ion (act: process): telecommunicat*ion*
-ish (of; like): fiend*ish*

-ism (system): commun*ism*
-ist (agent; doer): evangel*ist*
-ite (native of; follower): Brooklyn*ite*
-itis (inflammation; disease): bronch*itis*
-ity (condition; degree): alkalin*ity*
-ive (tending toward): act*ive*
-ize (cause to be; render): system*ize*
-kin (small): lamb*kin*
-kinesis (division; movement): cyto*kinesis*
-lepsy (fit; seizure): epi*lepsy*
-less (without): home*less*
-let (small): pamph*let*
-like (resembling): child*like*
-ling (characterized by): found*ling*
-lith (stone): mono*lith*
-lithic (stone): neo*lithic*
-logical (adjective form of -*logy*): bio*logical*
-logy (study of): theo*logy*
-ly (like; characterized by): week*ly*
-mancy (divination): oneiro*mancy*
-mania (exaggerated enthusiasm): letter*mania*
-ment (act; process): manage*ment*
-meter (measuring device): speedo*meter*
-metry (science of measuring): trigono*metry*
-most (most): ut*most*
-ness (state; quality): dark*ness*
-nomy (body of knowledge): agro*nomy*
-odont (tooth; teeth): acro*dont*
-oid (resembling): human*oid*
-opsy (examining): bi*opsy*
-or (performer of action): edit*or*
-ory (place for; something used as): dormit*ory*
-osis (abnormal condition): psych*osis*
-ous (characterized by): courag*eous*
-petal (moving toward): centri*petal*
-phagy (eating; consumption of): dys*phagy*
-phony (sound): sym*phony*
-plastic (forming; growing): proto*plastic*
-proof (able to resist): fool*proof*
-rrhea (flow; discharge): dia*rrhea*
-sect (cut; divide): bi*sect*

-ship (state; condition): governor*ship*
-some (characterized by): hand*some*
-sphere (shape of sphere): hemi*sphere*
-state (regulating device): thermo*stat*
-stead (place): home*stead*
-ster (one who is; belongs to): gang*ster*
-tion (act; process): cancella*tion*
-tomy (cutting): appendec*tomy*
-tor (doer): vic*tor*
-tude (state of being): alti*tude*
-ule (small): caps*ule*
-ure (act; process): expos*ure*
-urgy (technology; working at): metall*urgy*
-vorous (eating; feeding): carni*vorous*
-ward (direction): for*ward*
-ways (manage; direction): side*ways*
-wide (extent): nation*wide*
-work (product; production): piece*work*
-worthy (characterized by): trust*worthy*
-zoan (member of scientific group): proto*zoan*

47

Guide to Writing Compounds

The term *compounds* refers to two or more words combined or used together to form a new word or to modify another word. Most people have problems not in understanding the usage but in deciding whether to hyphenate the pertinent words, write them separately, or combine them as a solid compound (no space or hyphen). Authorities do not always agree on the appropriate style, but the following guidelines are consistent with contemporary writing styles. Chapter 48 lists some common compounds and illustrates the preferred spelling.

OPEN COMPOUNDS

Although most compounds are written solid or hyphenated, they should be written open, as separate words, in a few instances. Leave the words open when a number is combined with a possessive noun, in the case of a foreign phrase or a scientific compound; and when the words of the compound are capitalized.

six weeks' leave
a *per diem* assessment
sodium chloride solution
Stone Age tools

Leave open any adverb-adjective compound in which the adverb ends in *-ly,* any compound consisting of two adverbs and an adjective, and any adverb-adjective compound that follows the noun it modifies. Also, leave open well-known compounds such as *social security* before and after a noun.

a *carefully constructed* puzzle
a *very well received* speech
a house that is *well built*
the *public relations* effort

Write temporary compounds with the word *master* open. Also, leave open descriptions of relationships and *quasi* noun compounds.

master artist (but: *masterpiece*)
fellow employee
father figure
quasi corporation

Spell most compound titles such as *surgeon general* open (but see "Hyphenated Compounds"), and leave open a color term in which the first element modifies the second.

attorney general
judge advocate general
emerald green
yellowish orange

Also, write temporary object-gerund compounds open (but see "Hyphenated Compounds").

Better *problem solving* is necessary.
The *decision making* was faulty.

SOLID COMPOUNDS

Write words that have been combined to form a specialized term solid.

bookkeeper
checkbook
footnote
headache
greenhouse

Most prefixes and suffixes are written closed, except before a proper noun or when a vowel such as *i* is doubled. In particular, close compounds with *grand-* (relation), *-like* (unless it forms three *l*'s), *-fold,* and *-score* (unless numerals are used). Write compounds with *-wide* solid unless they are too long.

antigovernment (but: *anti-intelligence*)
postgraduate
grandmother
catlike
twofold
fivescore
statewide

Write most compounds with *-one* closed, unless a different meaning is intended. Also, close personal pronouns and words with *-body, -thing,* or *-where.*

Anyone may come. (but: *Any one* of the members may come.)
Somebody is responsible.
Thanks for *everything.*
He works *somewhere* else.

Write certain verb-preposition compounds closed; hyphenate others such as *follow-up, mix-up,* and *runner-up.* Write most compounds with *-back, down-, -out,* and *-over* solid. Because many terms with suffixes are hyphenated, however, consult a dictionary when in doubt.

backup	showdown
checkup	blackout
setup	fallout
drawback	workout
flashback	carryover
throwback	leftover
breakdown	turnover
countdown	

Some compound verbs are written solid, but others are hyphenated. When in doubt, consult a dictionary or book of grammar.

to *downgrade*
to *proofread*
to *whitewash*

HYPHENATED COMPOUNDS

Usually, a hyphen is used with most affixes such as *all-, cross-, ex-, -add, quasi-* (adjective), *self-,* and *vice-.* But consult a dictionary when in doubt.

all-around
cross-country
ex-mayor
quasi-judicial situation
self-concept (but: *selfsame, selfless,* etc.)
twenty-five-odd complaints
vice-chairperson

Use a hyphen in a compound if it helps in clarity.

recreation
re-create (to create again)

Nouns of equal value are hyphenated when the person or thing has the characteristics of both nouns.

city-state
owner-operator
secretary-treasurer

Hyphenate most compounds before a noun, except as explained in "Open Compounds."

well-kept secret
first-rate presentation
American-Mexican border
happy-go-lucky student
ever-loyal secretary
six-, eight-, and *ten-story* buildings

With numbers, hyphenate twenty-one to ninety-nine and adjective compounds before a noun. Hyphenate fractions unless the numerator or denominator already is a fraction or the fraction is used as a noun.

forty-second
thirty-first enrollment

24-inch ruler
nineteenth-century novel
five-sixteenth diameter
She cut *one-fourth* of the pattern.
seven *ninety-sixths*

Hyphenate *in-law* and *great-* relatives and name descriptions with a prepositional phrase.

sister-in-law
great-grandmother
stick-in-the-mud

48

Common Compounds

This list illustrates the spelling of common compounds. But because of the many exceptions to the rules for spelling compounds (see Chapter 47), you need to place a compound in the context of a sentence to be certain whether it should be spelled open or closed or whether it should be hyphenated.

Most of the compounds below that are not designated as adjectives or verbs are shown in their noun forms.

aforementioned
aforesaid
after-hours
aftertaste
afterthought
air-condition (v.)
air conditioner
airspace
airtight
all-around
all-important
all right (adv.)
all-time
also-ran
anti-intellectual
antiwar
anybody
anyhow
anyone

anyplace
anything
attorney general
audiofrequency
audiovisual
backup
ball bearing
ballpark; ball park
ballplayer
ball-point
bankbook
beforehand
billboard
birthplace
birthrate
blood stream,
   bloodstream
blue book, bluebook
blue-collar (adj.)

blue jeans, bluejeans
blueprint
blue ribbon
boardinghouse
bondholder
bookbinding
bookcase
bookend, book end
bookkeeping
bookkeeper
bookmaker
bookseller
bookshop
bookstore
bottom-line (adj.)
boxcar
box office
box spring
brainpower

brainstorm
brain trust
brainwash
breadwinner
break-in
breakout
breakthrough
breakup
briefcase
broadcast
broken-down
buildup
built-in
burnout
businessperson
buttonhole
by-election
bylaw
byline
bypass
by-product
campground
cardboard
card-carrying (adj.)
car pool
carryall
carryover
caseload
case study
casework
cashbook
castoff
catchall
catchword
catlike
checkbook
check-in
checklist
check mark
checkout
checkpoint

checkup
city-state
class-conscious (adj.)
classmate
classroom
clean-cut
cleanup
clear-cut
clearing house,
    clearinghouse
clipboard
closeout
close-up
coauthor
coed
coeducation
coexist
cold-blooded
coldshoulder
colorfast
comeback
common-law (adj.)
common sense
consciousness-raising
co-op
co-opt
copy edit
copywriter
costar
cost-effective (adj.)
countdown
court-martial
courtroom
courtyard
crackdown
crack-up
cross-examine
cross-index
crossover
cross-reference
crossroad

cross section
day care
day labor
daytime
deadline
deathbed
death rate
deluxe
devil-may-care
diehard
direct-action (adj.)
dive-bomb
double-check (v.)
double-cross (v.)
double entry
double-space (v.)
downplay
downtime
downtown
dry-clean (v.)
dry cleaner
dry goods
everybody
everything
everywhere
ex officio
ex-president
extracurricular
eye opener
eyewitness
fairway
fair-weather (adj.)
farfetched (adj.)
filmmaker
filmstrip
fingertip
firehouse
fireproof
fire station
first aid
first-rate (adj.)

foolproof
foothold
free lance
free-lance (adj.)
free trade
free will
garden-variety (adj.)
ghostwriter
good-bye
goodwill
grandmother
groundwork
grown-up
half-hour
halftime
halfway
handbook
handmade
handyman
headhunter
head-hunting
headline
high rise
high tech
holdover
holdup
hometown
horsepower
ill-advised (adj.)
inasmuch as
insofar as
interrelate
jawbone
jet lag
job lot
journeyman
keepsake
keypunch
keystroke
labor intensive
labor saving

landholder
landowner
lawmaker
layoff
layout
lead time
leave-taking
letterhead
lifeline
life-style
lightweight
lineup
looseleaf
loudspeaker
lowdown
manpower
markdown
marketplace
moneylender
moneymaker
moreover
nation-state
nationwide
nearby
network
nevertheless
newfound
newlywed
newscast
newsstand
newsworthy
nightlife
nonessential
nonetheless
no nonsense
nonprofit
no one
noontime
notebook
noteworthy
notwithstanding

nowadays
odd lot
offhand
officeholder
offset
once-over
one-half
one-upsmanship
on-line (adj.)
outbid
out of date
overall
overrate
paperwork
passbook
passerby
payroll
percent
pipeline
postmark
postmaster
postwar
preeminent
president-elect
prodemocratic
proofread
proof sheet
pseudointellectual
pushbutton
put-down
putoff
put-on
readout
recap
rewrite
rollback
roundup
rundown
salesclerk
salesperson
say-so

schoolteacher
scratchpad
self-concern
semiconscious
sendoff
send-up
setback
setup
shortcut
short-term (adj.)
showdown
sideline
standby
stand-in
statewide
stockbroker
stock market
stockpile

stopgap
subcommittee
subdivision
takeoff
takeout
takeover
taxpayer
textbook
thereafter
throwback
tie-in
tie-up
timecard
timesaving (adj.)
timetable
titleholder
trade-in
trademark

trade-off
transcontinental
turnover
twofold
underrate
underway (adj.)
vice-president
viewfinder
viewpoint
waterpower
wavelength
wildlife
windup
workday
work force
work load
wristwatch
yearbook

49

Guide to Word Division

When you want to divide a word at the end of a line, first determine the syllables in the word and then divide the word according to the rules in this chapter. Spelling dictionaries that show both pronunciation and word division are useful when you need to distinguish between words such as *pre-sent* (to give or introduce) and *pres-ent* (as a gift).

Although the rules given here are followed by particular writers and publishers, some persons and organizations rate speed and ease of production as well as conservation of space above correctness in word division. As a result, it is not uncommon to see some of these rules violated in printed material.

SYLLABLES AND LETTERS

Do not divide words pronounced as one syllable or fewer than five letters.

gained (*not* gain-ed)
into (*not* in-to)
only (*not* on-ly)
through (*not* th-rough)

Do not separate a single letter from the front or end of a word.

abate-ment (*not* a-batement)
around (*not* a-round)
tro-phy (*not* troph-y)

When a word has a one-letter syllable within it (not at the beginning or end), divide the word after the one-letter syllable. *Caution:* This does not pertain to the suffixes *-able* and *-ible.* The rule that suffixes should not be divided within themselves applies in that case.

acti-vate
busi-ness
con-sider-able (*not* considera-ble)
reduc-ible (*not* reduci-ble)

When there are two vowels together within a word, each sounded separately, divide the word between them.

courte-ous
experi-ence
levi-athan
situ-ation

Divide a word only if you can keep three or more characters (including punctuation) on the top line or carry three or more characters to the bottom line.

ad-mit
break-*up*
dit-*to*
ex-cept

PREFIXES AND SUFFIXES

Divide a word only after a prefix or before a suffix, not within the affix.

anti-welfare (*not* an-tiwelfare)
trans-national (*not* tr-ansnational)
appli-*cable* (*not* applica-ble)
trust-*worthy* (*not* trustwor-thy)

When a word is formed by doubling the consonant before adding a word ending, divide the word between the two consonants. But if the original word already has a double consonant, divide it after the double letter.

begin, begin-ner
deter, deter-rence
mill, mill-ing
spell, spell-er

NAMES

Avoid dividing names, but if it is necessary, divide only between the first and last names.

Donald / Hartwell (*not* Donald Hart-well)
Jennifer / Stevens (*not* Jen-nifer Stevens)

ABBREVIATIONS AND CONTRACTIONS

Do not divide abbreviations, initialisms, or acronyms, and do not divide words that are contractions.

admin. (*not* ad-min.)
asap (*not* as-ap)
NATO (*not* NA-TO)
doesn't (*not* does-n't)

NUMBERS

Avoid dividing numbers, but if it is necessary, divide only at the comma (if any).

3,592,-645 (*not* 3,5-92,645)
1990 (*not* 19-90)

Generally, avoid dividing any figures. Specifically, avoid separating figures and associated abbreviations or words. But if it is necessary to divide a date, separate only between the day and year.

16 mm (*not* 16 / mm)
page 15 (*not* page / 15)

January 1, / 1991 (*not* January / 1, 1991)
2400 East / Avenue (*not* 2400 / East Avenue)

Divide numbered or lettered items only before a number or letter.

(1) love, / (2) honor, and (3) trust
(*not* [1] love, [2] / honor, and [3] trust)

DASHES AND HYPHENS

When you must divide a line where a dash is positioned, always keep the dash on the top line.

It is permissible to divide a word—
　　but only when necessary.

The proper use of abbreviations depends upon the nature of the text.

—*Words into Type* 3rd ed.
(Englewood Cliffs, N.J.: Prentice-Hall, 1974), p. 100.

Part VIII

ABBREVIATED FORMS OF WORDS

50 Guide to Abbreviating

51 General Forms

52 Technical Forms

53 Organizations

54 Academic Degrees

55 States

56 Countries

57 Signs and Symbols

Guide to Abbreviating

Authorities, professions, businesses, and individuals differ in their style of abbreviating words. Although you should follow the form preferred by your employer or profession, in the absence of guidelines you should follow contemporary style. Currently, the trend is to use fewer periods and fewer capital letters. Contemporary style is explained in the sections below, along with examples, and additional examples of abbreviations for general words, technical words, organizations, academic degrees, states, countries, and signs and symbols are given in Chapters 50 to 57.

FORMS OF ABBREVIATION

An *abbreviation* is a shortened form of a written word or phrase, formed by omitting letters in a word or by combining the initials of the first or other letters in the key words of a phrase.

The term *acronym* refers to the initials of key words combined to form an abbreviation that is pronounced as a word in itself.

SALT, *Strategic Arms Limitation Talks*
ARM, *Adjustable Rate Mortgage*

When each individual letter is pronounced, the result is called *initials* or *initialism*.

TLC, *tender loving care*
RPL, *Rocket Propulsion Laboratory*

WHEN TO USE ABBREVIATIONS

Abbreviations are appropriate as a form of shorthand

1. In note taking and rough drafts
2. As a code in record keeping (such as a file designation)
3. On business forms (such as a purchase order)
4. In footnotes, bibliographies, and other references
5. In tabular and graphics material
6. In various scientific and technical writing

The use of abbreviations in technical applications and in business forms and record keeping is increasing.

WHEN NOT TO USE ABBREVIATIONS

Abbreviations are considered inappropriate in formal, general writing. Both technical and nontechnical terms should be spelled out.

In certain long documents (such as a formal report), some employers permit the use of organizational abbreviations and popular acronyms if the names are repeated many times in the text. In such cases, the initials should appear in parentheses on first use.

National Arts Foundation (NAF)

But even when the name is repeated many times, it is still not necessary to use the abbreviation *NAF.* One could refer to the *foundation* if a shorter version is desired.

The trend is to avoid abbreviations completely in formal, general writing (but *see* "Words That Are Always Abbreviated").

WORDS THAT ARE ALWAYS ABBREVIATED

Certain words are always abbreviated in the United States, and some are always abbreviated except in various social situations.

1. It is customary to abbreviate personal and professional titles such as *Mr., Mrs., Messrs.,* and *Dr.*

2. Designations such as *Jr., Sr.,* and *Esq.* are abbreviated after a name except in certain formal situations (such as a formal calling card).

3. Scholarly degrees such as *Ph.D.* and *M.D.* are abbreviated after a name.

4. Compass points such as *S.W.* are abbreviated after a street address (*4310 Cactus Drive, S.W.,* but *4310 West Avenue*).

5. Two-letter state abbreviations such as *NY* are required by the U.S. Postal Service for optical character sorting.

6. Time designations such as *A.D.* and *P.M.* are abbreviated except on formal invitations, where *o'clock* is used instead.

7. The abbreviation *RSVP* rather than the phrase *Répondez s'il vous plaît* is always used on formal invitations.

ABBREVIATING NUMBERS

When abbreviating numbers, follow these rules:

1. Abbreviate inclusive numbers above one hundred except in the cases stated below in items 2, 3, and 4.

1990–91; 241–46; 505–6

2. Do not abbreviate inclusive numbers when the first number ends in two zeros.

1900–1990; 200–246; 500–506

3. Do not abbreviate inclusive numbers when the second number begins with different digits.

1889–1990; 241–346; 505–606

4. Do not abbreviate inclusive numbers or use a hyphen with the words *from, to,* or *between.*

from 1989 *to* 1990
between 241 *and* 246

SPELLING OF ABBREVIATIONS

Some words and phrases have more than one correct form of abbreviation, and some abbreviations refer to different words or phrases. The abbreviation *v.* and *vb.*, for example, are both used as short forms of *verb.* The abbreviation *v.*, however, also refers to *verse, verso,* and *versus.*

Since organizations and individuals differ in their preferred style, follow the version used by your employer in business and professional situations. When in doubt, consult a book of abbreviations such as *The New American Dictionary of Abbreviations* (New American Library, 1990) or a library reference work such as *Acronyms, Initialisms & Abbreviations Dictionary* (Gale Research Company, current year).

CAPITALIZATION OF ABBREVIATIONS

Organizations and individuals also differ in capitalization of abbreviations, although the trend is toward fewer capital letters. Proper nouns, however, are always capitalized in abbreviated form. The abbreviations of some words that are used as both common nouns and proper nouns may be in small letters or capitals, depending on the intended usage.

FDR, *Franklin Delano Roosevelt*
YWCA, *Young Women's Christian Association*
SAM, *Student Accountability Model*
asap, *as soon as possible*
Fri., *Friday*
mgr., *manager*
Ast, *Atlantic standard time*
cps, *characters per second*
CPS, *Certified Professional Secretary*
cap, CAP, *computer-aided production*
eat, EAT, *estimated arrival time*

In the last two examples above, there is a choice between small letters and all capitals. Although the trend is toward the use of small letters, if your employer requires the use of all capitals, follow that style consistently throughout your work.

PUNCTUATION OF ABBREVIATIONS

The trend is to use less punctuation, although organizations and individuals may vary in their preferences. Some abbreviations are always punctuated, for example, academic degrees, states, and personal and professional titles. Country names used as adjectives are generally punctuated, although the abbreviation *USSR* is commonly used as a noun without periods (the word *Soviet* is used as an adjective more than the abbreviation *USSR*).

Some abbreviations, especially technical ones such as *km* for *kilometer,* are not punctuated. Also, initialisms such as *JFK* for *John Fitzgerald Kennedy* or *ssae* for *stamped, self-addressed envelope* are usually not punctuated. Any abbreviation such as *in.* for *inch* that also spells an actual word, however, such as the preposition *in* should have a period after it to avoid confusion with that word.

True abbreviations such as *coef.* for *coefficient* (in which the end of the word is dropped) should be punctuated. But when letters within a word are dropped as in *acct* or *acct.* for *accountant,* the abbreviation may or may not be punctuated depending on the user's preferred style. Some users rigidly follow the rule of not punctuating such forms; other users treat an abbreviation formed from dropped letters the same as one formed by dropping the end of a word and use a period in both cases.

Contractions such as *don't* for *do not* should not have a period. Also, a short form such as *memo* for *memorandum* that has been accepted as a word in itself should not be punctuated.

Sc.D., doctor of science degree
Dr. Brown, Doctor Brown
U.S. government, United States government
N.Y., New York
Ger., Germany
pat., patent; patrol; pattern
bfr, bfr., buffer
did., data item description
mm, millimeter
ia, impedance angle; international angstrom

51

General Forms

Most general abbreviations such as *equip. (equipment)* or *nfa (no further action)* should be used only in note taking or on certain business forms or records. In letters, reports, articles, and other written material, words and phrases should be spelled out.

a	absent; account; acre; at
aa	always afloat; author's alteration(s)
a&a	additions and amendments
aac	average annual cost
aae	average annual earnings
aap	advise if able to proceed; affirmative action program
AAP	affirmative action program
aar	after action report; against all risks
a&b	assault and battery
abbr.	abbreviate(d); abbreviation
abi	abstracted business information
ABM	antiballistic missile
abr.	abridged; abridgment
ac	air conditioning; average cost
a/c	account; account current; air conditioning
access.	accessory
accom.	accommodation
accomp.	accomplish
accred.	accredited
acct.	account(ant)(ing)
accum.	accumulate

achiev.	achievement
ack	accidentally killed
ack.	acknowledge; acknowledgment
ACM	advanced cruise missile
acn	all concerned notified; assignment control number
a/c pay.	accounts payable
a/c rec.	accounts receivable
acron.	acronym
ACS	Address Change Service
act.	acting; action; actor; actress; actual; actuarial; actuary; actuating
act. val.	actual value
act. wt.	actual weight
acv	actual cash value
ad	active duty; after drain; air dried; after date; athletic director
a&d	accounting and disbursing; ascending and descending
A.D.	in the year of our Lord (Latin *Anno Domini*)
ada	average daily attendance
adcon	advance concepts; advise or issue instructions to all concerned
add.	addenda; addendum; address; average daily dose
ade	automatic data entry; average daily enrollment
adeda	advise earliest date; advise effective date
ad fin.	to the end (Latin *ad finem*)
ad hom.	to the man (Latin *ad hominem*)
ad id.	both the same; likewise (Latin *ad idem*)
ad inf.	to infinity (Latin *ad infinitum*)
ad init.	at the beginning (Latin *ad initium*)
ad int.	in the interim or meantime (Latin *ad interim*)
adj.	adjacent; adjective; adjust; adjutant
ad lib.	at one's pleasure; freely to the degree desired (Latin *ad libitum*)
ad loc.	to or at this place (Latin *ad locum*)
adm	action description memo; average daily membership
ADM	air defense missile; air-launched decoy missile
admin.	administration; administrative; administrator
admx.	administrator
ad naus.	dull to the point of nausea (Latin *ad nauseam*)
ad neut.	until neutral (Latin *ad neutralizandum*)
adsap	advise as soon as possible

ad sat.	to saturation (Latin *ad saturandum*)
adsc	average daily service charge
Adt	Atlantic daylight time
adv.	advance; advantage; adverb; advertising
adv. chgs.	advance charges
adv. frt.	advance freight
advof	advise this office
adv. pmt.	advance payment
aec	additional extended coverage; at earliest convenience
aep	accrued expenditure paid
afc	average fixed cost
aff.	affairs
afsd.	aforesaid
ag.	agricultural; agriculture
agb	any good brand
agi	adjusted gross income; annual general inspection
agit. bene	shake well (Latin *agita bene*)
agric.	agricultural; agriculture
agt.	agent
agy.	agency
a&h	accident and health; alive and healthy
a.h.v.	at this word (Latin *ad hunc vocum*)
a&i	abstracting and indexing; accident and indemnity
aia	advise if available
AIDS	acquired immune deficiency syndrome
air.	artist in residence
aka	also known as
alc	on the menu (French *a la carte*)
ALCM	air-launched cruise missile
alcon	all concerned
ald	a later date; acceptable limit for dispersion
alf	alien life force; automatic letter facer
alg.	algebra; algebraic
all.	above lower limit
alloc.	allocate; allocation
Alp.	Alpine
alpha.	alphabetical
Alps	Alpine Mountains
a.m.	before noon (Latin *ante meridiem*)
a&m	agricultural and mechanical; ancient and modern; architectural and mechanical

Am.	America(n)
amb.	ambassador; amber; ambient; ambulance
am. cur.	a friend at court (Latin *amicus curiae*)
Amer.	America(n)
amo	advance material order; airmail only
amr	automatic message routing
amsl	above mean sea level
an.	above named; annual
an.	before (Latin *ante*); year (Latin *anno*)
anat.	anatomy
ang.	angiogram; angle; angular
ann.	year (Latin *anno*); years (Latin *anni*)
anniv.	anniversary (Latin *anniversarium*)
annot.	annotate(d); annotation
anon.	nameless (Latin *anonymous*)
ant.	antenna; anterior; antique; antonym
anvo	accept no verbal orders
ao	access opening; antioxidant; area of operations; accuracy only; account of; arresting officer
a/o	account of
aob	alcohol on breath; angle on the bow; annual operating budget; any other business; at or below
aod	as of date
aok	all okay (everything in good order)
aor	area of responsibility
a/or	and/or
aos	acquisition of signal; add or subtract
ap	above proof; access panel; action potential; advanced placement; aiming point; as prescribed; attached processor; author's proof; average product
a/p	authority to pay; authority to purchase; allied papers; authority to pay
apart.	apartment
apc	average propensity to consume
aper.	aperture
apos.	apostrophe
app.	apparatus; apparel; apparent; appeal; append(age)(ed)(ix); appetite; applause; applied; apprentice; approach; approve
appl.	applicable; application; applied
appr.	approval; approve(d)

appt.	appointment
apr	annual percentage rate
APR	annual percentage rate
aps	average propensity to save
apt.	apartment
aq	accomplishment quotient; achievement quotient; any quantity
ar	achievement ratio; all rail; all risks; allocated reserve; armed robbery; artificial respiration; average revenue
a/r	all risks; armed robbery; at the rate of
arfor	area forcast
arith.	arithmetic
ARM	adjustable-rate mortgage; antiradar missile; antiradiation missile
aro	after receipt of order
art.	advanced research and technology; artery; article; artillery; artist(ic)(ry); automatic reporting telephone
as.	alloy steel; at sight
a/s	after sight; alongside
ASC	All Saver Certificate
asl	above sea level
Asl	American sign language
asr	airport surveillance radar; air-sea rescue; answer and receive; available supply rate
assd.	assigned
ast	absolute space time
Ast	Atlantic standard time
At	Atlantic time
A/t	American terms
ata	actual time of arrival; air to air
atar	above transmitted and received
ATBM	advanced technology ballistic missile; antitactical ballistic missile
atiob	as this is our best
Atl.	Atlanta; Atlantic
ATM	automated teller machine
ato	according to others
atp	at any price (French *á tout prix*)
atten.	attention
atv	all-terrain vehicle
aureq	authority is requested

autopilot	automatic pilot
aux.	auxiliary
av	acid value; assessed valuation; audiovisual;
av.	avenue; average
AV	Authorized Version
ava	audiovisual aids
avail.	available; availability
avc	average variable cost
ave.	avenue
a/w	actual weight; all-water; all-weather
a&w	alive and well
awiy	as we informed you
awk.	awkward
awol	absent without leave; absent without official leave
AWOL	absent without leave; absent without official leave
ax.	axiom(atic)
b.	born; brother
b/a	billed at; budget authorized
ba&f	budget, accounting, and finance
bal	blood alcohol level
bal.	balance; balcony
bar.	barometer; barometric
b/b	bail bond
b&b	bed and board; bed and breakfast
bbq	barbecue
bc	back course; bad check; between centers; bills for collection; birth control; budgeted cost; building center; bulk carrier
b/c	bales of cotton; bills for collection; birth control; broadcast
b&c	buildings and contents
B.C.	before Christ
bdi	both days included
b&e	breaking and entering
beg.	begin(ning)
bev.	bevel; beverage
bf	backfeed; boldface
b.f.	genuine; in good faith; without fraud or deception (Latin *bona fide*)
b/f	black female; brought forward
b&g	buildings and grounds
b&i	bankruptcy and insolvency

bib.	bibliography; biblical
bio.	biographical; biography; biological; biology
biog.	biographer; biographical; biography
bionics	biology and electronics
biz	business
bk.	bank; book
bkpt.	bankrupt
b/l	basic letter; bill of lading; blueline; blueprint
bldg.	building
blk.	black; block(ing)
bll	below lower limit
bls.	bales
blvd.	boulevard
bm	birthmark; board measure; book of the month
bo	back order; blackout; body odor; branch office
b/o	back order; brought over; budget outlay
bop	balance of payments; best operating procedure
br	bank rate; bill of rights; builder's risk
b/r	bills receivable
brf.	brief(ing)
brkt.	bracket
BRM	business reply mail
Bros.	Brothers
bs	backspace
bskt.	basket
b/st	bill of sight
b&t	bath and toilet
bta	best time available; better than average
btf	balance to follow
b/tf	balance transferred
btw.	between
btwn.	between
bu.	bureau
bull.	bulletin
bur.	bureau
bus.	business
b/v	book value; brick veneer
BVD	Bradley, Vorhees & Day (suits of underwear)
b.w.	please turn over (German *bitte wenden*)
b/w	black and white; bread and water
byo	bring your own

byob	bring your own bottle
c	about; calorie; candle, carat; cent; century; chapter; child
C	Centigrade
ca	about; civil authorities; current assets
c/a	capital account; current account
cad.	cadet; cash against documents; computer-aided design; contract-award date
CAD	computer-aided design
cad/cam	computer-aided design/computer-aided manufacturing
CAD/CAM	computer-aided design/computer-aided manufacturing
caf	clerical, administrative, and fiscal; cost and freight; cost, assurance, and freight
cal	computer-aided learning
CAL	computer-aided learning
cal.	calendar; caliber; calorie
cap.	capacity; capital; capital letter; capitol; capsule; client assessment package; computer-aided production
CAP	computer-aided production
caps.	capital letters
catv	cable television; community antenna television
CATV	community antenna television
cav.	warning; writ of suspension (Latin *caveat*)
cav. emp.	let the buyer beware (Latin *caveat emptor*)
CB	citizen's band (radio)
cbd	cash before delivery
cbx	computerized branch exchange; computerized business exchange
CBX	computerized branch exchange; computerized business exchange
cc	carbon copy; chief complaint; color code; command and control
c/c	center to center; current account
c/d	carried down; cash against documents; certificate of deposit
c&d	carpets and drapes; collection and delivery
CD	certificate of deposit
cdst	central daylight saving time
cdt	central daylight time
cent.	century; hundred (Latin *centum*)
ceo	chief executive officer
CEO	chief executive officer

cert.	certificate; certify
cf.	compare (Latin *confer*)
c/f	carried forward
c&f	clearing and forwarding; cost and freight
cf&c	cost, freight, and commission
cfi	cost, freight, and insurance
ch.	chair; chapter; chief
chap.	chapter
ci	coefficient of intelligence; cost and insurance; counter-intelligence
c/i	certificate of insurance
c&i	cost and insurance; cowboys and Indians
cia	cash in advance
cir.	circle; circuit; circular
cit.	citation
ck.	cask; check; cork
c/l	carload lot; cash letter; combat loss
c&lc	capital and lowercase (small) letters
c.m.	cause of death (Latin *causa mortis*)
c/m	current month
co.	company; county
c/o	care of; carried over; cash order; complains/complaints of
c.o.d.	cash on delivery
C.O.D.	cash on delivery
coh	cash on hand
cola	cost-of-living adjustment; cost-of-living allowance
COLA	cost-of-living adjustment; cost-of-living allowance
com.	comedy; comma; command; commercial; commission; committee; common; communication; communism
conf.	confer(ence); confidential
cong.	congress
Cong.	Congress (U.S.)
cont.	against (Latin *contra*)
coop.	cooperation
co-op	cooperative
copr.	copyright
cor.	body (Latin *corpus*)
corres.	correspond(ence)(ent)(ing)
cos	cash on shipment
cpa	closest point of approach; cost planning and appraisal; critical path analysis

CPA	certified public accountant; critical path analysis
CPI	consumer price index
CPS	certified professional secretary
cr.	credit; creek; crown
c/r	company risk; correction requirement
cr. bal.	credit balance
CRIS	Carrier Route Information System
crt	cathode ray tube
CRT	cathode ray tube
cs	caesarean section; capital stock; center section; current series
c&sc	caps and small caps (capital and small capital letters)
cst	cargo ships and tankers; central standard time; combined station power; convulsive shock therapy
ct	cellular therapy; central time; central timing; corrected therapy
ct.	cent; court
ct.	hundred (Latin *centum*)
c/t	certificate of title
ctn.	carton
cto	canceled to order
ctr.	center; counter
ctw.	counterweight
cub.	control unit busy
cur.	curiosity; currency; current
curr.	currency; current
cust.	custard; custodian; custody; custom(er)
cv	capital value; carrier vehicle; collection voucher
c/w	counterweight
cwo	cash with order
cwt	counterweight; hundredweight
cx	central exchange; chest X ray; correct copy
CX	central exchange
cy	calendar year; current year
d	daughter; day; degree; died
da	days after acceptance; delayed action; deposit account; discharge afloat; district attorney; do not answer; documents against acceptance; documents attached; doesn't answer
d/a	deposit account

DA	district attorney
dad.	dispense as directed
daf	discharge afloat
dalpo	do all possible
dam.	damage
dap	data analysis package; data automation proposal; do anything possible; documents against payment
das	delivered alongside ship
dat	day (date) after tomorrow
db	day book; delayed broadcast; distribution board; double bed
db.	debit
d/b	documentary bill
dba	doing business as/at
dbb	dinner, bed, breakfast
dbi	database index; development-at-birth index
dbk.	debark; drawback
db. rts.	debenture rights
dbw/f	doing business with and for
dc	data collection; dead center; deck cargo; deviation clauses; digital computer; direct credit; double column; down center
d/c	deviation clause; double column; drift correction
d&c	dilation and curettage
dco	draft collection only
dd	days after date; deferred delivery; delayed delivery; double draft; drydock; due date
d'd	deceased
d/d	dated; delivered at dock; demand draft; developer/demonstrator; domicile to domicile; due date
ddt	digital data transmission
de	deflection error; direct elimination; direct entry; double entry
d/e	date of establishment
dealer prep.	dealer preparation
deb.	debenture; debit
dec.	deceased; deciduous; decimal; decision; decorate; decrease
declar.	declaration
ded	date expected delivery

deduct.	deduction
def.	defeat(ed); defect(ion)(or); defend(ant); defense; defer(red); definite; definition; deflect(ing)(ion); defrost(er)(ing); defunct
defic.	deficiency; deficit
deg.	degenerate; degree
degen.	degeneration
del.	delegate; delegation; delete; deletion; deliberate; deliberation; delineate(d); delineation; deliver(y)
dele.	delete
dely.	delivery
dem.	demand; democracy; democrat(ic); demolish; demolition; demonstrate; demonstration; demote; demotion
demo	demolition; demonstration
democ.	democracy
demod.	demodulator
dep	do everything possible
dep.	depart(ment)(ure); depend(ency)(ent); depose; deposit(or); depot; deputy
depr.	depreciation; depression
dept.	depart(ment)(ure)
des.	descend(ed)(ing); desert; design(er); designate; designation; desire; dessert
descr.	description
dest.	destination; destroy(er); destruction
det.	detach(ment); detail; detect(ive)(or); determinant; determine
dev.	develop(er)(ment); deviate; deviation; deviator
devel.	develop(er)(ment)
d. ex m.	godlike device; god from a machine (Latin *deus ex machina*)
df	damage free; dead freight; decontamination factor; disposition form
d/f	defogging; direct flow
dia	date of initial appointment; due in assets
diag.	diagnose; diagnosis; diagnostic; diagonal; diagram
dial.	dialect(ical)(ician)(ics)
diam.	diameter
dict.	dictate(d); dictation; diction(ary)
die.	died in emergency room
DIE	died in emergency room

diff.	diff(erence)(ential); diffuse(er)
dig.	digest(ion)(ive)
dip.	diphtheria; diploma; diplomat
dir.	direct(ion)(or)
dis	delivered into store
dis.	discount(ed)
disc.	discount
disco	discotheque
diss.	dissent(er); dissertation
diw	dead in water
diy	do it yourself
dj	disc jockey; dust jacket
D-J	Dow-Jones (average)
dk.	dark; deck; dock
dkt.	docket
dl	data link; day letter; demand loan; driver's license
d/l	data link; demand loan
dld.	delivered
dlo	dead-letter office; difference in longitude; dispatch loading only
DLO	dead-letter office
dlp	date of last payment
dls.	dollars
dlx.	deluxe
dly.	daily; delay; dolly
d/m	date and month; day and month; density/moisture
dn	debit note
d/n	debit note
DNA	desoxyribonucleic acid
dnl	do not load
dnr	does not run; do not renew
do.	days off; delivery order; direct order; ditto; dropout; dual ownership
d-o	dropout
d/o	delivery order; disbursing officer
doa	date of arrival; date of availability; dead on arrival; direction of approach; disposal of assets
dob	date of birth
Dom.	of the Lord (Latin *Dominicus*)
dom. ex.	domestic exchange
dos	date of sale

doz.	dozen
dp	data processing; deal pending; departure point; dewpoint; displaced person; distribution point
d/p	delivery papers; documents against payment
dpa	deferred payment account
dplx.	duplex
dpp	deferred payment plan
dr	differential rate; dining room
dr.	debit; doctor; dram; drill; drive
d/r	deposit receipt
drk.	dark
ds	days after sight; dead-air space; debenture stock; domestic service; double strength
d.s.	documents signed
dso	direct shipment order
ds&r	data storage and retrieval; document search and retrieval
dss	documents signed; dry surface storage
dst	daylight saving time
dta	daily travel allowance
dtc	design to cost; direct to consumer
dtp	desktop publishing
DTP	desktop publishing
d/tr	documents against trust receipt
dtx.	detoxification
dudat	due date
dui	driving under the influence (of alcohol/drugs)
dup.	duplicate; duplicating; duplication
dupl.	duplicate; duplication
d/v	declared value
D.V.	God willing (Latin *Deo volente*)
dw	deadweight; delivered weight; double weight; dumbwaiter
d/w	dock warrant
dwc	deadweight capacity
dwi	driving while intoxicated
dyb	do your best
dyu	do your utmost
ea.	each
eac	estimate at completion
ead	equipment allowance deduction; estimated availability date

eaf	emergency action file
eal	estimated average life
eaon	except as otherwise noted
eas	estimated air speed
eat.	estimated arrival time; earnings after taxes
EAT	estimated arrival time
ec.	economics
ecd	estimated completion date
econ.	economic(s); economist; economy
ecr	energy consumption rate
ed.	edit(or)(ion); edited by; editorial; educate(d); education
e&d	exploration and development
edd	estimated delivery date; expected date of delivery
edit.	editing; edition; editor; editorial
ed. note	editorial note; editor's note
eds.	editors
edt	eastern daylight time
ee	errors excepted; eye and ear
EE	Early English
eeo	equal employment opportunity
eer	energy efficiency ratio
efa	essential fatty acids
e.g.	for example (Latin *exempli gratia*)
e/i	endorsement irregular
el	each layer; educational level; extra line
elab.	elaborate(d); elaborating; elaboration
elec.	electric(al)(ian)(ity)
elect.	election; elector(al)(ate)
elem.	element(ary)
elev.	elevate(d)(ion); elevator
ellip.	elliptic(al)
emerg.	emergency
emerit.	retired with honor (Latin *emeritus*)
e.m.p.	as or in the manner prescribed (Latin *ex modo prescripto*)
emr	educable mentally retarded
enc.	enclose(d); enclosure; encumbrance
encl.	enclose(d); enclosure
ency.	encyclopedia
end.	endorse(ment)
env.	envelop(e); envoy
eo	end of operation

eo	by authority of his or her office (Latin *ex officio*)
eoa	effective on or about; examination, opinion, advice
eod	every other day
eoe	equal opportunity employer
e&oe	errors and omissions excepted
eohp	except as otherwise herein provided
eom	end of message; end of month; every other month
eooe	error or omission excepted
eoq	end of quarter
eot	end of transmission
eov	end of volume
epig.	epigram
eps	earnings per share; emergency power supply
epte	existed prior to entry
Eq.	Equator
equip.	equipment
equiv.	equivalent
e/r	editing/reviewing; en route
ERA	Equal Rights Amendment
err.	error; erroneous
err. & app.	errors and appeals
Esl	English as a second language
Esq.	Esquire
est	eastern standard time; electroshock therapy
est.	estate; estimate(d); estimation
estab.	establish(ed)(ment)
et	eastern time; educational therapy; elapsed time; electric/ electronic typewriter; extraterrestrial
eta	estimated time of arrival
et al.	and elsewhere (Latin *et alibi*); and others (Latin *et alia*)
etc.	and so on; and so forth (Latin *et cetera*)
et seq.	and following (Latin *et sequens*)
et ux.	and wife (Latin *et uxor*)
Eur.	Europe(an)
ev	earned value; exposure value
eval.	evaluate; evaluation
evap.	evaporate; evaporation
eve.	evening
e/w	equipped with
ex. af.	of affinity (Latin *ex afinis*)
exam.	examination; examine(r)

ex cath.	from the seat of authority (Latin *ex cathedra*)
exch.	exchange
excl.	exclude; exclusion; exclusive
ex int.	ex (without) interest
ex off.	by authority of his or her office (Latin *ex officio*)
exp.	expansion; expenditure; expense; export; express
ex p.	on one side only (Latin *ex parte*)
f	family; farthing; father; female
f.	folio; following page
F	Fahrenheit
faa	free of all average
fac	fast as can
fact.	factory
faq	fair average quality; free at quay
fas	free alongside ship
fath.	fathom
fax	facsimile (transmission/machine)
fb	freight bill; fullback
f/b	feedback; female black; front to back
fc	fixed cost; follow copy; free and clear
f/c	free and clear
f&c	fire and casualty (insurance)
f&d	freight and demurrage
fed.	federal; federated; federation
ff	far afield; folded flat; form feed
f/f	face to face; flip-flop
ffa	free for all; free from alongside; for further assignment
ffwd	fast forward
fga	foreign general average; free of general average
fic	freight, insurance, carriage
fifo	first in, first out
filo	first in, last out
fka	formerly known as
fl.	flourished (Latin *floruit*)
fn.	footnote
f/n	freight note
fna	for necessary action
fo	fade out; firm offer; firm order; free out; full out terms
f/o	for credit of; firm offer; for orders
fob	free on board
foc	free of charge; free on car

fod	free of damage
fol.	folio; follow(ing)
fol.	leaf (Latin *folium*)
foq	free on quay
fow	free on wharf
fp	fire policy; fixed price; floating policy; fully paid
freq.	frequency; frequent(ly)
fruc.	fruit (Latin *fructus*)
f/s	financial statement; first stage
ft	free of tax; free trade; full terms
f&t	fire and theft (insurance)
fv.	back of the page (Latin *folio verso*)
fwd.	forward
fx	foreign exchange
FY	fiscal year
fyi	for your information
FYI	for your information
fyr	for your reference
FYR	for your reference
g/a	general average; ground to air
gaq	general air quality
gar	gross annual return
gav	gross annual value
g/av	general average
gbo	goods in bad order
gdp	gross domestic product
GDP	gross domestic product
gep	gross energy product
gi	government issue; gross income; gross inventory
gigo	garbage in, garbage out
Gk.	Greek
gne	gross national expenditure
GNE	gross national expenditure
gni	gross national income
GNI	gross national income
gnp	gross national product
GNP	gross national product
govt.	government
gov't.	government
gr.	grain; great; gross
gro.	gross

gtc	good till canceled
gtw	good this week
g/w	gross wt.
h.a.	in this year (Latin *hoc anno*)
hab. corp.	may you have the body (Latin *habeas corpus*)
hb	halfback; handbook
h/b	handbook
h'back	hatchback
h/back	hardback
hc	hard copy; hydrocarbon
h.c.	tonight (Latin *hac nocte*)
h-d	heavy duty; high density
hdl.	handle
hdqrs.	headquarters
hdwe.	hardware
h/f	held for
hi fi	high fidelity
HIV	human immunodeficiency virus
h.l.	in this place (Latin *hoc loco*)
hlg.	halogen
hmo	health maintenance organization
HMO	health maintenance organization
h/r	heart rate
ht	half title; halftone; high tension; high tide
i&a	indexing and abstracting
iae	in any event
iatr	is amended to read
iaw	in accordance with
ibid.	in the same place (Latin *ibidem*)
ICBM	intercontinental ballistic missile
ico	in case of
icw	in connection with
id.	the same (Latin *idem*)
id. ac	the same as (Latin *idem ac*)
i.e.	that is (Latin *id est*)
ifo	in favor of; in front of
iia	if incorrect, advise
i/l	import license
illus.	illusion; illustrate(d); illustration; illustrator
indef.	indefinite

inf.	infinity
inf.	below (Latin *infra*)
in-out	input-output
in re	in regard to
int.	interest
INTELPOST	international post
introd.	introduction
i/o	in and/or over; input/output; instead of
i&o	input and output
IOU	I owe you
iow	in other words
i/p	input
IQ	import quota; intelligence quotient
i.q.e.d.	that which was to be proved (Latin *id quod erat demon-strandum*)
IRBM	intermediate range ballistic missile
ISBN	International Standard Book Number
it.	information technology; item
ital.	italics
iv	increased value; intravenous; invoice value
i.v.	under the word (Latin *in verbo*)
i/v	increased value
j.	journal
j/a	joint account
jds	job data sheet
je	job estimate
j/f	jigs and fixtures
JFK	John Fitzgerald Kennedy
jt	joint tenant
kia	killed in action
KIA	killed in action
k-o	knockout
KO	knockout
l.	line
lang.	language
lat.	lateral; latitude
lc	lowercase (small letters)
l.c.	in the place cited (Latin *loco citato*)
lcl	less than carload lot
lifo	last in, first out

lit.	liter; literacy; literal(ly); literary; literate; literature; litter; little
loc	letter of credit
loc. primo cit.	in the place first cited (Latin *loco primo citato*)
lp	long play
LP	long play
lr	letter report; long range
l.s.	place of the seal (Latin *locus sigilli*)
ltr.	letter
lux.	luxurious; luxury
lv.	leave
m	male; married; masculine; noon (Latin *meridies*)
M	money supply
M.	mister (French *Messieur*)
ma	machine account; mental age; monthly account
mad.	mind-altering drug; mutual(ly) assured destruction
MAD	mutual(ly) assured destruction
mag.	magazine
mag.	great (Latin *magnus*)
mag. op.	major work (Latin *magnum opus*)
maitre d'	head waiter (French *maitre d'hotel*)
mart.	maintenance analysis and review technique
MART	maintenance analysis and review technique
masc.	masculine
masc.	male (Latin *masculus*)
math	mathematics
math.	mathematician
mbo	management by objectives (technique)
MBO	management by objectives (technique)
m-d	manic-depressive
m/d	market day; memorandum of deposit; month(s) after date
Mesd.	Ladies (French *Mesdames*)
Messrs.	Gentlemen (French *Messieurs*).
m/f	male or female
m&f	male and female
mfg.	manufacturing
mfr.	manufacture(d)(r)
mgr.	manager
Mgr.	Monseigneur (French *Monsignor*); Monsignore (Italian *Monsignor*)

mia	missing in action
MIA	missing in action
min.	minimum; minister; minor(ity); minute
MIRV	multiple independently targeted (targetable) reentry vehicle
mkt.	market
Mlle.	Miss (French *Mademoiselle*)
Mlles.	Misses (French *Mesdemoiselles*)
m.m.	with the necessary changes (Latin *mutatis mutandis*)
Mme.	Missus (French *Madame*)
Mmes.	Ladies (French *Mesdames*)
mort.	mortal(ity); mortgage; mortician; mortuary
MP	member of Parliament; military police; mounted police
ms	months after sight; multiple sclerosis
ms.	manuscript
m/s	months after sight
m&s	maintenance and supply
MS	multiple sclerosis
mss.	manuscripts
mst	mean solar time; mountain standard time
mt	mountain time
n	note; number
n.	note; number
na	not applicable; not authorized; not available
n.a.n.	unless it is otherwise noted (Latin *nisi aliter notetur*)
natl.	national
nat'l	national
n/c	no charge; numerical control
NC	numerical control
nco	no-cost option; noncommissioned officer
NCO	noncommissioned officer
nd	next day; no date; no decision; no discount
nde	near-death experience
nec.	necessary
nf	no funds
n/f	no funds
nfa	no further action
ng	no go; no good; not given; not good
nl	new line; no liability; not licensed; not listed
n/n	no number; not to be noted
no.	number

n/o	no orders
noa	not otherwise authorized
nohp	not otherwise herein provided
nol. con.	do not want to contend (Latin *nolo contendere*)
nol. pros.	do not want to prosecute (Latin *nolle prosequi*)
non obs.	notwithstanding (Latin *non obstante*)
non seq.	it does not follow (Latin *non sequitor*)
no op.	no opinion
nop	not otherwise provided for
nos	not otherwise specified
np	no place; no publisher; notary public; note payable
n.p.	no place; no publisher
n/p	net proceeds
ns	new series; not specified
NS	new style
N.S.	new style
n/t	new terms
ntp	no title page
o/a	on account; on or about
oac	on approved credit
ob.	died (Latin *obiit*)
obit.	obituary
oc	office copy; on camera; open charter
o/c	overcharge
o/d	on demand; overdraft
oka	otherwise known as
o/o	on order; order of
op	old prices; open policy; out of print
op. cit.	in the work cited (Latin *opere citato*)
OR	operating room
os	old series; operating system; out of stock
o.s.	old series
o/s	out of service; out of stock
OS	old style
O.S.	old style
pa	particular average; pending availability; private account
p/a	per annum; power of attorney
pass.	here and there (Latin *passim*)
pax.	private automatic exchange
PAX	private automatic exchange

pbx	private branch exchange
PBX	private branch exchange
pc	percent; personal computer; petty cash; prices current
PC	personal computer
pd.	paid
p.d.	by the day (Latin *per diem*)
p/f	portfolio
p&i	principal and interest
pin.	personal identification number
PIN	personal identification number
pl.	plural; plate
p&l	profit and loss
pls.	please
p.m.	afternoon and night (Latin *post meridiem*)
pmt.	payment
pn	part number; promissory note
p/n	part number; please note; promissory note
p/o	part of
por	payable on receipt
pp.	pages
ppd.	prepaid
prep.	preparation; preparatory; prepare; preposition
pro tem.	for the time being (Latin *pro tempore*)
P.S.	written after (Latin *post scriptum*)
Pst	Pacific standard time
Pt	Pacific time
pto	please turn over
pvt.	private
px	please exchange; post exchange
q&a	question and answer
q.e.	which is (Latin *quod est*)
q.e.d.	that which was to be proved or demonstrated (Latin *quod erat demonstrandum*)
q.v.	which see (Latin *quod vide*)
r	recto; reigned
rcd.	received
r&d	research and development
R&D	research and development
r/e	rate of exchange
ref.	refer(ee)(ence): reform(atory); refraction; refresher
repr.	reprint(ed)

rev.	reverend; reverse(d); review(ed); revise(d); revision; revolution
rna	ribonucleic acid
RNA	ribonucleic acid
roa	received on account; return on assets
roi	return on investment
rom.	roman (type style)
rop	run of paper; run of press
r&r	rape and robbery; rest and recreation; rest and recupera-tion; rock and roll
RSVP	please reply (French *répondez s'il vous plaît*)
R.S.V.P.	please reply (French *répondez s'il vous plaît*)
rv	recreation vehicle; reentry vehicle
RV	recreation vehicle; reentry vehicle
/s/	signed
sa	subject to approval
sae	self-adressed envelope
SALT	Strategic Arms Limitation Talks
salv.	salvage
sanr	subject to approval—no risks
sare	self-addressed return envelope
sase	self-addressed stamped envelope
sb	small business; switchboard
sc	separate; small caps (small capital letters); statistical control
sc.	to wit; namely (Latin *scilicet*)
s/c	single column
scat.	supersonic commercial air transport
SCAT	supersonic comercial air transport
scc	specific clauses and conditions
sch.	schedule; school
sci.	science; scientific; scientist
sci-fi	science fiction
script.	scriptural; scripture
sd	standard deviation; sudden death
s.d.	without date (Latin *sine die*)
se	single entry; standard error; straightedge
sect.	section; sector
sec'y	secretary
s.e.e.o.	excepting errors and omissions (Latin *salvis erroribus et omissis*)

seq.	the following (Latin *sequens*); it follows (Latin *sequitur*)
ser.	serial; series
serv.	service
sgd.	signed
s/h	shorthand
shr.	share
s.h.v.	under this work (Latin *sub hoc voce*)
sig.	signal(ing); signature
sim.	similar; simile; simulate
sit.	stopping in transit
SI unit	International System of Units (French *Systeme Interna-tional unit*)
s/l	self-loading
s&l	savings and loan
slr	self-loading rifle; single-lens reflex
smat	see me about this
smaze	smoke and haze
sm. caps	small capitals (small capital letters)
smist	smoke and mist
smog	smoke and fog
smsa	standard metropolitan statistical area
SMSA	standard metropolitan statistical area
smust	smoke and dust
s/n	serial number; service number; stock number
so.	seller's option; senior officer; sex offender; shipping order; ship's option; shop order; south(ern); standing order; supply office(r)
s-o	shutoff
s/o	shipping order; son of
sob.	see order blank
sol.	solution (Latin *solutio*)
sop.	soprano; standard operating procedure
sp	self-propelled; selling price; single purpose; special purpose; standard practice; starting point; stop payment
sp. del.	special delivery
spec.	special(ly)(ty); specie(s); specific(ally)(ation); specimen; spectacle; speculation
sq.	squadron; square
sqd.	squad
srac	short-run average cost
SRAM	short-range attack missile

srm	standard reference material
SRM	short-range missile
ss	sample size; single signal; single source; social security; solid state; stainless steel; steamship; supersonic; suspended sentence
ss.	namely (Latin *scilicet*); written above (Latin *supra scriptum*)
s/s	same size
s to s	ship to shore; station to station
ssd	signed, sealed, and delivered
SSM	surface-to-surface missile
st	stock tansfer; surface tension; survival time
st.	saint; stanza; state; street
st.	let it (copy crossed out) stand (Latin *stet*)
s&t	science and technology
stat.	statistic(al); statuary; statue; statute
stat.	immediately (Latin *statim*)
std.	standard
steno.	stenographer; stenography; stenotype
stereo	stereophonic
sto	standard temperature and pressure; standing order
stud.	student
sup.	above (Latin *supra*)
supp.	supplement
suppl.	supplement
supv.	supervise; supervisor
s.v.	under the word (Latin *sub verbo*)
s-w	shortwave
s/w	seaworthy; standard weight
s&w	salaries and wages; surveillance and warning
swm	standards, weights, and measures
swoc	subject word out of context
syd	sum of the year's digits
sys.	system(atic)(atization)(atize)(ic)(s)
t	temperature
T	temperature
ta	target area; teaching assistant; time and attention; travel allowance
t/a	trading as
tab.	table; tablet; tabulate(d); tabulation; tabulator

targ.	target
taw	twice a week
tax.	taxation; taxes; taxonomy
tb	time base; trial balance; tuberculosis
t&b	top and bottom
tba	to be announced; to be approved; to be assigned; to be audited
tbb	to be billed
tbo	to be ordered
tbsn.	tablespoon
tbsp.	tablespoon
tc	terra cotta; total cost; true course
tcb	take care of business
td	technical director; time delay; time of departure; touchdown
t/d	table of distribution; time deposit
telecom.	telecommunication
telecon	telephone communication
temp.	temper(ature)(ed)(ing); temporary
tf	till forbidden
t/f	true/false
t&h	transportation and handling
tho'	though
thou.	thousand
thro'	through
thru	through
'til	until
tl	time limit; time line; total load; transmission line; truck load(ing)
t/l	total loss
TLC	tender loving care
tm	trademark
to.	telephone order; turn off
t/o	takeoff
toc	table of contents
tod	time of day; time of delivery
tp	title page
tr.	transpose
t/r	transmit/receive
trad.	traditional
treas.	treasure(r); treasury

ts	time sharing; traffic signal; typescript; type specification
TV	television
typ.	typical; typing; typist; typographer; typography; type-writer
type.	typewriter; typewriting
u.	university
uc	uppercase (capital letters)
ucb	unless caused by
ufa	until further advised
ufn	until further notice
ufo	unidentified flying object
UFO	unidentified flying object
ugt.	urgent
u&lc	upper and lowercase (capital and small letters)
univ.	universal; university
uo	undelivered orders
u/o	used on
us.	unconditional stimulus; under seal; undersize; uniform sales
usc	under separate cover
usu.	usual(ly)
u.s.w.	and so forth (German *und so weiter*)
ut	universal time
u/t	untrained
u-v	ultraviolet
u/w	underwater; under way; underwriter; used with
ux.	wife (Latin *uuxor*)
v.	verb; verse; verso; versus
var.	variable; variant; variation; variety
vb.	verb(al)
vet.	veteran; veterinarian; veterinary
vg	very good
vib.	vibrate; vibration; vibratory
vid.	see (Latin *vide*)
vip	very important person; very important people
vis.	viscera; visible; visibility; visual
vit.	vital; vitamin
viz.	namely (Latin *videlicet*)
vol.	volume; volunteer
voy.	voyage

vr	variable response
vs.	versus
v.s.	see above (Latin *vide supra*)
war.	warrant; with all risks
warr.	warranty
WASP	white Anglo-Saxon Protestant
wats	wide-area telephone service
WATS	Wide Area Telecommunications Service
w/b	westbound
wc	working capital; workers' compensation
w/c	with corrections
w/e	weekend
wf	wrong font
wip	work in process; work in progress
wk.	walk; weak; week; work; wreck
wo	wait order; without; work order; write out; written order
w/o	without
woh	work on hand
wp	will proceed; word processing; working paper; working party
w/p	without prejudice
wpi	wholesale price index
WPI	wholesale price index
ww	warehouse warrant; waterworks; wrong word
xch	exchange
xp	express paid
xref	cross-reference
xs	cross section; extra strong
yb	yearbook
y/o	years old
yob	year of birth
yod	year of death
yr.	year
ytd	year to date
z	zero; zone
zn.	zone
zo	zero output

52

Technical Forms

The use of technical forms in many areas of science and technology is increasing. Technical abbreviations include shortened words such as *amp.* for *ampere,* acronyms such as *ARE* for *air reactor experiment,* and initialisms such as *ia* for *impedance angle.* But the term should be spelled out in formal usage and in nontechnical material.

a	ampere; arc; atgto (prefix: one quintillionth)
A	absolute
Å	angstrom
abamp	absolute ampere
abm	automated batch mixing
ABM	automated batch mixing
abp	absolute boiling point; actual block processor
ABP	actual block processor
ac	alternating current; automatic analog computer; axio-cervical
acc	accumulator
ACC	accumulator
accw	alternating current continuous wave
ace.	alcohol-chloroform-ether; automatic circuit exchange
acet.	acetone
acf	advanced communication function
ACL	Audit Command Language
acm	area-composition machine; automatic coding machine
acr	abandon call and retry

acu	address control unit; automatic calling unit
acw	alternating continuous wave
a/d	analog to digital
ADABAS	Adapatable Data Base System
adaline	adaptive linear neuron
adc	analog-to-digital converter
ADC	analog-to-digital converter
ADDR	address
ade	automatic data entry
ADIS	Automatic Data Interchange System
ADJ	adjust
adl	automatic data link
ADL	automatic data link
ADR	adder
ADV	advance
aei	azimuth error indicator
aex	automatic electronic exchange
af	audiofidelity; audiofrequency; autofocus
agd	axial gear differential
agw	actual gross weight
agz	actual ground zero
ah	ampere hour
a-h	ampere-hour
Ah	ampere-hour; hyperopic astigmatism
ahm	ampere-hour meter
ahp	air horsepower; aviation horsepower
ai	azimuth indicator
alcom	algebraic compiler; algebraic computer
ALERT	Automatic Linguistic Extraction and Retrieval Technique
ALGOL	Algebraically Oriented Language; Algorithmic Language
ALP	assembly language program
alphanumeric	alphabetical and numerical
alt.	alternator; altimeter
altran	algebraic translator
a/m	ampere per meter; auto/manual
A/m	ampere per meter
amp	average mean pressure
amp.	ampere; amplification; amplifier; amplitude
amp. hr.	ampere hour
amp-turns	ampere-turns
amr	automatic message routing

AMR	automatic message routing
amu	atomic mass unit
anacom	analog computer
antilog.	antilogarithm
ao	axio-occlusal
aoi	angle of incidence
aor	angle of reflection
aos	add or subtract; angle of sight
a/p	after perpendicular; angle point
apa	axial pressure angle
a-part.	alpha particle(s)
aper.	aperture
apf	animal protein factor
apoth.	apothecaries; apothecary
apt.	automatically programmed tools
APT	Automatic Programmed Tools
apu	auxiliary power unit
ar	achievement ratio; address register; aspect ratio; auditory reception
AR	address register
arcos	arc cosine
are.	air reactor experiment
ARE	air reactor experiment
aru	analog remote unit; audio response unit
asc	automatic sequence control; automatic switching center; auxiliary swtich closed
ASCII	American Standard Code for Information Interchange
asi	air-speed indicator; azimuthal speed indicator
asm	auxiliary-storage management
assmblr.	assembler
asr	answer-send-receive; automatic send-receive
ast	absolute space time
ast. t	astronomical time
at.	ampere-ton; ampere-turn; atmosphere
At	ampere-ton; ampere-turn
atl	analog threshold logic
at. m	atomic mass
at/m	ampere turns per meter
At/m	ampere turns per meter
at. no.	atomic number
at. vol.	atomic volume

at. wt.	atomic weight
AUTOVON	automatic voice network
av.	average; avoirdupois
avdp.	avoirdupois
aw	atomic weight
a/w	actual weight
ax.	axial; axes; axiom; axis
az.	azimuth
azi.	azimuth
azm.	azimuth
b	bit
ba	binary add
BA	binary add
bac	binary asymmetric channel
BAC	binary asymmetric channel
BAM	basic access method
bar.	barometer; barometric; base address register; buffer address register
BAR	buffer address register
BASIC	Beginner's All-Purpose Symbolic Instruction
bau	basic assembly unit; British absolute unit
bbl.	barrel
bbp	building-block principle
bc	binary code; binary counter; bioconversion
bcd	binary-coded data; binary-coded decimal
bd.	baud
bdl.	bundle
bev	billion electron volts
BeV	billion electorn volts
bex	broadbank exchange
bfe	beam-forming electrode
bfr.	buffer
bhp	boiler horsepower; brake horsepower
bi	bacteriological index; burn index; buffer index
bi.	binary
BI	binary
bit.	binary digit
biu	basic information unit
bix	binary information exchange
BIZNET	(American) Business Network

bjf	batch-job format
bl	baseline
bl.	bale
bm	basal metabolism; board measure; body mass; bone mar-row; buffer mark; buffer modules
BM	buffer mark; buffer modules
bmep	brake mean effective pressure
bn	binary number (system)
BN	binary number (system)
bof	beginning of file
BOF	beginning of file
bot	beginning of tape
BOT	beginning of tape
b/p	blood pressure
bpi	bits per inch; bytes per inch
bps	bits per second; bytes per second
bpu	base production unit
br.	branch
BR	branch
bs	backspace (character); binary subtraction
BS	backspace (character)
BSAM	Basic Sequential Access Method
bsc	basic message switching center; binary synchronous communication
bsd	bit storage density
btl	beginning tape level
btp	body temperature and pressure
btu	basic transmission unit; British thermal unit
Btu	British thermal unit
BTU	British thermal unit
bu	base unit
bu.	bushel
bwa	backward-wave amplifier; bent-wire antenna
bw/d	barrels of water per day
bw/h	barrels of water per hour
bw/m	barrels of water per minute
bwo	backward-wave oscillator
c	calorie (large); carbohydrates; centi (prefix: one-hun-dredth); coefficient; computer; cycle; speed of light
C	calculated weight; candle; Celsius; Centigrade

cad.	cartridge-activated device; computer-aided design
CAD	computer-aided design
cad/cam	computer-aided design/computer-aided manufacturing
CAD/CAM	computer-aided design/computer-aided manufacturing
cal	computer-aided learning; conversational algebraic language
cal.	calorie (small)
CAL	computer-aided learning; Conversational Algebraic Language
cam.	central-address memory; computer-addressed memory; computer-aided manufacturing
CAM	computer-aided manufacturing
CAN	cancel (character)
cap.	computer-aided production
CAP	computer-aided production
car.	computer-assisted retrieval
CAR	computer-assisted retrieval
CARR	carriage
caw	cam-action wheel; channel address word
c-b	circuit breaker
cbfm	constant bandwidth frequency modulation
cbx	computerized branch exchange; computerized business exchange
CBX	computerized branch exchange; computerized business exchange
ccb	command control block; convertible circuit breaker
ccc	central computer complex; command control console; computer-command control
cce	carbon-chloroform extract
ccr	command control receiver; computer character recognition; control circuit resistance
ccv	closed-circuit voltage
Cd	coefficient of drag
cdb	current data bit
cdc	call-directing code
ce	carbon equivalent; circular error; compass error
c-e	chloroform-ether
c of *e*	coefficient of elasticity
cea	circular error average
cep	circle of equal probability; circle of error probability
cet	cumulative elapsed time

cf	centrifugal force
cfc	chlorofluorocarbon
cff	computer forms feeder; critical flicker frequency
cfp	computer forms printer
cg	center of gravity; centigram
c of g	center of gravity
cgf	center-of-gravity factor
cgh	computer-generated hologram
cgl	center-of-gravity locator; corrected geomagnetic latitude
c-h	candle-hour
char.	character
CHAR	character
chr	candle-hour
ci	coefficient of intelligence
cic	cardioinhibitor center; command input coupler
ciu	computer interface unit
c/km	cents per kilometer
cl	centiliter
cla	communication line adaptor
cll	circuit load logic
clp	command language processor
CLP	command language processor
CLS	close
clu	central logic unit
cm	center of mass; centimeter; communications multiplexor
c/m	communications multiplexer; control and monitoring; cycles per minute
cm^2	square centimeter
cm^3	cubic centimeter
cml	circuit micrologic; current mode logic
CMND	command
CMP	compare
cmw	critical minimum weight
c/n	carbon to nitrogen (ratio); carrier to noise (ratio)
cnl	circuit net loss
co	carbon monoxide; cardiac output; coenzyme; corneal opacity
coax.	coaxial
COBOL	Common Business-Oriented Language
coef.	coefficient
cof	coefficient of friction

COINS	Computerized Information System
compac	computer program for automatic control
co Q	coenzyme Q
cos.	cosine
cot.	card or tape reader; cotangent
cotan.	cotangent
cp	candlepower; capillary pressure; carotid pulse; center of pressure; central processor
c/p	control panel
cpa	critical-path analysis
cpe	circular probable error
cph	characters per hour; cycles per hour
cpi	characters per inch
cpl	characters per line; common program language
cpm	cards per minute; characters per minute; commutative principle of multiplication; condensed particulate matter; counts per minute; critical path method; cycles per minute
cp/m	control program/microcomputers
cpr	cardiopulmonary resuscitation
cps	central processing system; characters per second; critical path scheduling; cycles per second
cpu	central processing unit
CPU	central processing unit
crf	control relay forward; cortiocotropin-releasing factor
crm	critical reaction measure; crucial reaction measure
crt	cathod-ray tube
CRT	cathode-ray tube
crtu	combined receiving and transmitting unit
c/s	call signal; cycles per second
csect	control section; cross section
csk	countersink
csl	computer-simulation language; computer-sensitive language
CSMP	Continuous System Modeling Program
CSMPS	Computerized Scientific Management Planning System
csr	circumsolar radiation
cst	channel status indicator; channel status table; convulsive shock therapy
csu	central statistical unit; circuit-switching unit; constant-speed unit

csw	continuous seismic wave
ct	contrast threshold; control transformer; current transformer
ctc	carbon tetrachloride
cte	coefficient of thermal expansion
ctf	cytotoxic factor
ctk	capacity-ton kilometer
ctm	capacity-ton mile; centrifugal turning moment; communications terminal modules
ctpt.	counterpart; counterpoint
CTRL	control
ctu	centigrade thermal unit; central terminal unit
ctw.	counterweight
ctx	computer telex exchange
cub.	control unit busy
cum	central unit memory
cv	coefficient of variation
cvs	cardiovascular system
cw	call waiting; continuous wave; cubic weight
c/w	chainwheel; counterweight
cwo	continuous-wave oscillator
cwp	communicating word processor
CWP	communicating word processor
cwt	centum weight; counterweight; hundredweight
cwv	continuous-wave video
cx	central exchange; control transmitter
CX	central exchange
cyb.	cybernetics
cyc.	cycle
CZm	compass azimuth
d	day, deci (prefix: one-tenth)
da	deka (prefix: ten); density altitude; drift angle
d to a	digital to analog
dag	dekagram
dal	dekaliter
dam.	dekameter; direct-access method
DAM	direct-access method
dam^2	square dekameter
dam^3	cubic dekameter
dart.	datagraphic automated retrieval technique

DART	datagraphic automated retrieval technique
datacom	data communications
dav	data above voice
db	decibel; diode block
dB	decibel
dbam	database-access method
DBAM	database-access method
dbc	diameter bolt circle
dbu	decibel unit
dBu	decibel unit
d-bug	debug(ged)(ging)
dc	digital computer; direct current; directional coupler; drift correction
dcd	differential current density
dctl	direct coupled transistor logic
dex	double convex
dd	digital data; digital display
ddc	direct digital control
dde	direct data entry
ddis	data display
ddl	data definition language; data description language; digital data link
ddm	data demand module
ddr	direct debit
dds	digital display scope; digital dynamics simulator
decit	decimal digit
del.	delete
DEL	delete (character)
de/me	decoding memory
d/f	defogging; direct flow
dfa	digital fault analysis
dfd	data function diagram
dfg	digital function generator; diode function generator
dg	decigram
dgs	designated ground zero
dhp	developed horsepower
diam.	diameter
dian	digital analog
didad	digital data display
di/do.	data input/data output
dig. r-o	digital readout

diox.	dioxygen
dir. coup.	directional coupler
div	data in voice; digits in voice
div.	divide; division
dks	dekastere
dl	data link; deciliter
d/l	data link
dlu	digitizer logic unit
dm	decimeter; delta modulation; demand meter
d-max.	density maximum
dmb	dual-mode bus
dmc	digital microcircuit
dmpi	desired mean point of impact
dms	digital multiplex switching
dna	desoxyribonucleic acid
DNA	desoxyribonucleic acid
do.	diamine oxidase; disolved oxygen
dohc	double overhead cam; dual overhead cam
dos	disk operating system
DOS	Disk Operating System
dov	data over voice
dp	data processing; dewpoint; diametral pitch; diffusion pressure
dr.	dram
dri	data rate indicator; data reduction interpreter
dro	destructive readout
drs	data-reduction system
drt	data-review technique
ds	data set
DS	data set
dscb	data set control block
ds&r	data storage and retrieval
dtl	diode transistor logic
dtr	data terminal ready; distribution tape reel
DTR	data terminal ready
duv	data under voice
dv	dependent variable
dvl	direct voice line
dvm	digital voltmeter
dvom	digital volt ohmmeter
dw	deadweight

dwc	deadweight capacity
dwt	deadweight ton; pennyweight
dyn.	dyne
dyno.	dynamometer
eb	electron beam
ebcdic	extended binary-coded decimal interchange code
EBCDIC	Extended Binary-Coded Decimal Interchange Code
ecm	extended core memory
ecr	energy consumption rate
ect	electronconvulsive therapy
edac	error detection and correction
edc	electronic digital computer; error detection and correction
edp	electronic data processing
EDP	electronic data processing
eer	energy-efficiency ratio
efi	electronic fuel injection
ehd	electrohydradynamics
ehp	effective horsepower
eht	extra high frequency; extremely high frequency
ekg	electrocardiogram
EKG	electrocardiogram
ekv	electron kilovolt
ekw	electrical kilowatt
elf.	extra low frequency; extremely low frequency
elv	extra low voltage; extremely low voltage
e/m	(specific) electron mass
e of m	error of measurement
emf	electromotive force
Emos	Earth's mean orbital speed
ems	expected mean squares
emux	electronic multiplexer
emv	electron megavolt
eo	end of operation
EO	end of operation
e-o	electro-optical
eob	end of block (character)
EOB	end of block (character)
eof	end of file
EOF	end of file
eoj	end of job
EOJ	end of job

eolb	end-of-line block
EOLB	end-of-line block
eom	end of message
EOM	end of message
eor	end of record; end of run
EOR	end of record; end of run
eot	end of tape; end of transmission
EOT	end of tape; end of transmission
erf	error function
erp	effective radiated power
esc	escape (character)
ESC	escape (character)
esd	echo-sounding device; estimated standard deviation
esl	expected significance level
est	electroshock therapy
etb	end-of-transmission block (character)
ETB	end-of-transmission block (character)
etx	end of text (character)
ETX	end of text (character)
eu	electron unit
ev	electron volt; exposure value
eV	electron volt
evt	effective visual transmission
ez	electrical zero
e/z	equal zero
f	farad; fathom; feedback; feet
F	Fahrenheit; farad; fathom; feedback
fa	fatty acid; folic acid; free aperture
fath.	fathom
fax	fuel air explosion
f-b	full-bore
f/b	feedback; front to back (ratio)
fbm	board foot measure
fc	foot-candle
fca	frequency control and analysis
fdb	field dynamic braking
fde	field decelerator
fdm	frequency division multiplexing
FDOS	Floppy Disk Operating System
fe	format effective

FE	format effective
felv	feline complex leukemia virus
ff	form feed
FF	form feed
ffwd	full-speed forward
fhp	fractional horsepower
fl	flow line; fluid loss; fluorescent level; focal length
fL	foot-lambert
fl. dr.	fluid dram
fl. oz.	fluid ounce
fl. pt.	fluid pint
fl./rt.	flow rate
fm	frequency modulation
FM	freqeuncy modulation
fnp	fusion point
FORTRAN	Formula Translation
fov	field of view
f&r	feed and return; force and rhythm
fs	file separation
FS	file separation
ft.	feet; foot
ft.^{2}	square feet; square foot
ft.^{3}	cubic feet; cubic foot
f/t	freight ton
ft. H_2O	conventional foot of water
ft.-lb.	foot-pound
ft.-lbf	foot-pound force
fufo	fly under, fly out
fwt.	featherweight
g	glucose; gram; gravity (acceleration of)
G	gauss; giga (prefix: one billion)
gal.	gallon
galv.	galvanometer
gaser	gamma-ray laser
gasid	gas and acid
gasphyxiation	gas and asphyxiation
g at. wt.	gram atomic weight
Gb	gilbert
gc	geographical coordinates; gigacycle; gyrocompass
g cal.	gram calorie
GECREF	Geographic Reference (system)

GEOIS	Geographic Information System
gert	graphical evaluation and review technique
GERT	Graphical Evaluation and Review Technique
gev	gigaelectronvolt
GeV	gigaelectronvolt
gew	gram equivalent weight
g-force	gravity force(s)
gg	gamma globulin
g gr.	great gross
ghx	ground heat exchange
GHz	gigahertz
gill	gill
g ion	gram ion
giq	giant imperial quart
GIS	Geographic Information System; Global Information System
gj	gigajoule
gm-aw	gram atomic weight
gmv	gram molecular volume
gmw	gram molecular weight
g-n	glucose-nitrogen (ratio)
goa	gyroscope output amplifier
gor	gas-oil ratio
gox	gaseous oxygen
gpu	ground power unit
gr.	grain; gross
g-r	gamma ray
grtm	gross-ton mile
gs	ground speed
gsd	grid sphere drag
gsr	galvanic skin reflex; galvanic skin response
gtm	gross ton mile
gtow	gross takeoff weight
gtw	gross ton weight
GV	gigavolt
Gv	gigavolt
gvt	gravity vacuum tube
gvw	gross vehicle weight
gw	gigawatt; ground wave
g/w	gross weight
Gw	gigawatt

gwh	gigawatt hour
GWh	gigawatt hour
gz	ground zero
h	hectare; hecto (prefix: one hundred); height; hour
H	henry
ha	hectare; hour angle; hour aspect; humic acid
Hb	hemoglobin
hc	hydrocarbon
hepa	high-efficiency particulate air (filter)
hf	high frequency; hyperfocal
HF	high frequency
hhp	hydraulic horsepower
hi-T	high torque
hl	hectoliter
hlg.	halogen
hm	hectometer
hp	high pressure; horizontal parallax; horsepower
hph	horsepower-hour
hv	high velocity; high voltage
hz	hertz
Hz	hertz
ia	impedance angle; international angstrom
iae	integral absolute error
iao	intermittent aortic occlusion
ibw	information bandwidth
ic	input circuit; integrated circuit
i/c	intercom
icff	intercommunication flip-flop
icr	iron-core reactor
id	inside diameter
idac	interim digital-analog converter
idp	information data processing; input data processing; integrated data processing
ie	ion exchange
if.	information feedback; interferon; intermediate frequency
ig	inertial guidance
i gal.	imperial gallon
ihp	indicated horsepower
ihph	indicated horsepower hour

ildf	integrated logistic data file
ilf	inductive loss factor
im	impulse modulation; intensity modulation
imp. gal.	imperial gallon
in.	inch
INDN	indication
INDR	indicator
in. H$_2$O	conventional inch of water
inr	impact noise rating; impact noise ratio
INT	initial
i/o	input/output
i&o	input and output
iob	input-output buffer
i/p	input
ipa	intermediate power amplifier; internal power amplifier
ipfm	integral pulse frequency modulation
ir	infrared
i&r	information and retrieval
ise	integral square error
is&r	information storage and retrieval
ixc	interexchange
J	joule
jds	job data sheet
j/f	jigs and fixtures
k	about one thousand (computer storage capacity); carat (karat); Kelvin; kilo (prefix: one thousand); knot
K	about one thousand (computer storage capacity)
kb	keyboard; kilobit; kilobyte
kbar	kilobar
kbe	keyboard entry
kbtu	kilo British thermal unit
kc	kilocycle
kcal	kilocalorie
ke	kinetic energy
kev	kiloelectronvolt; one thousand electron volts
keV	kiloelectronvolt
kg	kilogram
kG	kilogauss
kg cal.	kilogram calorie

kg-f	kilogram-force
kgm	kilogram meter
khp	kilohorsepower
khz	kilohertz
kHz	kilohertz
kilohm	kilo-ohm
kΩ	kilo-ohm
kj	kilojoule
kJ	kilojoule
kK	kilokelvin
kl	kiloliter
km	kilometer
kmw	kilomegawatt
kmwhr	kilomegawatt-hour
kn	kilonewton; knot
kPa	kilopascal
kr	kiloroentgen
krad	kilorad
ksia	thousand square inches absolute
kt	karet (caret); kiloton
kv	kilovolt
kV	kilovolt
kva	kilovoltampere
kVa	kilovoltampere
kV/a	kilovolts per ampere
kvah	kilovolt-ampere-hour
kvam	kilovolt ampere meter
kvar	kilovar; kilovolt ampere reactive
kvarh	kilovar hour
kvm	kilovolt meter
kvp	kilovolt peak
kw	kilowatt
kW	kilowatt
kwh	kilowatt hour
kWh	kilowatt hour
kwhr	kilowatt hour
kwm	kilowatt meter
kwr	kilowatt reactive
l	line; liter; locus
L	lambert
LAN	local area network

lb	line buffer
lb.	pound
lb. ap.	apothecaries' pound
lb. avdp.	avoirdupois pound
lb. cal.	pound calorie
lbf	pound-force
lb.-f	pound-force
lb. ft.	pound foot
lb. in.	pound inch
lbl.	label
LBL	label
lbs.	pounds
lbs. t	pounds thrust
lc	liquid crystal; low calorie; low carbon
lcd	liquid crystal display; lowest common denominator
LCD	liquid crystal display
lcf	least common factor; lowest common factor
lcm	large-core memory; least common multiple; lowest common multiple
l-d	low density
lf	line feed; low frequency
lft	linear feet; linear foot
lg	large grain; long grain; low grade
lg. tn.	long ton
LH_2	liquid hydrogen
lha	local hour angle
lHe	liquid helium
lhr	lumen hour
li	line item; longitudinal interval
linac	linear accelerator
lin. ft.	linear feet; linear foot
ll	lower limit
l/l	line by line; lower limit
llr	line of least resistance
lm	lumen
lms	least mean square; lumen second; lunar mass spectrometer
lmt	length, mass, time
lna	low-noise amplifier
lnp	lunar neutron probe
lab.	line of balance

loc   locus of control
lo-d   low density
log.   logarithm
lop.   line of position
los   line of sight; loss of signal
loxygen   liquid oxygen
lp   latent period; light perception; linear programming; low
                 pressure
lpcw   long-pulse continuous wave
lpo   liquid phase oxidation
lq   linear quantifier; lowest quartile
lsb   lest significant bit
lsc   least significant character
lsd   last significant data; last significant digit; least significant
                 difference; least significance digit
lsg   list set generator
lt   line terminator; long ton; low temperature; low tension;
                 low torque
ltm   low thermal mass
lv   low viscosity; low voltage
lvr   line voltage regulator
lw   long wave

m   mega (prefix: one million); meter; milli (prefix: one-
                 thousandth)
m^2 square meter
m^3 cubic meter
M   money (supply); thousand
ma   milliampere
mA   milliampere
mÅ   milliangstrom
mad.   mean absolute deviation
mae   mean absolute error
mamp   milliampere
mar.   memory address register; minimal angle resolution
mas   milliampere second
mb   macrobiotic; megabyte; memory buffer; millibar
mbar   millibar
mbps   megabits per second; million bits per second
mbr   memory buffer register
mbs   magnetron beam switching

mb/s	megabits per second
mbt	mean body temperature
mc	magnetic center; master control; megacycle; metric carat; millicycle
mcg	microgram
mc hr.	millicurie hour
mci	megacurie
mcvf	multichannel voice frequency
m-d	modulator-demodulator
mdn.	median
mdt	mean down time
m/e	mechanical/electrical
mean max.	mean maximum
mei	marginal efficiency of investment
mep	mean effective pressure
mev	million electron volts
meV	megaelectronvolts
mf	medium frequency; millifarad
mF	millifarad
mftL	millifoot lamberts
mg	megagram; milligram
mG	milligauss
mgn	micrograin
mgtrn	magnetron
mgw	maximum gross weight
mh	magnetic heading; millihenry
mH	millihenry
mhz	megahertz; millihertz
mHz	megahertz; millihertz
mi.	mile
mi.^{2}	square mile
mi.^{3}	cubic mile
mic	micrometer
mil.	mileage; million
mil. m/t	million metric tons
min.	minute
mJ	megajoule; millijoule
mK	millikelvin
ml	machine language; millilambert; milliliter
mL	millilambert
mlr	main line of resistance; multiple linear regression

mm	megameter; millimeter; millimicron
mm²	square millimeter
mm³	cubic millimeter
mmx	memory multiplexer
mnls	modified new least squares
moa	minute of angle
moddem	modulator-demodulator
moe	measuare of effectiveness
mol. wt.	molecular weight
mot	mean operating time
mΩ	megaohm
mp	manifold pressure; melting point
mpx	multiplex
mr	milliroentgen
mR	milliroentgen
mrad	megarad; millirad
mre	mean radial error
mrt	mean radiant temperature
ms	mean square; metric system; millisecond
msc	most significant character
msd	most significant digit
mse	mean square error
msg	monosodium glutamate
MSG	monosodium glutamate
mst	mean solar time
mt	machine translation; maximum torque; mean time; megaton; metric ton
mte	maximum thermal energy
mux	multiplex(or)
mv	mean variation; megavolt; millivolt
mV	megavolt; millivolt
mva	mean vertical acceleration; megavolt ampere
mw	megawatt; milliwatt; molecular weight
mW	megawatt; milliwatt
mwh	milliwatt hour
mWhr	milliwatt hour
mwr	mean width ratio
mx	multiplex
µ	micro (prefix: one-millionth)
µa	microampere

μbar	microbar
μF	microfarad
μg	microgram
μH	microhenry
μin	microinch
μm	micrometer
μs	microsecond
μv	microvolt
μV	microvolt
μw	microwatt
μW	microwatt
n	nano (prefix: one-billionth)
N	newton
na	nanoampere; nucleic acid
NA	nucleic acid
n-bomb	neutron bomb
N-bomb	neutron bomb; nuclear bomb
nc	nitrocellulose; nuclear capability; numerical code; numerical control
NC	numerical control
ndw	net deadweight
negatron	negative electron
neutron	neutral ion
nF	nanofarad
ng	nitroglycerine
nhp	nominal horsepower
nls	new least squares; nonlinear system
nm	nanometer; neuromuscular; nuclear megaton
Nm	newton meter
nmi	nautical mile
nrl	normal rated load
nrp	normal rated power
ns	nanosecond; neuropsychiatric
nsd	no significant deviation; noise suppression device
n/t	net tonnage
ntc	negative temperature coefficient
ntm	net ton mile
nt. wt.	net weight
nw	nanowatt
n/w	net weight

nW	nanowatt
nwt	net weight
nzg	nonzero test
oc	open circuit
ocr	optical character reader; optical character recognition
OCR	optical characcater reader
odt	on-line debugging technique
olc	on-line computer
olrt	on-line real time
ols	ordinary least squares
o/p	output
opn.	open; operation
OPN	open
os	oil solvent; operating system
OS	operating system
oz.	ounce
oz. ap.	apothecaries' ounce
oz. avd.	avoirdupois ounce
ozf	ounce-force
oz.-f	ounce-force
oz. t	ounce troy
p	pico (prefix: one-trillionth); probability
pa	paper advance; picoampere; power amplifier
Pa	pascal
pabx	private automatic branch exchange
PABX	private automatic branch exchange
par.	parallax; perimeter acquisition radar; precision approach radar
param.	parameter; parametric
pax.	private automatic exchange
PAX	private automatic exchange
p/bhp	pounds per brake horsepower
pbx	personal business exchange; private branch exchange
PBX	private branch exchange
pc	percent; personal computer; pitch circle; point of curve; printed circuit; program counter; pulsating current
PC	personal computer
p/c	percent(age); processor controller; pulse counter
pct.	percent
pd	pitch diameter; pulse duration

pdm	pulse-delta modulation
pe	photoelectric; probable error; program element
PERT	Program Evaluation and Review Technique
pf	performance factor; picofarad; pneumatic float; pulse frequency
pF	picofarad
pfd	personal flotation device
pfm	power factor meter; pulse frequency modulation
pfr	peak flow rate
pk	psychokinesis
p/l	payload
pm	primary memory; pulse modulation
p-m	permanent magnet; phase modulation
p/m	parts per million; pounds per minute
pmbx	private manual branch exchange
PMBX	private manual branch exchange
pmm	pulse mode multiplex
pmx	private manual exchange
PMX	private manual exchange
po	power oscillator
pos	product of sums
pot.	point of tangency; potentiometer
ppb	parts per billion
pph	pulses per hour
ppm	parts per million; pulse position modulation
pr	percentile rank
ps	picosecond; pressure sensitive; pulmonary stenosis
psec	picosecond
ptc	positive temperature coefficient
ptm	pulse-time modulation
pw	packed weight; picowatt; pulse width
pW	picowatt
p-wave	pressure wave
pwt.	pennyweight
ql	quintal
qt.	quart
R	rankine; roentgen
r/a	radioactive
rad.	radian; radius
ram.	random-access memory

RAM	random-access memory
rd.	rad
rem	recognition memory
REM	recognition memory
rf	radio frequency
ri	random interval; retrograde inversion
rkva	reactive volt-ampere
rms	root mean square
rmse	root mean square error
Rn	radon
rna	ribonucleic acid
RNA	ribonucleic acid
rom	read-only memory
ROM	read-only memory
rps	revolutions per second
r-sq.	r-squared
r-s ratio	response-stimulus ratio
rss	root-sum square
rtn.	routine
RTN	routine
rvm	reactive voltmeter
s	second
sam.	sequential-access method; serial access memory; synchronous
SAM	sequential-access method
s/c	short circuit
scn.	scan
SCN	scan
sd	standard deviation
se	spherical equivalent; standard error
s-ft.	second-foot
shf	superhigh frequency
shp	shaft horsepower
sh. tn.	short ton
slf	straight-line frequency
s/n	signal to noise (ratio)
so.	shift out
SO	shift out
sop.	sum of products
sqc	statistical quality control
sq. rt.	square root

st	short ton
sta. mi.	statute miles
sw	shipper's weight
s-w	shortwave
s/w	standard weight
syd	sum of the years' digits
t	tonne (metric); troy
T	tera (prefix: one trillion)
t-a	toxin-antitoxin
tan.	tangent
t/c	temporary coefficient
tgn.	tangent
thp	thrust horsepower
tmw	thermal megawatts
ton	ton
twx	teletypewriter exchange
TWX	Teletypewriter Exchange (now Telex II)
u	(unified) atomic mass unit
uhf	ultrahigh frequency
UHF	ultrahigh frequency
ulf	ultralow frequency
USASCII	USA Standard Code for Information Interchange
uv	ultraviolet
u-v	ultraviolet
v	volt
V	volt
va	voltampere
v-a	volt-ampere
VA	voltampere
vf	video frequency
vhf	very high frequency
VHF	very high frequency
vhs	video home system
vm	voltmeter
vof	variable operating frequency
w	watt
W	watt
w/d	weight displacement (ratio)
wh	watt hour

Wh	watt hour
wpc	watts per candle
x	unknown quantity
xcvr	transceiver
xhf	extrahigh frequency
xmt	transmit
yd.	yard
yd.^{2}	square yard
yd.^{3}	cubic yard
z	zero
zf	zero frequency
zg	zero gravity
zn.	zenith

53

Organizations

Abbreviations of organizations frequently are formed by combining the first initials of key words in the organization. These initials are written in capital letters without periods or spaces between them. Generally, abbreviations of organizations should not be used in formal writing. In informal writing, if they are used, spell out the name of the organization the first time it is mentioned (or the first time in each chapter in the case of a larger work) and put the initials in parentheses after the spelled out name: *Computer Systems of Massachusetts (CSM)*.

AA	Addicts Anonymous; Alcoholics Anonymous
AAA	American Academy of Advertising; America Anthropological Association; American Automobile Association
AAAS	American Academy of Arts and Sciences; American Association for the Advancement of Science
AADS	American Academy of Dental Science
AAG	Association of American Geographers
AAHA	American Animal Hospital Association; American Association of Handwriting Analysts; American Association of Homes for the Aging; American Association of Hospital Accountants
AAIE	American Association of Industrial Editors; American Association of Industrial Engineers
AARP	American Association of Retired Persons
AASM	Association of American Steel Manufacturers

AAUP   American Association of University Presses; American Association of University Professors
AAUW   American Association of University Women
ABA   American Bankers Association; American Bar Association; American Booksellers Association
ABC   American Broadcasting Company; Audit Bureau of Circulation
ABCA   American Business Communications Association
ABT   American Board of Trade
ACAE   American Council for the Arts in Education
ACE   American Cinema Editors; American Council on Education; Army Corps of Engineers; Association for Community Education
ACES   Americans for the Competitive Enterprise System; Area Cooperative Educational Service
ACET   Advisory Committee on Electronics and Telecommunications
ACFA   American Cat Fanciers Association; Association of Commercial Finance Attorneys
ACHR   American Council of Human Rights
ACLO   Association of Cooperative Library Organizations
ACLU   American Civil Liberties Union; American College of Life Underwriters
ACM   American College of Musicians; Associated Colleges of the Midwest; Association for Computing Machinery
ACOC   Air Command Operations Center
ACPE   Association for Continuing Professional Education
ACRR   American Council on Race Relations
ACS   American Cancer Society; American Ceramic Society; American Chemical Society; American College of Surgeons; Association of Clinical Scientists
ACSOC   Acoustical Society of America
ACSSN   Association of Colleges and Secondary Schools for Negroes
ACTA   American Community Theatre Association
ACTI   Advisory Committee on Technology Innovation
ACTSU   Association of Computer Time-Sharing Users
ACU   American Church Union; American Congregational Union; American Conservation Union; American Conservative Union
ACUG   Association of Computer User Groups

ADA	American Dairy Association; American Dental Association; American Dermatological Association; American Diabetes Association; American Dietetic Association; Americans for Democratic Action; Atomic Development Authority; Automobile Dealers Association
ADAA	American Dental Assistants Association; Art Dealers Association of America
ADBA	American Dog Breeders Association
ADCI	American Die Casting Institute
ADCIS	Association for the Development of Computer-Based Instruction Systems
ADDS	Alcohol and Drug Dependence Service
ADEA	American Driver Education Association
ADHA	American Dental Hygienists Association
ADS	Alzheimer's Disease Society; American Daffodil Society; American Dahlia Society; American Dental Society; American Denture Society
ADTI	American Dinner Theatre Institute
ADTS	Automatic Data and Telecommunications Service
AEA	Actors' Equity Association; Adult Education Association; American Economic Association; American Education Association; Atomic Energy Authority
AEC	Army Electronics Command; Atomic Energy Commission
AEI	American Enterprise Institute
AELC	Association of Evangelical Lutheran Churches
AESC	American Engineering Standards Committee
AETA	American Educational Theatre Association
AFA	Actors Fund of America; Advertising Federation of America; Air Force Association; American Forensic Association; American Forestry Association
AFB	American Farm Bureau; American Foundation for the Blind
AFBF	American Farm Bureau Federation
AFC	American Football Conference
AFL	American Football League
AFL-CIO	American Federation of Labor and Congress of Industrial Organizations
AFNE	Americans for Nuclear Energy
AFO	Atlantic Fleet Organization
AFPC	American Food for Peace Council
AFRASEC	Afro-Asian Organization for Economic Cooperation

AFSB	American Federation of Small Business
AFSC	American Friends Service Committee
AFT	American Federation of Teachers
AFTC	American Fair Trade Council
AFTRA	American Federation of Television and Radio Artists
AGAC	American Guild of Authors and Composers
AGCA	Associated General Contractors of America
AGS	American Gem Society; American Geographical Society; American Geriatrics Society; American Gynecological Society; American Association of Graduate Schools
AHA	American Heart Association; American Historical Association; Animal Hospital Association; American Humane Association
AHL	American Hockey League
AI	Amnesty International; Astrologers International
AIA	Aerospace Industries Association; American Institute of Accountants; American Institute of Aeronautics; American Institute of Architects
AIAA	Aerospace Industries Association of America; American Industrial Arts Association; American Institute of Aeronautics and Astronautics
AIB	American Institute of Banking
AICR	American Institute for Cancer Research
AIDA	American Indian Development Association
AIEE	American Institute of Electrical Engineers
AIGA	American Institute of Graphic Arts
AIIE	American Institute of Industrial Engineers
AIME	American Institute of Mechanical Engineers
AIO	Americans for Indian Opportunity
AIPO	American Institute of Public Opinion
AKC	American Kennel Club
ALA	American Legion Auxiliary; American Library Association; American Livestock Association; American Lung Association; Authors League of America
ALDA	American Land Development Association
ALEOA	American Law Enforcement Officers Association
ALGU	Association of Land Grant Colleges and Universities
ALI	American Law Institute; American Liberties Institute
ALRA	Abortion Law Reform Association
ALRB	Agricultural Labor Relations Board; Agricultural Labor Relations Bureau
ALTA	American Land Title Association

AMA	Aircraft Manufacturers Association; American Machinery Association; American Management Association; American Maritime Association; American Marketing Association; American Medical Association; American Motel Association; American Municipal Association; Automobile Manufacturers Association
AMEME	Association of Mining, Electrical, and Mechanical Engineers
AMI	American Marine Institutes; American Military Institute
AMIA	American Mutual Insurance Alliance
AMOCO	American Oil Company
AMPS	Associated Music Publishers
AMPTP	Association of Motion Picture and Television Producers
AMS	Administrative Management Society; American Mathematical Society; American Meteorological Society; American Musicological Society
AMVETS	American Veterans (World War II, Korea, Vietnam)
ANC	African National Congress; American News Company; Arlington National Cemetery
ANG	Air National Guard; American Newspaper Guild
ANGUS	Air National Guard of the United States
ANHA	American Nursing Home Association
ANL	Argonne National Laboratory
ANMC	American National Metric Council
ANP	Associated Negro Press
ANPA	American Newspaper Publishers Association
ANRC	American National Red Cross
ANSC	American National Standards Committee
ANSI	American National Standards Institute
AP	Associated Press
APCA	Air Pollution Control Association
APCB	Air Pollution Control Board
APG	Aberdeen Proving Ground
APL	Applied Physics Laboratory
APLA	American Patent Law Association
APTC	Allied Printing Trades Council
APWU	American Postal Workers Union
AQAB	Air Quality Advisory Board
ARBA	American Road Builders Association
ARC	Agricultural Relations Council; Agricultural Research Council; American Red Cross
ARCO	Atlantic Richfield Company

ARDA   American Railway Development Association
AREA   American Railway Engineering Association
ARIA   Adult Reading Improvement Association
ARTA   Association of Retail Travel Agents
ARTCC   Air Route Traffic Control Center
ARU   American Railway Union
ASA   Acoustical Society of America; African Studies Association; Amateur Softball Association; Amateur Swimming Association; American Society of Appraisers; American Society of Auctioneers; American Sociological Association; American Softball Association; American Standards Association; American Statistical Association; American Surgical Association; Atomic Security Agency
ASB   Air Safety Board
ASC   American Security Council; American Society of Cinematographers; American Society of Criminology; American Society for Cybernetics
ASCAP   American Society of Composers, Authors, and Publishers
ASCE   American Society of Civil Engineers
ASCHE   American Society of Chemical Engineers
ASCN   American Society of Clinical Nutrition
ASDS   American Society of Dental Surgeons
ASE   American Stock Exchange
ASFA   American Steel Foundrymen's Association
ASFH   Albert Schweitzer Friendship House
ASG   American Society of Genetics
ASHA   American School Health Association; American Social Hygiene Association; American Speech and Hearing Association
ASI   Aerospace Studies Institute; American Society of Indexers; American Statistics Institute
ASIL   American Society of International Law
ASJA   American Society of Journalists and Authors
ASLA   American Savings and Loan Association; American Society of Landscape Architects
ASM   American Society for Metals
ASME   American Society of Magazine Editors; American Society of Mechanical Engineers
ASNE   American Society of Newspaper Editors
ASO   American School of Orthodontists; American Symphony Orchestra

ASOL	American Symphony Orchestra League
ASPCA	American Society for the Prevention of Cruelty to Animals
ASPCC	American Society for the Prevention of Cruelty to Children
ASQC	American Society for Quality Control
ASSE	American Society of Safety Engineers; American Society of Sanitary Engineers
ASSOCHAM	Associated Chambers of Commerce
ASTA	American Society of Travel Agents
ASTE	American Society of Tool Engineers
ASTME	American Society of Tool and Manufacturing Engineers
ASU	American Secular Union; American Student Union
ASZ	American Society of Zoologists
ATAS	Academy of Television Arts and Sciences
ATB	Air Transportation Board
ATCB	Air Traffic Control Board
ATESL	Association of Teachers of English as a Second Language
ATF	American Type Founders
ATLA	American Trial Lawyers Association
ATSC	American Traffic Safety Council
ATSU	Association of Time-Sharing Users
AT&T	American Telephone & Telegraph
ATWE	Association of Technical Writers and Editors
AU	Atheists United
AUCTU	All-Union Council of Trade Unions
AUT	Association of University Teachers
AVC	American Veterans Committee
AVMA	American Veterinary Medical Association
AWA	American Watch Association; American Wine Association; American Woman's Association; Aviation/Space Writers Association
AWBA	American World Boxing Association
AWI	Animal Welfare Institute
AWL	Animal Welfare League
AWMF	Andrew W. Mellon Foundation
BA	Bank of America; Bureau of Accounts
BAA	Bureau of African Affairs
BAC	Black Action Committee; Bureau of Air Commerce; Business Advisory Council
BAPSA	Broadcast Advertising Producers Society of America
BATF	Bureau of Alcohol, Tobacco, and Firearms
BBA	Big Brothers of America

BBB	Better Business Bureau
BBHF	B'nai B'rith Hillel Foundations
BBL	Big Brothers League
BBWAA	Baseball Writers' Association of America
BC	Bureau of the Census
BC/BS	Blue Cross/Blue Shield
BEMA	Business Equipment Manufacturers Association
BEP	Bureau of Engraving and Printing
BES	Bureau of Employment Security
BETA	Business Equipment Trade Association
BEWT	Bureau of East-West Trade
BFI	Business Forms Institute
BFUSA	Baseball Federation of the United States of America
BGA	Better Government Association
BH	Board of Health
BHE	Board of Higher Education
BIA	Braille Institute of America; Building Industry Association; Bureau of Indian Affairs
BIAA	Bureau of Inter-American Affairs
BIAC	Business and Industry Advisory Committee
BIB	Bureau of International Broadcasting
BILA	Bureau of International Labor Affairs
BLE	Brotherhood of Locomotive Engineers
BLM	Bureau of Land Management
BLS	Bureau of Labor Statistics
BM	Bureau of Medicine; Bureau of Mines; Bureau of the Mint
BNA	Bureau of National Affairs
BNDD	Bureau of Narcotics and Dangerous Drugs
BNF	Brand Name Foundation
BOB	Bureau of the Budget
BOMC	Book of the Month Club
BOT	Board of Trade
BPP	Black Panther Party
BPWA	Business and Professional Women's Association
BR	Bureau of Reclamation
BRS	Bertrand Russell Society; Bureau of Railroad Safety; Buyers' Research Syndicate
BS	Bureau of Ships; Bureau of Standards
BSA	Bibliographical Society of America; Boy Scouts of America; Boy Scouts Association; Bureau of Supplies and Accounts

BSU	Black Students Union
BTA	Board of Tax Appeals
BTL	Bell Telephone Laboratories
BW	Business Week
BWA	Baptist World Alliance; Baseball Writers Association
CAA	Civil Aeronautics Administration; Civil Aeronautics Authority; Collectors of American Art; Community Action Agencies; Custom Agents Association
CAAA	Composers, Authors, and Artists of America
CAD	Civil Air Defense
CAEU	Council of Arab Economic Unity
CAG	Civil Air Guard; Composers-Authors Guild; Concert Artists Guild
CAGI	Compressed Air and Gas Institute
CAL	Center for Applied Linguistics; Citizens Action League
CAN	Citizens Against Noise
CANA	Clergy Against Nuclear Arms
CAP	Civil Air Patrol; Combat Air Patrol; Consumer Action Panel
CARE	Citizens Association for Racial Equality
CASB	Cost-Accounting Standards Board
CAT	Civil Air Transport
CATCC	Carrier Air Traffic Control Center
CAU	Congress of American Unions; Consumer Affairs Union
CB	Census Bureau; Children's Bureau; Consultants Bureau
CBBB	Council of Better Business Bureaus
CBE	Council for Basic Education; Council of Basic Education; Council of Biology Editors
CBEMA	Computer and Business Equipment Manufacturers Association
CBO	Congressional Budget Office
CBOT	Chicago Board of Trade
CBS	Columbia Broadcasting System
CBT	Chicago Board of Trade
CCCA	Classic Car Clubs of America; Conservative Christian Churches of America
CCHE	Central Council for Health Education; Coordinating Council for Higher Education
CCIA	Consumer Credit Insurance Association
CCJ	Center for Criminal Justice
CCL	Council for Civil Liberties

CCR	Commission on Civil Rights
CCRKBA	Citizens Committee for the Right to Keep and Bear Arms
CCSB	Credit Card Service Bureau
CCUS	Chamber of Commerce of the United States
CDA	Catholic Daughters of America; Child Development Association
CDF	Children's Defense Fund; Civil Defense Force; Community Development Foundation
CDMB	Civil Defense Mobilization Board
CDNS	Chicago Daily News Service
CE	Church of England; Corps of Engineers
CEARC	Computer Education and Applied Research Center
CEC	Civil Engineer Corps; Commodity Exchange Commission; Consolidated Edison Company; Consulting Engineers Council
CECR	Center for Environmental Conflict Resolution
CEEB	College Entrance Examination Board
CEEC	Council for European Economic Cooperation
CEG	Coalition for Economic Growth
CEIP	Carnegie Endowment for International Peace
CEMA	Council for Economic Mutual Assistance; Council for Encouragement of Music and the Arts
CENTO	Central Treaty Organization
CEP	Council on Economic Priorities
CEPR	Center for Educational Policy Research
CEQ	Council on Environmental Quality
CF	Conservation Foundation
CFAT	Carnegie Foundation for the Advancement of Teaching
CFPTS	Coalition for Peace Through Strength
CFTC	Commodity Futures Trading Commission
CGA	Coast Guard Academy
CH	Carnegie Hall
CHA	Catholic Hospital Association; Child Health Association; Community Health Association
CHL	Central Hockey League
CHR	Commission on Human Rights
CIA	Central Intelligence Agency; Commerce and Industry Association; Culinary Institute of America
CIL	Center for Independent Living
CIO	Congress of Industrial Organizations
CLC	Cost of Living Council

CLGA	Composers and Lyricists Guild of America
CLR	Council on Library Research
CLRA	Consumer Law Reform Association
CLUSA	Cooperative League of the USA
CLW	Council for a Livable World
CM	Common Market
CMEA	Council for Mutual Economic Assistance
COLC	Cost of Living Council
CORE	Congress of Racial Equality
COSR	Committee on Space Research
COST	Congressional Office of Science and Technology
COSW	Citizen's Organization for a Sane World
CPD	Committee on the Present Danger
CPSC	Consumer Product Safety Commission
CRA	Community Redevelopment Agency
CRB	Civilian Review Board
CRC	Civil Rights Commission
CRE	Commission for Racial Equality
CRS	Coast Radio Service; Community Relations Service; Congressional Research Service
CSC	Central Security Council; Civil Service Commission
CSIR	Council of Scientific and Industrial Research
CUA	Council on Urban Affairs
CURE	Citizens United for Racial Equality
CWA	Civil Works Administration; Communication Workers of America; Crime Writers Association
CWL	Catholic Women's League
CWLA	Child Welfare League of America
CYMA	Catholic Young Men's Association
DA	Department of Agriculture; Department of the Army
DAR	Daughters of the American Revolution
DBC	Drum and Bugle Corps
DC	Department of Commerce; Diners Club
DCP	Department of Consumer Protection
DDEM	Dwight D. Eisenhower Museum
DEA	Drug Enforcement Administration
DECUS	Digital Equipment Computer Users Society
DEQ	Department of Environmental Quality
DFG	Department of Fish and Game
DGTA	Dry Goods Trade Association
DHUD	Department of Housing and Urban Development

DI   Department of the Interior
DJ   Department of Justice
DL   Department of Labor
DMA   Direct Mail Association
DMAA   Direct Mail Advertising Association
DMMA   Direct Mail/Marketing Association
DN   Department of the Navy
DOD   Department of Defense
DOE   Department of Education; Department of Energy
DOI   Department of Industry; Department of the Interior
DOJ   Department of Justice
DOL   Department of Labor
DON   Department of the Navy
DOS   Department of State
DOT   Department of Tourism; Department of Transportation
DOW   Dow Chemical Company
DPS   Department of Public Safety
DPW   Department of Public Works
DS   Delta Society; Department of Sanitation; Department of
              State
DT   Department of Tourism; Department of Transportation;
              Department of the Treasury
DWP   Department of Water and Power

EAB   Ethnic Affairs Bureau
EAIC   East African Industrial Council
EATA   East Asia Travel Association
EBC   Educational Broadcasting Corporation
EBS   Emergency Broadcasting System
ECF   Edgar Cayce Foundation
ECM   European Common Market
ECME   Economic Commission for the Middle East
ECSC   European Coal and Steel Community
EDB   Economic Development Board; Energy Development
              Board
EDDS   Electronic Devices Data Service
EDS   Electric Devices Society; English Dialect Society; Environ-
              mental Data Services
EDU   European Democratic Union
EEC   European Economic Community
EEOC   Economic Employment Opportunity Committee; Equal
              Employment Opportunity Commission

EFA	Epilepsy Foundation of America; Evangelical Friends Alliance
EFTA	European Free Trade Association
EHL	Eastern Hockey League
EK	Eastman Kodak
ELEC	European League for Economic Cooperation
ENA	English Newspaper Association
EOC	Economic Opportunity Commission; Equal Opportunity Commission
EOP	Executive Office of the President
EPA	Economic Planning Agency; Environmental Protection Agency; Evangelical Press Association
EPI	Environmental Policy Institute
EPO	Emergency Planning Office
EQB	Environmental Quality Board
EQC	Environmental Quality Council
ERCA	Educational Research Council of America
ESA	Ecological Society of America; Economic Stabilization Agency; Employment Standards Administration; Engineers and Scientists of America; European Space Agency
ETO	Energy Technology Office
ETUC	European Trade Union Confederation
EWA	East and West Association; Education Writers Association
EXIMBANK	Export-Import Bank
FAA	Federal Aviation Agency; Film Artists' Association
FAAR	Feminist Alliance Against Rape
FASB	Financial Accounting Standards Board
FAT	Folk Arts Theater
FBI	Federal Bureau of Investigation; Food Business Institute
FBLA	Future Business Leaders of America
FCIC	Farm Crop Insurance Corporation
FD	Foundation for the Disabled
FDA	Food and Drug Administration
FDIC	Federal Deposit Insurance Corporation
FEI	Free Enterprise Institute
FEMA	Farm Equipment Manufacturers Association; Federal Emergency Management Agency; Fire Equipment Manufacturers Association; Foundry Equipment Manufacturers Association
FEPC	Fair Employment Practices Commission

FERA	Federal Emergency Relief Administration
FERC	Federal Energy Regulatory Commission
FFA	Future Farmers of America
FGA	Freer Gallery of Art
FHA	Farmers Home Administration; Federal Highway Administration; Federal Housing Administration; Future Homemakers of America
FHAA	Field Hockey Association of America
FISC	Financial Industries Service Corporation
FJA	Future Journalists of America
FLA	Federal Loan Administration; Federal Loan Agency
FLB	Federal Land Bank
FLRA	Federal Labor Relations Authority
FMC	Federal Maritime Commission; Federated Motor(ing) Club; Federated Mountain Club; Ford Motor Company
FNMA	Federal National Mortgage Association
FOR	Foundation for Ocean Research
FPC	Federal Power Commission; Food Packaging Council; Friends Peace Committee
FRB	Federal Reserve Bank; Federal Reserve Board
FRC	Federal Radio Commission; Foreign Relations Council
FS	Foreign Service; Forest Service; Friends Society
FSC	Family Services Bureau; Federal Safety Council; Food Standards Committee
FSIC	Federal Savings Insurance Corporation
FSLA	Federal Savings and Loan Association
FSLIC	Federal Savings and Loan Insurance Corporation
FTA	Free Trade Association; Future Teachers of America
FTC	Fair Trade Commission; Federal Trade Commission
FTL	Federal Telecommunications Laboratory
FUA	Farm Underwriters Association
FWAA	Football Writers Association of America
FWPCA	Federal Water Pollution Control Administration
FWQA	Federal Water Quality Association
FWRC	Federal Water Resources Council
GA	Gamblers Anonymous; Geographical Association; Geologists Association
GAA	Gay Activists Alliance; General Aviation Association
GAO	General Accounting Office; General Auditing Office; Government Accounting Office
GBF	Great Books Foundation

GD	General Dynamics
GEC	General Electric Company
GFTU	General Federation of Trade Unions
GHI	Good Housekeeping Institute
GIA	Goodwill Industries of America
GIO	Government Information Organization; Government Insurance Office
GMA	Gallery of Modern Art; Grocery Manufacturers of America
GMC	General Motors Corporation; Gulf Maritime Company
GP	Gallup Poll
GPO	Government Printing Office
GRA	Governmental Research Association
GRC	Gale Research Company; Government Research Corporation; Gulf Research Corporation
GRO	Greenwich Royal Observatory
GSA	General Services Administration; Geological Society of America; Girl Scouts of America
HARM	Humans Against Rape and Molestation
HBA	Hollywood Bowl Association; Hospital Benefit Association; Housing Builders Association
HBS	Harvard Business School
HEC	Hydro-Electric Commission
HEPC	Hydro-Electric Power Commission
HF	Hall of Fame
HFM	Henry Ford Museum
HL	House of Lords
HLS	Harvard Law School
HMO	Health Maintenance Organization
HMSO	His (Her) Majesty's Stationery Office
HP	House of Parliament
HR	House of Representatives
HRC	Human Rights Commission
HSA	Health Services Administration; Hispanic Society of America; Hospital Savings Association
HSUS	Humane Society of the United States
HU	Harvard University
HUAC	House Un-American Activities Committee
HUD	Housing and Urban Development (Department of)
HUP	Harvard University Press
IACA	Independent Air Carriers Association

IAS	Institute for Advanced Study; International Accountants Society
IAT	Institute for Applied Technology
IAW	International Alliance of Women
IBA	Independent Bankers Association; Independent Broadcasting Association; International Bar Association; Investment Bankers Association
IBC	International Broadcasting Corporation
IBEW	International Brotherhood of Electrical Workers
IBSA	International Bible Student Association
IBU	International Broadcasting Union
ICAA	International Council on Alcohol and Addictions
ICBO	Interracial Council for Business Opportunities
ICC	Indian Claims Commission; International Chamber of Commerce; International Control Commission; Interstate Commerce Commission
ICS	Indian Civil Service; Institution of Computer Sciences; International College of Surgeons
ICWU	International Chemical Workers Union
IDA	Industrial Development Agency
IDB	Industrial Development Board
IDEA	International Drug Enforcement Association
IDR	Institute for Dream Research
IEE	Institute of Electrical Engineers; Institute of Electronic Engineering
IEEE	Institute of Electrical and Electronic Engineers
IFA	Industrial Forestry Association; Industry Film Association; International Federation of Actors
IGA	Independent Grocers Alliance
ILC	International Law Commission
ILHR	International League of Human Rights
ILO	International Labor Organization
IMA	Industrial Marketing Association; International Management Association
IMF	International Monetary Fund
IMS	Industrial Management Society
INP	International News Photos
INS	Immigration and Naturalization Service; International News Service
INSTAAR	Institute of Arctic and Alpine Research
INTELSAT	International Telecommunications Satellite Organization

INTERPOL	International Criminal Police Organization
IOBB	Independent Order of B'nai B'rith
IOC	International Olympic Committee
IOS	Investors Overseas Services
IPCA	Industrial Pest Control Association
IRAB	Institute for Research in Animal Behavior
IRAC	Industrial Relations Advisory Committee
IRB	Industrial Relations Bureau; Industrial Review Board; Insurance Rating Board
IRC	Industrial Relations Council; International Red Cross
IRN	Independent Radio News
IRO	International Refugee Organization; International Relief Organization
IRR	Institute of Race Relations
IRS	Internal Revenue Service; International Rorschach Society
ISA	Instrument Society of America; International Standards Association; International Student Association
ISO	International Standards Organization
ISTA	Institute of Science and Technology
ISWA	International Science Writers Association
ITA	Independent Teachers Association; International Trade Administration
ITB	Industrial Training Board
ITC	Industrial Training Council; International Trade Commission
ITNA	Independent Television News Association
IT&T	International Telephone and Telegraph
IVA	International Volleyball Association
IWW	Industrial Workers of the World
IYF	International Youth Federation
JAMA	Japan Automobile Manufacturers Association
JBS	John Birch Society
JCC	Job Corps Center; Junior Chamber of Commerce
JDS	John Dewey Society; Joint Defense Staff
JEC	Joint Economic Committee
JF	Jewish Federation
JPGM	J. Paul Getty Museum
JRC	Junior Red Cross
JSC	Johnson Space Center
KC	Knights of Columbus

KCPA	Kennedy Center for the Performing Arts
KFC	Kentucky Fried Chicken
KI	Kiwanis International
KKK	Ku Klux Klan
LAC	League of Arab Countries
LACL	Latin America Citizens League
LACM	Latin America Common Market
LAM	London Academy of Music
LAW	League of American Writers
LC	Library of Congress
LCRT	Lincoln Center Repertory Theater
LCSA	Lewis and Clark Society of America
LEAA	Law Enforcement Assistance Administration
LEDC	League for Emotionally Disturbed Children
LHW	League of Hispanic Women
LI	Lions International
LIAA	Life Insurance Association of America
LIC	Liquor Industry Council
LIO	Lions International Organization; Livestock Improvement Organization
LL	Little League
LLL	Lawrence Livermore Laboratories
LMA	League for Mutual Aid
LN	League of Nations
LO	Lowell Observatory
LPA	Labor Party Association; Little People of America
LPE	London Press Exchange
LPGA	Ladies Professional Golf Association
LRC	Law Reform Commission
LRL	Lawrence Radiation Laboratory; Lunar Receiving Laboratory
LSA	Labor Services Agency; Land Settlement Association; Leukemia Society of America; Linguistic Society of America
LUC	Land Use Commission
LWF	Lutheran World Federation
LWV	League of Women Voters
MA	Manpower Administration; Maritime Administration; Metric Association; Mountaineering Association
MAA	Mathematical Association of America; Mutual Aid Association; Motel Association of America

MADD	Mothers Against Drunk Drivers; Mothers Against Drunk Driving
MAES	Mexican American Engineering Society
MANFED	Manufacturers Federation
MANWA	Mexican-American National Women's Association
MAPI	Machinery and Allied Products Institute
MARAD	Maritime Administration
MASH	Mobile Army Surgical Hospital
MAUS	Metric Association of the United States
MBAA	Master Brewers Association of America
MBS	Motor Business Society; Music Broadcasting Society; Mutual Broadcasting System
MC	Manpower Commission; Maritime Commission
MCA	Music Corporation of America; Music Critics Association
MCB	Metric Conversion Board; Metric Conversion Bureau
MCBA	Master Car Builders' Association
MCTA	Motor Carriers Traffic Association
MEC	Monetary and Economic Council
MEDIA	Manufacturers Educational Drug Information Association
MEPC	Maritime Environment Protection Committee
METO	Middle East Treaty Organization
MFA	Master Fencers Association; Museum of Fine Arts
MFTB	Motor Freight Traffic Bureau
MFW	Maritime Federation of the World
MGIC	Mortgage Guarantee Insurance Corporation
MGM	Metro-Goldwyn-Mayer
MHA	Marine Historical Association; Mental Health Administration; Mental Health Association; Mental Health Authority; Multiple Handicapped Association
MIO	Metric Information Office
MIPTC	Men's International Professional Tennis Council
MIT	Massachusetts Institute of Technology
MLA	Marine Librarians Association; Master Locksmiths Association; Medical Library Association; Modern Language Association; Music Library Association
MLAA	Modern Language Association of America
MLBPA	Major League Baseball Players Association
MLC	Meat and Livestock Commission
MM	Moral Majority
MMA	Metropolitan Museum of Art; Museum of Modern Art; Music Masters Association; Minute Men of America

MOA	Metropolitan Opera Association; Music Operators of America
MOCA	Museum of Contemporary Art
MOG	Metropolitan Opera Guild
MOMS	Mothers for Moral Stability
MPA	Magazine Publishers Association; Medical Procurement Agency; Mobile Press Association; Modern Poetry Association; Motion Picture Alliance; Music Publishers Association
MPB	Missing Persons Bureau
MPDA	Motion Picture Distributors Association
MRCA	Market Research Corporation of America
MRS	Market Research Society
MRUA	Mobile Radio Users' Association
MS	Manuscript Society; Metallurgical Society; Meteoritical Society
MSC	Manned Spacecraft Center; Maple Syrup Council; Medical Service Corps
MSFC	Marshall Space Flight Center
MSG	Madison Square Garden
MSS	Movement Shorthand Society; Multiple Sclerosis Society
MTA	Manpower Training Association; Market Technicians Association; Metropolitan Transit Authority; Motor Trade Association; Music Teachers Association
MTBA	Machine Tool Builders' Association
MTRF	Mark Twain Research Foundation
MTTA	Machine Tool Trades' Association
MVMA	Motor Vehicle Manufacturers Association
MWA	Mystery Writers of America
MWIA	Medical Women's International Association
MWL	Mutual Welfare League
MWO	Mount Wilson Observatory
NAA	National Aeronautic Association; National Association of Accountants; National Auctioneers Association; National Automobile Association
NAAB	National Architectural Accrediting Board
NAACP	National Association for the Advancement of Colored People
NAADC	North American Area Defense Command
NAB	National Alliance of Businessmen; National Association of Broadcasters; National Association of Businessmen; Newspaper Advertising Bureau

NABA	North American Benefit Association
NABP	National Association of Book Publishers
NABS	National Association of Barber Schools; National Association of Black Students
NAC	National Arts Club; National Association of Chiropodists; North Atlantic Council; Northeast Air Command
NACA	National Air Carrier Association; National Armored Car Association
NACB	National Association of Convention Bureaus
NACH	National Advisory Council for the Handicapped
NADA	National Association of Drug Addiction; National Automobile Dealers Association
NADF	National Alzheimer's Disease Foundation
NAF	National Abortion Foundation; National Amputation Foundation; National Arts Foundation
NAFD	National Association of Funeral Directors
NAG	Negro Actors Guild
NAHB	National Association of Home Builders
NAHC	National Advisory Health Council; National Anti-Hunger Coalition
NALS	National Association of Legal Secretaries
NAMSB	National Association of Mutual Savings Banks
NANA	North American Newspaper Alliance
NAPA	National Association of Performing Artists; National Association of Purchasing Agents
NAR	National Association of Realtors
NARAS	National Academy of Recording Arts and Sciences
NARP	National Association of Railroad Passengers
NARS	National Archives and Records Service
NAS	National Academy of Sciences; National Agricultural Society; National Audubon Society
NASA	National Aeronautics and Space Administration; National Appliance Service Association; North American Sailing Association
NASL	North America Soccer League
NASM	National Air and Space Museum; National Association of Schools of Music
NASRC	National Association of State Racing Commissioners
NATA	National Association of Tax Accountants; National Association of Tax Administrators; North Atlantic Treaty Alliance
NATAS	National Academy of Television Arts and Sciences

NATO	National Association of Taxicab Owners; National Association of Theater Owners; National Association of Trailer Owners; National Association of Travel Organizations; North Atlantic Treaty Organization
NAVH	National Association for the Visually Handicapped
NAWA	National Association of Women Artists
NAWF	National Aborigine Welfare Fund; North American Wildlife Foundation
NAWPA	North American Water and Power Alliance
NBA	National Band Association; National Bankers Association; National Bar Association; National Basketball Association; National Boat Association; National Bowling Association; National Boxing Association; National Button Association
NBC	National Basketball Congress; National Book Committee; National Broadcasting Commission; National Broadcasting Company; Nigerian Broadcasting Corporation
NBCA	National Baseball Congress of America; National Beagle Club of America
NBEA	National Business Education Association
NBL	National Basketball League; National Book League
NBME	National Board of Medical Examiners
NBPC	National Border Patrol Council
NBS	National Bureau of Standards; National Broadcasting Service
NBTA	National Business Teachers Association
NCA	National Chiropractic Association; National Civic Association; National Council on the Aging; National Council on Alcoholism; National Council on the Arts; National Credit Association
NCAA	National Collegiate Athletic Association
NCAI	National Congress of American Indians; National Council on Alcoholism, Inc.
NCAPC	National Center for Air Pollution Control
NCCD	National Council on Crime and Delinquency
NCDC	National Center for Disease Control; National Communicable Disease Center
NCFA	National Commission of Fine Arts; National Consumer Finance Association
NCL	National Consumers League
NCMC	National Center on Missing Children

NCMDA	National Commission on Marijuana and Drug Abuse
NCOA	National Council on the Aging
NCR	National Cash Register
NCS	National Cartoonists Society; Numerical Control Society
NCUF	National Computer Users Forum
NCW	National Council of Women
NEC	National Economic Council
NEGRO	National Economic Growth and Reconstruction Organization
NEIC	National Earthquake Information Center; National Energy Information Center
NERA	National Emergency Relief Administration
NEWS	New England Wildflower Society
NFAC	National Food and Agricultural Council
NFAL	National Foundation of Arts and Letters
NFBF	National Farm Bureau Federation
NFC	National Football Conference
NFMD	National Foundation for the March of Dimes
NFU	National Farmers Union
NG	National Guard
NGA	National Gallery of Art; National Governors Association
NGAUS	National Guard Association of the United States
NGS	National Geodetic Survey; National Geographic Society
NHA	National Health Association; National Hockey Association; National Housing Administration; New Homemakers of America
NHC	National Health Council
NHL	National Hockey League
NHS	National Health Service; National Historical Society; National Honor Society
NIAL	National Institute of Arts and Letters
NIH	National Institutes of Health
NIPH	National Institute of Public Health
NIWU	National Industrial Workers Union
NKF	National Kidney Foundation
NLAA	National Legal Aid Association
NLRB	National Labor Relations Board
NLTA	National Lawn Tennis Association
NMCB	National Metric Conversion Board
NMTA	National Metal Trades Association
NMTBA	National Machine Tool Builders' Association

NNS	National Newspaper Syndicate
NOC	National Oceanographic Council; National Olympic Committee
NOSTA	National Ocean Science and Technology Agency
NOW	National Organization for Women
NOWAPA	North American Water and Power Alliance
NPA	National Parenthood Association; National Parks Association; National Pet Association; National Petroleum Association; National Pharmaceutical Association; National Pilots Association; National Planning Association; Newspaper Publishers Association
NPC	National Patent Council; National Peoples Congress; National Press Club
NPF	National Park Foundation; National Parkinson Foundation; National Piano Foundation; National Poetry Foundation
NPPA	National Press Photographers Association
NPRA	National Parks and Recreation Association
NPS	Narcotics Prevention Service; National Parks Service
NRA	National Racing Authority; National Recovery Administration; National Recreation Association; National Rehabilitation Association; National Restaurant Association; National Rifle Association; Naval Reserve Association
NRAA	National Rifle Association of America
NRC	National Racquetball Club; National Republican Club; National Research Council; Nuclear Regulatory Commission; Nuclear Research Council
NRECA	National Rural Electric Cooperative Association
NRFA	National Retail Furniture Association
NRFL	National Rugby Football League
NRLC	National Right to Life Committee
NRPA	National Recreation and Park Association
NSF	National Science Foundation
NSL	National Standards Laboratory
NSNA	National Student Nurses Association
NSPCC	National Society for the Prevention of Cruelty to Children
NSRA	National Shoe Retailers Association; National Shorthand Reporters Association
NSTA	National Science Teachers Association
NTDPMA	National Tool, Die, and Precision Machining Association
NTL	National Tennis League; National Training Laboratories

NUP	Negro Universities Press
NWA	National Wrestling Alliance
NWBA	National Wheelchair Basketball Association
NWF	National Wildlife Federation
NWRO	National Welfare Rights Organization
NWS	National Weather Service
OAAA	Outdoor Advertising Association of America
OAAU	Organization of Afro-American Unity
OAS	Organization of American States
OAU	Organization for African Unity
OCA	Office of Consumer Affairs
OCAS	Organization of Central American States
OEC	Office of Energy Conservation
OECD	Organization for Economic Cooperation and Development
OEEC	Organization for European Economic Cooperation
OEMA	Office Equipment Manufacturers Association
OEO	Office of Economic Opportunity
OEP	Office of Energy Planning; Office of Emergency Preparedness
OGE	Office of Government Ethics
OIAA	Office of Inter-American Affairs
OIE	Office of Indian Education
OMAT	Office of Manpower, Automation, and Training
ONA	Overseas News Agency
OPC	Overseas Press Club
OPEC	Oil Producer's Economic Cartel; Organization of Petroleum Exporting Countries
OPMA	Office Products Manufacturers Association
OPS	Office of Price Stabilization
ORC	Officers Reserve Corps; Offshore Racing Council; Opinion Research Corporation
OST	Office of Science and Technology
OTC	Organization for Trade Cooperation; Overseas Telecommunications Commission
OUP	Oxford University Press
OWAA	Outdoor Writers' Association of America
OWAEC	Organization for West African Economic Cooperation
PA	Parents Anonymous
PAAC	Public Arts Advisory Council
PAB	Price Adjustment Board

PAU	Pan American Union
PAW	People for the American Way
PBA	Professional Bookmen of America; Professional Bowlers Association
PC	Peace Corps
PCPF	President's Council on Physical Fitness
PDF	Parkinson's Disease Foundation
PECUSA	Presidential Ethics Commission
PEN	Poets, Playwrights, Editors, Essayists, and Novelists
PETA	People for the Ethical Treatment of Animals
PGA	Professional Golfers Association
PHS	Public Health Service
PI	Plastics Institute
PIA	Plastics Institute of America; Printing Industries of America
PIMA	Paper Industry Management Association
PLAV	Polish Legion of American Veterans
PMU	Pattern Makers Union
PNAC	President's National Advisory Committee
PNCC	President's National Crime Commission
POPS	People Opposed to Pornography in Schools
POS	Patent Office Society
POWER	Professionals Organized for Women's Equal Rights
PPFA	Planned Parenthood Federation of America
PPL	Police Protective League
PRA	Psychological Research Association; Public Roads Administration; Puerto Rico Association
PRC	Postal Rate Commission
PSA	Photographic Society of America; Poetry Society of America; Public Service Administration; Public Service Association
PSAL	Public School Athletic League
PSC	Product Safety Commission; Public Service Commission
PSI	Professional Secretaries International
PSM	People for Self Management
PSRO	Professional Services Review Organization; Professional Standards Review Organization
PSSC	Public Service Satellite Consortium
PTA	Parent-Teacher Association; Protestant Teachers Association
PTO	Patent and Trademark Office
PUB	Public Utilities Board

PUC	Public Utilities Commission
PWP	Parents without Partners
QAB	Quality Assurance Board
QBAA	Quality Brands Associates of America
QBAC	Quality Bakers of America Cooperative
RAB	Radio Advertising Bureau
RBA	Roadside Business Association
RCB	Retail Credit Bureau
RCC	Rape Crisis Center; Rescue Control Center
RCOA	Radio Club of America; Record Club of America
RDA	Railway Development Association
REA	Railway Express Agency; Rural Education Association; Rural Electrification Administration
RFL	Rugby Football League
RFU	Rugby Football Union
RGA	Republican Governors Association; Rubber Growers' Association
RHA	Rural Housing Alliance
RIMR	Rockefeller Institute for Medical Research
RJA	Retail Jewelers of America
RLCA	Rural Letter Carriers' Association
RNA	Romantic Novelists' Association
ROA	Reserve Officers Association; Retired Officers Association
ROTC	Reserve Officers Training Corps
RPL	Rocket Propulsion Laboratory
RPO	Royal Philharmonic Orchestra
RRB	Railroad Retirement Board
RRF	Reading Reform Foundation
RRI	Rubber Research Institute
RSROAA	Roller Skating Rink Operators Association of America
RTES	Radio and Television Executives Society
RTNA	Radio and Television News Association
RTS	Rubber Traders Society
RVIA	Recreation Vehicle Industry Association
RWG	Radio Writers' Guild
SA	Salvation Army; Society of Actuaries; Sugar Association
SAAA	Salvation Army Association of America
SABE	Society for Automation in Business Education
SABW	Society of American Business Writers
SACO	Sino-American Cooperative Organization

SADD	Students Against Drunk Drivers
SAE	Society for the Advancement of Education; Society of American Etchers; Society of Automotive Engineers
SAG	Screen Actors Guild
SAI	Schizophrenics Anonymous International
SAR	Sons of the American Revolution
SAST	Society for the Advancement of Space Travel
SATO	South American Travel Organization; Southern African Treaty Organization
SATW	Society of American Travel Writers
SBA	Small Business Administration; Small Businesses Association
SBFA	Small Business Foundation of America
SBME	Society of Business Magazine Editors; State Board of Medical Examiners
SC	Security Council
SCBW	Society of Children's Book Writers
SCF	Save the Children Federation
SCORE	Service Corps of Retired Executives
SCOTUS	Supreme Court of the United States
SCS	Society of Civil Servants; Society for a Clinical Surgery; Society for Computer Simulation; Soil Conservation Service
SCSA	Soil Conservation Society of America
SCUS	Supreme Court of the United States
SCV	Sons of Confederate Veterans
SDA	Social Democratic Alliance; Students for Democratic Action
SEATO	Southeast Asia Treaty Organization
SEC	Securities and Exchange Commission
SEE	Society of Environmental Engineers
SEG	Screen Extras Guild; Society of Economic Geologists
SENI	Society for the Encouragement of National Industry
SFA	Saks Fifth Avenue; Scientific Film Association; Soroptimist Federation of the Americas; Speech Foundation of America; Symphony Foundation of America
SFWA	Science Fiction Writers of America
SGO	Surgeon General's Office
SHHV	Society for Health and Human Values
SI	Society of Illustrators

SIE	Society of Industrial Engineers
SIN	Society for International Numismatics
SIS	Shut-In-Society
SITU	Society for the Investigation of the Unexplained
S-K	Sloan-Kettering
SKCC	Sloan-Kettering Cancer Center
SLAM	Society's League Against Molestation
SMW	Society of Magazine Writers
SNCC	Student Non-Violent Coordinating Committee
SOAR	Save Our American Resources; Society of Authors' Representatives
SOC	Save Our Children
SPAB	Society for the Protection of Ancient Buildings
SPARS	Women's Coast Guard Reserve
SPCA	Society for the Prevention of Cruelty to Animals
SPCC	Society for the Prevention of Cruelty to Children
SPCH	Society for the Prevention of Cruelty to Homosexuals
SPCW	Society for the Prevention of Cruelty to Women
SPJ	Society of Professional Journalists
SPS	Society of Plastic Surgeons
SRC	Science Research Council; Signal Reserve Corps
SSFC	Severe Storms Forecast Center
SSP	Society for Scholarly Publishing; Society of St. Paul
STC	Satellite Television Corporation; Satellite Tracking Committee; Society for Technical Communication
STW	Society of Technical Writers
STWE	Society of Technical Writers and Editors
SUNOCO	Sun Oil Company
SZA	Student Zionist Association
SZO	Student Zionist Organization
TCUS	Tax Court of the United States
TEB	Tax Exemption Board
TIA	Tax Institute of America
TLA	Theatre Library Association; Trial Lawyers Association
TLS	The Law Society
TMF	The Menninger Foundation
TMIF	Three-Mile Island Facility
TNA	The National Archives
TOA	Theatre Owners of America; The Orchestral Association
TPF	Thomas Paine Foundation

TVA	Tennessee Valley Authority
TWA	Textile Waste Association; Toy Wholesalers Association; Trans World Airlines
TWU	Transport Workers Union
TWUA	Textile Workers Union of America; Transport Workers Union of America
UAC	Urban Affairs Council
UCP	United Cerebral Palsy
UFON	Unidentified Flying Objects Network
UL	Universal League
UMTA	Urban Mass Transportation Administration
UN	United Nations
UNARCO	United Nations Narcotics Commission
UNCF	United Nations Children's Fund; United Negro College Fund
UNESCO	United Nations Educational, Scientific, and Cultural Organization
UNFAO	United Nations Food and Agricultural Organization
UNIDO	United Nations Industrial Development Organization
UNRRA	United Nations Relief and Rehabilitation Administration
UNSC	United Nations Security Council
UNTC	United Nations Trusteeship Council
UPS	United Parcel Service
UPSW	Union of Postal Service Workers
URA	Urban Redevelopment Authority; Urban Renewal Administration
USA	United States of America; United States Army; United Steelworkers of America
USBS	United States Bureau of Standards
USCC	United States Chamber of Commerce
USCRC	United States Civil Rights Commission
USCSC	United States Civil Service Commission
USDA	United States Department of Agriculture
USDC	United States Department of Commerce
USDE	United States Department of Education; United States Department of Energy
USDEA	United States Drug Enforcement Agency
USDHUD	United States Department of Housing and Urban Development
USDI	United States Department of the Interior
USDJ	United States Department of Justice

USDL	United States Department of Labor
USDT	United States Department of Transportation
USFWS	United States Fish and Wildlife Service
USGPO	United States Government Printing Office
USGS	United States Geological Survey
USIA	United States Information Agency
USI&NS	United States Immigration and Naturalization Service
USIS	United States Information Service
USM	United States Mint
USO	United Service Organization
USS	United States Senate
USWA	United Steel Workers of America
USWB	United States Weather Bureau
UWP	Up with People
VA	Veterans Administration
VFW	Veterans of Foreign Wars
VOA	Voice of America
WGA	Writers' Guild of America
WHA	World Hockey Association
WHO	World Health Organization
WMB	War Mobilization Board
WPBL	Women's Professional Basketball League
WPC	World Peace Council
WWI	Weight Watchers International
ZOA	Zionist Organization of America
ZS	Zoological Society

54

Academic Degrees

In spite of the trend toward little or no punctuation in abbreviations, academic degrees are still punctuated in the United States. Although the initial letters are capitalized (*Ph.D.*), the spelled-out version should be written with small letters (*doctor of philosophy*) in text material. Initials should be used after a name in mailing addresses (*John Doe, M.D.,* not *John Doe, Medical Doctor*).

A.A.	associate in accounting; associate in arts
A.A.Ag.	associate of arts in agriculture
A.A.A.S.	associate in arts and science
A.A.F.A.	associate in arts in fine arts
A.Agric.	associate in agriculture
A.A.H.E.	associate in arts in home economics
A.B.	bachelor of arts
A.E.	associate in education; associate in engineering
A.Ed.	associate in education
A.Eng.	associate in engineering
A.F.A.	associate in fine arts
A.M.	master of arts
A.M.L.S.	master of arts in library science
A.Sc.	associate in science
A.S.S.	associate in secretarial science; associate in secretarial studies
B.A.	bachelor of arts (Latin *Baccalaureus Artium*)
B.A.Ed.	bachelor of arts in education

B.Ag.	bachelor of agriculture
B.Agr.	bachelor of agriculture
B.A.I.	bachelor of engineering (Latin *Baccalaureus in Arte Ingeniaria*)
B.Ar.	bachelor of architecture
B.B.A.	bachelor of business administration
B.C.	bachelor of chemistry; bachelor of commerce
B.C.L.	bachelor of civil law
B.E.	bachelor of education; bachelor of engineering
B.F.	bachelor of finance; bachelor of forestry
B.F.A.	bachelor of fine arts
B.I.E.	bachelor of industrial engineering
B.Lit(t).	bachelor of literature; bachelor of letters (Latin *Baccalaureus Literarum*)
B.L.S.	bachelor of library science; bachelor of library service
B.M.	bachelor of medicine; bachelor of music
B.Med.	bachelor of medicine
B.Med.Sci.	bachelor of medical science
B.Mus.	bachelor of music
B.N.	bachelor of nursing
B.P.	bachelor of pharmacy; bachelor of philosophy
B.Pharm.	bachelor of pharmacy
B.Phil.	bachelor of philosophy
B.Phys.	bachelor of physics
B.Ps.	bachelor in psychology
B.S.	bachelor of science
B.Sc.	bachelor of science
B.S.Dent.	bachelor of science in dentistry
B.S.Ec.	bachelor of science in economics
B.S.Ed.	bachelor of science in education
B.S.E.E.	bachelor of science in electrical engineering
B.S.Eng.	bachelor of science in engineering
B.S.Fin.	bachelor of science in finance
B.S.Ind.Art.	bachelor of science in industrial art
B.S.J.	bachelor of science in journalism
B.S.M.E.	bachelor of science in mechanical engineering; bachelor of science in music education
B.S.Med.	bachelor of science in medicine
B.S.N.	bachelor of science in nursing
B.Soc.Sci.	bachelor of social science
B.S.P.	bachelor of science in pharmacy

B.S.Pharm.	bachelor of science in pharmacy
B.S.Phys.Ed.	bachelor of science in physical education
B.S.S.S.	bachelor of science in secretarial studies; bachelor of science in social science
B.S.W.	bachelor of social work
B.Th.	bachelor of theology
B.Vet.Med.	bachelor of veterinary medicine
Ch.D.	doctor of chemistry
D.Ag.	doctor of agriculture
D.Bi.Sc.	doctor of biological sciences
D.C.	doctor of chiropractic
D.Civ.L.	doctor of civil law
D.C.L.	doctor of canon law; doctor of civil law
D.D.	doctor of divinity
D.D.S.	doctor of dental science
D.Ed.	doctor of education
D.Eng.	doctor of engineering
D.F.A.	doctor of fine arts
D.L.S.	doctor of library science; doctor of library service
D.M.	doctor of mathematics; doctor of medicine; doctor of music; doctor of musicology
D.Math.	doctor of mathematics
D.Med.	doctor of medicine
D.M.L.	doctor of modern languages
D.M.S.	doctor of medical science
D.Mus.	doctor of music
D.M.V.	doctor of veterinary medicine
D.O.	doctor of optometry; doctor of osteopathy
D.P.	doctor of pharmacy; doctor of podiatry
D.P.E.	doctor of physical education
D.P.H.	doctor of public health
D.Pharm.	doctor of pharmacy
D.Psych.	doctor of psychology
Dr.Jur.	doctor of law (Latin *Doctor Juris*)
D.S.	doctor of science
D.Sc.	doctor of science
D.S.E.	doctor of science in economics
D.Sur.	doctor of surgery
D.S.W.	doctor of social welfare
D.T.	doctor of theology
D.Th.	doctor of theology

D.V.M.	doctor of veterinary medicine
Ed.B.	bachelor of education
Ed.D.	doctor of eduction
Ed.M.	master of education
Eng.D.	doctor of engineering
J.D.	doctor of jurisprudence; doctor of law(s) (Latin *Juris* or *Jurum Doctor*)
L.B.	bachelor of letters (Latin *Baccalaureus Litterarum*)
LL.B.	bachelor of laws (Latin *Legum Baccalaureus*)
LL.D.	doctor of laws (Latin *Legum Doctor*)
LL.M.	master of laws (Latin *Legum Magister*)
L.S.D.	doctor of library science
M.A.	master of arts (Latin *Magister Artium*)
M.A.S.	master of applied science
M.A.Sc.	master of applied science
M.B.	bachelor of medicine
M.B.A.	master of business administration
M.Chir.	master of surgery (Latin *Magister Chirugiae*)
M.C.L.	master of civil law
M.D.	doctor of medicine
M.Div.	master of divinity
M.D.S.	master of dental surgery
M.D.Sc.	master of dental science
M.E.	master of education
M.Ed.	master of education
M.E.E.	master of electrical engineering
M.F.	master of forestry
M.F.A.	master of fine arts
M.H.E.	master of home economics
M.Hor.	master of horticulture
M.I.E.	master of industrial engineering
M.L.A.	master of landscape architecture
M.Lit.	master of letters; master of literature
M.L.S.	master of library science
M.M.	master of music
M.Med.	master of medicine
M.N.	master of nursing
M.N.S.	master of nutritional science
M.P.A.	master of professional accounting; master of public administration; master of public works
M.P.E.	master of physical education

M.Ph.	master of philosophy
M.S.	master of science; master of surgery
M.S.B.A.	master of science in business administration
M.Sc.	master of science
M.S.E.	master of sanitary engineering; master of science in education; master of science in engineering
M.S.Ed.	master of science in education
M.S.Eng.	master of science in engineering
M.S.H.A.	master of science in hospital administration
M.Soc.Sci.	master of social science
M.S.Pharm.	master of science in pharmacy
M.S.S.	master of social science
M.S.W.	master of social welfare; master of social work
M.Th.	master of theology
Mus.D.	doctor of music
M.V.E.	master of vocational education
M.Vet.Med.	master of veterinary medicine
Phar.B.	bachelor of pharmacy
Phar.D.	doctor of pharmacy
Phar.M.	master of pharmacy (Latin *Pharmaciae Magister*)
Ph.B.	bachelor of philosophy (Latin *Philosophiae Baccalaureus*)
Ph.D.	doctor of philosophy (Latin *Philosophiae Doctor*)
Pod.D.	doctor of podiatry
S.B.	bachelor of science
Sc.B.	bachelor of science (Latin *Scientiae Baccalaureus*)
Sc.D.	doctor of science (Latin *Scientiae Doctor*)
Sci.D.	doctor of science
Sc.M.	master of science (Latin *Scientiae Magister*)
S.M.	master of science (Latin *Scientiae Magister*)
Th.D.	doctor of theology (Latin *Theologiae Doctor*)
Th.M.	master of theology (Latin *Theologiae Magister*)
V.M.D.	doctor of veterinary medicine (Latin *Veterinariae Medicinae Doctor*)

55

States

The following list includes, in addition to the fifty American states, the U.S. territories and possessions of American Samoa, the Canal Zone (the Panama Canal will revert to Panama in 1999), Guam, Puerto Rico, and the Virgin Islands. The two-letter postal abbreviations are required by the U.S. Postal Service for optical character reading and sorting. Traditional abbreviations are used in note taking and record keeping as well as in footnotes, bibliographies, and tabular material. But the names of states and territories should be spelled out in formal usage and in general text discussion.

	Traditional	*Postal*
Alabama	Ala.	AL
Alaska	Alaska	AK
American Samoa	Amer. Samoa	AS
Arizona	Ariz.	AZ
Arkansas	Ark.	AR
California	Calif.	CA
Canal Zone	C.Z.	CZ
Colorado	Colo.	CO
Connecticut	Conn.	CT
Delaware	Del.	DE
District of Columbia	D.C.	DC
Florida	Fla.	FL
Georgia	Ga.	GA
Guam	Guam	GU
Hawaii	Hawaii	HI
Idaho	Idaho	ID

Illinois	Ill.	IL
Indiana	Ind.	IN
Iowa	Iowa	IA
Kansas	Kans.	KS
Kentucky	Ky.	KY
Louisiana	La.	LA
Maine	Maine	ME
Maryland	Md.	MD
Massachusetts	Mass.	MA
Michigan	Mich.	MI
Minnesota	Minn.	MN
Mississippi	Miss.	MS
Missouri	Mo.	MO
Montana	Mont.	MT
Nebraska	Nebr.	NE
Nevada	Nev.	NV
New Hampshire	N.H.	NH
New Jersey	N.J.	NJ
New Mexico	N.Mex.	NM
New York	N.Y.	NY
North Carolina	N.C.	NC
North Dakota	N.Dak.	ND
Ohio	Ohio	OH
Oklahoma	Okla.	OK
Oregon	Oreg.	OR
Pennsylvania	Pa.	PA
Puerto Rico	P.R.	PR
Rhode Island	R.I.	RI
South Carolina	S.C.	SC
South Dakota	S.Dak.	SD
Tennessee	Tenn.	TN
Texas	Tex.	TX
Utah	Utah	UT
Vermont	Vt.	VT
Virginia	Va.	VA
Virgin Islands	V.I.	VI
Washington	Wash.	WA
West Virginia	W.Va.	WV
Wisconsin	Wis.	WI
Wyoming	Wyo.	WY

56

Countries

Abbreviations for the principal foreign countries of the world are found in most atlases as well as in almanacs and other descriptive material. Authorities vary in their preferred spelling of country abbreviations, but the following examples are widely accepted for use in footnotes, bibliographies, and tabular material. The names of countries should be spelled out in formal usage and in general text discussions.

Afghanistan	Afghan.
Albania	Alb.
Algeria	Alg.
Andorra	And.
Angola	Ang.
Antigua	Ant.
Argentina	Argen.
Australia	Aust., Austl.
Austria	Aus.
Bahamas, The	Bah.
Bahrain	Bah.
Bangladesh	Bangla.
Barbuda	Barbuda, Bar.
Barbados	Barb.
Belgium	Belg.
Belize	Bel.
Benin	Benin, Ben.
Bhutan	Bhu.
Bolivia	Bol.

Botswana	Botswana, Bots.
Brazil	Braz.
Bulgaria	Bulg.
Burma	Bur.
Burundi	Burun.
Cameroon	Cam.
Canada	Can.
Cape Verde	C.V., CV
Central African Empire	C.A.E., CAE, C. Afr. Emp.
Chad	Chad
Chile	Chile
China	Chin.
Colombia	Col., Colom.
Comoros	Comoros, Com.
Congo	Congo, Cong.
Costa Rica	C.R., CR
Cuba	Cuba
Cyprus	Cyp.
Czechoslovakia	Czech.
Denmark	Den.
Djibouti	Djib.
Dominica	Dom.
Dominican Republic	D.R., DR, Dom. Rep.
Ecuador	Ecua.
Egypt	Egyp.
El Salvador	El. Sal.
Equatorial Guinea	E.G., EG, Eq. Guin.
Estonia	Est.
Ethiopia	Eth.
Fiji	Fiji
Finland	Fin.
France	Fr.
Gabon	Gab.
Gambia	Gam.
German Democratic Republic	G.D.R., GDR (E.Ger.)
Germany, Federal Republic of	F.R.G., FRG (W.Ger.)
Germany	Ger.
Ghana	Ghana
Greece	Greece
Grenada	Gren.
Guatemala	Guat.

Guinea	Guinea
Guinea-Bissau	Guinea-Bissau
Guyana	Guy.
Haiti	Haiti
Honduras	Hond.
Hungary	Hung.
Iceland	Ice.
India	Ind.
Indonesia	Indon.
Iran	Ir.
Iraq	Iraq
Ireland	Ir.
Israel	Isr.
Italy	It.
Ivory Coast	I.C., IC, Iv. Cst.
Jamaica	Jam.
Japan	Jap.
Jordan	Jord.
Kampuchea (Cambodia)	Kamp. (Cambod.)
Kenya	Ken.
Kiribati	Kir.
Korea, North	N.Kor.
Korea, South	S.Kor.
Kuwait	Kuw.
Laos	Laos
Latvia	Lat.
Lebanon	Leb.
Lesotho	Leso.
Liberia	Lib., Liberia
Libya	Lib.
Liechtenstein	Liech.
Lithuania	Lith.
Luxembourg	Lux.
Madagascar	Madag.
Malawi	Malawi, Mal.
Malaysia	Mal.
Maldives	Mald.
Mali	Mali
Malta	Mal.
Mauritania	Maurit.
Mauritius	Maur.

Mexico	Mex.
Monaco	Mon.
Mongolia	Mong.
Morocco	Mor.
Mozambique	Mozam.
Nauru	Nau.
Nepal	Nep.
Netherlands, The	Neth.
New Zealand	N.Z., NZ
Nicaragua	Nica.
Niger	Nig.
Nigeria	Nig.
Norway	Nor.
Oman	Om.
Pakistan	Pak.
Panama	Pan.
Papua New Guinea	Pap. N.G., Pap. NG
Paraguay	Para.
Peru	Peru
Philippines	Phil.
Poland	Pol.
Portugal	Port.
Quatar	Quatar, Qua.
Romania	Rom.
Rwanda	Rwanda
Saint Lucia	S.L., SL, St. Lu.
Saint Vincent and the Grenadines	St. V.&G., St. V&G
San Marino	S.M., SM
São Tomé and Principe	São Tomé and Principe
Saudi Arabia	S.A., SA
Senegal	Seneg.
Seychelles	Seychelles, Sey.
Sierra Leone	S.L., SL
Singapore	Sing.
Solomon Islands	S.I., SI
Somalia	Som.
South Africa	S.A., SA, S.Afr.
Spain	Sp.
Sri Lanka (Ceylon)	S.L., SL, Sri Lan. (Cey.)
Sudan	Sud.

Suriname	Suri.
Swaziland	Swaz.
Sweden	Swed.
Switzerland	Switz.
Syria	Syr.
Tanzania	Tanz.
Thailand	Thai., Thail.
Tobago	Tob.
Togo	To.
Tonga	Ton.
Trinidad	Trin.
Tunisia	Tun.
Turkey	Turk.
Tuvalu	Tuv.
Uganda	Ugan.
Union of Soviet Socialist Republics	U.S.S.R., USSR
United Arab Emirates	U.A.E., UAE
United Kingdom	U.K., UK
Upper Volta	U.V., UV
Uruguay	Uru.
Vanuatu	Vanu.
Vatican City	V.C., VC
Venezuela	Venez.
Vietnam	Viet.
Western Samoa	W.S., WS
Yemen (South Yemen)	S.Yem.
Yemen (Arab Republic)	Yem.
Yugoslavia	Yug.
Zaire	Zai.
Zambia	Zam.
Zimbabwe	Zimb.

57

Signs and Symbols

Signs and symbols are commonplace in scientific and technical writing. They are also used freely in tabular material and in graphs and charts.

ACCENTS

◌́ acute
◌̆ breve
◌̧ cedilla
◌̂ circumflex
◌̈ dieresis
◌̀ grave
◌̄ macron
◌̃ tilde

CHEMICAL

‰ salinity
℩ minim
⇋ exchange
↑ gas

ELECTRICAL

ℜ reluctance
↔ reaction goes both right and left
↕ reaction goes both up and down
↨ reversible
→ direction of flow; yields
→ direct current
⇌ electrical current
⇌ reversible reaction
⇌ reversible reaction
⇌ alternating current
⇌ alternating current
⇌ reversible reaction beginning at left
⇌ reversible reaction beginning at right

ELECTRICAL—Con.

Ω ohm; omega
MΩ megohm; omega
μΩ microohm; mu omega
ω angular frequency, solid angle; omega
Φ magnetic flux; phi
Ψ dielectric flux; electrostatic flux; psi
γ conductivity; gamma
ρ resistivity; rho
Λ equivalent conductivity
℗ horsepower

MATHEMATICAL

— vinculum (above letters)
∺ geometrical proportion
−: difference, excess
‖ parallel
∥s parallels
∦ not parallels
| | absolute value
· multiplied by
: is to; ratio
+ divided by
∴ therefore; hence
∵ because
:: proportion; as
≪ is dominated by

MATHEMATICAL—Con.

> greater than
⊏ greater than
≥ greater than or equal to
≧ greater than or equal to
≷ greater than or less than
≯ is not greater than
< less than
⊐ less than
≶ less than or greater than
≮ is not less than
⋖ smaller than
≤ less than or equal to
≦ less than or equal to
≧ or ≥ greater than or equal to
≲ equal to or less than
≦ equal to or less than
≩ is not greater than equal to or less than
≳ equal to or greater than
≩ is not less than equal to or greater than
⊥ equilateral
⊥ perpendicular to
⊢ assertion sign
≐ approaches
≑ approaches a limit
⩗ equal angles
≠ not equal to
≡ identical with
≢ not identical with
⑉ score
≈ or ≒ nearly equal to
= equal to
∼ difference
≃ perspective to
≅ congruent to approximately equal
≏ difference between
⇔ geometrically equivalent to
(included in
) excluded from
⊂ is contained in
∪ logical sum or union
∩ logical product or intersection
√ radical
√ root

MATHEMATICAL—Con.

∛ square root
∛ cube root
∜ fourth root
∜ fifth root
∜ sixth root
π pi
ε base (2.718) of natural system of logarithms; epsilon
ε is a member of; dielectric constant; mean error; epsilon
+ plus
➕ bold plus
− minus
➖ bold minus
/ shill(ing); slash; virgule
± plus or minus
∓ minus or plus
× multiplied by
= bold equal
number
℀ per
% percent
∫ integral
| single bond
╲ single bond
╱ single bond
‖ double bond
╲╲ double bond
╱╱ double bond
⬡ benzene ring
∂ or δ differential; variation
∂ Italian differential
→ approaches limit of
∼ cycle sine
↳ horizontal integral
∮ contour integral
∝ variation; varies as
Π product
Σ summation of; sum; sigma
! or ⌊ factorial product

MEASURE

℔ pound
℥ dram
ƒ℥ fluid dram
℥ ounce
ƒ℥ fluid ounce
O pint

MISCELLANEOUS

§ section
† dagger
‡ double dagger
%c account of
% care of
/X/ score
¶ paragraph
þ Anglo-Saxon
₵ center line
♂ conjunction
⊥ perpendicular to
″ or " ditto
∝ variation
℞ recipe
] move right
[move left
◯ or ⊙ or ① annual
⊙⊙ or ② biennial
∈ element of
℈ scruple
ƒ function
! exclamation mark
⊞ plus in square
♃ perennial
φ diameter
c̄ mean value of c
U mathmodifier
⊂ mathmodifier
⊡ dot in square
△ dot in triangle
⊠ station mark
@ at

PLANETS

☿ Mercury
♀ Venus
⊕ Earth
♂ Mars
♃ Jupiter
♄ Saturn
♅ Uranus
♆ Neptune
♇ Pluto
☊ dragon's head, as-
      cending   node
☋ dragon's tail, de-
      scending node
♂ conjunction
☍ opposition
⊙ or ⊙ Sun
♁ Sun's lower limb

PLANETS—Con.

☉ Sun's upper limb
☉ solar corona
⊕ solar halo
☽ Moon
● new Moon
☽ first quarter
◖ first quarter
◗ third quarter
◑ last quarter
☾ last quarter
◐ last quarter
◯ full Moon
◍ full Moon
⊖ eclipse of Moon
⊽ lunar halo
∪ lunar corona
⚳ Ceres
⚴ Juno

PUNCTUATION

{ } braces
[ ] brackets
( ) parentheses
⟨ ⟩ square parentheses;
      angle brackets
¡ Spanish open quote
¿ Spanish open quote

GEOLOGIC SYSTEMS [1]

Q Quaternary
T Tertiary
K Cretaceous
J Jurassic
Ᵽ Triassic
P Permian
P Pennsylvanian
M Mississippian
D Devonian
S Silurian
O Ordovician
Ɛ Cambrian
pƐ Precambrian
C Carboniferous

WEATHER

T thunder
R thunderstorm;
      sheet lightning
≺ sheet lightning

---

[1] Standard letter symbols used by the Geological Survey on geologic maps. Capital letter indicates the system and one or more lowercased letters designate the formation and member where used.

WEATHER—Con.

↓ precipitate
⊕ rain
← floating ice crystals
↔ ice needles
▲ hail
⊗ sleet
∾ glazed frost
⊔ hoarfrost
∨ frostwork
✳ snow or sextile
⊠ snow on ground
⊹ drifting snow (low)
≡ fog
∞ haze
△ Aurora

ZODIAC

♈ Aries; Ram
♉ Taurus; Bull
♊ Gemini; Twins
♋ Cancer; Crab
♌ Leo; Lion
♍ Virgo; Virgin
♎ Libra; Balance
♏ Scorpio; Scorpion
♐ Sagittarius; Archer
♑ Capricornus; Goat
♒ Aquarius; Water bearer
♓ Pisces; Fishes

PROOFREADER MARKS

Margin Symbol	Text Marking	Meaning
ℓ	trust**ℯ**	Delete
ℓ̄	me*e*n	Delete and close up.
stet.	~~new issue of~~ ℓ	Let it stand.
noᶈ	college,⌐(Students believe	No paragraph.
#	reading∧and	Add space.
out, sc	cunning∧let us	Something missing; see copy.
sp. out	②people	Spell out.
◠	semi ⌣colon	Close up.
[	[the sign	Move left.
]	the]ign	Move right.
tr.	re*mo*al	Transpose.
‖	‖write the government and	Line up, or align.
¶	mailing.⌐Therefore	New paragraph.
②	1895∧	Question to author.

Margin Symbol	*Text Marking*	*Meaning*
?	Do you agree‸	Insert question mark.
!	Amazing‸	Insert exclamation mark.
|=|	non‸European	Insert hyphen.
ᵛ/ᵛ	as she said,‸perhaps‸	Insert quotation marks.
⌃;	noticed‸in fact	Insert semicolon.
⌃⌄	the following list‸	Insert colon.
⌃	pens, pencils‸and	Insert comma.
⊙	your car‸	Insert period.
⌄	the members‸	Insert apostrophe.
t	/oo	Change to t.
caps(or≡)	<u>Title</u>	set in capital letters.
lc.	P̸REFACE	Set in lowercase letters.
bf(or ⌣⌣)	<u>Management and administration</u>	Set in boldface type.
ital(or—)	<u>Word-Usage Book</u>	Set in Italic type.
s.c.(or=)	<u>a.m.</u> or <u>p.m.</u>	Set in small capital letters.
C & SC	<u>Capitalization</u> <u>Rules</u>	Set in caps and small caps.
√√√	k√e√y√factors	Correct spacing.
☐	☐ List the following	Indent one em.
(rom)	(Index)	Change to roman type.
⌄5	note⌄5/	Set as superior number.
⌃2	H⌃2O	Set as inferior number.
Ɛ/Ǝ	‸x + y‸	Insert brackets.
Ɛ/Ǝ	‸x + y‸	Insert parentheses.
¦M	as shown¦they M	One-em dash.

Translation is at best an echo.

—George Borrow
Lavengro (1851)

Part IX

FOREIGN WORDS AND TERMS

58 Greek and Latin Roots and English Derivatives

59 A Dictionary of Foreign Terms

60 Overused Foreign Terms

61 Familiar Foreign Words That Do Not Need Accents

62 Alphabets of Familiar Foreign Languages

63 Currencies of the World

64 Nouns and Adjectives Denoting Nationality

58

Greek and Latin Roots and English Derivatives

Both Greek and Latin roots are abundant in the English language. Most scientific terms, for instance, are derived from Greek, and Latin origins are evident in all types of writing. To form English words, you need only take the Greek or Latin root (such as the Latin root *jure,* meaning law, or to swear) and add a beginning or ending, or both, to form the desired English derivative (per*jury*). Notice that since a consonant (*y*) follows the root, the final *e* in *jure* is dropped. With the Greek root *gnost,* referring to intelligence, one would retain all letters in "dia*gnost*ic." Refer to the lists below for further examples. Each list gives the Greek or Latin root, its meaning, and an example of an English-language derivative.

GREEK

age (to drive, to struggle): ant*age*onize
anth (to bloom, flower): chrys*anth*emum
ast (star): *ast*ronomy
bapt (to baptize, to dip): *bapt*ism
card (heart, stomach): *card*iogram
chrome (color): mono*chrome*
caust (to burn): holo*caust*
deme (common people): *deme*ocracy
derm (skin): epi*derm*is
ech (echo, sound): *ech*o
game (to marry, marriage): poly*game*ous
gnost (knowledge, intelligence, judgment): dia*gnost*ic
hede (base, seat): cat*hed*ral

herm (solitary): *herm*it
kine (to move, motion): hyper*kine*tic
lemm (argument, preposition): di*lemm*a
mach (contrivance, means): *mach*ine
morph (beauty, form, outward appearance): anthropo*morph*ism
narc (numbness, stupor): *narc*otic
neur (nerve, sinew): *neur*itis
oil (olive): *oil*y
phone (sound, speech, voice): tele*phone*
rrhage (to burst forth): hemo*rrhage*
scope (to see, watcher): micro*scop*ic
taut ("this the same"): *taut*ology
techn (art, craft, skill): poly*techn*ic

LATIN

aud (to hear): *aud*ience
act (to drive, to do): re*act*or
amb (to walk, to go about): *amb*ulance
batt (to beat): *batt*le
bi (two): *bi*nocular
carn (flesh): in*carn*ation
cumb (to lie down): suc*cumb*
doct (to teach): in*doct*rinate
duc (to lead): in*duc*e
feder (league, treaty): con*feder*ate
form (contour, form, shape): con*form*ity
grad (to go, to step): *grad*ual
her (to stick): ad*her*e
just (just): in*just*ice
lat (to bear, to carry): trans*lat*ion
magn (great): *magn*itude
mod (measure): *mod*icum
mut (to change): *mut*ation
pend (to hang, hanging): im*pend*ing
ple (to fill, full): com*ple*te
port (to carry): trans*port*
rupt (to break): dis*rupt*ive
spec (to look): in*spec*t
voc (to call, voice): *voc*al
viv (to live): re*viv*e

59

A Dictionary of Foreign Terms

Although some people overuse foreign terms (see Chapter 60), it is nevertheless useful to be able to recognize those words and phrases that are used in English-language discourse. French and Latin terms, in particular, are employed in various professions, and the following list includes examples of the words and phrases frequently used professionally and socially. Chapter 61 lists familiar foreign words that do not need to be accented in general writing.

à bon marche: at a bargain price
a la carte: according to a menu with items priced separately
a la mode: topped with ice cream
amour: love
a priori: reasoned from self-evident propositions
apropos of: concerning
à propos de rien: apropos of nothing
atelier: workshop; studio
attache: diplomatic official
au contraire: to the contrary
au naturel: naked; uncooked
au revoir: good-bye
aussitôt dit, aussitôt fair: no sooner said than done
autre temps: other times
avec plaisir: with pleasure

baroque: ornate
barranca, barranco: deep gully; a steep bank or bluff

belles-lettres: literature
bête noire: something or someone feared or disliked
bona fide: in good faith; genuine
bonhomie: good nature
bon jour: good day; hello
bon soir: good evening; good night

cache: something hidden
camaraderie: goodwill
carpe diem: enjoy the present
carte blanche: unconditional power
causa sine qua non: an indispensable condition
caveat emptor: Let the buyer beware.
c'est-à-dire: that is to say
c'est la vie: such is life
chacun à son goût: everyone to his own taste
chef de cuisine: head cook
chef d'oeuvre: masterpiece
cherchez la femme: Look for the woman.
cloisonne: enameled decoration
cogito ergo sum: I think, therefore, I am.
communique: official report
connoisseur: expert
cortege: funeral procession
coterie: exclusive group
coup d'etat: sudden overthrow
coûte que coûte: cost what it may
critique: critical review

debacle: sudden collapse
debonair: suave; urbane
degustibus non est disputandum: There is no arguing about tastes.
Dei gratia: by the grace of God
denouement: climax; outcome
Deo gratias: Thanks be to God.
Deo volente: God willing
de riguer: customary; fashionable
de trop: too much; too many; superfluous
Deus vobiscum: God be with you.
Dominus vobiscum: The Lord be with you.
dossier: documents pertaining to a particular subject
double entendre: two meanings

ecce homo: behold the man

effendi: man of property; authority; education (eastern Mediterranean)

elan: vigorous spirit or enthusiasm

en famille: in one's family; informally

ennui: boredom

en plein jour: in full daylight; openly

en rapport: in sympathy or agreement

entourage: attendants

entré nous: between us; confidentially

e pluribus unum: one out of many

ersatz: imitation

et cetera: and so forth

ex cathedra: with the authority derived from one's office

ex more: according to custom

ex officio: by virtue of or because of an office

fait accompli: an accomplished fact or deed

finis: finished

gauche: tactless

gratis: free

habitué: regular

hauteur: haughty manner

hoc anno: in this year

honi soit quit mal y pense: Shame to him who thinks evil of it.

humanum est errare: To err is human.

impasse: deadlock

in extremis: at the point of death

ingenue: innocent girl

in loco parentis: in the place of a parent

in medias res: in or into the middle of a sequence of events

in omnia paratus: prepared for all things

in perpetuum: forever

in propria persona: in one's own person

in rerum natura: in the nature of things

in situ: in its place

in statu quo: in the state in which it was before

inter alia: among other things

in toto: altogether; entirely

ipso jure: by the law itself

jure divino: by divine law

jus canonicum: canon law
justitia omnibus: justice for all
j'y suis, j'y reste: Here I am, here I stay.

kapellmeister: director of choir or orchestra

laissez-faire: governmental policy of noninterference
laus Deo: Praise be to God.
le roi est mort, vive le roi: The king is dead! Long live the king!
le style, c'est l'homme: The style is the man.
le tout ensemble: the whole (taken) together
liaison: affair
locus in quo: the place in which
loquitur: he or she speaks

macabre: ghastly; dwelling on the gruesome
ma foi: Really!
mea culpa: acknowledgment of personal fault or error
menage à trois: an arrangement whereby three persons live together
  and share sexual relations
melee: free-for-all
mens sana in corpore: a sound mind in a healthy body
mi casa es su casa: My house is your house.
mise en scène: a stage setting; environment
modus operandi: method of operating
mon ami: my friend
morituri te salutamus: We who are about to die salute you.
mutatis mutandis: the necessary changes having been made

nee: born
nemine contradicente: no one contradicting
nemine dissentiente: no one dissenting
n'est-ce pas? Isn't that so?
nolens volens: whether willing or not
nom de guerre: a pseudonym
non de plume: pen name; pseudonym
nouveau riche: newly rich
nuance: subtle distinction

obiit: He or she died.
objet d'art: a work of art
omnia vincit amor: Love conquers all.
opere citato: in the work cited

panache: stylish

par excellence: best of a kind
pari passu: with equal pace
parvenue: upstart
pasha: man of high rank or office (e.g., in Turkey or North Africa)
pax vobiscum: peace be with you
per se: in or of itself
persona grata: fully acceptable
piece de resistance: an outstanding accomplishment
pied-à-terre: part-time or temporary lodging
pince-nez: eyeglasses clipped to one's nose
pis aller: the last resort
pleno jure: with full authority
plus ça change, plus c'est la même chose: The more it changes, the more it's the same thing.
potpourri: mixture; medley
précis: summary
primus inter pares: first among equals
pro forma: done in a perfunctory way
pro tempore: for the time being; temporarily
protege: someone trained by a person of experience or prominence
quod vide: which see
quo jure? by what right?

raconteur: storyteller
raison d'être: reason for existing or being
recherche: choice
remuda: herd of horses from which ones to be used are chosen
rendezvous: place for a meeting; the meeting itself
requiescat in pace: May he or she rest in peace.
ricochet: rebound
risque: suggestive
rococo: elaborate; ornate

salon: elegant home or room; fashionable gathering of notables in the home of a prominent person
sans doute: without doubt
sans gene: without embarrassment
sans pareil: without equal
sans peine: without difficulty
sans souci: carefree
savoir-faire: know-how; knowledge
secundum: according to

semper idem: always the same
semper paratus: always ready
sine die: without a day specified (for a future meeting)
sine qua non: something essential
sub verbo: under the word
summum bonum: the greatest good
suo jure: in one's own right
suo loco: in one's rightful place
suum cuique: to each his own

table d'hôte: meal served to all guests at a certain time for a certain
   price
tant mieux: so much the better
tant pis: so much the worse
tempora mutantur: Times change.
tempus fugit: Time flies.
tete-a-tete: private conversation
trattoria: restaurant

ut infra: as below
ut supra: as above

vale: farewell
verbatim et literatim: word for word and letter for letter
voila: look! see!

weltschmerz: mental depression or apathy caused by comparing the
   actual state of the world with an ideal state

60

Overused Foreign Terms

Many foreign words and expressions (such as *rendezvous* or *status quo*) are familiar to most people. Some of them have been used so widely that they have become anglicized. Chapter 61, for instance, lists foreign terms that have become so much a part of the English language that they may properly be written without accents. Some foreign terms, however, are needlessly used by writers and speakers primarily for effect to impress the reader or listener. Often the terms are used so much that they become pretentious and annoying. The following list contains terms that should be used sparingly, if at all; in most contexts, the English equivalent is preferred.

a priori: reasoned from self-evident propositions
apropos of: concerning
au contraire: to the contrary
belles-lettres: literature
bona fide: genuine
carte blanche: unconditional power
chef d'oeuvre: masterpiece
communique: communication
coup d'etat: sudden overthrow
critique: critical review
entré nous: between us
ersatz: imitation
et cetera: and so forth
finis: finished
gratis: free

inter alia: among other things
in toto: altogether; entirely
melee: free-for-all
modus operandi: method of operating
nom de plume: pen name; pseudonym
nouveau riche: newly rich
objet d'art: work of art
par excellence: best of a kind
per se: in or of itself
piece de resistance: outstanding accomplishment
raison d'être: reason for existing or being
savoir-faire: know-how; knowledge
sine qua non: essential

61

Familiar Foreign Words That Do Not Need Accents

Most foreign words use diacritical marks as an essential part of their spelling, for example, *chargé, doña, entrepôt, père.* But diacritical marks are not required with foreign terms that have become completely anglicized (they also need not be italicized). Although some writers still use accents on some of the following words, contemporary style generally recommends that diacritical marks be omitted in these cases.

abaca	chateau	debacle
aide memoire	cliche	debris
a la carte	cloisonne	debut
a la king	comedienne	debutante
a la mode	comme ci	decollete
angstrom	comme ca	dejeuner
aperitif	communique	denouement
applique	confrere	depot
apropos	consomme	dos-a-dos
auto(s)-da-fe	cortege	eclair
blase	coulee	eclat
boutonniere	coup de grace	ecru
brassiere	coup d'etat	elan
cabana	coupe	elite
cafe	creme	entree
cafeteria	crepe	etude
caique	crepe de chine	facade
canape	critique	faience
cause celebre	critiquing	fete

fiance (masc., fem.)

frappe

garcon

glace

grille

gruyere

habitue

ingenue

jardiniere

litterateur

materiel

matinee

melange

melee

menage

mesalliance

metier

moire

naive

naivete

nee

opera bouffe

opera comique

papier mache

piece de resistance

pleiade

porte cochere

porte lumiere

portiere

pousse cafe

premiere

protege (masc., fem.)

puree

rale

recherche

regime

risque (masc., fem.)

role

rotisserie

roue

saute

seance

senor

smorgasbord

soiree

souffle

suede

table d'hote

tete-a-tete

tragedienne

vicuna

vis-a-vis

62

Alphabets of Familiar Foreign Languages

With increasing international communication and expanding commercial relations with other nations, there is a mounting need at least to recognize certain words and characters in other languages. The alphabets of seven familiar foreign languages are presented in this chapter to help those whose interest in language extends beyond the United States.

FRENCH

Alphabet and pronunciation

A	a	⎫ between *a* in pat and *o* in pot
À	à	⎭
A	â	*a* in hah
B	b	*b*
C	c	*c* in city before *e, i, y* (=*s*); *c* in car, elsewhere (=*k*)
Ç	ç	*c* in city (=*s*)
D	d	*d*
E	e	*e* in met when followed by two consonants, or by a single final consonant, digraph, or consonantal unit; silent when final and in *-ent,* third person plural verb ending; *e* in moment, before a single consonant, digraph, or consonantal unit, followed by a vowel
È	è	*e* in met
Ê	ê	*e* in met or there
Ë	ë	dieresis indicates that preceding vowel has its usual value and does not form a diphthong with *e*
É	é	*a* in late
F	f	*f*

G	g	*s* in pleasure (=*zh*) before *e, i, y; g* in game elsewhere
H	h	silent
I	i	*ee* in meet
Î	î	*ee* in meet
Ï	ï	*y* in yet, between vowels; *ee* in meet elsewhere
J	j	*s* in pleasure (=*zh*)
K	k	*k*
L	l	*l;* silent in a few cases—*gentil, outil, fils;* frequently letters *il* in final position, and after vowel, and *ill* before vowel pronounced like *y* in yet—*travail, fille*
M	m	*m*
N	n	*n; -ent,* third person plural verb ending, is silent
O	o	*o* in no when final; *o* in for elsewhere
Ô	ô	*o* in no
P	p	*p*
Q	q	*q* in quick (=*k*)
R	r	sound made by scraping of air between back of tongue and roof of mouth; silent when final in ending *-er*
S	s	*z* between vowels; usually silent when final; *s* elsewhere
T	t	*t* with few exceptions; usually silent when final.
U	u	
Û	û	} like German *ü* (*ee* with lips rounded as for *oo*) in Esaü; usually silent after *g* and *q* before *e, i, y*
Ü	ü	
V	v	*v*
W	w	*w* or *v*
X	x	*gz* at the beginning of word (Xavier, xylophone) and sometimes between vowels (exister); otherwise *ks*
Y	y	*ee*
Z	z	*z;* usually silent when final

Abbreviations

a.	accepté, accepted
a.c.	année courante, current year
art.	article, article
av.	avec, with
B.B.	billet de bank, bank note
c (c^es)	centime(s), centime(s)
c.à-d.	c'est-à-dire, that is (i.e.)
ch.	chapitre, chapter
ch. de f.	chemin de fer, railway
Cie, Cie	compagnie, company
C.V.	cheval vapeur, H.P.
C., c., c^te	compte, account
f., fr.(s)	franc, franc(s)

h.	heure, hour
J.-C.	Jésus-Christ, Jesus Christ
M., MM.	Monsieur, Messieurs, Mr., Messrs.
Mme	Madame, Mrs.
Mlle	Mademoiselle, Miss
Mgr	monseigneur, my lord
N.-D.	Notre Dame, Our Lady
N.D.L.R.	note de la rédaction, editor's note.
p.ex.	par exemple, for example
p.f.s.a.	pour faire ses adieux, to say goodby
R.F.	République française, French Republic
R.S.V.P.,	répondez, s'il vous plaît, please answer
or	
r.s.v.p.	
S.A.R.	Son Altesse Royale, His Royal Highness
S.E.	Son Excellence, His Excellency
S.E.O.	sauf erreur ou omission, error or omission excepted
S.M.	Sa Majesté, His Majesty
S.A.,	Société anonyme, similar to limited liability company
Soc. an^e	
S.S.	Sa Sainteté, His Holiness
s.v.p.	s'il vous plaît, please
t., T.	tome, book
tît.	tître, title
t.s.v.p.	tournez, s'il vous plaît, please turn
voy., v.	voyez, voir, see
Vve	veuve, widow
1er	premier *(m.)*, first
1ère	première *(f.)*, first
IIe, 2^e	deuxième, second

Abbreviations of metric terms

Mm	mégamètre	m^2	mètre carré
hkm	hectokilomètre	mm	millimètre
mam	myriamètre	mm^2	millimètre carré
km	kilomètre	mm^3	millimètre cube
hm	hectomètre	ha	hectare
dam	décamètre	a	are
m	mètre	ca	centiare
dm	décimètre	dast	décastère
cm	centimètre	st	stère

NOTE: The period is not used when the last letter in the abbreviation is the last letter of the complete word.

dst	décistère	mg	milligramme
t	tonne	kl	kilolitre
q	quintal	hl	hectolitre
kg	kilogramme	dal	décalitre
hg	hectogramme	l	litre
dag	décagramme	dl	décilitre
g	gramme	cl	centilitre
dg	décigramme	ml	millilitre
cg	centigramme		

Cardinal numbers

un, *m.* ⎱ une, *f,* ⎰	one
deux	two
trois	three
quatre	four
cinq	five
six	six
sept	seven
huit	eight
neuf	nine
dix	ten
onze	eleven
douze	twelve
treize	thirteen
quatorze	fourteen
quinze	fifteen
seize	sixteen
dix-sept	seventeen
dix-huit	eighteen
dix-neuf	nineteen
vingt	twenty
vingt et un	twenty-one
vingt-deux, etc.	twenty-two, etc.
trente	thirty
trente et un	thirty-one
trente-deux, etc.	thirty-two, etc.
quarante	forty
cinquante	fifty
soixante	sixty
soixante-dix	seventy
soixante et onze	seventy-one
soixante-douze	seventy-two

soixante-treize	seventy-three
soixante-quatorze	seventy-four
soixante-quinze	seventy-five
soixante-seize	seventy-six
soixante-dix-sept	seventy-seven
soixante-dix-huit	seventy-eight
soixante-dix-neuf	seventy-nine
quatre-vingts	eighty
quatre-vingt-un	eighty-one
quatre-vingt-deux	eighty-two
quatre-vingt-trois	eighty-three
quatre-vingt-quatre	eighty-four
quatre-vingt-cinq	eighty-five
quatre-vingt-six, etc.	eighty-six, etc.
quatre-vingt-dix	ninety
quatre-vingt-onze, etc.	ninety-one, etc.
quatre-vingt-dix-sept	ninety-seven
quatre-vingt-dix-huit	ninety-eight
quatre-vingt-dix-neuf	ninety-nine
cent	hundred
cent un, etc.	one hundred and one, etc.
deux cents, etc.	two hundred, etc.
mille (mil)	thousand
million	million
milliard	billion

Ordinal numbers

premier, *m.* } *première,* f. }	*first*
second, *m.*; seconde, *f.* } deuxième }	second
troisième	third
quatrième	fourth
cinquième	fifth
sixième	sixth
septième	seventh
huitième	eighth
neuvième	ninth
dixième	tenth
onzième, etc.	eleventh, etc.
vingt et unième	twenty-first
vingt-deuxième, etc.	twenty-second, etc.
centième	hundredth

Months

janvier (janv.)	January
février (fév.)	February
mars	March
avril (av.)	April
mai	May
juin	June
juillet (juil.)	July
août	August
septembre (sept.)	September
octobre (oct.)	October
novembre (nov.)	November
décembre (déc.)	December

Days

dimanche	Sunday
lundi	Monday
mardi	Tuesday
mercredi	Wednesday
jeudi	Thursday
vendredi	Friday
samedi	Saturday

Seasons

printemps	spring
été	summer
automne	autumn
hiver	winter

Time

seconde	second
minute	minute
demi-heure	half an hour
heure	hour
jour	day
semaine	week
mois	month
année	year
saison	season

GERMAN

Alphabet and pronunciation[1]

A	a	short: *a* like *u* in cup; long: *a* in father
Ä	ä	short: *e* in bet; long: *e* in there or *a* in bad
B	b	*b*; at end of word or syllable, bulb or as *p* in lip
C	c	before *e, i, ä* and usually *y*, as *ts* in bits; before other vowels, as *c* in can (=*k*)
D	d	*d*; at end of word or syllable, as *t* in hit
E	e	short: *e* in bet; long: somewhat like *a* in gate; in unstressed syllables, like *e* in aspen
F	f	*f*
G	g	*g*; at end of word after *e, ei,* and *i,* many Germans pronounce *g* like German *ch* (see under consonant sequences)
H	h	*h*; at end of word or syllable or before consonant, merely shows that preceding vowel is long; between vowels *h* has the effect of a dieresis
I	i	short: *i* in bit; long: *ee* in meet
J	j	*y* in yes
K	k	*k*
L	l	*l* in let
M	m	*m*
N	n	*n*
O	o	short: between *o* in not and *u* in nut; long: *o* in tone
Ö	ö	short: as in French neuf; (as in fur) long (tongue in long *e* position, lips in long *o* position): *u* in hurt or *eu* in fur
P	p	*p*; after initial *s*, as *p* in spin
Q	q	*k*; *qu* pronounced as *kv*
R	r	*r* in three or parade; at end of word or syllable, usually as in alter
S	s	before vowel, as *z* in zoo or *s* in rose; at end of word, as *s* in miss; before *p* or *t* at beginning of word, as *sh* in ship
T	t	*t*; after initial *s*, as *t* in stop
U	u	short: *oo* in cook; long: *oo* in boot
Ü	ü	short: tongue in short *u* position, lips in short *i* position; long (tongue in long *u* position, lips in long *i* position): *u* in French du
V	v	*v* of *f* at beginning of words, *f* at beginning and end of words; elsewhere usually *v*
W	w	*v*
X	x	*x* (= *ks*)
Y	y	short and long: as German *i* or German *ü*; occasionally (before vowel) as *y* in yet
Z	z	*ts* in bits

[1]All German vowels are pronounced short or long. German spelling does not consistently indicate vowel quantity, but two dependable conversion rules may be mentioned. A double vowel and a vowel followed by a single consonant are pronounced long; a single vowel followed by a double consonant is pronounced short. Consonant quantity is fairly stable; a double consonant does not indicate a lengthened sound.

Abbreviations

a.	an, am, an der, on (the), at (the)
a.a.O.	am angeführten Ort, in the place cited (loc. cit.)
Abb.	Abbildung, illustration, figure
Abk.	Abkürzung, abbreviation
Abt.	Abteilung, section
a.d.	an der, on the
a.D.	außer Dienst, retired
Adr.	Adresse, address
A.G.	Aktiengesellschaft, corporation
allg.	allgemein, general(ly)
Anm.	Anmerkung, note
Art.	Artikel, article
Aufl.	auflage, edition
b.	bei, beim, near, with, c/o
Bd.	Band, volume
bes.	besonders, especially
betr.	betreffs, betreffend, concerning
bez.	bezüglich, respecting
Bez.	Bezirk, district
bezw., bzw.	beziehungsweise, respectively
Blg.	Beilage, enclosure
b.w.	bitte wenden, please turn page
ca.	circa, zirka, about
d.Ä.	der Ältere, Sr.
ders.	derselbe, the same
dgl.	dergleichen, the like, of that kind
d.h.	das heißt, that is, i.e.
d.i.	das ist, that is, i.e.
d.J.	der Jüngere, junior; dieses Jahres, of this year
DM	Deutsche Mark, mark (after World War II)
d.M.	dieses Monats, of the . . . instant
do.	ditto, the same
Dr.	Doktor, doctor
Dtzd.	Dutzend, dozen
einschl.	einschließlich, including, inclusive
entspr.	entsprechend, corresponding
e.V.	eingetragener Verein, incorporated society or association
ev.	evangelisch, Protestant
evtl.	eventuell, perhaps, possibly
Fa.	Firma, firm
ff.	folgende (Seiten), following (pages)
F.f.	Fortsetzung folgt, to be continued
Forts.	Fortsetzung, continuation
Frl.	Fräulein, Miss

geb.	geboren, born; gebunden, bound; geborene, née
Gebr.	Gebrüder, Brothers
gef.	gefälligst, kindly
gegr.	gegründet, founded
ges., gesch.	gesetzlich geschützt, registered trademark
G.m.b.H.	Gesellschaft mit beschränkter Haftung, Ltd., or Inc.
hrsg.	herausgegeben, edited or published
i.	in, im, in, in the
Ing.	Ingenieur, engineer
inkl.	inklusive, inclusive, included
insb.	insbesondere, in particular
Kap.	Kapitel, chapter
kath.	kathalisch, Catholic
Kl.	Klasse, class
lfd.	laufend, current
Lfg.	Lieferung, fascicle
M.	Mark, mark (coin)
m.E.	meines Erachtens, in my opinion
Nachf.	Nachfolger, successor(s)
nachm.	nachmittags, p.m., afternoon
näml.	nämlich, namely, i.e.
NB	(nota bene) beachte, note, remark (P.S.)
n.Chr.	nach Christus, A.D.
n.F.	neue Folge, new series
No., Nr.	Numero, number
no., ntto.	Netto, net
od.	oder, or
ö., österr.	österreichisch, Austrian
p.A.	per Adresse, care of (c/o)
Pf.	Pfennig, penny
Pfd.	Pfund, pound (lb.)
PS	Pferdestärke, horsepower
resp.	respektiv, respectively
rglm.	regelmäißg, regular
S.	Seite, page
s.	siehe, see (cf.)
sel.	selig, late
Skt., St.	Sankt, Saint
s.o.	siehe oben, see above
sog.	sogenannt, so called
Sp.	Spalte, column
St.	Stück, individual piece
staatl.	staatlich, State or Federal
Str.	Strasse, street
s.u.	siehe unten, see below

T.	Teil, part
teilw.	teilweise, partly
u.	und, and
u.a.	und andere, and others; unter anderem, among other things; unter andern, among others (inter alia)
u.a.m.	und andere mehr, and many others
U.A.w.g.	Um Antwort wird gebeten, an answer is requested
usw.	und so weiter, and so forth, etc.
v.	(vide) siehe, see (cf.); von, of, from, by
v.Chr.	vor Christus, B.C.
Verf.	Verfasser, author
Verl.	Verleger, publisher
vgl.	vergleiche, compare
v.H.	vom Hundert, percent (%)
v.J.	vorigen Jahres, of last year
v.M.	vorigen Monats, of last month
vorm.	vormittags, morning, a.m.
Vors.	Vorsitzender, chairman
w.o.	wie oben, as above
Wwe.	Witwe, widow
z.	zu, zum, zur, to, to the, at
z.B.	zum Beispiel, for example
z.H.	zu Händen, attention of
Ztschr.	Zeitschrift, periodical
z.T.	zum Teil, in part
zus.	zusammen, together
z.Z.	zur Zeit, at the time, acting (e.g., secretary)

Cardinal numbers

eins	one
zwei	two
drei	three
vier	four
fünf	five
sechs	six
sieben	seven
acht	eight
neun	nine
zehn	ten
elf	eleven
zwölf	twelve
dreizehn	thirteen
vierzehn	fourteen
fünfzehn	fifteen
sechzehn	sixteen

siebzehn	seventeen
achtzehn	eighteen
neunzehn	nineteen
zwanzig	twenty
einundzwanzig	twenty-one
zweiundzwanzig	twenty-two
dreiundzwanzig, etc.	twenty-three, etc.
dreißig	thirty
vierzig	forty
fünfzig	fifty
sechzig	sixty
siebzig	seventy
achtzig	eighty
neunzig	ninety
hundert	hundred
hundertundeins	one hundred and one
hundertundzwei, etc.	one hundred and two, etc.
zweihundert, etc.	two hundred, etc.
tausend	thousand

Ordinal numbers

erste	first
zweite	second
dritte	third
vierte	fourth
fünfte	fifth
sechste	sixth
siebente	seventh
achte	eighth
neunte	ninth
zehnte	tenth
elfte	eleventh
zwölfte	twelfth
dreizehnte, etc.	thirteenth, etc.
zwanzigste	twentieth
einundzwanzigste	twenty-first
zweiundzwanzigste, etc.	twenty-second, etc.
dreißigste	thirtieth, etc.
vierzigste, etc.	fortieth
hundertste	hundredth
hundertunderste, etc.	one hundred and first, etc.
zweihundertste	two hundredth
tausendste	thousandth

After ordinal numbers a period is placed where in English the form would be 1st, 2d, etc., as *1. Heft; 2. Band.*

Months

Januar (Jan.)	January
Februar (Feb.)	February
März	March
April (Apr.)	April
Mai	May
Juni (Jun.)	June
Juli (Jul.)	July
August (Aug.)	August
September (Sept.)	September
Oktober (Okt.)	October
November (Nov.)	November
Dezember (Dez.)	December

Days

Sonntag	Sunday
Montag	Monday
Dienstag	Tuesday
Mittwoch	Wednesday
Donnerstag	Thursday
Freitag	Friday
Sonnabend, Samstag	Saturday

Seasons

Frühling	spring
Sommer	summer
Herbst	autumn
Winter	winter

Time

Stunde	hour
Tag	day
Woche	week
Monat	month
Jahr	year

GREEK (Modern)

Alphabet and pronunciation

A	α	$\mathscr{A}\,a$	alpha	*a* in father
B	β	$\mathscr{B}\,b$	beta	*v*
Γ	γ	$\mathscr{T}\,\gamma$	gamma	*y* in yes before αι, ε, ει, η, ι, οι, υ, υι; *ng* in singer before γ, κ, ξ, χ; somewhat like *g* in go everywhere else

Δ δ	delta	*th* in this, except in νδρ, pronounced *ndr*
E ε	epsilon	*e* in met
Z ζ	zeta	*z*
H η	eta	*ee* in eel; *y* in yet, when after a consonant and before a vowel
Θ θ	theta	*th* in thin
I ι	iota	*ee* in eel; *y* in yet when initial or after a consonant, before a vowel
K κ	kappa	*k*
Λ λ	lambda	*l*
M μ	mu	*m*
N ν	nu	*n*
Ξ ξ	xi	*x* (=ks)
O o	omicron	*o* in for
Π π	pi	*p*
P ρ	rho	*r*, somewhat like the Scotch trilled *r*
Σ σ s[1]	sigma	*z* before β, γ, δ, λ, μ, ν, ρ; *s* everywhere else
T τ	tau	*t*
Y υ	upsilon	*ee* in eel; *y* in yet, after a consonant and before a vowel
φ φ	phi	*f*
X χ	chi	like a strong *h* (like German *ch*)
Ψ ψ	psi	*ps*
Ω ω	omega	*o* in or

[1] The character σ is used in initial and medial positions in a word; the character *s*, in the final position.

Abbreviations

A.E.	ΑὐτοῦἘξοχότης, His Excellency
A.M.	Αὐσοῦ Μεγαλειότης, His Majesty
Β.Δ.	Βασιλικὸν Διάταγμα, Royal Decree
βλ.	βλέπε, see
δηλ.	δηλαδή, that is, namely, to wit
δρ.	δραχμή, drachma

δράμ.	δράμιον, dram
Δ.Φ.	Διδάκτωρ Φιλοσοφίας, Ph. D.
Δ.Ν.	Διδάκτωρ Νομικῆς, LL. D.
ἔ.ἀ.	ἔνθα ἀνωτέρω, loc. cit.
ἰδ.	ἰδέ, see
I. X.	'Ιησοῦς Χριστός, Jesus Christ
Καθ.	Καθηγητής, Prof.
Κοs.	Κύριος, Mr.
Κα.	Κυρία, Mrs.
κτλ.	καὶ τὰ λοιπά, etc.
κ. τ. ὅ.	καὶ τά ὅμοια, and the like
κφλ.	κεφάλαιον, chapter
λπτ.	λεπτά, lepta
μέρ.	μέρος, part
μ. μ.	μετὰ μεσημβρίαν, p.m.
μ. Χ.	μετὰ Χριστόν, A.D.
Ν. Δ.	Νέα Διαθήκη, New Testament; Νομοθετικὸν Διάταγμα, Legislative Ordinance
ν. ἡμ.	νέον ἡμερολόγιον, New Calendar
Ο΄	'Εβδομήκοντα, Septuagint
Π. Δ.	παλαιὰ Διαθήκη, Old Testament; Προεδρικὸν Διάταγμα, Presidential Order
πλ.	πληθυντικός, plural
π. μ.	πρὸ μεσημβρίας, a.m.
πρβλ.	παράβαλε, compare, cf.
π. Χ.	πρὸ Χριστοῦ, B.C.
π. χ.	παραδείγματος χάριν, for example, e.g.
σεβ.	σεβαστός, Hon.
σελ.	σελίς, page
στήλ.	στήλη, column
σύγκρ.	σύγκρινε, compare, cf.
τ. ἔ.	τοῦτ' ἔστιν, that is, i.e.
τόμ.	τόμος, volume
Τ. Σ.	τόποσσφραγίδος, L.S., locosigilli
τρ. ἔτ.	τρέχοντος ἔτους, current year
φ.	φύλλον, folio
χιλ.	χιλιόμετρον, kilometer

Cardinal numbers

εἷς (ἕνας), μία, ἕν(α)	one
δύο	two
τρεῖς, τρία	three
τέσσαρες -α	four
πέντε	five
ἕξ(ι)	six
ἑπτά (ἑφτά)	seven

ὀκτὼ	eight
ἐννέα	nine
δέκα	ten
ἔνδεκα	eleven
δώδεκα	twelve
δεκατρεῖς (m. and f.), δεκατρία (n.)	thirteen
δεκατέσσαρες (m. and f.), δεκατέσσαρα (n.)	fourteen
δεκαπέντε, etc.	fifteen, etc.
εἴκοσι	twenty
εἴκοσι ἕνα (m. and n.), εἴκοσι μία (f.)	twenty-one
εἴκοσι δύο, etc.	twenty-two, etc.
τριά(κο)ντα	thirty
σαράντα	forty
πενῆντα	fifty
ἑξῆντα	sixty
ἑβδομῆντα	seventy
ὀγδῶντα	eighty
ἐνενῆντα	ninety
ἑκατόν	one hundred
ἑκατὸν ἕνας, etc.	one hundred and one, etc.
διακόσια	two hundred
τριακόσια	three hundred
τέτρακόσια, etc.	four hundred, etc.
χίλια	thousand
δύο χιλιάδες, etc.	two thousand, etc.
ἕν ἑκατομμύριον	one million

NOTE. Modern Greek uses the Arabic figures for ordinary number work. When Western languages use Roman numerals, the Modern Greek uses the same scheme of letters as used in Classical Greek.

Ordinal numbers

πρῶτος	first
δεύτερος	second
τρίτος	third
τέταρτος	fourth
πέμπτος	fifth
ἔκτος	sixth
ἔβδομος	seventh
ὄγδοος	eighth
ἔννατος	ninth
δέκατος	tenth
ἑνδέκατος	eleventh

δωδέκατος	twelfth
δέκατος τρίτος, etc.	thirteenth, etc.
εἰκοστὸς	twentieth
εἰκοστὸς πρῶτος, etc.	twenty-first, etc.
τριακοστὸς	thirtieth
τεσσαρακοστὸς	fortieth
πεντηκοστὸς	fiftieth
ἑξηκοστὸς	sixtieth
ἑβδομηκοστὸς	seventieth
ὀγδοηκοστὸς	eightieth
ἐνενηκοστὸς, etc.	ninetieth, etc.
ἑκατοστὸς	hundredth
χιλιοστὸς	thousandth
ἑκατομμυριοστὸς	millionth

Months

Ἰανουάριος	January
Φεβρουάριος	February
Μάρτιος	March
Ἀπρίλιος	April
Μάϊος	May
Ἰούνιος	June
Ἰούλιος	July
Αὔγουστος	August
Σεπτέμβριος	September
Ὀκτώβριος	October
Νοέμβριος	November
Δεκέμβριος	December

Days

Κυριακή	Sunday
Δευτέρα	Monday
Τρίτη	Tuesday
Τετάρτη	Wednesday
Πέμπτη	Thursday
Παρασκευὴ	Friday
Σάββατο(ν)	Saturday

Seasons

ἄνοιξις	spring
καλοκαῖρι	summer
φθινόπωρον	autumn
χειμών (χειμῶνας)	winter

Time

ὥρα	hour
ἡμέρα	day

ἑβδομὰs   week
μήναs   month
ἔsοs   year

ITALIAN

Alphabet and pronunciation

A   a   *a* in far
B   b   *b*; all consonant letters may be doubled, and then pronounced
                long, as *n(k)n* in penknife, etc.
C   c   *c* in scan (=*k*) before *a, o, u,* and consonants; before *e* or *i,* similar
                to *ch* in chant; *cia, cie, cio,* and *ciu* pronounced as *cha* in chart,
                che in check or *cha* in chafe, *cho* in chortle, and *chu* in Manchu,
                respectively; *ccia,* etc., sound like *tch,* etc.; *scia, scie, scio,* and
                sciu pronounced as *sha* in sharp, *she* in shepherd, *sho* in show,
                and *sho* in shoe, respectively
D   D   *d*
E   e   *a* in grate; *e* in bell
F   f   *f*
G   g   *g* in gay before *a, o, u,* and consonants; before *e* or *i* like *j; gia, gie,*
                gio, and *giu* pronounced as *ja* in jar, *je* in jet, between *ja* in jaw
                and *jo* in joke, and *ju* in jury, respectively; *ggia,* etc., sound like *d*
                plus *ja,* etc.
H   h   silent, but makes a preceding *c* or *g* hard
I   i   *e* in me; *i* preceded by *c, sc,* or *g* and followed by *a, o,* or *u* is silent
                unless stressed; before or after more highly stressed vowel, *i* is
                similar to *y* in yes and in boy, respectively
J   j   *y* in yes; now obsolete and replaced by *i*
K   k   *k*; only in foreign words
L   l   *l* in million
M   m   *m*
N   n   *n*
O   o   *o* in note; *aw* in saw
P   p   *p* in spin
Q   q   always with following *u; qu* pronounced as in quick
R   r   *r* in three
S   s   *s*; usually *z* between two vowels; *scia, scie, scio,* and *sciu* are
                pronounced *sha, she, sho,* and *shu,* respectively
T   t   *t* in step
U   u   *oo* in coo; before or after more highly stressed vowel, *u* is similar
                to *w* in wet and how, respectively
V   v   *v*
W   w   } only in foreign words
X   x
Y   y   *i*; only in foreign words
Z   z   *ts* in quarts or *ds* in adz

Abbreviations

a/c.	a conto, account
a.c.	anno corrente, current year
a.D.	anno Domini, in the year of our Lord
a.m., ant.	antimeridiano, a.m.
a.p.	anno passato, last year
c.m.	corrente mese, instant
C.ᵃ	Compagnia, company
d.C.	dopo Cristo, after Christ
Dep. prov.	Deputato provinciale, member of the provincial parliament
disp.	dispensa, number, part
ecc.	eccetera, etc.
Ed.	Edizione, edition; Editore, editor
es.	esempio, example
fasc.	fascicolo, number, part
f(err).	ferrovia, railroad
f.co	franco, post free
F.lli	Fratelli, brothers
Giun.	Giuniore, junior
I. Cl.	prima classe, first class
Ill.mo	Illustrissimo, most illustrious
lit., ₤	lire
LL. MM.	Loro Maestà, Their Majesties
N.ⁱ	Numeri, numbers
N.º	Numero, number
On.	Onorevole, Honorable
p.m., pom.	pomeridiane, p.m.

Cardinal numbers

uno	one
due	two
tre	three
quattro	four
cinque	five
sei	six
sette	seven
otto	eight
nove	nine
dieci	ten
undici	eleven
dodici	twelve
tredici	thirteen
quattordici	fourteen
quindici	fifteen
sedici	sixteen

diciassette diciasette }	seventeen
diciotto	eighteen
diciannove dicianove }	nineteen
venti	twenty
ventuno	twenty-one
ventidue	twenty-two
ventitrè, etc.	twenty-three, etc.
ventotto, etc.	twenty-eight, etc.
trenta	thirty
quaranta	forty
cinquanta	fifty
sessanta	sixty
settanta	seventy
ottanta	eighty
novanta	ninety
novantuno, etc.	ninety-one, etc.
cento	hundred
cent(o)uno, etc.	one hundred and one, etc.
duecento, etc.	two hundred, etc.
mille, mila	thousand
duemila, etc.	two thousand, etc.

Ordinal numbers

primo, -a	first
secondo	second
terzo	third
quarto	fourth
quinto	fifth
sesto	sixth
settimo	seventh
ottavo	eighth
nono	ninth
decimo	tenth
decimo primo undicesimo }	eleventh
dodicesimo	twelfth
tredicesimo	thirteenth
quattordicesimo decimo quarto, etc. }	fourteenth, etc.
ventesimo	twentieth
ventunesimo ventesimo primo, etc. }	twenty-first, etc.
trentesimo	thirtieth

quarantesimo	fortieth
cinquantesimo	fiftieth
sessantesimo, etc.	sixtieth, etc.
centesimo	hundredth
centesimo primo, etc.	one hundred and first, etc.
duecentesimo	two hundredth
trecentesimo, etc.	three hundredth, etc.
millesimo	thousandth

Months

gennaio (genn.)	January
febbraio (febb.)	February
marzo	March
aprile	April
maggio (magg.)	May
giugno	June
luglio	July
agosto	August
settembre (sett.)	September
ottobre (ott.)	October
novembre (nov.)	November
dicembre (dic.)	December

Days

domenica	Sunday
lunedì	Monday
martedì	Tuesday
mercoledì	Wednesday
giovedì	Thursday
venerdì	Friday
sabato	Saturday

Seasons

primavera	spring
estate	summer
autunno	autumn
inverno	winter

Time

ora	hour
giorno	day
settimana	week
mese	month
anno	year

LATIN

Alphabet and pronunciation

A	a	long: *ah*; short: *o* in hot
B	b	*b*
C	c	*k*
D	d	*d*
E	e	long: *e* in there; short: *e* in met
F	f	*f*
G	g	*g* in go
H	h	*h*
I	i	long: *ee*; short: *i* in sit
J	j	*y* in yet
K	k	*k*
L	l	*l*
M	m	*m*
N	n	*n*
O	o	long: *o* in note; short: *o* in fort
P	p	*p*
Q	q	*k*
R	r	*r*
S	s	*s*
T	t	*t*
U	u	long: *oo* in food; short: *oo* in good; like *w* after *q*, and usually after other consonants before another vowel
V	v	*w*
X	x	*ks*
Y	y	*ee*; *i* as for *i*
Z	z	*z*

Abbreviations

a., annus, year; ante, before

A.A.C., anno ante Christum, in the year before Christ

A.A.S., Academiae Americanae Socius, Fellow of the American Academy [Academy of Arts and Sciences]

A.B., artium baccalaureus, bachelor of arts

ab init., ab initio, from the beginning

abs. re., absente reo, the defendant being absent

A.C., ante Christum, before Christ

A.D., anno Domini, in the year of our Lord

a.d., ante diem, before the day

ad fin., ad finem, at the end, to one end

ad h.l., ad hunc locum, to this place, on this passage

ad inf., ad infinitum, to infinity

ad init., ad initium, at the beginning

ad int., ad interim, in the meantime

ad lib., ad libitum, at pleasure

ad loc., ad locum, at the place

ad val., ad valorem, according to value

A.I., anno inventionis, in the year of the discovery

al., alia, alii, other things, other persons

A.M., anno mundi, in the year of the world; Annus mirabilis, the wonderful year [1666]; a.m., ante meridiem, before noon

an., anno, in the year; ante, before

ann., annales, annals; anni, years

A.R.S.S., Antiquariorum Regiae Societatis Socius, Fellow of the Royal Society of Antiquaries

A.U.C., anno urbis conditae, ab urbe conolita, in [the year from] the building of the City [Rome], 753 B.C.

B.A., baccalaureus artium, bachelor of arts

B. Sc., baccalaureus scientiae, bachelor of science

C., centum, a hundred; condemno, I condemn, find guilty

c., circa, about

cent., centum, a hundred

cf., confer, compare

C.M., chirurgiae magister, master of surgery

coch., cochlear, a spoon, spoonful

coch. amp., cochlear amplum, a tablespoonful

coch. mag., cochlear magnum, a large spoonful

coch. med., cochlear medium, a dessert spoonful

coch. parv., cochlear parvum, a teaspoonful

con., contra, against; conjunx, wife

C.P.S., custos privati sigilli, keeper of the privy seal

C.S., custos sigilli, keeper of the seal

cwt., c. for centum, wt. for weight, hundredweight

D., Deus, God; Dominus, Lord; d., decretum, a decree; denarius, a penny; da, give

D.D., divinitatis doctor, doctor of divinity

D.G., Dei gratia, by the grace of God; Deo gratias, thanks to God

D.N., Dominus noster, our Lord

D. Sc., doctor scientiae, doctor of science

d.s.p., deccessit sine prole, died without issue

D.V., Deo volente, God willing

dwt., d. for denarius, wt. for weight pennyweight

e.g., exempli gratia, for example

et al., et alibi, and elsewhere; et alli, or aliae, and others

etc., et cetera, and others, and so forth

et seq., et sequentes, and those that follow

et ux., et uxor, and wife

F., filius, son

f., fiat, let it be made; forte, strong

fac., factum similis, facsimile, an exact copy

fasc., fasciculus, a bundle

fl., flores, flowers; floruit, flourished; fluidus, fluid

f.r., folio recto, right-hand page

F.R.S., Fraternitatis Regiae Socius, Fellow of the Royal Society

f.v., folio verso, on the back of the leaf

guttat., guttatim, by drops

H., hora, hour

h.a., hoc anno, in this year; hujus anni, this year's

hab. corp., habeas corpus, have the body—a writ

h.e., hic est, this is; hoc est, that is

h.m., hoc mense, in this month; huius mensis, this month's

h.q., hoc quaere, look for this

H.R.I.P., hic requiescat in pace, here rests in peace

H.S., hic sepultus, here is buried; hic situs, here lies; h.s., hoc sensu, in this sense

H.S.S., Historiae Societatis Socius, Fellow of the Historical Society

h.t., hoc tempore, at this time; hoc titulo, in or under this title

I, Idus, the Ides; i., id, that; immortalis, immortal

ib. or ibid., ibidem, in the same place

id., idem, the same

i.e., id est, that is

imp., imprimatur, sanction, let it be printed

I.N.D., in nomine Dei, in the name of God

in f., in fine, at the end

inf., infra, below

init., initio, in the beginning

in lim., in limine, on the threshold, at the outset

in loc., in loco, in its place

in loc. cit., in loco citato, in the place cited

in pr., in principio, in the beginning

in trans., in transitu, on the way

i.q., idem quod, the same as

i.q.e.d., id quod erat demonstrandum, what was to be proved

J., judex, judge

J.C.D., juris civilis doctor, doctor of civil law

J.D., jurum doctor, doctor of laws

J.U.D., juris utriusque doctor, doctor of both civil and canon law

L., liber, a book; locus, a place

£, libra, pound; placed before figures, thus £10; if l., to be placed after, as 40l.

L.A.M., liberalium artium magister, master of the liberal arts

L.B., baccalaureus literarum, bachelor of letters

lb., libra, pound (singular and plural)

L.H.D., literarum humaniorum doctor, doctor of the more humane letters

Litt. D., literarum doctor, doctor of letters

LL.B., legum baccalaureus, bachelor of laws

LL.D., legum doctor, doctor of laws

LL.M., legum magister, master of laws

loc. cit., loco citato, in the place cited

loq., loquitur, he, or she, speaks

L.S., locus sigillli, the place of the seal

l.s.c., loco supra citato, in the place above cited

£ s. d., librae, solidi, denarii, pounds, shillings, pence

M., magister, master; manipulus, handful; medicinae, of medicine; m., meridies, noon

M.A., magister artium, master of arts

M.B., medicine baccalaureus, bachelor of medicine

M. Ch., magister chirurgiae, master of surgery

M.D., medicinae doctor, doctor of medicine

m.m., mutatis mutandis, with the necessary changes

m.n., mutato nomine, the name being changed

MS., manuscriptum, manuscript; MSS., manuscripta, manuscripts

Mus. B., musicae baccalaureus, bachelor of music

Mus. D., musicae doctor, doctor of music

Mus. M., musicae magister, master of music

N., Nepos, grandson; nomen, name; nomina, names; noster, our; n., natus, born; nocte, at night

N.B., nota bene, mark well

ni. pri., nisi prius, unless before

nob., nobis, for (or on) our part

nol. pros., nolle prosequi, will not prosecute

non cul, non culpabilis, not guilty

n.l., non licet, it is not permitted; non liquet, it is not clear; non longe, not far

non obs., non obstante, notwithstanding

non pros., non prosequitur, he does not prosecute

non seq., non sequitur, it does not follow logically

O., octarius, a pint

ob., obiit, he, or she, died; obiter, incidentally

ob. s.p., obiit sine prole, died without issue

o.c., opere citato, in the work cited

op., opus, work; opera, works

op. cit., opere citato, in the work cited

P., papa, pope; pater, father; pontifex, bishop; populus, people; p., partim, in part; per, by, for; pius, holy; pondere, by weight; post, after; primus, first; pro, for

p.a., or per ann., per annum, yearly; pro anno, for the year

p. ae., partes aequales, equal parts

pass., passim, everywhere

percent., per centum, by the hundred

pil., pilula, pill

Ph. B., philosophiae baccalaureus, bachelor of philosophy

P.M., post mortem, after death

p.m., post meridiem, afternoon

pro tem., pro tempore, for the time being

prox., proximo, in or of the next [month]

P.S., postscriptum, postscript; P.SS., postscripta, postscripts

q.d., quasi dicat, as if one should say; quasi dictum, as if said; quasi dixisset, as if he
     had said

q.e., quod est, which is

Q.E.D., quod erat demonstrandum, which was to be demonstrated

Q.E.F., quod erat faciendum, which was to be done

Q.E.I., quod erat inveniendum, which was to be found out

q.l., quantum libet, as much as you please

q. pl., quantum placet, as much as seems good

q.s., quantum sufficit, sufficient quantity

q.v., quantum vis, as much as you will; quem, quam, quod vide, which see; qq. v.,
     quos, quas, or quae vide, which see (plural)

R., regina, queen; recto, right-hand page; respublica, commonwealth

℞, recipe, take

R.I.P., requiescat, or requiescant, in pace, may he, she, or they, rest in peace

R.P.D., rerum politicarum doctor, doctor of political science

rr., rarissime, very rarely

R.S.S., Regiae Societatis Sodalis, Fellow of the Royal Society

S., sepultus, buried; situs, lies; societas, society; socius or sodalis, fellow; s., semi,
     half; solidus, shilling

s.a., sine anno, without date; secundum artem, according to art

S.A.S., Societatis Antiquariorum Socius, Fellow of the Society of Antiquaries

sc., scilicet, namely; sculpsit, he, or she, carved or engraved it

Sc. B., scientiae baccalaureus, bachelor of science

Sc. D., scientiae doctor, doctor of science

S.D., salutem dicit, sends greetings

s.d., sine die, indefinitely

sec., secundum, according to

sec. leg., secundum legem, according to law

sec. nat., secundum naturam, according to nature, or naturally

sec. reg., secundum regulam, according to rule

seq., sequens, sequentes, sequentia, the following

S.H.S., Societatis Historiae Socius, Fellow of the Historical Society

s.h.v., sub hac voce or sub hoc verbo, under this word

s.l.a.n., sine loco, anno, vel nomine, without place, date, or name

s.l.p., sine legitima prole, without lawful issue

s.m.p., sine mascula prole, without male issue

s.n., sine nomine, without name

s.p., sine prole, without issue

S.P.A.S., Societatis Philosophiae Americanae Socius, Fellow of the American Phil-
osophical Society

s.p.s., sine prole superstite, without surviving issue

S.R.S., Societatis Regiae Socius or Sodalis, Fellow of the Royal Society

ss, scilicet, namely (in law)

S.S.C., Societas Sanctae Crucis, Society of the Holy Cross

stat., statim, immediately

S.T.B., sacrae theologiae baccalaureus, bachelor of sacred theology

S.T.D., sacrae theologiae doctor, doctor of sacred theology

S.T.P., sacrae theologiae professor, professor of sacred theology

sub., subaudi, understand, supply

sup., supra, above

t. or temp., tempore, in the time of

tal. qual., talis qualis, just as they come; average quality

U.J.D., utriusque juris doctor, doctor of both civil and canon law

ult., ultimo, last month (may be abbreviated in writing but should be spelled out in
printing)

ung., unguentum, ointment

u.s., ubi supra, in the place above mentioned

ut dict, ut dictum, as directed

ut sup., ut supra, as above

ux., uxor, wife

v., versus, against; vide, see; voce, voice, word

v. —— a., vixit —— annos, lived [so many] years

verb. sap., verbum [satis] sapienti, a word to the wise suffices

v.g., verbi gratia, for example

viz, videlicet, namely

v.s., vide supra, see above

Cardinal numbers

unus, una, unum	one
duo, duae, duo	two
tres, tria	three
quattuor	four
quinque	five
sex	six
septem	seven
octo	eight
novem	nine
decem	ten
undecim	eleven
duodecim	twelve

tredecim	thirteen
quattuordecim	fourteen
quindecim	fifteen
sedecim	sixteen
septendecim	seventeen
duodeviginti	eighteen
undeviginti	nineteen
viginti	twenty
viginti unus, etc.	twenty-one, etc.
duodetriginta	twenty-eight
undetriginta	twenty-nine
triginta	thirty
quadraginta	forty
quinquaginta	fifty
sexaginta	sixty
septuaginta	seventy
octoginta	eighty
nonaginta	ninety
centum	hundred
centum et unus, etc.	hundred and one, etc.
ducenti, -ae, -a	two hundred
trecenti	three hundred
quadringenti	four hundred
quingenti	five hundred
sescenti	six hundred
septingenti	seven hundred
octingenti	eight hundred
nongenti	nine hundred
mille	thousand

Ordinal numbers

primus	first
secundus	second
tertius	third
quartus	fourth
quintus	fifth
sextus	sixth
septimus	seventh
octavus	eighth
nonus	ninth
decimus	tenth
undecimus	eleventh
duodecimus	twelfth

tertius decimus, etc.	thirteenth, etc.
duodevicesimus	eighteenth
undevicesimus	nineteenth
vicesimus, vigesimus	twentieth
vicesimus primus, etc.	twenty-first, etc.
centesimus	hundredth
millesimus	thousandth

Months

Januarius	January
Februarius	February
Martius	March
Aprilis	April
Maius	May
Junius	June
Julius	July
Augustus	August
September	September
October	October
November	November
December	December

Days

dies solis	
dies dominica	Sunday
dies lunae	Monday
dies Martis	Tuesday
dies Mercurii	Wednesday
dies Iovis	Thursday
dies Veneris	Friday
dies Saturni	Saturday

Seasons

ver	spring
aestas	summer
autumus	autumn
hiems	winter

Time

hora	hour
dies	day
hebdomas	week
mensis	month
annus	year
saeculum	century

RUSSIAN

Alphabet, transliteration,[1] and pronunciation

А	а	a	*a* in far [2]
Б	б	b	*b*
В	в	v	*v*
Г	г	g	*g* in go [3]
Д	д	d	*d*
Е	е	ye, e [4]	*ye* in yell, *e* in fell [5]
Ё	ё	yë, ë [6]	*yo* in yore, *o* in order [7]
Ж	ж	zh	*z* in azure
З	з	z	*z* in zeal
И	и	i	*i* in machine [8]
Й	й	y	*y* in boy
К	к	k	*k*
Л	л	l	*l*
М	м	m	*m*
Н	н	n	*n*
О	о	o	*o* in order [9]
П	п	p	*p*
Р	р	r	*r*
С	с	s	*s* in so
Т	т	t	*t*
У	у	u	*u* like the *oo* in Moon.
Ф	ф	f	*f*
Х	х	kh	*h* in how, but stronger, or *ch* in Scottish loch
Ц	ц	ts	*ts* in hats
Ч	ч	ch	*ch* in church
Ш	ш	sh	*sh* in shoe
Щ	щ	shch	*sh* plus *ch*, somewhat like *sti* in question
Ъ	ъ	ʺ [10]	([11])
Ы	ы	y	*y* in rhythm
Ь	ь	ʹ [12]	([13])
Э	э	e	*e* in elder
Ю	ю	yu	*u* in union
Я	я	ya	*ya* in yard

[1] U.S. Board on Geographic Names transliteration, 1944. (See p. 526 for Slavic transliteration as a whole.)

[2] When stressed; when unstressed, like *a* in sofa.

[3] Also pronounced as *v* in the genitive ending -го; often used for original *h* in non-Russian words, but is pronounced as *g* by Russians.

[4] *Ye* initially, after vowels, and after ъ, ь.

[5] Pronounced as *i* in habit, or the same sound with preceding *y*, when unstressed.

[6] *Yë* as for *ye*. The sign ё is not considered a separate letter of the alphabet, and the ¨ is often omitted. Transliterate as *ë*, *yë* when printed in Russian as *ë*; otherwise use *e*, *ye*.

[7] Only stressed.

[8] Like *i* in habit when unstressed; like *yie* in yield after a vowel and after ь.

[9] Like *o* in abbot when unstressed.

[10] The symbol ʺ (double apostrophe), not a repetition of the line above.

[11] No sound; used only after certain prefixes before the vowel letters е, ё, я, ю. Formerly used also at the end of all words now ending in a consonant letter. See Note on Old Spelling, p. 473.

[12] ʹ (apostrophe).

[13] Palatalizes a preceding consonant, giving a sound resembling the consonant plus *y*, somewhat as in English meet you, did you.

Abbreviations

амер.	американский, American		г.	год, year; город, city; господин, Mr.
АН	Академия наук, Academy of Sciences		г-жа	госпожа, Mrs.
б.г.	без года, no date		гл.	глава, chapter
б.м.	без места, no place		гр.	гражданин, citizen; гражданка, citizen (female)
ВКП (б)	Всесоюзная Коммунистическая Партия (большевиков) All-Union Communist Party (Bolshevik)		до н. э.	до нашей эры, B.C.
			ж. д.	железная дорога, railroad
			и т. д.	и так далее etc.
км.	километр, kilometer		СССР	Союз Советских Социалистических Республик, Union of Soviet Socialist Republics
КПСС	Коммунистическая партия Советского, Союза, Communist Party of the Soviet Union		с. ст.	старый стиль, old style
			США	Соединенные Штаты Америки, United States of America
м.	метр, meter			
мм.	миллиметр, millimeter		ст.	статья, article; столбец, column
н. ст.	новый стиль, new style		стр.	страница, page
н. э.	нашей эры, A.D.		т.	том, volume; товарищ, comrade
обл.	область, oblast		т.е.	то есть, that is
отд.	отделение, section		ЦК	Центральный Комитет, Central Committee
по Р. Х.	по Рождестве Христове, anno Domini		ч.	часть, part
см.	сентиметр, centimeter; смотри, see, cf.			

Cardinal numbers

один, одна, одно *m., f., n.*	one		семнадцать	seventeen
два, две *m. & n., f.*	two		восемнадцать	eighteen
три	three		девятнадцать	nineteen
четыре	four		двадцать	twenty
пять	five		двадцать один, etc.	twenty-one, etc.
шесть	six		тридцать	thirty
семь	seven		сорок	forty
восемь	eight		пятьдесят, etc.	fifty, etc.
девять	nine		девяносто	ninety
десять	ten		сто	hundred
одиннадцать	eleven		сто один, etc.	one hundred and one, etc.
двенадцать	twelve		двести	two hundred
тринадцать	thirteen		триста, etc.	three hundred, etc.
четырнадцать	fourteen		пятьсот, etc.	five hundred, etc.
пятнадцать	fifteen		тысяча	thousand
шестнадцать	sixteen			

Ordinal numbers [1]

первый	first		шестнадцатый	sixteenth
второй	second		семнадцатый	seventeenth
третий	third		восемнадцатый	eighteenth
четвёртый	fourth		девятнадцатый	nineteenth
пятый	fifth		двадцатый	twentieth
шестой	sixth		двадцать первый	twenty-first
седьмой	seventh		сотый	hundredth
восьмой	eighth		сто первый, etc.	one hundred and first, etc.
девятый	ninth			
десятый	tenth		двухсотый	two hundredth
одиннадцатый	eleventh		трехсотый	three hundredth
двенадцатый	twelfth		четырехсотый	four hundredth
тринадцатый	thirteenth		пятьсотый, etc.	five hundredth, etc.
четырнадцатый	fourteenth			
пятнадцатый	fifteenth		тысячный	thousandth

[1] The ordinal numbers here given are of the masculine gender. To convert them to feminine or neuter, it is only necessary to effect the proper gender changes: For the feminine, change ый to ая, ий to ья, ой to ая. For the neuter, change ый to ое, ий to ье, and ой to ое.

Months

январь (Янв.)	January	июль	July
февраль (Февр.)	February	август (Авг.)	August
март	March	сентябрь (Сент.)	September
апрель (Апр.)	April	октябрь (Окт.)	October
май	May	ноябрь	November
июнь	June	декабрь (Дек.)	December

Days

воскресенье	Sunday	четверг	Thursday
понедельник	Monday	пятница	Friday
вторник	Tuesday	суббота	Saturday
среда	Wednesday		

Seasons

весна	spring	осень	autumn
лето	summer	зима	winter

Time

час	hour	месяц	month
день	day	год	year
неделя	week		

SPANISH

Alphabet and pronunciation

A	a	*a* in watt; *ai* as in aisle
B	b	*b*, at beginning of words and after *m*; more like *v* everywhere else
C	c	*c* in car, before *a, o, u,* and consonants; before *e, i* pronounced as *s* in so, in Spanish America; as *th* in thin, in Spain
Ch	ch	*ch* in chart
D	d	*d*
E	e	*e* in met; *ei* as in vein
F	f	*f*
G	g	*g* in go, before *a, o, u,* and consonants; like strong *h* before *e* and *i; gu* like *gw* before *a, o; gü* like *gw* before *e, i*
H	h	not pronounced
I	i	*i* in machine; *y* in yet, before and after vowels
J	j	*h*, but with more friction (same as *g* before *e, i*)
K	k	*k*; only in foreign words
L	l	*l* in lily
LL	ll	*y* in yet, in most of Spanish America; *lli* in million, in Spain, Colombia, and Ecuador
M	m	*m*
N	n	*n; nv* like *mb* in lumber
Ñ	ñ	*ny* in canyon
O	o	*o* in obey; *oi* as in oil
P	p	*p*
Q	q	always followed by silent *u, qu* being pronounced *k*
R	r	*r*, like tongue-tap *r* in British pronunciation of very
Rr	rr	*r* trilled, as in Scotch English or Italian
S	s	*s* in so, before most consonants and between vowels; *z* in zeal, before voiced consonants (*b, d, g, l, m, n, r, y*)
T	t	*t*
U	u	*u* in rule (=*oo* as in coo); *w* in wet, before vowels; silent in *que, qui, qu*
V	v	*b* at beginning of words; more like *v* everywhere else
W	w	*w, v*; only in foreign words
X	x	*x* in ax (=*ks*), between vowels, *s* before consonants
Y	y	*y* in yet, initially and between vowels; *ay* as *ai* in aisle; *ey* as in they; *oy* as in boy
Z	z	*s* in so, in Spanish America; *th* in thin, in Spain

Abbreviations

a. de J. C.	antes de Jesucristo
a.m.	ante meridiano
C.A.	Centro América

Cía.	Compañía
cm.	centímetro
d. de J. C.	después de Jesucristo
D.	Don
D.F.	Distrito Federal
Dr., Dra.	Doctor, Doctora
E.	Este
EE.UU.	Estados Unidos
E.U.A.	Estados Unidos de América
Excmo., Excma.	Excelentísimo, Excelentísima
Gral.	General
Hnos.	Hermanos
Ilmo., Ilma.	Ilustrísimo, Ilustrísima
kg.	kilógramo
km.	kilómetro
Lic.	Licenciado
m.	metro, metros
m/n	moneda nacional
Mons.	Monseñor
M.S.	Manuscrito
M.S.S.	Manuscritos
N.	Norte
N.B.	Nota bene
N. de la R.	Nota de la Redacción
N. del A.	Nota del Autor
N. del T.	Nota del Traductor
no.	número
N.S.	Nuestro Señor, Nuestra Señora
núm.	número
O.	Oeste
pág., págs.	página, páginas
Pbro.	Presbítero
P.D.	Post Data
P.ej.	Por ejemplo
p.m.	pasado meridiano
Prov.	Provincia
Q.E.P.D.	Que en paz descanse
R.P.	Reverendo Padre
S.	Sur
S.A.	Sociedad Anónima
S.A.R.	Su Alteza Real
S.E.	Su Excelencia
S.E. u O.	Salvo error u omisión
S.M.	Su Majestad

Sr., Sres.	Señor, Señores
Sra., Sras.	Señora, Señoras
S.R.L.	Sociedad de Responsabilidad Limitada
Srta.	Señorita
S.S.	Su Santidad
S.S.S.	Su seguro servidor, Su segura servidora
Sta., Sto.	Santa, Santo
T.	Tomo
Ud., Uds.	Usted, Ustedes
V.° B.°	Visto bueno

Cardinal numbers

uno, una	one
dos	two
tres	three
cuatro	four
cinco	five
seis	six
siete	seven
ocho	eight
nueve	nine
diez	ten
once	eleven
doce	twelve
trece	thirteen
catorce	fourteen
quince	fifteen
diez y seis, dieciséis	sixteen
diez y siete, diecisiete, etc.	seventeen, etc.
veinte	twenty
veinte y uno (veintiuno)	twenty-one
veinte y dos, veintidós, etc.	twenty-two, etc.
treinta	thirty
cuarenta	forty
cincuenta	fifty
sesenta	sixty
setenta	seventy
ochenta	eighty
noventa	ninety
ciento, cien	hundred
ciento uno, etc.	one hundred and one, etc.
doscientos, -as, etc.	two hundred, etc.
quinientos, -as	five hundred

seiscientos, -as	six hundred
setecientos, -as	seven hundred
ochocientos, -as	eight hundred
novecientos, -as	nine hundred
mil	thousand

Round millions preceding units of quantity are followed by the preposition de: *tres millones de pesos, 3,000,000 de pesos.*

Ordinal numbers

prim(er)o, -a (1°)	first
segundo, -a (2°)	second
tercero, tercer	third
cuarto	fourth
quinto	fifth
sexto	sixth
sé(p)timo	seventh
octavo	eighth
noveno, nono	ninth
décimo	tenth
undécimo	eleventh
duodécimo	twelfth
décimotercio	thirteenth
décimocuarto, etc.	fourteenth, etc.
vigésimo	twentieth
vigésimo primero, etc.	twenty-first, etc.
trigésimo	thirtieth
cuadragésimo	fortieth
quincuagésimo	fiftieth
sexagésimo	sixtieth
septuagésimo	seventieth
octogésimo	eightieth
nonagésimo	ninetieth
centésimo	hundredth
centésimo primo, etc.	one hundred and first, etc.
ducentésimo	two hundredth
tricentésimo	three hundredth
cuadringentésimo	four hundredth
quingentésimo	five hundredth
sexcentésimo	six hundredth
septingentésimo	seven hundredeth
octingentésimo	eight hundredth
noningentésimo	nine hundredth
milésimo	thousandth

Months

enero	January
febrero	February
marzo	March
abril	April
mayo	May
junio	June
julio	July
agosto	August
se(p)tiembre	September
octubre	October
noviembre	November
diciembre	December

Days

domingo	Sunday
lunes	Monday
martes	Tuesday
miércoles	Wednesday
jueves	Thursday
viernes	Friday
sábado	Saturday

Seasons

primavera	spring
verano	summer
otoño	autumn
invierno	winter

Time

hora	hour
día	day
semana	week
mes	month
año	year
siglo	century

63

Currencies of the World

The currency of a country is referred to in terms of its basic monetary unit, such as the *dollar* in the United States. In addition, books, magazines, and newspapers sometimes refer to a country's principal fractional unit, such as the *cent* in the United States. The literature may also use symbols, instead of words, such as *$* for *dollar*. The following list is based on a compilation of currencies by the State Department and the International Monetary Fund.

FOREIGN MONEY

Country or area	Basic monetary unit		Principal fractional unit	
	Name	Symbol	Name	Abbreviation or symbol
Afghanistan	Afghani	Af	Pul	
Albania	Lek	L	Quintar	
Algeria	Dinar	DA	Centime	
Andorra	French franc	Fr. F.	French centime	
	Spanish peseta	Sp. Ptas.[1]	Spanish centimo	
Angola	Kwanza	Kz	Lwei	
Antigua and Barbuda	Dollar	EC$	Cent	
Argentina	Peso	M$N	Centavo	Ctvo.
Australia	Dollar	A$	Cent	
Austria	Schilling	S	Groschen	
Bahamas, The	Dollar	B$	Cent	
Bahrain	Dinar	BD	Fil	
Bangladesh	Taka	Tk	Paise	
Barbados	Dollar	Bds$	Cent	
Belgium	Franc	BF	Centime	
Belize	Dollar	$B	Cent	
Benin	Franc	CFAF	Centime	
Bermuda	Dollar	$B	Cent	

364

FOREIGN MONEY—Continued

Country or area	Basic monetary unit		Principal fractional unit	
	Name	Symbol	Name	Abbreviation or symbol
Bhutan	Ngultruns	N	Tikchung	
Bolivia	Peso Boliviana	$b	Centavo	Ctvo.
Botswana	Pula	P	Thebe	
Brazil	New cruzeiro	NCr$	Centavo	Ctvo.
Brunei	Dollar	B$	Cent	
Bulgaria	Lev	L	Stotinka	
Burma	Kyat	K	Pya	
Burundi	Franc	FBu	Centime	
Cameroon	Franc	CFAF	. . . do	
Canada	Dollar	$ or Can$	Cent	C, ct.
Cape Verde	Escudo	C.V. Esc	Centavo	
Central African Republic	Franc	CFAF	Centime	
Chad	Franc	CFAF	. . . do	
Chile	Peso	Ch$	Centavo	
China	Yuan	¥	Fen	
Colombia	Peso	Col$	Centavo	Ctvo.
Comoros	Franc	CFAF	Centime	
Congo	. . . do	CFAF	. . . do	
Cook Islands	New Zealand dollar	NZ$	Cent	
Costa Rica	Colon	¢	Centimo	Ctmo.
Cuba	Peso	$	Centavo	Ctvo.
Cyprus	Pound	£ or £C	Mil	
Czechoslovakia	Koruna	Kcs	Haler	
Dahomey	Franc	CFAF	Centime	
Denmark	Krone	DKr	Øre	
Djibouti	Franc	DF	Centime	
Dominica	Dollar	EC$	Cent	
Dominican Republic	Peso	RD$	Centavo	Ctvo.
Ecuador	Sucre	S/	. . . do	Ctvo.
Egypt	Pound	£E	Piaster	
El Salvador	Colon	¢	Centavo	Ctvo.
Equatorial Guinea	Ekuele	EK	Centimo	
Estonia	Ruble		. . . . Kopek	
Ethiopia	Birr	EB	Cent	
Falkland Islands	Pound	£	Shilling	
Faroe Islands	Danish krone	DKr	Øre	
Fiji	Dollar	$F	Cent	
Finland	Finnmark	Fimr	Penni	Pia.
France	Franc	F	Centime	
French Guiana	. . . do	F	. . . do	
French Polynesia	. . . do	CFPF	. . . do	
Gabon	. . . do	CFAF	. . . do	
Gambia, The	Dalasi	DD	Butut	
Germany	Mark	DME	Pfennig	Pf.
Ghana	Cedi	₡	Pesewa	P.
Gibraltar	Pound	£	Shilling	

FOREIGN MONEY—Continued

Country or area	Basic monetary unit		Principal fractional unit	
	Name	Symbol	Name	Abbreviation or symbol
Greece	Drachma	Dr	Lepton	
Greenland	Danish krone	DKr	Øre	
Grenada	Dollar	EC$	Cent	
Guadeloupe	Franc	F	Centime	
Guatemala	Quetzal	Q	Centavo	Ctvo.
Guinea	Syli	GS	Cauri	
Guyana	Dollar	G$	Cent	
Haiti	Gourde	G	Centime	
Honduras	Lempira	L	Centavo	Ctvo.
Hong Kong	Dollar	HK$	Cent	
Hungary	Forint	Ft	Filler	
Iceland	Krona	IKr	Eyrir	
India	Rupee	Rs	Paisa	
Indonesia	Rupiah	Rp	Sen	
Iran	Rial	Rls[2]	Dinar	
Iraq	Dinar	ID	Fil	
Ireland	Pound	£ or £Ir	Shilling	S., d.
Israel	Shekel	I£	Agrirot	
Italy	Lira	Lit	Centesimo	Ctmo.
Ivory Coast	Franc	CFAF	Centime	
Jamaica	Dollar	J$	Cent	
Japan	Yen	¥	Sen	
Jordan	Dinar	JD	Fil	
Kampuchea	Riel	KR		
Kenya	Shilling	K Sh	Cent	
Kiribati	Australian dollar	A$	. . . do	
Korea	Chon	W	Chun	
Kuwait	Dinar	KD	Fil	
Laos	Kip	K	At	
Latvia	Ruble	R	Kopek	
Lebanon	Pound	LL	Piaster	
Lesotho	Rand	R	Cent	
Liberia	Dollar	$	. . . do	
Libya	Dinar	LD	Milleme	
Liechtenstein	Swiss franc	Sw F	Centime	
Lithuania	Ruble	R	Kopek	
Luxembourg	Franc	Lux F	Centime	
Macao	Pataca	P	Avo	
Madagascar	Franc	FMG	Centime	
Malawi	Kwacha	K	Tambal	
Malaysia	Ringgits	M$	Sen	
Maldives	Rupee	Mal Re	Lari	
Mali	Franc	MF		
Malta	Pound	£M	Cent	
Martinique	Franc	F	Centime	
Mauritania	Ouguiya	UM	Khoum	
Mauritius	Rupee	Mau Rs[3]	Cent	

FOREIGN MONEY—Continued

Country or area	Basic monetary unit		Principal fractional unit	
	Name	Symbol	Name	Abbreviation or symbol
Mexico	Peso	Mex$	Centavo	Ctvo.
Monaco.............	French franc	Fr	Centime.........	
Mongolia............	Tugrik	Tug	Möngö	
Montserrat	Dollar	EC$	Cent	
Morocco	Dirham	DH	Centime.........	
Mozambique	Escudo	M. Esc	Centavo	
Nauru	Australian dollar	$A	Cent	
Nepal	Rupee	NRs[1]	Pice	
Netherlands	Guilder	f.	Cent	
Netherlands Antilles	...do	NAE	...do	
New Caledonia	Franc	CFPF	Centime.........	
New Zealand.........	Dollar	$NZ	Cent	
Nicaragua	Cordoba	C$	Centavo	Ctvo.
Niger	Franc	CFAF	Centime.........	
Nigeria	Naira.............	₦	Kobo	k.
Norway	Krone	NKr	Øre	
Oman	Riyal	ORls	Baiza	
Pakistan	Rupee	PRs	Paisa	
Panama.............	Balboa	B	Centesimo	Ctmo.
Paraguay............	Guarani	G	Centimo	Ctmo.
Papua New Guinea	Kina	K	Toca	
Peru	Sol	S/	Centavo	Ctvo.
Philippines	Peso	₱	...do	Ctvo.
Poland	Zloty	Zl	Grosz..........	
Portugal	Escudo	Esc	Centavo	
Qatar	Riyal	QRls	Dirham	
Reunion	French franc	F	Centime.........	
Romania	Leu	L	Ban	
Rwanda.............	Franc	RF	Centime.........	
St. Christopher-Nevis ...	Dollar	EC$	Cent	
St. Lucia	...do	EC$	...do	
St. Pierre and Miquelon .	Franc	CFAF	Centime.........	
St. Vincent and the Grenadines	Dollar	EC$	Cent	
San Marino	Italian lira	Lit	Centesimo	
Sao Tome e Principe ...	Dobra	Db	Centavo	
Saudi Arabia	Riyal	SRls[2]	Halala	
Senegal.............	Franc	CFAF	Centime.........	
Seychelles	Rupee	Sey Rs[3]	Cent	
Sierra Leone	Leone	Le	...do	
Singapore	Dollar	S$	...do	
Solomon Islands	Dollar	SI$	...do	
Somalia.............	Shilling	So. Sh.	...do	
South Africa	Rand	R	Cent	
Spain	Peseta	Ptas[1]	Centimo	
Sri Lanka	Rupee	Cey Rs[3]	Cent	
Sudan	Pound	£S	Piaster	

FOREIGN MONEY—Continued

Country or area	Basic monetary unit		Principal fractional unit	
	Name	Symbol	Name	Abbreviation or symbol
Suriname	Guilder	Sur. f.	Cent	
Swaziland	Lilangeni (emalangeni, plural)	E	...do	
Sweden	Krona	SKr	Öre	
Switzerland	Franc	SwF	Centime	
Syria	Pound	£Syr	Piaster	
Tanzania	Shilling	T Sh	Cent	
Thailand	Baht	B	Satang	
Taiwan	New Taiwan dollar	NT$	Cent	
Togo	Franc	CFAF	Centime	
Tonga	Pa'anga	T$	Seniti	
Trinidad and Tobago	Dollar	TT$	Cent	
Tunisia	Dinar	D	Millime	
Turkey	Lira	TL	Kurus	
Tuvalu	Australian dollar	A$	Cent	
Uganda	Shilling	U Sh	...do	
U.S.S.R.	Ruble	R	Kopek	
United Arab Emirates	Dirham	UD	Fil	
United Kingdom	Pound	£ *or* £ stg.	Shilling	S., d.
United States	Dollar	$ *or* US$	Cent	
Upper Volta	Franc	CFAF	Centime	
Uruguay	Peso	N$	Centesimo	
Vanatu	Franc	FNH	Centime	
Vatican City	Italian lira	Lit	Centesimo Ctmo...	
Venezuela	Bolivar	Bs	Centimo	
Vietnam	Dông	VND	Hao	
Wallis and Futuna	Franc	CFPF	Centime	
Western Samoa	Tala	WS$	Cent	
Yemen (Aden)	Dinar	SYD	Fil	
Yemen (Sanaa)	Rial	Y Rls[2]	...do	
Yugoslavia	Dinar	Din	Para	
Zaire	Zaire	Z	Likuta	
Zambia	Kwacha	K	Ngwee	S., d.
Zimbabwe	Dollar	Z$	Cent	

[1]Singular: Pta.
[2]Singular: Rl.
[3]Singular: Re.

64

Nouns and Adjectives Denoting Nationality

Although every literate person in the United States knows that the proper noun or adjective form of a citizen is *American,* not everyone could give the correct words for citizens of Singapore or Yemen. The following list of nouns and adjectives denotes nationality by country or region.

NOUNS AND ADJECTIVES DENOTING NATIONALITY

Country or region	Noun (plural ending in parentheses)	Adjective
Afghanistan	Afghan(s)	Afghan.
Albania	Albanian(s)	Albanian.
Algeria	Algerian(s)	Algerian.
Andorra	Andorran(s)	Andorran.
Angola	Angolan(s)	Angolan.
Antigua and Barbuda	Antiguan(s)	Antiguan.
Argentina	Argentine(s)	Argentine.
Australia	Australian(s)	Australian.
Austria	Austrian(s)	Austrian.
Bahamas, The	Bahamian(s)	Bahamian.
Bahrain (State of)	Bahraini(s)	Bahraini.
Bangladesh	Bangladeshi(s)	Bangladesh.
Barbados	Barbadian(s)	Barbadian.
Belgium	Belgian(s)	Belgian.
Belize	Belizean(s)	Belizean.
Benin	Beninese (singular, plural)	Beninese.
Bermuda	Bermudan(s)	Bermudan.
Bhutan	Bhutanese (singular, plural)	Bhutanese.
Bolivia	Bolivian(s)	Bolivian.

NOUNS AND ADJECTIVES DENOTING NATIONALITY

Country or region	Noun (plural ending in parentheses)	Adjective
Botswana	Motswana (singular), Botswana (plural)	Botswana.
Brazil	Brazilian(s)	Brazilian.
Brunei	Bruneian(s)	Bruneian.
Bulgaria	Bulgarian(s)	Bulgarian.
Burma	Burman(s)	Burmese.
Burundi	Burundian(s)	Burundi.
Cameroon	Cameroonian(s)	Cameroonian.
Canada	Canadian(s)	Canadian.
Cape Verde	Cape Verdean(s)	Cape Verdean.
Central African Republic	Central African(s)	Central African.
Chad	Chadian(s)	Chadian.
Chile	Chilean(s)	Chilean.
China	Chinese (singular, plural)	Chinese.
Colombia	Colombian(s)	Colombian.
Comoro Islands	Comoran(s)	Comoran.
Congo	Congolese (singular, plural)	Congolese *or* Congo.
Cook Islands	Cook Islander(s)	Cook Islander.
Costa Rica	Costa Rican(s)	Costa Rican.
Cuba	Cuban(s)	Cuban.
Cyprus	Cypriot(s)	Cypriot.
Czechoslovakia	Czechoslovak(s)	Czechoslovak.
Denmark	Dane(s)	Danish.
Djibouti	Afar(s), Issa(s)	Afar, Issa.
Dominica	Dominican(s)	Dominican.
Dominican Republic	...do	do.
Ecuador	Ecuadorean(s)	Ecuadorean.
Egypt	Egyptian(s)	Egyptian.
El Salvador	Salvadoran(s)	Salvadoran.
Equatorial Guinea	Equatorial Guinean(s)	Equatorial Guinean.
Estonia	Estonian(s)	Estonian.
Ethiopia	Ethiopian(s)	Ethiopian.
Falkland Islands	Falkland Islander(s)	Falkland Island.
Faroe Islands	Faroese (singular, plural)	Faroese.
Fiji	Fijian(s)	Fijian.
Finland	Finn(s)	Finnish.
France	Frenchman(men)	French.
French Guiana	French Guianese (singular, plural)	French Guiana.
French Polynesia	French Polynesian(s)	French Polynesian.
Gabon	Gabonese (singular, plural)	Gabonese.
Gambia, Republic of The	Gambian(s)	Gambian.
Germany	German(s)	German.
Ghana	Ghanaian(s)	Ghanaian.
Gibraltar	Gibraltarian(s)	Gibraltar.

NOUNS AND ADJECTIVES DENOTING NATIONALITY

Country or region	Noun (plural ending in parentheses)	Adjective
Greece	Greek(s)	Greek.
Greenland	Greenlander(s)	Greenlandic.
Grenada	Grenadian(s)	Grenadian.
Guadeloupe	Guadeloupian(s)	Guadeloupe.
Guatemala	Guatemalan(s)	Guatemalan.
Guinea	Guinean(s)	Guinea.
Guinea-Bissau	Guinean(s)	Guinean.
Guyana	Guyanese (singular, plural)	Guyanese.
Haiti	Haitian(s)	Haitian.
Honduras	Honduran(s)	Honduran.
Hong Kong		Hong Kong.
Hungary	Hungarian(s)	Hungarian.
Iceland	Icelander(s)	Icelandic.
India	Indian(s)	Indian.
Indonesia	Indonesian(s)	Indonesian.
Iran	Iranian(s)	Iranian.
Iraq	Iraqi(s)	Iraqi.
Ireland	Irishman(men), Irish (collective, plural)	Irish.
Israel	Israeli(s)	Israeli.
Italy	Italian(s)	Italian.
Ivory Coast	Ivorian(s)	Ivorain.
Jamaica	Jamaican(s)	Jamaican.
Japan	Japanese (singular, plural)	Japanese.
Jordan	Jordanian(s)	Jordanian.
Kampuchea	Kampuchean(s)	Kampuchean.
Kenya	Kenyan(s)	Kenyan.
Khmer Republic	Cambodian(s) *or* Khmer (singular, plural)	Cambodian *or* Khmer.
Kiribati	Kiribatian(s)	Kiribati.
Korea	Korean(s)	Korean.
Kuwait	Kuwait(s)	Kuwaiti.
Laos	Lao *or* Laotian (singular), Laotians (plural)	Lao *or* Laotian.
Latvia	Latvian(s)	Latvian.
Lebanon	Lebanese (singular, plural)	Lebanese.
Lesotho	Masotho (singular), Basotho (plural)	Basotho.
Liberia	Liberian(s)	Liberian.
Libya	Libyan(s)	Libyan.
Liechtenstein	Liechtenstiner(s)	Liechtenstein.
Lithuania	Lithuanian(s)	Lithuanian.
Luxembourg	Luxembourger(s)	Luxembourg.
Macau	Macanese (singular, plural)	Macau.
Madagascar	Malagasy (singular, plural)	Malagasy.
Malawi	Malawian(s)	Malawian.

NOUNS AND ADJECTIVES DENOTING NATIONALITY

Country or region	Noun (plural ending in parentheses)	Adjective
Malaysia	Malaysian(s)	Malaysian.
Maldives	Maldivian(s)	Maldivian.
Mali	Malian(s)	Malian.
Malta	Maltese (singular, plural)	Maltese.
Martinique	Martiniquais (singular, plural)	Martiniquais
Mauritania	Mauritanian(s)	Mauritanian.
Mauritius	Mauritian(s)	Mauritian.
Mexico	Mexican(s)	Mexican.
Monaco	Monacan(s) (Monegasque(s)	Monacan *or* Monegasque.
Mongolia	Mongolian(s)	Mongolian.
Morocco	Moroccan(s)	Moroccan.
Mozambique	Mozambican(s)	Mozambican.
Nauru	Nauruan(s)	Nauruan.
Nepal	Nepalese (singular, plural)	Nepalese.
Netherlands	Netherlander(s)	Netherlands.
Netherlands Antilles	Netherlands Antillean(s)	Netherlands Antillean.
New Caledonia	New Caledonian(s)	New Caledonian.
New Zealand	New Zealander(s)	New Zealand.
Nicaragua	Nicaraguan(s)	Nicaraguan.
Niger	Nigerois (singular, plural)	Niger.
Nigeria	Nigerien(s) (singular, plural)	Nigerian.
Norway	Norwegian(s)	Norwegian.
Oman	Omani(s)	Omani.
Pakistan	Pakistani(s)	Pakistani.
Panama	Panamanian(s)	Panamanian.
Papua New Guinea	Papua New Guinean(s)	Papua New Guinean.
Paraguay	Paraguayan(s)	Paraguayan.
Peru	Peruvian(s)	Peruvian.
Philippines	Filipino(s)	Philippine.
Poland	Pole(s)	Polish.
Portugal	Portuguese (singular, plural)	Portuguese.
Qatar	Qatari(s)	Qatari.
Reunion	Reunionese (singular, plural)	Reunionese.
Romania	Romanian(s)	Romanian.
Rwanda	Rwandan(s)	Rwandan.
St. Christopher-Nevis	Kittsian(s), Nevisians(s)	Kittsian, Nevisian.
St. Lucia	St. Lucian(s)	St. Lucian.
Sao Tome e Principe	Sao Tomean(s)	Sao Tomean.
St. Vincent and The Grenadines	St. Vincentian(s) *or* Vincentian(s)	St. Vincentian *or* Vincentian.
San Marino	Sanmarinese (singular, plural)	Sanmarinese.
Saudi Arabia	Saudi(s)	Saudi Arabian *or* Saudi.
Senegal	Senegalese (singular, plural)	Senegalese.
Seychelles	Seychellois (singular, plural)	Seychelles.
Sierra Leone	Sierra Leonean(s)	Sierra Leonean.
Singapore	Singaporean(s)	Singapore.

NOUNS AND ADJECTIVES DENOTING NATIONALITY

Country or region	Noun (plural ending in parentheses)	Adjective
Solomon Islands	Solomon Islander(s)	Solomon Islander.
Somalia	Somali (singular, plural)	Somali.
South Africa	South African(s)	South African.
Spain	Spaniard(s)	Spanish.
Sri Lanka	Sri Lankan(s)	Sri Lankan.
Sudan	Sudanese (singular, plural)	Sudanese.
Suriname	Surinamer(s)	Surinamese.
Swaziland	Swazi (singular, plural)	Swazi.
Sweden	Swede(s)	Swedish.
Switzerland	Swiss (singular, plural)	Swiss.
Syria	Syrian(s)	Syrian.
Taiwan	Chinese (singular, plural)	Chinese.
Tanzania	Tanzanian(s)	Tanzanian.
Thailand	Thai (singular, plural)	Thai.
Togo	Togolese (singular, plural)	Togolese.
Tonga	Tongan(s)	Tongan.
Trinidad and Tobago	Trinidadian(s), Tobagan(s)	Trinidadian; Tobagar.
Tunisia	Tunisian(s)	Tunisian.
Turkey	Turk(s)	Turkish.
Tuvalu	Tuvaluan(s)	Tuvaluan.
Uganda	Ugandan(s)	Ugandan.
Union of Soviet Socialist Republics	Soviet(s)	Soviet.
United Arab Emirates	Emirian(s)	Emirian.
United Kingdom	Briton(s), British (collective plural)	British.
United States of America	American(s)	American.
Upper Volta	Upper Voltan(s)	Upper Voltan.
Uruguay	Uruguayan(s)	Uruguayan.
Vanuatu	Vanuatuan(s)	Vanuatuan.
Vatican City		
Venezuela	Venezuelan(s)	Venezuelan.
Vietnam	Vietnamese (singular, plural)	Vietnamese.
Wallis and Futuna Islands	Wallisian(s), Futunan(s) *or* Wallis and Futuna Islander(s)	Wallisian, Futunan *or* Wallis and Futuna Islander.
Western Samoa	Western Samoan(s)	Western Samoa.
Yemen (Aden)	Yemini (singular, plural)	Yemeni.
Yemen (Sanaa)	Yemeni(s)	Do.
Yugoslavia	Yugoslav(s)	Yugoslav.
Zaire	Zairian(s)	Zairian.
Zambia	Zambian(s)	Zambian.
Zimbabwe	Zimbabwean(s)	Zimbabwean.

Heaven and earth shall pass away, but my words shall not pass away.

—Matthew 24:35

Part X

FAMOUS WORDS

65 Quotable Words for All Occasions

65

Quotable Words for All Occasions

Have you ever wanted to make a point more forceful or memorable by using words that have gained acclaim either through their impact or because of the fame associated with the original speaker or writer? Most of us have. Whether we are making a speech or writing something, and whether we are at school, at work, or in a social situation, we like to appear clever and knowledgeable and want to lend importance to our remarks. Books of quotations are invaluable for this purpose, and this chapter provides a wide-ranging collection of quotable words to draw on for virtually any occasion. The more than 500 famous expressions, including well-known proverbs from various countries, are organized under alphabetical headings such as "Freedom," "Honesty," "Opportunity," "Sin," and "Work."

ACHIEVEMENT

The reward of a thing well done is to have done it.

RALPH WALDO EMERSON

Well done is better than well said.

BENJAMIN FRANKLIN

ACTION

Experience is the child of Thought, and Thought is the child of Action.

BENJAMIN FRANKLIN

Everyone is responsible for his own actions.

INDIAN PROVERB

AGE

Age is a sorry travelling companion.

DANISH PROVERB

The essence of age is intellect.

RALPH WALDO EMERSON

Youth is a blunder; manhood is a struggle; old age a regret.

RALPH WALDO EMERSON

Gather ye rosebuds while ye may.

ROBERT HERRICK

AMBITION

Hitch your wagon to a star.

RALPH WALDO EMERSON

No thing is so commonplace as to wish to be remarkable.

OLIVER WENDELL HOLMES

I would sooner fail than not be among the greatest.

JOHN KEATS

ANGER

Never forget what a man says to you when he is angry.

HENRY WARD BEECHER

He who conquers his anger has conquered an enemy.

GERMAN PROVERB

No man can think clearly when his fists are clenched.

GEORGE JEAN NATHAN

ART

Art distills sensation and embodies it with enhanced meaning in memorable form.

JACQUES BARZUM

Art is a jealous mistress.

RALPH WALDO EMERSON

Art has no enemy but ignorance.

ENGLISH PROVERB

Great art is precisely that which never was nor will be taught; it is preeminently and finally the expression of the spirits of great men.

JOHN RUSKIN

ATHEISM

The equal toleration of all religions . . . is the same things as atheism.

POPE LEO XIII

I was a freethinker before I knew how to think.

GEORGE BERNARD SHAW

BEAUTY

Beauty without virtue is like a rose without a scent.

DANISH PROVERB

Beauty is not caused. It is.

EMILY DICKINSON

Beauty is truth, truth beauty.

JOHN KEATS

What is beautiful is good, and who is good will soon be beautiful.

SAPPHO

BEHAVIOR

Be civil to all; sociable to many; familiar to few; Friend to One; enemy to none.

BENJAMIN FRANKLIN

A mirror, in which everyone shows his image.

JOHANN W. GOETHE

BOOKS

Some books are to be tasted, others to be swallowed, and some few to be chewed and digested.

FRANCIS BACON

In the highest civilization, the book is still the highest delight.

RALPH WALDO EMERSON

I cannot live without books.

THOMAS JEFFERSON

BROTHERHOOD

All for one and one for all.

ALEXANDRE DUMAS

Finally, be ye all of one mind.

PETER 3:8

BUSINESS

The business of America is business.

CALVIN COOLIDGE

Business? That's very simple—it's other people's money.

ALEXANDRE DUMAS

Few people do business well who do nothing else.

LORD CHESTERFIELD

Be not slothful in business.

ROMANS 12:11

Never do business with a relative.

TURKISH PROVERB

CAPITALISM

Capital as such is not evil; it is its wrong use that is evil.

MOHANDAS GANDHI

Under capitalism man exploits man; under socialism the reverse is true.

POLISH PROVERB

CAUSE

Take away the cause and the effect must cease.

ENGLISH PROVERB

That which follows ever conforms to that which went before.

MARCUS AURELIUS

Everything in nature is a cause from which there flows some effect.

BARUCH SPINOZA

CERTAINTY

I am certain of nothing but the holiness of the heart's affections and the truth of imagination.

JOHN KEATS

The only certainty is that nothing is certain.

PLINY I

CHANCE

He who trusts all things to chance makes a lottery of his life.

ENGLISH PROVERB

There is no such thing.

JOHANN C. SCHILLER

A word devoid of sense; nothing can exist without a cause.

VOLTAIRE

CHARACTER

That which reveals moral purpose, exposing the class of things a man chooses or avoids.

ARISTOTLE

Every man has three characters—that which he exhibits, that which he has, and that which he thinks he has.

ALPHONSE KARR

The measure of a man's real character is what he would do if he knew he would never be found out.

THOMAS B. MACAULAY

Even a child is known by his doings, whether his work be pure, and whether it be right.

PROVERBS 20:11

CIVILIZATION

Civilization is a method of living, an attitude of equal respect for all men.

JANE ADDAMS

Increased means and increased leisure are the two civilizers of man.

BENJAMIN DISRAELI

A decent provision for the poor is the true test of civilization.

SAMUEL JOHNSON

A civilization without culture and art is no civilization.

NELSON A. ROCKEFELLER

COMMON SENSE

What the world calls wisdom.

SAMUEL TAYLOR COLERIDGE

If the clouds be full of rain, they empty themselves on the earth; and if the tree fall toward the south, or toward the north, in the place where the tree falls, there it shall be. He who observes the wind shall not sow; and he who regards the clouds shall not reap.

ECCLESIASTES 11:3–4

Genius is homespun.

ALFRED NORTH WHITEHEAD

CONSCIENCE

Conscience serves for a thousand witnesses.

CHINESE PROVERB

A man's conscience and his judgment is the same thing.

THOMAS HOBBES

Conscience is the inner voice that warns us that someone may be looking.

H. L. MENCKEN

The voice of the soul.

JEAN-JACQUES ROUSSEAU

CONSISTENCY

Consistency of action is the measure of greatness.

INDIAN PROVERB

The foolish and the dead alone never change their opinion.

JAMES RUSSELL LOWELL

The only man who can change his mind is a man that's got one.

EDWARD NOYES WESTCOTT

CONSTITUTION

We are under a Constitution, but the Constitution is what the judges say it is.

CHARLES EVANS HUGHES

Constitutions are checks upon the hasty action of a majority.

WILLIAM HOWARD TAFT

CONVERSATION

Silence is the one great art of conversation.

WILLIAM HAZLITT

It takes a great man to make a good listener.

SIR ARTHUR HELPS

COURAGE

To know how to say what other people only think, is what makes men poets and sages; and to dare to say what others only dare to think, makes men martyrs or reformers.

ELIZABETH RUNDLE CHARLES

That virtue which champions the cause of right.

CICERO

Courage is fire, and bullying is smoke.

BENJAMIN DISRAELI

Damn the torpedoes, full speed ahead!

REAR ADMIRAL DAVID G. FARRAGUT

Who has no courage must have legs.

ITALIAN PROVERB

I have not yet begun to fight.

CAPTAIN JOHN PAUL JONES

The soul that knows it not, knows no release / From little things.

AMELIA EARHART PUTNAM

COWARDICE

To know what is right and not do it.

CONFUCIUS

To sin by silence.

ABRAHAM LINCOLN

To evade danger is not cowardice.

PHILIPPINE PROVERB

Cowards die many times before their deaths; / The valiant never taste of death but once.

WILLIAM SHAKESPEARE

CREATIVITY

No great thing is created suddenly.

EPICTETUS

In creating, the only hard thing's to begin.

JAMES RUSSELL LOWELL

It is not the finding of a thing, but the making something out of it after it is found.

JAMES RUSSELL LOWELL

CRISIS

These are the times that try men's souls.

THOMAS PAINE

The crisis of yesterday is the joke of tomorrow.

H. G. WELLS

CRITIC

A wise skepticism is the first attribute of a good critic.

JAMES RUSSELL LOWELL

A man who leaves no turn unstoned.

GEORGE BERNARD SHAW

Criticism comes easier than craftsmanship.

ZEUXIS

CULTURE

Culture, the acquainting ourselves with the best that has been known and said in the world.

MATTHEW ARNOLD

The great law of culture is: Let each become all that he was created capable of being.

THOMAS CARLYLE

Imparts both light and sweetness to the soul which has the eyes to see.

PHILO

CYNIC

One who never sees a good quality in a man, and never fails to see a bad one.

HENRY WARD BEECHER

What is a cynic? A man who knows the price of everything and the value of nothing.

OSCAR WILDE

DANGER

Better pass a danger once than be always in fear.

ENGLISH PROVERB

He that always fears danger always feels it.

ENGLISH PROVERB

DEATH

The long habit of living indisposeth us for dying.

SIR THOMAS BROWNE

The life of the dead consists in being present in the minds of the living.

CICERO

O death; where is thy sting? O grave, where is thy victory?

1 CORINTHIANS 15:55

I weep not for the silent dead, / Their pains are past, their sorrows o'er.

HELEN D'ARCY CRANSTOUN

The dead don't die. They look on and help.

D. H. LAWRENCE

Dust thou art, to dust returnest.

HENRY WADSWORTH LONGFELLOW

DEMOCRACY

Democracy arose from men's thinking that if they are equal in any respect, they are equal absolutely.

ARISTOTLE

Democracy is a device that insures we shall be governed no better than we deserve.

GEORGE BERNARD SHAW

DIETING

To lengthen thy life, lessen thy meals.

BENJAMIN FRANKLIN

One must eat to live, not live to eat.

MOLIERE

Everything I like is either illegal, immoral, or fattening.

ALEXANDER WOOLLCOTT

ECONOMICS

If you would know the Value of Money, go and try to borrow some.

BENJAMIN FRANKLIN

We have always known that heedless self-interest was bad morals; we know now that it is bad economics.

FRANKLIN D. ROOSEVELT

EDUCATION

Education is life, not books.

AFRICAN PROVERB

Train up a child in the way he should go; and when he is old, he will not depart from it.

PROVERBS 22:6

That which gives a man his liberty.

SENECA

Learn to live, and live to learn.

BAYARD TAYLOR

ENEMY

Every man is his own chief enemy.

ANACHARSIS

He that has no enemies has no friends.

ENGLISH PROVERB

He that is not with me is against me.

LUKE 11:23

ENVY

You shall not covet your neighbor's house, you shall not covet your neighbor's wife, nor his manservant, nor his maidservant, nor his ox, nor his ass, nor anything that is your neighbor's.

EXODUS 20:17

Envy always implies conscious inferiority wherever it resides.

PLINY I

Envy sees the sea but not the rocks.

RUSSIAN PROVERB

ETERNITY

The sum of all sums.

LUCRETIUS

I am the things that are, and those that are to be, and those that have been.

PROCLUS

ETHICS

Expedients are for the hour, but principles are for the ages.

HENRY WARD BEECHER

This above all: to thine own self be true.

WILLIAM SHAKESPEARE

There is only one morality, as there is only one geometry.

VOLTAIRE

EVIL

Who does not punish evil invites it.

GERMAN PROVERB

In every evil there is something good.

RUSSIAN PROVERB

EXPERIENCE

Experience is the comb nature gives us when we are bald.

BELGIAN PROVERB

Experience is the best teacher.

GERMAN PROVERB

I know of no way of judging the future but by the past.

PATRICK HENRY

FAILURE

They fail, and they alone, who have not striven.

THOMAS BAILEY ALDRICH

Failure comes only when we forget our ideals and objectives and principles.

JAWAHARLAL NEHRU

Failure teaches you more than success.

RUSSIAN PROVERB

FAITH

Man prefers to believe what he prefers to be true.

FRANCIS BACON

The substance of things hoped for, the evidence of things not seen.

HEBREWS 11:1

Faith can move mountains.

RUSSIAN PROVERB

Believing where we cannot prove.

ALFRED LORD TENNYSON

FAMILY

Nothing is so soothing to our self-esteem as to find our bad traits in our forbears. It seems to absolve us.

VAN WYCK BROOKS

It is not observed in history that families improve with time.

GEORGE WILLIAM CURTIS

The first and essential cell of human society.

POPE JOHN XXIII

Every family has its own ugly member.

RUSSIAN PROVERB

The family is one of nature's masterpieces.

GEORGE SANTAYANA

FATE

Fate leads the willing but drives the stubborn.

ENGLISH PROVERB

Whatever the universal nature assigns to any man at any time.

MARCUS AURELIUS

What must be shall be.

SENECA

FEAR

Wise fear begets care.

ENGLISH PROVERB

Let us never negotiate out of fear. But let us never fear to negotiate.

JOHN F. KENNEDY

The first thing on earth to make gods.

LUCRETIUS

Nothing is so much to be feared as fear.

HENRY DAVID THOREAU

FOOD

Tell me what you eat, and I will tell you what you are.

ANTHELME BRILLAT-SAVARIN

A Jug of Wine, a Loaf of Bread—and Thou.

EDWARD FITZGERALD

An army marches on its stomach.

NAPOLEON BONAPARTE (ATTRIBUTED)

FOOL

Fools rush in where angels fear to tread.

ENGLISH PROVERB

A fool and his money are soon parted.

JAMES HOWELL

There is no fool like an old fool.

JOHN LYLY

One who does not suspect himself.

JOSÉ ORTEGA Y GASSET

Let us be thankful for the fools. But for them the rest of us could not succeed.

MARK TWAIN

FORGIVENESS

He that cannot forgive others breaks the bridge over which he must pass himself.

THOMAS FULLER

We should forgive our enemies, but only after they have been hanged first.

HEINRICH HEINE

The offender never pardons.

GEORGE HERBERT

FREEDOM

So far as a man thinks, he is free.

RALPH WALDO EMERSON

You shall know the truth, and the truth shall make you free.

JOHN 8:32

Pursuing our own good in our own way, so long as we do not attempt to deprive others of theirs, or impede their efforts to obtain it.

JOHN STUART MILL

The Bible and Church have been the greatest stumbling blocks in the way of women's emancipation.

ELIZABETH CADY STANTON

FRIEND

I do not want people to be very agreeable, as it saves me the trouble of liking them a great deal.

JANE AUSTEN

If we all said to people's faces what we say behind one another's backs, society would be impossible.

HONORÉ DE BALZAC

We walk alone in the world. Friends, such as we desire, are dreams and fables.

RALPH WALDO EMERSON

The only way to have a friend is to be one.

RALPH WALDO EMERSON

A friend to all is a friend to none.

ENGLISH PROVERB

A friend in need is a friend indeed.

ENGLISH PROVERB

The enemy of my enemy.

FRENCH PROVERB

FUTURE

If a man takes no thought about what is distant, he will find sorrow at hand.

CONFUCIUS

One generation cannot bind another.

THOMAS JEFFERSON

The trouble with our times is that the future is not what it used to be.

PAUL VALÉRY

GAMBLING

No gambler was ever yet a happy man.

WILLIAM COBBETT

The roulette table pays nobody except him who keeps it.

GEORGE BERNARD SHAW

GENIUS

Genius is one percent inspiration and 99 percent perspiration.

THOMAS A. EDISON

If we wish to know the force of human genius we should read Shakespeare. If we wish to see the insignificance of human learning we may study his commentators.

WILLIAM HAZLITT

The state of mental disease arising from the undue predominance of some one of the faculties.

EDGAR ALLEN POE

GLORY

Consists not in never failing, but in rising every time we fail.

RALPH WALDO EMERSON

Military glory—the attractive rainbow that rises in showers of blood.

ABRAHAM LINCOLN

There's no glory without sacrifice.

PHILIPPINE PROVERB

GOD

For science, God is simply the stream of tendency by which all things seek to fulfill the law of their being.

MATTHEW ARNOLD

God helps them that help themselves.

ENGLISH PROVERB

Existence is God!

JOHANN W. GOETHE

Ultimate reality.

PHILO

GOOD

He knows best what good is that has endured evil.

ENGLISH PROVERB

Out of a great evil often comes a great good.

ITALIAN PROVERB

GOVERNMENT

The people. From this element spring all governments.

JOHN QUINCY ADAMS

Government is best which governs least.

AMERICAN PROVERB

The worst thing in this world, next to anarchy, is government.

HENRY WARD BEECHER

Government is not an exact science.

LOUIS D. BRANDEIS

We are the government you and I.

THEODORE ROOSEVELT

A form of association that defends and protects the person and property of each with the common force of all.

JEAN-JACQUES ROUSSEAU

GREATNESS

Greatness lies not in being strong, but in the right use of strength.

HENRY WARD BEECHER

To be great is to be misunderstood.

RALPH WALDO EMERSON

Some are born great, some achieve greatness and some have greatness thrust upon 'em.

WILLIAM SHAKESPEARE

HAPPINESS

Show me a thoroughly satisfied man—and I will show you a failure.

THOMAS A. EDISON

The way to be happy is to make others so.

ROBERT G. INGERSOLL

It is all within yourself, in your way of thinking.

MARCUS AURELIUS

A good bank account, a good cook, and a good digestion.

JEAN-JACQUES ROUSSEAU

HATRED

Hating people is like burning down your own house to get rid of a rat.

HARRY EMERSON FOSDICK

All men kill the thing they hate, too, unless, of course, it kills them first.

JAMES THURBER

HEALTH

Medical men . . . having merely entered into a tacit agreement to call all sorts of maladies . . . by one name; so that one sort of treatment may serve for all, and their practice be thereby greatly simplified.

JANE WELSH CARLYLE

Health is not a condition of matter, but of mind.

MARY BAKER EDDY

Early to bed, and early to rise, makes a man healthy, wealthy and wise.

BENJAMIN FRANKLIN

The less you think about your health the better.

OLIVER WENDELL HOLMES

Health is . . . a blessing that money cannot buy.

IZAAK WALTON

HEART

In every man's heart there is a sleeping lion.

ARMENIAN PROVERB

Faint heart never won fair lady.

ENGLISH PROVERB

HISTORY

History is only a confused heap of facts.

LORD CHESTERFIELD

What history teaches us is that men have never learned anything from it.

GEORG WILHELM HEGEL

Those who cannot remember the past are condemned to repeat it.

GEORGE SANTAYANA

HONESTY

Honesty is the best policy.

ENGLISH PROVERB

Honesty may be dear bought, but can never be a dear pennyworth.

ENGLISH PROVERB

HOPE

Hope for the best and prepare for the worst.

ENGLISH PROVERB

He that lives on hope has a slender diet.

SCOTTISH PROVERB

HUMAN

I am more and more convinced that man is a dangerous creature; and that power ... like the grave, cries "Give, give!"

ABIGAIL (SMITH) ADAMS

The only animal that can remain on friendly terms with the victims he intends to eat until he eats them.

SAMUEL BUTLER

Every man for himself.

ENGLISH PROVERB

Every man has his value.

FRENCH PROVERB

Man is nature's sole mistake.

W. S. GILBERT

A worm.

JOB 25:6

Children of a larger size.

SENECA

The more I see of man, the more I like dogs.

MME. DE STAËL

HUMANITY

Let us have but one end in view, the welfare of humanity.

JOHN COMENIUS

The more humanity advances, the more it is degraded.

GUSTAVE FLAUBERT

Rejoice with them that do rejoice, and weep with them that weep.

ROMANS 12:15

HUMAN NATURE

There is no crime of which one cannot image oneself to be the author.

JOHANN W. VON GOETHE

Human action can be modified to some extent, but human nature cannot be changed.

ABRAHAM LINCOLN

HUMOR

Man is distinguished from all other creatures by the faculty of laughter.

JOSEPH ADDISON

Men will let you abuse them if only you will make them laugh.

HENRY WARD BEECHER

Wit is the salt of conversation, not the food.

WILLIAM HAZLITT

Wit sometimes enables us to act rudely with impunity.

DUC DE LA ROCHEFOUCAULD

Laugh and the world laughs with you; / Weep and you weep alone.

ELLA WHEELER WILCOX

IGNORANCE

I have never met a man so ignorant that I couldn't learn something from him.

GALILEO GALILEI

Most ignorance is vincible ignorance. We don't know because we don't want to know.

ALDOUS HUXLEY

IMMORTALITY

We are miserable enough in this life, without the absurdity of speculating upon another.

LORD BYRON

Man is the only animal that contemplates death, and also the only animal that shows any sign of doubt of its finality.

WILLIAM ERNEST HOCKING

A hope beyond the shadow of a dream.

JOHN KEATS

INDIVIDUALITY

Nature never rhymes her children, nor makes two men alike.

RALPH WALDO EMERSON

The strongest man in the world is he who stands alone.

HENRIK IBSEN

Whatever you may be sure of, be sure of this—that you are dreadfully like other people.

JAMES RUSSELL LOWELL

We forfeit three-fourths of ourselves in order to be like other people.

ARTHUS SCHOPENHAUER

If a man does not keep pace with his companions, perhaps it is because he hears a different drummer.

HENRY DAVID THOREAU

INNOCENCE

The truly innocent are those who not only are guiltless themselves but think others are.

JOSH BILLINGS

Innocence itself sometimes has need of a mask.

ENGLISH PROVERB

To have no guilt at heart, no wrong-doing to turn us pale.

HORACE

INTELLECTUAL

An intellectual is someone whose mind watches itself.

ALBERT CAMUS

Swollen in head, weak in legs, sharp in tongue.

MAO TSE-TUNG

JOY

After joy comes sorrow.

ENGLISH PROVERB

Joy and sorrow are sisters.

GREEK PROVERB

JUSTICE

When one has been threatened with a great injustice, one accepts a smaller as a favour.

JANE WELSH CARLYLE

To give everyone his due.

CICERO

One man's justice is another man's injustice.

RALPH WALDO EMERSON

Eye for eye, tooth for tooth, hand for hand, foot for foot.

EXODUS 21:24

Justice has nothing to do with expediency.

WOODROW WILSON

KNOWLEDGE

Knowledge is power.

FRANCIS BACON

He that increase knowledge increases sorrow.

INDIAN PROVERB

To know that we know what we know, and that we do not know what we do not know, that is true knowledge.

HENRY DAVID THOREAU

LAUGHTER

Laughter is satanic, and, . . . is born of Man's conception of his own superiority.

CHARLES BAUDELAIRE

And if I laugh at any mortal thing, / 'Tis that I may not weep.

LORD BYRON

No one is more profoundly sad than he who laughs too much.

JEAN PAUL RICHTER

Laugh, and the world laughs with you; / Weep, and you weep alone.

ELLA WHEELER WILCOX

LAW

You cannot live without the lawyers, and certainly you cannot die without them.

JOSEPH H. CHOATE

Anyone who takes it on himself, on his own authority, to break a bad law, thereby authorizes everybody else to break the good ones.

DENIS DIDEROT

Possession is nine points of the law.

THOMAS FULLER

There is no law but has a hole in it for those who can find it out.

GERMAN PROVERB

For whoever shall keep the whole law, and yet offend in one point, he is guilty of all.

JAMES 2:10

Ignorance of the law excuses no man.

JOHN SELDEN

Not made for a righteous man, but for the lawless and disobedient, for the ungodly and for sinners.

TIMOTHY 1:9

"LAWS"

You can fool most of the people most of the time.

P. T. BARNUM

Live within your income, even if you have to borrow to do so.

JOHN BILLINGS

Anytime you don't want anything, you get it.

CALVIN COOLIDGE

If you can't convince them, confuse them.

HARRY S. TRUMAN

LEARNING

The second half of a man's life is made up of nothing but the habits he has acquired during the first half.

FEODOR DOSTOEVSKI

Learning is the eye of the mind.

ENGLISH PROVERB

A little learning is a dangerous thing.

ALEXANDER POPE

LIBERTY

The unhampered translation of will into act.

DANTE

Give me liberty or give me death!

PATRICK HENRY

It has been observed that they who most loudly clamour for liberty do not most liberally grant it.

SAMUEL JOHNSON

Liberty in the lowest rank of every nation is little more than the choice of working or starving.

SAMUEL JOHNSON

O Liberty! Liberty! what crimes are committed in thy name!

MADAM ROLAND

LIES

There are a terrible lot of lies going about the world, and the worst of it is that half of them are true.

WINSTON CHURCHILL

Better a lie that heals than a truth that wounds.

CZECH PROVERB

A lie begets a lie.

ENGLISH PROVERB

We lie loudest when we lie to ourselves.

ERIC HOFFER

LIFE

Life has its ups and downs.

AMERICAN PROVERB

Life consists not in holding good cards but in playing those you do hold well.

JOSH BILLINGS

Life is an incurable disease.

ABRAHAM COWLEY

Then give to the world the best you have, / And the best will come back to you.

MARY AINGE DE VERE

If I can stop one heart from breaking, / I shall not live in vain.

EMILY DICKINSON

Life is too short to waste.

RALPH WALDO EMERSON

While there's life there's hope.

ENGLISH PROVERB

A little credulity helps one on through life very smoothly.

ELIZABETH CLEGHORN GASKELL

I slept and dreamed that life was beauty. / I woke—and found that life was duty.

ELLEN STURGIS HOOPER

A predicament which precedes death.

HENRY JAMES

It better befits a man to laugh at life than to lament over it.

SENECA

The mass of men lead lives of quiet desperation.

HENRY DAVID THOREAU

LOVE

All is fair in love and war.

ENGLISH PROVERB

Love is blind.

ENGLISH PROVERB

Life's greatest happiness is to be convinced we are loved.

VICTOR HUGO

It is a man's peculiar duty to love even those who wrong him.

MARCUS AURELIUS

True love is like ghosts, which everybody talks about and few have seen.

DUC DE LA ROCHEFOUCAULD

'Tis better to have loved and lost / Than never to have loved at all.

ALFRED LORD TENNYSON

Love conquers all.

VIRGIL

LUCK

Better be born lucky than rich.

JOHN CLARKE

Shallow men believe in luck.

RALPH WALDO EMERSON

An ounce of luck is worth a pound of wisdom.

FRENCH PROVERB

One's good luck is another's misfortune.

YIDDISH PROVERB

MANNERS

Manners make the man.

ENGLISH PROVERB

Civility costs nothing and buys everything.

LADY MARY WORTLEY MONTAGU

The art of making those people easy with whom we converse.

JONATHAN SWIFT

There are few things that so touch us with instinctive revulsion as a breach of decorum.

THORSTEIN VEBLEN

MARRIAGE

Marriages are made in heaven.

ENGLISH PROVERB

An edifice that must be rebuilt every day.

EMILE HERZOG

Marriage may be compared to a cage: the birds outside frantic to get in and those inside frantic to get out.

MICHEL DE MONTAIGNE

Marriage is popular because it combines the maximum of temptation with the maximum of opportunity.

GEORGE BERNARD SHAW

MATURITY

To mature is to go on creating oneself endlessly.

HENRI BERGSON

When I was a child, I spoke as a child, I understood as a child, I thought as a child; but when I became a man, I put away childish things.

1 CORINTHIANS 13:11–12

MONEY

That which gives a man thirty years more of dignity.

CHINESE PROVERB

Money governs the world.

ENGLISH PROVERB

Money talks.

ENGLISH PROVERB

The cause of good things to a good man, of evil things to a bad man.

PHILO

For the love of money is the root of all evil.

1 TIMOTHY 6:10

MORALITY

Morality is a private and costly luxury.

HENRY BROOKS ADAMS

A terribly thin covering of ice over a sea of primitive barbarity.

KARL BARTH

I ought, or I ought not, constitute the whole of morality.

CHARLES DARWIN

I have to live for others and not for myself; that's middle class morality.

GEORGE BERNARD SHAW

MUSIC

Music is well said to be the speech of angels.

THOMAS CARLYLE

Music has charms to soothe a savage breast.

WILLIAM CONGREVE

The universal language of mankind.

HENRY WADSWORTH LONGFELLOW

NATURE

The only love that does not deceive human hopes.

HONORÉ DE BALZAC

Nature is the true law.

ENGLISH PROVERB

Let us permit nature to have her way; she understands business better than we do.

MICHEL DE MONTAIGNE

Men and Nature must work hand in hand. The throwing out of balance of the resources of Nature throws out of balance also the lives of men.

FRANKLIN D. ROOSEVELT

NEIGHBOR

For what do we live, but to make sport for our neighbours, and laugh at them in our turn.

JANE AUSTEN

No man is an island.

JOHN DONNE

Nothing is fair or good alone.

RALPH WALDO EMERSON

Good fences make good neighbors.

ROBERT FROST

Thou shalt love thy neighbor as thyself.

LEVITICUS 19:18

OLD AGE

With age comes wisdom.

AMERICAN PROVERB

The pegs fall out, the tone is gone, and the harmony becomes dissonance.

ARISTOPHANES

Age makes many a man whiter, but not better.

DANISH PROVERB

To be out of war, out of debt, . . . out of the dentist's hands.

RALPH WALDO EMERSON

Young men want to be faithful and are not; old men want to be faithless and cannot.

OSCAR WILDE

OPINION

We are all of us, more or less, the slaves of opinion.

WILLIAM HAZLITT

It is difference of opinion which makes horse races.

MARK TWAIN

OPPORTUNITY

A wise man will make more opportunities than he finds.

SIR FRANCIS BACON

God helps them that help themselves.

BENJAMIN FRANKLIN

When the iron is hot, strike.

JOHN HEYWOOD

American has been another name for opportunity.

FREDERICK JACKSON TURNER

ORIGINALITY

I invent nothing. I rediscover.

AUGUSTE RODIN

There is nothing new under the sun.

ECCLESIASTES 1:9

My guess is that well over 80 percent of the human race goes through life without having a single original thought.

H. L. MENCKEN

PARENTS

Honor thy father and thy mother.

EXODUS 20:12

Parents we can have but once.

SAMUEL JOHNSON

All women become like their mothers. That is their tragedy. No man does. That's his.

OSCAR WILDE

PATIENCE

He that has no patience has nothing.

ENGLISH PROVERB

Patience is a virtue.

ENGLISH PROVERB

PATRIOTISM

Patriotism is as fierce as a fever, pitiless as the grave, blind as a stone, and irrational as a headless hen.

AMBROSE BIERCE

Patriotism is not enough. I must have no hatred or bitterness toward anyone.

EDITH CAVELL

Looking out for yourself by looking out for your country.

CALVIN COOLIDGE

Patriotism is the last refuge of a scoundrel.

SAMUEL JOHNSON

Ask not what your country can do for you; ask what you can do for your country.

JOHN F. KENNEDY

That pernicious sentiment, "Our country, right or wrong."

JAMES RUSSELL LOWELL

The Athenian democracy suffered much from that narrowness of patriotism which is the ruin of all nations.

H. G. WELLS

PEACE

There never was a good war or a bad peace.

BENJAMIN FRANKLIN

The mere absence of war is not peace.

JOHN F. KENNEDY

Peace, like charity, begins at home.

FRANKLIN D. ROOSEVELT

A bad peace is better than a good war.

RUSSIAN PROVERB

Peace begins just where ambition ends.

EDWARD YOUNG

PEOPLE

A people without faith in themselves cannot survive.

CHINESE PROVERB

The man in the street.

RALPH WALDO EMERSON

God must love the common man, he made so many of them.

ABRAHAM LINCOLN

The people are a many-headed beast.

ALEXANDER POPE

God must hate the common man, he made him so common.

PHILIP WYLIE

PESSIMIST

People who have an appetite for grief.

RALPH WALDO EMERSON

A man who thinks everybody as nasty as himself, and hates them for it.

GEORGE BERNARD SHAW

The optimist sees the doughnut / But the pessimist sees the hole.

McLANDBURGH WILSON

PHILOSOPHY

Philosophy: unintelligible answers to insoluble problems.

HENRY ADAMS

I believe that in actual fact, philosophy ranks before and above the natural sciences.

THOMAS MANN

PLEASURE

Every pleasure has a pain.

ENGLISH PROVERB

Everyone takes his pleasure where he finds it.

FRENCH PROVERB

POETRY

All that is worth remembering of life.

WILLIAM HAZLITT

Poetry is the art of uniting pleasure with truth.

SAMUEL JOHNSON

Vocal painting.

SIMONIDES

POLITICIAN

One who shrinks from the duties of private life to seek the publicity of public office.

ANONYMOUS

Any citizen with influence enough to get his old mother a job as char-woman in the City Hall.

H. L. MENCKEN

It is better to trust in the Lord than to put confidence in princes.

PSALM 118:9

POLITICS

Politics makes strange bedfellows.

AMERICAN PROVERB

The doctrine of the possible.

OTTO VON BISMARCK

A whip for the horse, a briddle for the ass, and a rod for the fool's back.

PROVERBS 26:3

The madness of many for the gain of a few.

JONATHAN SWIFT

POVERTY

You don't have to look for distress; it is screaming at you!

SAMUEL BECKETT

The poor you always have with you.

JOHN 12:8

Few, save the poor, feel for the poor.

LETITIA ELIZABETH LANDON

The poor is hated even of his own neighbor; but the rich has many friends.

PROVERBS 14:20

Very few people can afford to be poor.

GEORGE BERNARD SHAW

Poverty is no sin.

SPANISH PROVERB

PREJUDICE

Prejudices . . . are most difficult to eradicate from the heart whose soil has never been loosened or fertilized by education.

CHARLOTTE BRONTE

Prejudice is the child of ignorance.

WILLIAM HAZLITT

Those who deny freedom to others deserve it not for themselves.

ABRAHAM LINCOLN

It is never too late to give up our prejudices.

HENRY DAVID THOREAU

An opinion without judgment.

VOLTAIRE

PRIDE

Pride goeth before a fall.

ENGLISH PROVERB

Pride in prosperity turns to misery in adversity.

ENGLISH PROVERB

PRINCIPLES

You can't learn too soon that the most useful thing about a principle is that it can always be sacrificed to expediency.

SOMERSET MAUGHAM

It is easy to be tolerant of the principles of other people if you have none of your own.

SIR HERBERT SAMUEL

PROFIT

What is a man profited, if he shall gain the whole world, and lose his own soul?

MATTHEW 16:26

No man profiteth but by the loss of others.

MICHEL DE MONTAIGNE

There is no way of keeping profits up but by keeping wages down.

DAVID RICARDO

PROGRESS

All progress is based upon a universal innate desire on the part of every organism to live beyond its income.

SAMUEL BUTLER

The consequence of rapidly spending the planet's irreplaceable capital.

ALDOUS HUXLEY

Those who speak most of progress measure it by quantity and not quality.

GEORGE SANTAYANA

PUBLIC OPINION

Public opinion is no more than this. / What people think that other people think.

ALFRED AUSTIN

What we call public opinion is generally public sentiment.

BENJAMIN DISRAELI

With public sentiment, nothing can fail; without it, nothing can succeed.

ABRAHAM LINCOLN

QUOTATIONS

Quoting: The act of repeating erroneously the words of another.

AMBROSE BIERCE

The wise make proverbs and fools repeat them.

ISAAC D'ISRAELI

I quote others only the better to express myself.

MICHEL DE MONTAIGNE

RACE

Men are not superior by reason of the accidents of race or color. They are superior who have the best heart—the best brain.

ROBERT G. INGERSOLL

There is but one race—humanity.

GEORGE MOORE

Morality knows nothing of geographical boundaries or distinctions of race.

HERBERT SPENCER

RADICAL

A man with both feet planted firmly in the air.

FRANKLIN DELANO ROOSEVELT

The radical invents the views. When he has worn them out, the conservative adopts them.

MARK TWAIN

REALITY

Humankind cannot bear very much reality.

T. S. ELIOT

To seize the flying thought before it escapes us is our only touch with reality.

ELLEN GLASGOW

The pure concept of the understanding, that which corresponds to a sensation in general.

IMMANUEL KANT

And the most terrible reality brings us, with our suffering, the joy of a great discovery.

MARCEL PROUST

REASON

That by which the soul thinks and judges.

ARISTOTLE

He who will not reason, is a bigot; he who cannot is a fool; and he who dares not is a slave.

SIR WILLIAM DRUMMOND

Reason governs the wise man, and cudgels the fool.

ENGLISH PROVERB

Reason is not measured by size or height, but by principle.

EPICTETUS

Reason always means what some one else has got to say.

ELIZABETH CLEGHORN GASKELL

RELIGION

Religion: A daughter of Hope and Fear, explaining to Ignorance the nature of the Unknowable.

AMBROSE BIERCE

The most acceptable service of God is the doing of good to man.

BENJAMIN FRANKLIN

A disease, but a noble disease.

HERACLITUS

Every religion is good that teaches man to be good.

THOMAS PAINE

REVOLUTION

Revolutions are not made with rosewater.

ENGLISH PROVERB

The setting up of a new order contradictory to the old one.

JOSÉ ORTEGA Y GASSET

Repression is the seed of revolution.

DANIEL WEBSTER

RIGHT

Men, their rights and nothing more; women, their rights and nothing less.

SUSAN B. ANTHONY

The greatest good to the greatest number.

JEREMY BENTHAM

That which tends to the universal good.

FRANCIS HUTCHESON

Who is in the right fears, who is in the wrong hopes.

ITALIAN PROVERB

SATIRE

Sarcastic levity of tongue.

LORD BYRON

When there's more malice shown than matter.

BENJAMIN FRANKLIN

Satire is a sort of glass, wherein beholders do generally discover everybody's face but their own.

JONATHAN SWIFT

SELFISHNESS

That detestable vice which no one will forgive in others and no one is without in himself.

HENRY WARD BEECHER

Selfishness is the greatest curse of the human race.

WILLIAM EWART GLADSTONE

Self-interest is a fire which first consumes others and then self.

RUSSIAN PROVERB

To seek our own profit.

BARUCH SPINOZA

SEX

Give me chastity and continence, but not just now.

SAINT AUGUSTINE

The pleasure is momentary, the position ridiculous, and the expense damnable.

LORD CHESTERFIELD

An irresistible attraction and an overwhelming repugnance and disgust.

GEORGE BERNARD SHAW

SHAME

Who fears no shame comes to no honor.

DUTCH PROVERB

He that has no shame has no conscience.

ENGLISH PROVERB

SILENCE

Blessed is the man who, having nothing to say, abstains from giving in words evidence of the fact.

GEORGE ELIOT

Silence is golden.

ENGLISH PROVERB

Wisdom's best reply.

EURIPIDES

The best resolve for him who mistrusts himself.

DUC DE LA ROCHEFOUCAULD

SIN

That which we call sin in others is experiment for us.

RALPH WALDO EMERSON

Hate the sin but do not hate the person.

JAPANESE PROVERB

Man's self-desecration par excellence.

FRIEDRICH W. NIETZSCHE

SKEPTICISM

The first step on the road to philosophy.

DENIS DIDEROT

A wise skepticism is the first attribute of a good critic.

JAMES RUSSELL LOWELL

SOCIETY

It is not from top to bottom that societies die; it is from bottom to top.

HENRY GEORGE

In civilized society, we all depend upon each other.

SAMUEL JOHNSON

High society is for those who have stopped working and no longer have anything important to do.

WOODROW WILSON

SOLITUDE

I was never less alone than while by myself.

EDWARD GIBBON

One of the greatest necessities in America is to discover creative solitude.

CARL SANDBURG

I never found the companion that was so companionable as solitude.

HENRY DAVID THOREAU

STYLE

Have something to say, and say it as clearly as you can.

MATTHEW ARNOLD

The style is the man himself.

GEORGE DE BUFFON

SUCCESS

Success is its own reward.

AMERICAN PROVERB

Never fail to get what you desire; never to fall into what you would avoid.

EPICTETUS

Success is counted sweetest / By those who ne'er succeed.

EMILY DICKINSON

Why should we be in such desperate haste to succeed . . . ? If a man does not keep pace with his companions, perhaps it is because he hears a different drummer.

HENRY DAVID THOREAU

TACT

Tact consists in knowing how far to go too far.

JEAN COCTEAU

Tact is the ability to describe others as they see themselves.

ABRAHAM LINCOLN

TALK

Talk is cheap.

AMERICAN PROVERB

Much talk, little work.

DUTCH PROVERB

TEACHER

The man who can make hard things easy.

RALPH WALDO EMERSON

To teach is to learn.

JAPANESE PROVERB

He who can, does. He who cannot, teaches.

GEORGE BERNARD SHAW

THOUGHT

If you do not have thoughts you do not have understanding.

AFRICAN PROVERB

A strenuous art—few practice it: and then only at rare times.

DAVID BEN-GURION

Feelings gone to seed.

JOHN BURROUGHS

TIME

This time, like all times, is a very good one, if we but know what to do with it.

RALPH WALDO EMERSON

Time cures all things.

ENGLISH PROVERB

Time is an herb that cures all diseases.

BENJAMIN FRANKLIN

Time is money.

BENJAMIN FRANKLIN

TRAGEDY

The climax of every tragedy lies in the deafness of its heros.

ALBERT CAMUS

Herein lies the tragedy . . . that men know so little of men.

WILLIAM DU BOIS

Commonplace people dislike tragedy, because they dare not suffer and cannot exult.

JOHN MASEFIELD

TRAVEL

Travel in the younger sort, is a part of education; in the elder, a part of experience.

FRANCIS BACON

Travel makes a wise man better, but a fool worse.

ENGLISH PROVERB

The use of travelling is to regulate imagination by reality, and instead of thinking how things may be, to see them as they are.

SAMUEL JOHNSON

See on promontory, one mountain, one sea, one river, and see all.

SOCRATES

TROUBLE

Troubles don't last forever.

AFRICAN PROVERB

He that seeks trouble never misses.

ENGLISH PROVERB

Patience is the best remedy for every trouble.

PLAUTUS

TRUTH

Everything possible to believe is an image of truth.

WILLIAM BLAKE

The aim of the superior man.

CONFUCIUS

To write truth first on the tablet of one's own heart—this is the sanity and perfection of living.

MARY BAKER EDDY

Truth will prevail.

ENGLISH PROVERB

Truth is the nursing mother of genius.

MARGARET FULLER

You shall know the truth, and the truth shall make you free.

JOHN 8:32

UNIVERSE

Not a machine, but an organism, with an indwelling principle of life.

JOHN FISKE

The sum total of all sums total.

LUCRETIUS

The whole theory of the universe is directed unerringly to one single individual—namely to You.

WALT WHITMAN

UTOPIA

Straws to which those who cling have no real hope.

EMIL BRUNNER

The most magnificent promises of impossibilities.

THOMAS B. MACAULAY

From each according to his abilities, to each according to his needs.

KARL MARX

VIRTUE

Virtue is its own reward.

JOHN DRYDEN

Whatever behavior fits a given situation.

JOHANN W. GOETHE

To resist all temptation to evil.

THOMAS R. MALTHUS

I find that the best virtue I have has in it some tincture of vice.

MICHEL DE MONTAIGNE

WAR

War is much too important a matter to be left to the generals.

GEORGES CLEMENCEAU

Nation shall rise against nation, and kingdom against kingdom.

LUKE 21:10

War is hell.

WILLIAM T. SHERMAN

That mad game the world so loves to play.

JONATHAN SWIFT

WEALTH

It is to be regretted that the rich and powerful too often bend the acts of government to their selfish purposes.

ANDREW JACKSON

Those who condemn wealth are those who have none and see no chance of getting it.

WILLIAM PENN PATRICK

Wealth is a power usurped by the few to compel the many to labor for their benefit.

PERCY BYSSHE SHELLEY

The best wealth is health.

WELSH PROVERB

WILL

That by which the mind chooses anything.

JONATHAN EDWARDS

Where there's a will there's a way.

ENGLISH PROVERB

Nothing but the power, or ability, to prefer or choose.

JOHN LOCKE

Will and intellect are one and the same thing.

BARUCH SPINOZA

WISDOM

Wisdom comes by suffering.

AESCHYLUS

Common sense in an uncommon degree is what the world calls wisdom.

SAMUEL TAYLOR COLERIDGE

Too much wisdom is folly.

GERMAN PROVERB

The art of being wise is the art of knowing what to overlook.

WILLIAM JAMES

The beginning of wisdom is the definition of terms.

SOCRATES

WORDS

Words once spoken cannot be wiped out with a sponge.

DANISH PROVERB

I am sorry when any language is lost, because languages are the pedigree of nations.

SAMUEL JOHNSON

Weigh your words, do not count them.

SERBO-CROATIAN PROVERB

Man does not live by words alone, despite the fact that sometimes he has to eat them.

ADLAI E. STEVENSON

It is the man who determines what is said, not the words.

HENRY DAVID THOREAU

WORK

Do not put off today's work till tomorrow.

AFRICAN PROVERB

A remedy against all ills.

CHARLES BAUDELAIRE

The most dignified thing in the life of man.

DAVID BEN-GURION

Idleness and lack of occupation are the best things in the world to ruin the foolish.

DIO CHRYSOSTOM

There is no right to strike against the public safety by anybody, anywhere, any time.

CALVIN COOLIDGE

Work saves us from three great evils: boredom, vice and need.

Voltaire

WORRY

As a rule, men worry more about what they can't see than about what they can.

Julius Caesar

How much pain have cost us the evils which have never happened.

Thomas Jefferson

The misfortunes the hardest to bear are those which never come.

James Russell Lowell

YOUTH

Have exalted notions because they have not yet been humbled by life or learned its necessary limitations.

Aristotle

Young men think old men are fools, but old men know young men are fools.

George Chapman

A habit with some so long they cannot part with it.

Rudyard Kipling

A wonderful thing; what a crime to waste it on children.

George Bernard Shaw

Knowledge is of two kinds: we know a subject ourselves, or we know where we can find information upon it.

—BOSWELL
Life of Dr. Johnson, Vol. 1
(1791).

Part XI

REFERENCE POTPOURRI

66 Special Names, Words, and Terms

66

Special Names, Words, and Terms

Often in our daily lives we need or want to know the name of something but can't recall the correct word or term. We either don't know where to look or don't have the necessary reference book immediately available. This chapter consists of just such material. It provides a collection of names, words, and terms covering a variety of topics ranging from the correct names of the major languages of the world to the Latin terms for the trees of North America to the standard names of the principal vitamins and minerals.

Birthstones (page 435)
Flowers (page 435)
U.S. State Flowers (page 435)
U.S. State Birds (page 437)
U.S. National Parks (page 438)
Geologic Terms (page 442)
U.S. Physical Divisions (page 44:
U.S. Meridians and Base Lines (page 446)
The Planets (page 448)
Major Constellations (page 449)
The Brightest Stars (page 449)
Vitamins (page 450)
Minerals (page 450)
Amino Acids (page 450)
Common Generic Prescription Drugs (page 451)
Common Generic Nonprescriptic Drugs (page 452)
Metric Terms (page 453)
Popular Sports (page 454)
Common Mammals of North America (page 455)
Common Insects of North America (page 457)
Common Birds of North America (page 459)
Common Trees of North America (page 462)
Common Flowers of North America (page 466)
Large Islands of the World (page 469)
Large Oceans and Seas of the World (page 469)
Large Mountains of the World (page 470)
Large Rivers of the World (page 471)
Principal Languages of the World (page 472)
Capitals of the World (page 476)

BIRTHSTONES (*by month*)

January: garnet
February: amethyst
March: aquamarine or bloodstone
April: diamond
May: emerald
June: pearl, alexandrite, or moonstone
July: ruby
August: sardonyx or peridot
September: sapphire
October: opal or tourmaline
November: topaz
December: turquoise or lapis lazuli

FLOWERS (*by month*)

January: carnation or snowdrop
February: primrose
March: violet or daffodil
April: daisy or lily
May: hawthorn or lily of the valley
June: rose
July: water lily or larkspur
August: poppy
September: morning glory or dahlia
October: begonia or calendula
November: chrysanthemum
December: holly or poinsettia

U.S. STATE FLOWERS

Alabama: camellia
Alaska: forget-me-not
Arizona: saguaro cactus
Arkansas: apple blossom
California: golden poppy
Colorado: Rocky Mountain columbine
Connecticut: mountain laurel

Delaware: peach blossom
District of Columbia: American Beauty rose
Florida: orange blossom
Georgia: Cherokee rose
Hawaii: hibiscus
Idaho: syringa
Illinois: violet
Indiana: peony
Iowa: wild rose
Kansas: sunflower
Kentucky: goldenrod
Louisiana: magnolia
Maine: white pine cone and tassel
Maryland: black-eyed Susan
Massachusetts: mayflower
Michigan: apple blossom
Minnesota: pink and white lady slipper
Mississippi: magnolia
Missouri: hawthorn
Montana: bitter root
Nebraska: goldenrod
Nevada: sagebrush
New Hampshire: purple lilac
New Jersey: purple violet
New Mexico: yucca
New York: rose
North Carolina: dogwood
North Dakota: wild prairie rose
Ohio: scarlet carnation
Oklahoma: mistletoe
Oregon: Oregon grape
Pennsylvania: mountain laurel
Rhode Island: violet
South Carolina: Carolina yellow jessamine
South Dakota: American pasqueflower
Tennessee: Iris
Texas: bluebonnet
Utah: sego lily
Vermont: red clover
Virginia: flowering dogwood

Washington: western rhododendron
Wisconsin: wood violet
Wyoming: Indian paintbrush

U.S. STATE BIRDS

Alabama: yellowhammer
Alaska: willow ptarmigan
Arizona: cactus wren
Arkansas: mockingbird
California: California valley quail
Colorado: lark bunting
Connecticut: American robin
Delaware: blue hen chicken
District of Columbia: wood thrush
Florida: mockingbird
Georgia: brown thrasher
Hawaii: nene (Hawaiian goose)
Idaho: mountain bluebird
Illinois: cardinal
Indiana: cardinal
Iowa: eastern goldfinch
Kansas: western meadowlark
Kentucky: Kentucky cardinal
Louisiana: eastern brown pelican
Maine: chickadee
Maryland: Baltimore oriole
Massachusetts: chickadee
Michigan: robin
Minnesota: common loon
Mississippi: mockingbird
Missouri: bluebird
Montana: western meadowlark
Nebraska: meadowlark
Nevada: mountain bluebird
New Hampshire: purple finch
New Jersey: eastern goldfinch
New Mexico: roadrunner
New York: bluebird

North Carolina: cardinal
North Dakota: western meadowlark
Ohio: cardinal
Oklahoma: scissor-tailed flycatcher
Oregon: western meadowlark
Pennsylvania: ruffed grouse
Rhode Island: Rhode Island hen
South Carolina: Carolina wren
South Dakota: ring-necked pheasant
Tennessee: mockingbird
Texas: mockingbird
Utah: seagull
Vermont: hermit thrush
Virginia: cardinal
Washington: willow goldfinch
West Virginia: cardinal
Wisconsin: robin
Wyoming: meadowlark

U.S. NATIONAL PARKS (*by states*)

Alabama

Horseshoe Bend National Military Park

Alaska

Denali National Park and Preserve
Gates of the Arctic National Park and Preserve
Glacier Bay National Park and Preserve
Katmai National Park and Preserve
Kenai Fjords National Park
Klondike Gold Rush National Historical Park
Kobuk Valley National Park
Lake Clark National Park and Preserve
Sitka National Historical Park
Wrangell–St. Elias National Park and Preserve

Arizona

Grand Canyon National Park
Petrified Forest National Park

Arkansas

  Hot Springs National Park
  Pea Ridge National Military Park

California

  Channel Islands National Park
  Kings Canyon National Park
  Lassen Volcanic National Park
  Redwood National Park
  Sequoia National Park
  Yosemite National Park

Colorado

  Mesa Verde National Park
  Rocky Mountain National Park

Florida

  Biscayne National Park
  Everglades National Park

Georgia

  Chickamauga and Chattahooga National Military Park
  Kennesaw Mountain National Battlefield Park

Hawaii

  Hawaii Volcanoes National Park
  Kalaupapa National Historical Park
  Koloko-Honokohau National Historical Park
  Pu'uhonua o Honaurau National Historical Park

Idaho

  Nez Perce National Historical Park

Illinois

  George Rogers Clark National Historical Park

Kentucky

  Cumberland Gap National Historical Park
  Mammoth Cave National Park

Louisiana

  Chalmette National Historical Park
  Jean Lafitte National Historical Park and Preserve

Maine

  Acadia National Park

Maryland

  Chesapeake and Ohio Canal National Historical Park
  Morristown National Historic Park

Massachusetts

  Boston National Historical Park
  Lowell National Historical Park
  Minute Man National Historical Park

Michigan

  Isle Royal National Park

Minnesota

  Voyageurs National Park

Mississippi

  Vicksburg National Military Park

Montana

  Glacier National Park

New Mexico

  Carlsbad Caverns National Park
  Chaco Culture National Historical Park
  Guadalupe Mountains National Park

New York

  Saratoga National Historical Park

North Carolina

  Guilford Courthouse National Military Park

North Dakota

  Theodore Roosevelt National Park

Oregon

   Crater Lake National Park

Pennsylvania

   Gettysburg National Military Park
   Independence National Historical Park

South Carolina

   Kings Mountain National Military Park

South Dakota

   Badlands National Park
   Wind Cave National Park

Tennessee

   Fort Donelson National Military Park
   Great Smoky Mountains National Park
   Shiloh National Military Park

Texas

   Big Bend National Park
   Guadalupe Mountains National Park
   Lyndon B. Johnson National Historical Park
   San Antonio Missions National Historical Park

Utah

   Arches National Park
   Bryce Canyon National Park
   Canyonlands National Park
   Capitol Reef National Park
   Zion National Park

Virginia

   Appomattox Court House National Historical Park
   Colonial National Historical Park
   Fredricksburg and Spotsylvania County Battlefields Memorial
      National Military Park
   Manassas National Battlefield Park
   Richmond National Battlefield Park
   Shenandoah National Park

Washington

> Klondike Gold Rush National Historical Park
> Mount Rainier National Park
> North Cascades National Park
> Olympic National Park
> San Juan Island National Historical Park
> Harpers Ferry National Historical Park

Wyoming

> Grand Teton National Park
> Yellowstone National Park

GEOLOGIC TERMS

Alexandrian
Animikie
Atoka
Belt
Cambrian:
  Upper, Late
  Middle, Middle
  Lower, Early
Carboniferous Systems
Cayuga
Cenozoic
Cincinnatian
Chester
Coahuila
Comanche
Cretaceous:
  Upper, Late
  Lower, Early
Des Moines
Devonian:
  Upper, Late
  Middle, Middle
  Lower, Early
Eocene:
  upper, late

  middle, middle
  lower, early
glacial:
  interglacial
  postglacial
  preglacial
Glenarm
Grand Canyon
Grenville
Guadalupe
Gulf
Gunnison River
Holocene
Jurassic:
  Upper, Late
  Middle, Middle
  Lower, Early
Keweenawan
Kinderhook
Leonard
Little Willow
Llano
Meramec
Mesozoic:
  pre-Mesozoic

post-Mesozoic
Miocene:
  upper, late
  middle, middle
  lower, early
Mississippian:
  Upper, Late
  Lower, Early
Missouri
Mohawkian
Morrow
Niagara
Ochoa
Ocoee
Oligocene:
  upper, late
  middle, middle
  lower, early
Osage
Ordovician:
  Upper, Late
  Middle, Middle
  Lower, Early
Pahrump
Paleocene:
  upper, late
  middle, middle
  lower, early
Paleozoic
Pennsylvanian:
  Upper, Late

Middle, Middle
Lower, Early
Permian:
  Upper, Late
  Lower, Early
Pleistocene
Pliocene:
  upper, late
  middle, middle
  lower, early
Precambrian:
  upper
  middle
  lower
Quaternary
red beds
Shasta
Silurian:
  Upper, Late
  Middle, Middle
  Lower, Early
St. Croixan
Tertiary
Triassic:
  Upper, Late
  Middle, Middle
  Lower, Early
Virgil
Wolfcamp
Yavapai

U.S. PHYSICAL DIVISIONS

Division	*Province*	*Section*
Laurentian Upland	Superior Upland	
Atlantic Plain	Continental Shelf	
	Coastal Plain	Embayed section
		Sea Island section
		Floridian section

Division	*Province*	*Section*
		East Gulf Coastal Plain
		Mississippi Alluvial Plain
		West Gulf Coastal Plain
Appalachian Highlands	Piedmont province	Piedmont Upland
		Piedmont Lowland
	Blue Ridge province	Northern; Southern section
	Valley and Ridge province	
		Tennessee section
		Middle section
		Hudson Valley
	St. Lawrence Valley	Champlain section
		Northern section
	Appalachian Plateaus	
		Mohawk section
		Catskill section
		Southern New York section
		Allegheny Mountain section
		Kanawha section
		Cumberland Plateau
		Cumberland Mountain section
	New England province	
		Seaboard Lowland
		New England Upland
		White Mountain section
		Green Mountain section
		Taconic section
	Adirondack province	
Interior Plains	Interior Low Plateaus	
		Highland Rim
		Lexington Plain
		Nashville Basin

Division	Province	Section
	Central Lowland	Eastern lake section
		Western lake section
		Wisconsin Driftless section
		Till Plains
		Dissected Till Plains
		Osage Plains
	Great Plains	Missouri Plateau, glaciated
		Missouri Plateau, unglaciated
		Black Hills
		High Plains
		Plains Border
		Colorado Piedmont
		Raton section
		Pecos Valley
		Edwards Plateau
		Central Texas section
Interior Highlands	Ozark Plateaus	Springfield-Salem Plateaus
		Boston "Mountains"
	Ouachita province	Arkansas Valley
		Ouachita Mountains
Rocky Mountain System	Southern Rocky Mountain	
	Wyoming Basin	
	Middle Rocky Mountains	
	Northern Rocky Mountains	
Intermontane Plateaus	Columbia Plateaus	Walla Walla Plateau
		Blue Mountain section
		Payette section
		Snake River Plain
		Harney section
	Colorado Plateaus	High Plateaus of Utah
		Uinta Basin
		Canyon Lands

Division	*Province*	*Section*
		Navajo section
		Grand Canyon section
		Datil section
	Basin and Range province	
		Great Basin
		Sonoran Desert
		Salton Trough
		Mexican Highland
		Sacramento section
Pacific Mountain System		
	Sierra-Cascade Mountains	
		Northern Cascade Mountains
		Middle Cascade Mountains
		Southern Cascade Mountains
		Sierra Nevada
	Pacific Border province	
		Puget Trough
		Olympic Mountains
		Oregon Coast Range
		Klamath Mountains
		California Trough
		California Coast Ranges
		Los Angeles Ranges
	Lower Californian province	

U.S. MERIDIANS AND BASE LINES

First, second, etc., standard parallel
First, second, etc., guide meridian

First, second, etc., principal meridian

Auxiliary (first, second, etc.)
  meridian
Ashley Guide Meridian (Utah)
Beaverhead Guide Meridian
  (Montana)
Belt Mountain Guide Meridian
  (Montana)
Big Hole Guide Meridian (Montana)
Bitterroot Guide Meridian
  (Montana)
Black Hills base line (South Dakota)
Black Hills Guide Meridian (South
  Dakota)
Boise Meridian (Idaho)
Boulder Guide Meridian (Montana)
Browning Guide Meridian
  (Montana)
Buffalo Creek Guide Meridian
  (Montana)
Carson River Guide Meridian
  (Nevada)
Castle Valley Guide Meridian (Utah)
Chickasaw Meridian (Mississippi)
Choctaw base line (Mississippi)
Choctaw Meridian (Mississippi)
Cimarron Meridian (Oklahoma)
Colorado Guide Meridian (Utah)
Columbia Guide Meridian
  (Washington)
Colville Guide Meridian
  (Washington)
Copper River Meridian (Alaska)
Coulson Guide Meridian (Montana)
Deer Lodge Guide Meridian
  (Montana)
Deschutes Meridian (Oregon)
Emery Valley Guide Meridian
  (Utah)
Fairbanks Meridian (Alaska)

Flathead Guide Meridian (Montana)
Fort Belknap Guide Meridian
  (Montana)
Fremont Valley Guide Meridian
  (Utah)
Gila and Salt River Meridian
  (Arizona)
Grand River Guide Meridian (Utah)
Grande Ronde Guide Meridian
  (Oregon)
Green River Guide Meridian (Utah)
Haystack Butte Guide Meridian
  (Montana)
Helena Guide Meridian (Montana)
Henry Mountain Guide Meridian
  (Utah)
Horse Plains Guide Meridian
  (Montana)
Humboldt Meridian (California)
Humboldt River Guide Meridian
  (Nevada)
Huntsville Meridian
  (Alabama-Mississippi)
Indian Meridian (Oklahoma)
Jefferson Guide Meridian
  (Montana)
Judith Guide Meridian (Montana)
Kanab Guide Meridian (Utah)
Kolob Guide Meridian (Utah)
Little Porcupine Guide Meridian
  (Montana)
Louisiana Meridian (Louisiana)
Maginnis Guide Meridian
  (Montana)
Michigan Meridian (Michigan-Ohio)
Mount Diablo base line
  (California-Nevada)
Mount Diablo Meridian
  (California-Nevada)

Musselshell Guide Meridian
(Montana)
Navajo base line (Arizona-New
Mexico)
Navajo Meridian (Arizona-New
Mexico)
New Mexico Guide Meridian (New
Mexico-Colorado)
New Mexico Principal Meridian
(New Mexico-Colorado)
Panguitch Guide Meridian (Utah)
Passamari Guide Meridian
(Montana)
Pine Valley Guide Meridian (Utah)
Principal Meridian (Montana)
Red Rock Guide Meridian
(Montana)
Reese River Guide Meridian
(Nevada)
Ruby Valley Guide Meridian
(Nevada)
St. Helena Meridian (Louisiana)
St. Stephens base line
(Alabama-Mississippi)
St. Stephens Meridian
(Alabama-Mississippi)
Salt Lake Meridian (Utah)
San Bernardino base line
(California)

San Bernardino Meridian
(California)
Sevier Lake Guide Meridian (Utah)
Seward Meridian (Alaska)
Shields River Guide Meridian
(Montana)
Smith River Guide Meridian
(Montana)
Snake Valley Guide Meridian (Utah)
Square Butte Guide Meridian
(Montana)
Sweet Grass Guide Meridian
(Montana)
Tallahassee Meridian (Florida)
Teton Guide Meridian (Montana)
Uinta Special Meridian (Utah)
Ute Principal Meridian (Colorado)
Valley Creek Guide Meridian
(Montana)
Wah Wah Guide Meridian (Utah)
Washington Meridian (Mississippi)
Willamette Meridian
(Oregon-Washington)
Willow Springs Guide Meridian
(Utah)
Wind River Meridian (Wyoming)
Yantic Guide Meridian (Montana)
Yellowstone Guide Meridian
(Montana)

THE PLANETS

Earth
Jupiter
Mars
Mercury
Neptune
Pluto
Uranus
Saturn
Venus

MAJOR CONSTELLATIONS

Andromeda	Crux	Orion
Antlia	Cygnus	Pavo
Apus	Delphinus	Pegasus
Aquarius	Dorado	Perseus
Aquila	Draco	Phoenix
Ara	Equuleus	Pictor
Argo Navis	Eridanus	Pisces
Aries	Fornax	Pisces Austrinus
Auriga	Gemini	Puppis
Boötes	Grus	Pyxis
Caelum	Hercules	Reticulum
Camelopardus	Horologium	Sagitta
Cancer	Hydra	Sagittarius
Canes Venatici	Hydrus	Scorpius
Canis Major	Indus	Sculptor
Canis Minor	Lacerta	Scutum
Capricornus	Leo	Serpens
Carina	Leo Minor	Sextans
Cassiopeia	Lepus	Taurus
Centaurus	Libra	Telescopium
Cepheus	Lupus	Triangulum
Cetus	Lynx	Triangulum Australe
Chamaeleon	Lyra	Tucana
Circinus	Mensa	Ursa Major
Columba	Microscopium	Ursa Minor
Coma Berenices	Monoceos	Vela
Corona Australis	Musca	Virgo
Corona Borealis	Norma	Volans
Corvus	Octans	Vulpecula
Crater	Ophiuchus	

THE BRIGHTEST STARS
(*top thirty in order of brightness*)

Sirius	Arcturus	Altair
Canopus	Rigel	Betelgeuse
Alpha Centauri	Procyon	Aldebaran
Vega	Achennar	Spica
Capella	Beta Centari	Pollux

Antares
Fomalhaut
Deneb
Regulus
Beta Crucis

Eta Carinae
Alpha-one Crucis
Castor
Gamma Crucis
Epsilon Cannis Majoris

Epsilon Ursae Majoris
Bellatrix
Lambda Scorpii
Epsilon Carinae
Mira

VITAMINS

A
B-1 (thiamine)
B-2 (riboflavin)
B-3 (niacin)
B-5 (pantothenic acid)
B-6 (pyridoxine)
B-12 (cyanocobalamin)
B-15 (pangamic acid)
biotin

C (ascorbic acid)
choline
D
E
folic acid (folacin)
inositol
K
PABA (para-aminobenzoic acid)
P (bioflavonoids)

MINERALS

calcium
chlorine
chromium
cobalt
copper
fluroine (flourides)
iodine (iodide)

iron
magnesium
manganese
molybdenum
nickel
phosphorus

potassium
selenium
sodium
sulfur
vanadium
zinc

AMINO ACIDS

alanine
arginine
aspartic acid
cysteine
cystine
glutamic acid
glycine

histidine
hydroxyproline
isoleucine
leucine
lysine
methionine
phenylalanine

proline
serine
threonine
tryptophan
tyrosine
valine

COMMON GENERIC PRESCRIPTION DRUGS

acebutolol (angina attacks, high blood pressure)
acetohexamide (diabetes)
acetophenazine (nausea, vomiting, anxiety)
acyclovir [oral and topical] (herpes infections)
albuterol (asthma, allergies, bronchitis)
alprazolam (tension, depression)
amantadine (type-A flu, Parkinson's disease)
ambenonium (myasthenia gravis, urinary retention)
amiloride (potassium loss)
amiodarone (heartbeat irregularities)
amobarbitol (anxiety, insomnia)
amphetamine (sleepiness, hyperactivity)
anesthetics [topical and rectal] (hemorrhoids, proctitis)
anthralin [topical] (psoriasis, hair growth)
anticoagulants [oral] (abnormal blood clotting)
anticonvulsants, Dione type (petit mal seizures)
antifungals [vaginal] (vaginal infections)
antiglaucoma, long acting [opthalmic] (glaucoma)
antithytroid (overactive thyroid)
atenolol (migraine headaches, angina attacks)
benztropine (Parkinson's disease)
buspirone (anxiety, nervousness, tension)
carisoprodol (muscle spasms)
chloral hydrate (anxiety, insomnia)
chlorambucil (cancer)
chloroquine (malaria, arthritis, lupus)
chlorothiazine (fluid retention)
chlorpromazine (nausea, anxiety, agitation)
cholestyramine (cholesterol, excess bile)
cimetidene (ulcers)
conjugated estrogens (menopause, osteoporosis)
contraceptives [oral] (pregnancy, menstrual periods)
cyclandelate (poor blood flow)
cyclobenzaprine (muscle spasms, pain)
danazol (endometriosis, menstruation)
diazepam (nervousness, muscle spasm)
diflunisal (arthritis, gout)
digitalis preparations (congestive heart failure)
diphenoxylate and atrophine (diarrhea, cramps)
disulfiram (alcoholism)

doxylamine (hay fever, hives, rashes)
ergoloid mesylates (memory loss, confusion, depression)
ergonovine (postdelivery bleeding)
ergotamine (migraine headaches)
estrogen (menopause, hormone deficiency)
famotidine (ulcers, acid secretion)
fluoxetine (depression)
fluprednisolone (inflammation, asthma, emphysema)
flurazepam (insomnia, tension)
furosemide (high blood pressure)
methotrexate (rheumatoid arthritis, cancer)
nalidixic acid (urinary tract infection)
naltrexone (narcotic addiction)
natamycin (eye fungus infection)
narcotic and acetaminophen (pain)
neomycin (high blood cholesterol)
neostigmine (myasthenia gravis)
nicardipine (angina attacks, high blood pressure)
nicotine resin complex (smoking addiction)
penicillamine (rheumatoid arthritis)
prednisone (inflammation, asthma, kidney disease)

COMMON GENERIC NONPRESCRIPTION DRUGS

acetaminophen (moderate pain and fever)
adrenocorticoids [topical] (skin swelling and itching)
aluminum and magnesium antacids (gastritis, hiatal hernia)
aluminum, calcium, and magnesium antacids (peptic ulcers, hyper-
    acidity)
aluminum hydroxide (hyperacidity, heartburn, constipation)
aspirin (pain, fever, inflammation)
ascorbic acid (anemia, scurvy, acid urine)
benzoyl peroxide (acne, face wrinkles)
bisacodyl (constipation)
bismuth (subsalicylate-diarrhea, nausea)
caffeine (drowsiness, fatigue)
calcium carbonate (osteoporosis)
cascara (stool softener)
charcoal, activated (medication, poisonings)
clemastine (hay fever, rash, itching)
cyclezine (motion sickness)

cyclophosphamide (cancer, arthritis, skin disease)
danthron (constipation)
dextromethorphan (colds, flu, bronchitis)
gualifenesin (hay fever, cough, cold)
hyoscyamine (digestive system spasms)
ibuprofen (inflammation, pain)
insulin (diabetes)
kaolin and pectin (diarrhea, intestinal cramps)
lactulose (liver disease, constipation)
loperamide (diarrhea, colosomy discharge)
magnesium citrate (constipation)
magnesium sulfate (constipation)
magnesiam trisilicate (hiatal hernia)
meclizine (motion sickness)
niacin [nicotinic acid] (cholesterol, vertigo, pellegra)
pantothenic acid (vitamin B-5 deficiency)
phenylephine (allergies, colds, sinusitis)
simethicone (abdominal gas)
sodium phosphate (constipation)
sulindac (joint pain, inflammation)
terpin hydrate (cough, bronchial irritation)
vitamin A (sun exposure, eyes, skin)
vitamin B-1 [thiamin] (alcoholism, cirrhosis, beri-beri)
vitamin B-2 [riboflavin] (sores in mouth, itching skin)
vitamin B-12 [cyanocobalamin] (anemia, nerve damage)
vitamin C [ascorbic acid] (anemia, acid urine)
vitamin D (bone disease, low blood calcium)
vitamin E (fibrocystic disease of the breast)
vitamin K (bleeding disorders)
vitamins and fluoride (dental caries)
xlometazoline (nasal and throat congestion)

METRIC TERMS

Length

millimeter (0.001 m)
centimeter (0.01 m)
decimeter (0.1 m)
meter (1 m)
dekameter (10 m)

hectometer (100 m)
kilometer (1,000 m)

Area

centiare (1 m^2)
are (100 m^2)
hectare (10,000 m^2)

Weight   Capacity

    milligram (0.001 g)   milliliter (0.001 l)
    centigram (0.01 g)   centiliter (0.01 l)
    decigram (0.1 g)   deciliter (0.1 l)
    gram (1 g)   liter (1 l)
    dekagram (10 g)   dekaliter (10 l)
    hectogram (100 g)   hectoliter (100 l)
    kilogram (1,000 g)   kiloliter, or stere (1,000 l)
    metric ton (1,000,000 g)

POPULAR SPORTS

archery   ice skating
auto racing   figure
badminton   speed
baseball   judo
basketball   karate
bicycling   kayaking
billiards   kite flying
boating   lacrosse
  pleasure   motorcycle
  power   riding
  sailing   racing
boat racing   polo
bobsledding   racketball
bowling   roller skating
boxing   rowing
canoeing   scuba diving
fencing   shuffleboard
fishing   skeet shooting
football   skiing
golf   cross-country
gymnastics and tumbling   downhill
handball   skin diving
horseback riding   soccer
horse racing   surfing
horseshoe pitching   swimming
hunting   table tennis
ice hockey   target shooting

trap shooting
tennis
track and field
water skiing

weight lifting
wind surfing
wrestling

COMMON MAMMALS OF NORTH AMERICA

armadillo, nine-banded (*Dasypus novemcinctus*)
badger (*Taxidea taxus*)
bat, Brazilian free-tailed (*Tadarida brasiliensis*)
  hoary (*Lasiurus cinereus*)
  Indiana (*Myotis lucifugus*)
  red (*Lasiurus borealis*)
bear, black (*Ursus americanus*)
  grizzly (*Ursus arctos*)
  polar (*Ursus maritimus*)
beaver (*Castor canadensis*)
   mountain (*Aplodentia ruta*)
bison (*Bison bison*)
bobcat (*Felis rufus*)
caribou (*Rangifer tarandus*)
chipmunk, cliff (*Tamias dorsalis*)
    eastern (*Tamias striatus*)
    least (*Tamias minimus*)
coyote (*Canis latrans*)
deer, mule (*Odocoileus hemionus*)
  white-tailed (*Odocoileus virginianus*)
elk (*Cerus elaphus*)
ermine (*Mustela erminea*)
fisher (*Martes pennanti*)
fox, Arctic (*Alopex lagopus*)
  Channel Islands gray (*Urocyon littoralis*)
  gray (*Urocyon cinereoargenteus*)
  kit (*Vulpes macrotis*)
  red(*Vulpes vulpes*)
  swift (*Vulpes relox*)
goat, mountain (*Oreamnos americanus*)
gopher, plains pocket (*Geomys bursarius*)
hare, snowshoe (*Lepus americanus*)
jack rabbit, black-tailed (*Lepus californicus*)
   white-tailed (*Lepus townsendii*)

lion, mountain (*Felis concolor*)
lynx (*Felis lynx*)
marmot, hoary (*Marmota caligata*)
       Olympic (*Marmota olympus*)
       yellow bellied (*Marmota flaviventris*)
marten (*Martes americana*)
mink (*Mustela vison*)
mole, broad-footed (*Scapaneus latimanus*)
    eastern (*Scalopus aquaticus*)
    star-nosed (*Condylura cristata*)
moose (*Alces alces*)
mouse, deer (*Peromyscus maniculatus*)
      eastern harvest (*Reithrodontomys humulis*)
      house (*Mus musculus*)
      meadow jumping (*Zapus hudsonius*)
      western harvest (*Reithrodontomys megalotis*)
      western jumping (*Zapus princeps*)
      white-footed (*Peromyscus leucopus*)
muskrat (*Ondatra zibethicus*)
      round-tailed (*Neofiber alleni*)
opossum, Virginia (*Didelphis virginiana*)
otter, river (*Lutra canadensis*)
    sea (*Enhydra lutris*)
peccary, collared (*Tayassu tajacu*)
pocket gopher, plains (*Geomys bursarius*)
porcupine (*Erethizon dorsatum*)
prairie dog, black-tailed (*Cynomys ludovicianus*)
       white-tailed (*Cynomys leucurus*)
pronghorn (*Antilocapra americana*)
rabbit, brush [desert] (*Sylvilagus bachmani*)
    eastern cottontail (*Sylvilagus floridanus*)
    marsh (*Sylvilagus palustris*)
raccoon (*Procyon lotor*)
rat, black (*Rattus rattus*)
   Norway (*Rattus norvegicus*)
   Ord's kangaroo (*Dipodomys ordii*)
ringtail (*Bassariscus astutus*)
sea lion, California (*Zalophus californianus*)
      northern (*Eumetopias jubatus*)
seal, gray (*Halichoerus grypus*)
   harbor (*Phoca vitulina*)

sheep, bighorn (*Ovis canadensis*)
     Dall's (*Ovis dalli*)
shrew, least (*Cryptotis parva*)
     masked (*Sorex cinereus*)
     short-tailed (*Blarina brevicauda*)
     vagrant (*Sorex vagrans*)
skunk, eastern spotted (*Spilogale putorius*)
     striped (*Mephitus mephitus*)
     western spotted (*Spilogale gracilis*)
squirrel, Abert's (*Sciurus aberti*)
     Arizona gray (*Sciurus arizonensis*)
     California ground (*Spermophilus beecheyi*)
     Cascade golden-mantled ground (*Spermophilus saturatus*)
     Douglas' (*Tamiasciurus douglasii*)
     fox (*Sciurus niger*)
     golden-mantled ground (*Spermophilus lateralis*)
     gray (*Sciarus carolinensis*)
     northern flying (*Glaucomys sabrinus*)
     red (*Tamiasciurus hudsonicus*)
     southern flying (*Glaucomys volans*)
     thirteen-lined ground (*Spermophilus tridecemlineatus*)
     western gray (*Sciurus griseus*)
vole, meadow (*Microtus pennsylvanicus*)
     southern red-backed (*Clethrionomys gapperi*)
     western red-backed (*Clethrionomys occidentalis*)
weasel, long-tailed (*Musela frenata*)
wolf, gray (*Canis lupus*)
     red (*Canis rufus*)
wolverine (*Gulo gulo*)
wood chuck (*Marmota monax*)
woodrat, eastern (*Neotoma floridana*)

COMMON INSECTS OF NORTH AMERICA

admiral, red [butterfly] (*Vanessa atalanta*)
aphid (Family Aphididae)
argiope, black and yellow [spider] (*Argiope aurentia*)
backswimmer (Family Notonectidae)
bee, honey (*Apis mellifera*)
     bumble (*Bombus*)

beetle, asparagus (*Crioceris asparagi*)
     darkling (Family Tenebrionidae)
     eyed click (*Alaus*)
     ground (Family Carabidae)
     Japanese (*Popilla Japenica*)
     June (*Phyllophaga*)
     ladybird (Family Coccinellidae)
     pinacate (*Eleodes*)
     spotted asparagus (*Crioceris duodecimpunctata*)
     tiger (*Cicindela*)
     tortoise (Family Chrysomelidae)
     whiligig (*Gyrinus*)
borer, cottonwood [beetle] (*Plectrodera scalator*)
boxelder bug, eastern (*Leptocoris trivittatus*)
           western (*Leptocoris rubrolineatus*)
butterfly, European cabbage (*Artogeia rapae*)
caterpillar, California tent (*Malacosoma californicum*)
        eastern tent (*Malacosoma americanum*)
        Pacific tent (*Malacosoma constrictum*)
        wooly bear (*Pyrrharctica isabella*)
cicadas (Family Cicadidae)
cricket, snowy tree (*Oceanthus fultoni*)
     field (*Gryllus*)
earwig, European (*Forficula auricularia*)
firefly (Family Lampyridae)
fly, bee (Family Bombyliidae)
   black (*Simulium*)
   blow (Family Calliphoridae)
   crane (*Tipula*)
   deer (*Chrysops*)
   horse (*Tabanus*)
   house (*Musca domestica*)
   hover (Family Syrphidae)
   robber (Family Asilidae)
   vinegar (*Drosophila melanagaster*)
grasshopper, spur-throated (*Melanoplus*)
katydid, true (*Plerophylla camellifolia*)
leafhopper, scarlet and green (*Graphocephala coccinea*)
locust, Carolina (*Dissosteira carolina*)
mantis, praying (*Mantis religiosa*)
monarch [butterfly] (*Danaus plexippus*)

mosquito (Family Culicidae)
moth, apantesis tiger (*Apantesis*)
      luna (*Actias luna*)
      sheep (*Hemilenca eglanterina*)
      underwing (*Catocala*)
mud dauber, black and yellow (*Sceliphron caementarium*)
          blue (*Chalybion californicum*)
scorpion fly (*Panorpa*)
spider, American house (*Achaearanea tepidariorum*)
      black widow (*Latrodectus mactans*)
      grass (*Agelenopsis*)
      wolf (Family Lycosidae)
stink bug (Family Pentatomidae)
swallowtail, tiger [butterfly] (*Pterourus glaucus*)
        western tigar (*Plerourus glaucus*)
tarantula hawks [wasps] (*Pepsis*)
termites (Order Isoptera)
treehopper (*Buffalo-stictocephala*)
velvet-ants (Family Mutillidae)
viceroy [butterfly] (*Basilarchia archippus*)
wasp, paper (*Polistes*)
water striders (*Gerris*)
weevil, boll (*Anthonomus grandis*)
white tail (*Libellula lydia*)
wood nymph, large (*Cercyonis pegala*)
yellow jackets (*Vespula*)

COMMON BIRDS OF NORTH AMERICA

blackbird, Brewer's (*Euphagus cyanocephalus*)
        red-winged (*Aelaius phoeniceus*)
        rusty (*Euphagus carolinus*)
bluebird, mountain (*Sialia currucoides*)
        western (*Sialia mexicana*)
bobolink (*Dolichonyx oryzivorus*)
bunting, indigo (*Passerina cyancea*)
      lazuli (*Passerina amoena*)
      painted (*Passerina ciris*)
cardinal (*Cardinalis cardinalis*)
catbird, gray (*Dumetella carolinensis*)

chickadee, black-capped (*Parus atricapillus*)
   mountain (*Parus gambeli*)
coot, American (*Fulica americana*)
cowbird, bronzed (*Molothrus aeneus*)
   brown-headed (*Molothrus ater*)
creeper, brown (*Certhia americana*)
crow, American (*Corvus brachyrhynchos*)
cuckoo, black-billed (*Coccyzus erythropthalmus*)
   yellow-billed (*Coccyzus americanus*)
dipper, American (*Cinclus mexicanus*)
dove, mourning (*Zenaida macroura*)
   rock [pigeon] (*Columba livia*)
eagle, bald (*Haliaeetus leucocephalus*)
   golden (*Aquila chrysaetos*)
finch, house (*Carpodacus mexicannus*)
   purple (*Carpodacus purpurens*)
flicker, northern (*Colaptes auratus*)
   red-shafted (*Colaptes cafer collaris*)
flycatcher, great crested (*Myiarchus crinitus*)
   ash-throated (*Myiarchus cinerascens*)
goldfinch, American (*Carduelis tristis*)
   lesser (*Carduelis psaltria*)
goose, Canada (*Branta canadensis*)
grackle, common (*Quiscalus quiscula*)
grebe, pied-billed (*Podilymbus podiceps*)
   Clark's (*Aechmophorus clarkii*)
   western (*Aechmophorus occidentalis*)
grossbeak, black-headed (*Pheucticus melanocephalus*)
   evening (*Coccothraustes vespertinus*)
   rose-breasted (*Pheucticus ludovicianus*)
hawk, red-tailed (*Buteo jamicensis*)
   Swainson's (*Buteo swainsoni*)
heron, great blue (*Ardea herodias*)
hummingbird, rufous (*Selasphorus rufus*)
   ruby-throated (*Archilochus colubris*)
jay, blue (*Cyanocitta cristata*)
   Stellar's (*Cyanocitta stelleri*)
junco, dark-eyed (*Junco hyemalis*)
kestrel, American (*Falco sparverius*)
killdeer (*Charadrius vociferous*)

kingbird, western (*Tyrannus verticalis*)
kingfisher, belted (*Ceryle alcyon*)
kinglet, golden-crowned (*Regulus satrapa*)
            ruby-crowned (*Regulus calendula*)
lark, horned (*Eremophila alpestris*)
loon, common (*Gavia immer*)
magpie, black-billed (*Pica pica*)
            yellow-billed (*Pica nuttalli*)
mallard (*Anas platyrhynchos*)
martin, purple (*Progne subis*)
meadowlark, eastern (*Sturnella magna*)
                western (*Sturnella neglecta*)
mockingbird, northern (*Mimus polyglottos*)
nighthawk, common (*Chordeiles minor*)
nuthatch, brown-headed (*Sitta pusilla*)
            red-breasted (*Sitte canadensis*)
            white-breasted (*Sitta carolinensis*)
oriole, orchard (*Icterus spurius*)
            northern [Baltimore] (*Icterus galbula*)
pelican, brown (*Pelecanus occidentalis*)
pheasant, ring-necked (*Phasianus colchicus*)
phoebe, eastern (*Sayornis phoebe*)
pigeon, band-tailed (*Columba fasciata*)
            rock dove (*Columba livia*)
quail, California (*Callipepla californica*)
            Gambel's (*Callipepla gambelii*)
raven, common (*Corvus corax*)
roadrunner, greater (*Geococcyx californianus*)
robin, American (*Turdus migratorius*)
sandpiper, spotted (*Actitis macularia*)
sapsucker, yellow-bellied (*Sphyrapicus varius*)
shrike, loggerhead (*Lanius ludovicianus*)
            northern (*Lanius excubitor*)
siskin, pine (*Carduelis pinus*)
snipe, common (*Gallinago gallinago*)
sparrow, chipping (*Spizella passerina*)
            English (*Passer domesticus*)
            Lincoln's (*Melospiza lincolnii*)
            song (*Melospiza melodia*)
            white crowned (*Zonotrichia leucophrys*)

starling, European (*Sturnus vulgaris*)
swallow, barn (*Hirundo rustica*)
     cliff (*Hirundo pyrrhonota*)
swan, tundra (*Cygnus columbianus*)
     trumpter (*Cygnus buccinator*)
swift, chimney (*Chaetura pelagica*)
     white-throated (*Aeronautes saxatalis*)
tanager, scarlet (*Piranga olivacea*)
     western (*Piranga ludoviciana*)
teal, blue-winged (*Anas discors*)
     cinnamon (*Anas cyanoptera*)
thrasher, brown (*Toxostoma rufum*)
     curve billed (*Toxostoma curvirostre*)
thrush, gray-cheeked (*Catharus minimus*)
     hermit (*Catharus guttatus*)
     wood (*Hylocichla mustelina*)
towhee, green-tailed (*Pipilo chlorurus*)
     rufus-sided (*Pipilo erythrophthalmus*)
vireo, black-capped (*Vireo atricapillus*)
     gray (*Vireo vicinior*)
     solitary (*Vireo solitarius*)
warbler, black-throated green (*Dendroica virens*)
     yellow (*Dendroica petechia*)
     yellow-rumped (*Dendroica coronata*)
     yellow-throated (*Dendroica dominica*)
waxwing, bohemian (*Bombycilla garrulus*)
     cedar (*Bombycilla cedrorum*)
whip-poor-will (*Caprimulgus vociferus*)
woodpecker, acorn (*Melanerpes formicivorus*)
     downy (*Picoides pubescens*)
     red-bellied (*Melanerpes carolinus*)
     red-headed (*Melanerpes erythrocephalus*)
wren, cactus (*Campylorhynchus brunneicapillus*)
     house (*Troglodytes aedon*)
yellowthroat, common (*Geothlypis trichas*)

COMMON TREES OF NORTH AMERICA

acacia, sweet (*Acacia farnesiana*)
alder, red [Oregon alder, western alder] (*Alnus rubra*)
apple (*Malus sylvestris*)

ash, Arizona [velvet ash] (*Fraxinus velutina*)
   Oregon (*Fraxinus latifolia*)
   white (*Fraxinus americana*)
aspen, quaking (*Populus tremuloides*)
baldcypress (*Taxodium distichum*)
basswood, American [linden tree] (*Tilia americana*)
bayberry, southern [southern waxmyrtle] (*Myrica cerifera*)
beech, American (*Fagus grandiflora*)
birch, black (eastern) [sweet birch] (*Betula lenta*)
      black (western) [red birch, water birch] (*Betula occidentalis*)
      gray [white birch, wire birch] (*Betula populifolia*)
      paper (*Betula papyrifera*)
blackgum [black tupelo, pepperidge] (*Nyssa sylvatica*)
bodark [osage orange] (*Maclura pemifern*)
boxelder [ashleaf maple] (*Acer negundo*)
buckeye, Ohio (*Aesculus glabra*)
buckthorn, European (*Rhammus cathartica*)
catalpa, southern (*Catalpa bignonioides*)
cedar, Alaska [Alaska yellow cedar, nootka cypress] (*Chamaecyparis nootkatensis*)
      canoe [western red cedar, giant araborvitae] (*Thuja plicata*)
      eastern red (*Juniperus virginiana*)
      Oregon [Port Orford cedar, Lawson cypress, Lawson's false cypress] (*Chamaecyparis lawsoniana*)
      white, northern [eastern arborvitae] (*Thuja occidentalis*)
cherry, bitter [quinine cherry, wild cherry] (*Prunus emarginata*)
      choke, common [eastern and western chokecherry] (*Prunus virginiana*)
      fire [pin cherry] (*Prunus pensylvanica*)
chestnut, American (*Castanea dentata*)
      horse (*Hesculus hippocastanum*)
cottonwood, black [western balsam poplar] (*Populus trichocarpa*)
      Fremont (*Populus fremontii*)
      narrowleaf (*Populus angustifolia*)
      eastern (*Populus deltoides*)
cypress, Lawson [Port Orford cedar] (*Chamaecyparis lawsoniana*)
      Monterey (*Cypressus macrocarpa*)
      nootka [Alaska cedar] (*Chamaecyparis nootkatensis*)
dogwood, flowering (*Cornus florida*)
      Pacific (*Cornus nuttallii*)
      red-osier [red dogwood, kinnikinnik] (*Cornus stolonifera*)

elder, American (*Sambucus canadensis*)
    blue (*Sambucus cerulea*)
elm, American (*Ulmus americana*)
    slippery (*Ulmus rubra*)
eucalyptus, bluegum (*Eucalyptus globulus*)
fir, balsam (*Abies balsamea*)
    California red (*Abies magnifica*)
    Douglas (*Pseudotsuga meziesii*)
    grand (*Abies magnifica*)
    white (*Abies concolor*)
    subalpine (*Abies lasiocarpa*)
ginkgo (*Ginkgo biloba*)
hackberry (*Celtis occidentalis*)
hawthorne, black [Douglas hawthorne] (*Crataegus donglasii*)
    cockspar (*Crataegus crus-galli*)
hemlock, Alpine [mountain hemlock, black hemlock] (*Tsuga merten-siana*)
    eastern (*Tsuga canadensis*)
    western (*Tsuga heterophylla*)
hickory, bitternut (*Carya cordiformis*)
    shagbark (*Carya ovata*)
holly, American (*Ilex opaca*)
    English (*Ilex aquifolium*)
hophornbeam, eastern (*Ostrya virginiana*)
Joshua tree (*Yucca brevifolia*)
juniper, Rocky Mountain (*Juniperus scopulorum*)
    Utah (*Juniperus osteosperma*)
larch, eastern [tamarack, hackmatack] (*Larix laricina*)
    western [western tamarack] (*Larix occidentalis*)
locust, black (*Robinia pseudoacacia*)
    honey (*Gleditsia triacanthos*)
madrone, Pacific (*Arbutus meziesii*)
magnolia, southern (*Magnolia grandiflora*)
    swamp [swampbay, sweetbay] (*Magnolia virginiana*)
maple, ashleaf [boxelder] (*Acer negundo*)
    bigleaf [broadleaf maple, Oregon maple] (*Acer macrophyllum*)
    Norway (*Acer platanoides*)
    red (*Acer rubrum*)
    silver (*Acer saccharinum*)
    sugar (*Acer saccharum*)

mesquite, honey (*Prosopis glandulosa*)
mountain laurel (*Kalmia latifolia*)
mulberry, white (*Morus alba*)
oak, black [yellow oak; quercitron oak] (*Quereus velulina*)
    blue [mountain white oak] (*Quercus douglasii*)
    bur [mossy cup oak] (*Quercus macrocarpa*)
    California black [Kellog oak, black oak] (*Quercus kelloggii*)
    California live [coast live oak, encima] (*Quercus agrifolia*)
    canyon live oak [maul oak] (*Quercus chrysolepis*)
    Garry oak [Oregon white oak] (*Quercus garryana*)
    mountain white [blue oak] (*Quercus douglasii*)
    northern red (*Quercus rubra*)
    pin (*Quercus palustris*)
Osage orange [bodark] (*Maclura pomifera*)
paloverde, blue (*Cercidium floridum*)
pear (*Pyrus communis*)
pecan (*Carya illinoensis*)
pepperidge [black tupelo] (*Nyssa sylvatica*)
pepperwood [California laurel] (*Umbellularia californica*)
pine, eastern white (*Pinus strobus*)
    lodgepole (*Pinus contorta*)
    longleaf (*Pinus palustris*)
    Norway [red pine] (*Pinus resinosa*)
    pinyon (*Pinus edulis*)
    ponderosa (*Pinus ponderosa*)
    scotch (*Pinus sylvestris*)
    sugar (*Pinus lambertiana*)
    western white (*Pinus monticola*)
planetree, American [sycamore] (*Platanus occidentalis*)
      London (*Platanus x acerifolia* [x = hybrid])
plum, American (*Prunus americana*)
poplar, balsam (*Populus balsamifera*)
    Lombardy (*Populus nigra*)
    tulip [yellow poplar, tulip tree] (*Liriodedron tulipifera*)
    western balsam [black cottonwood] (*Populus trichocarpa*)
    white (*Populus alba*)
redwood (*Sequoia sempervirens*)
rhododendron, rosebay (*Rhododendrun maximum*)
saguaro (*Cereus giganteus*)
sassafras (*Sassafras albidum*)

sequoia, giant (*Sequoia dendron giganteum*)
spruce, black (*Picea mariana*)
      blue (*Picea pungens*)
      eastern [red spruce] (*Picea rubens*)
      Engelmann (*Picea engelmanrii*)
      Norway (*Picea abies*)
      sitka (*Picea sitchensis*)
      white (*Picea glauca*)
sumac, poison (*Toxicodendron vernix*)
      scarlet [smooth sumac] (*Rhus glabra*)
sycamore, California (*Platanus racemosa*)
tamarack [hackmatack, eastern larch] (*Larix laricina*)
      western [western larch] (*Larix occidentalis*)
tupelo, black [swamp tupelo, blackgum, pepperidge] (*Nyssa sylvatica*)
willow, bebb (*Salix bebbiana*)
      black (*Salix nigra*)
      fire [scouler willow] (*Salix scoulerana*)
      Pacific [western black willow, yellow willow] (*Lalix lasiandra*)
      weeping (*Salix babylonica*)
walnut, black (*Juglans nigra*)
waxmyrtle, southern [southern bayberry] (*Myrica cerifera*)
willow, pussy (*Salix discolor*)
witch-hazel (*Hamamelis virginiana*)
yew, Pacific (*Taxus brevifolia*)
yucca, soaptree (*Yucca elata*)

COMMON FLOWERS OF NORTH AMERICA

arrowhead (*Sagittaria latifolia*)
aster, stiff (*Aster linariifolius*)
azalea, flame (*Rhododendron calendulaceum*)
baby blue eyes (*Nemophila menziesii*)
bindweed (*Convolvulus arvensis*)
bitterroot (*Lewisia rediviva*)
black-eyed Susan (*Rudbeckia hirta*)
bloodroot (*Sanguinaria canadensis*)
bluebells, Virginia (*Mertensia virginica*)
blue flag (*Iris versicolor*)
brittlebush (*Encelia farinosa*)
bunchberry (*Cornus canadensis*)

buttercup, common (*Ranunculus acris*)
        subalpine (*Ranunculus eschscholtzii*)
butterfly weed (*Asclepias tuberosa*)
calypso (*Calypso bulbosa*)
camas, common (*Camassia quamash*)
        death (*Zigadenus nuttallii*)
cardinal flower (*Lobelia cardinalis*)
catnip (*Nepeta cataria*)
chicory (*Cichorium intybus*)
cinquefoil, Canadian dwarf (*Potentilla canadensis*)
clover, purple prairie (*Petalostemum purpureum*)
        white prairie (*Petalostemum candidum*)
        white sweet (*Melitotus alba*)
columbine, blue (*Aquilegia coerulea*)
        wild (*Aquilegia canadensis*)
coral root, striped (*Corallorhiza striata*)
daisy, oxeye (*Chrysanthemum leucanthemum*)
        tahoka (*Machaeranthera tanacetifolia*)
dandelion, common (*Taraxacum officinale*)
desert plume (*Stanleya pinnata*)
devil's claw, sand (*Proboscidea arenaria*)
Dutchman's breeches (*Dicentra cucullaria*)
evening primose (*Oenothera biennis*)
fairy duster (*Calliandra eriophylla*)
fireweed [great willow herb] (*Epilobium angustifolium*)
flax, wild blue (*Linum perenne*)
forget-me-not, true (*Myosotis scorpiodides*)
four o'clock, desert (*Mirabilis multiflora*)
foxglove, downey false (*Aureolaria virginica*)
fringe cups (*Tellima grandiflora*)
globemallow, scarlet (*Sphaeralcea coccinea*)
goldenrod, meadow (*Solidago canadensis*)
        tall (*Solidago altissima*)
heather, Brewer's mountain (*Phyllodoce breweri*)
        pink mountain (*Phyllodoce empetriformis*)
        white (*Cassiope mertensiana*)
honeysuckle, Japanese (*Lonicera japonica*)
        trumpet (*Lonicera sempervirens*)
iris, Rocky Mountain (*Iris missouriensis*)
Jack-in-the-pulpit (*Arisaema triphyllum*)
lady's slipper, yellow (*Cypripedium calceolus*)

larkspur, Nuttall's (*Delphinium nuttallianum*)
lily, Carolina (*Lilium michauxii*)
      leopard [panther] (*Lilium pardalinum*)
      sego (*Calochortus nuttallii*)
      tiger (*Lilium columbianum*)
      Turk's cap (*Lilium superbum*)
lupine, miniature (*Lupinus bicolor*)
      wild (*Lupinus perennis*)
marigold, desert (*Baileya multiradiata*)
            marsh [cowslip] (*Caltha palustris*)
mint, wild (*Mentha arvensis*)
mission bells (*Fritillaria lanceolata*)
monument plant (*Frasera speciosa*)
morning glory, common (*Ipomoea purpurea*)
                  ivy-leaved (*Ipomoea hederacea*)
mullein, moth (*Verbascum blattaria*)
            woolly (*Verbascum thapsus*)
orchid, large purple fringed (*Haberaria fimbriata*)
            small purple fringed (*Habenaria psycodes*)
paintbrush, desert (*Castilleja chromosa*)
            Indian (*Castilleja coccinea*)
pasqueflower (*Anemone patens*)
                  western (*Anemone occidentalis*)
penstemon, golden-beard (*Penstemen barbatus*)
            Rydberg's (*Penstemon rydbergii*)
phlox, long-leaved (*Phlox longifolia*)
            wild blue [wild sweet William] (*Phlox divaricata*)
pimpernel, scarlet [poorman's weatherglass] (*Anagellis arvensis*)
pink, fire [catchfly] (*Silene virginica*)
      moss (*Silene acaulis*)
poppy, California (*Eschscholtzia californica*)
            prickly (*Argemone polyanthemos*)
queen Anne's lace [wild carrot] (*Daucus carola*)
queen's cut [bride's bonnet] (*Clintonia uniflora*)
rose, woods' (*Rosa woodsii*)
      salt spray (*Rosa rugosa*)
sand verbene, desert (*Abronia villosa*)
shooting star, few-flowered (*Dodecatheon pulchellum*)
skunk cabbage (*Symplocarpus foetidus*)
skyrocket [desert trumpet] (*Scarlet gilia*)
            skunk flower (*Ipomopsis aggregata*)

St. Johnswort, common (*Hypericum perforatum*)
starflower, western (*Trientalis latifolia*)
strawberry, beach (*Fragaria chiloensis*)
        common (*Fragaria virginiana*)
        wood (*Fragaria vesca*)
sunflower, common (*Helianthus annaus*)
thistle, bull (*Cirsium vulgare*)
violet, common blue [meadow violet] (*Viola papilionacea*)
      stream [pioneer violet, smooth yellow violet] (*Viola glabella*)
water lily, fragrant (*Nymphaea odorata*)
      small white (*Nymphaea tetragona*)
wintergreen, spotted [stripped wintergreen] (*Chimaphila maculata*)
wood sorrel, yellow (*Oxalis grandis*)
yarrow (*Achillea millefolium*)
yucca, blue (*Yucca baccata*)

LARGE ISLANDS OF THE WORLD
(*over 10,000 square miles*)

Baffin Island (Canada)
Banks Island (Canada)
Borneo [Kalimantan] (Asia)
Celebes [Sulawesi] (Indonesia)
Cuba (North America)
Devon Island (Canada)
Ellesmere Island (Canada)
Great Britain (United Kingdom)
Greenland (North America)
Hainan Dao (China)
Hispaniola (North America)
Hokkaidō (Japan)
Honshū (Japan)
Iceland (Europe)
Ireland (Europe)
Java [Jawa] (Indonesia)
Kyūshū (Japan)
Luzon (Philippines)
Madagascar (Africa)
Melville Island (Canada)

Mindanao (Philippines)
New Britain (Papua New Guinea)
Newfoundland (Canada)
New Guinea (Asia-Oceania)
North Island (New Zealand)
Novaya Zemlya (Soviet Union)
Prince of Wales Island (Canada)
Sakhalin (Soviet Union)
Seram (Indonesia)
Southampton Island (Canada)
South Island (New Zealand)
Spitsbergen (Norway)
Sri Lanka (Asia)
Sumatra [Sumatera] (Indonesia)
Taiwan (Asia)
Tasmania (Australia)
Tierra del Fuego (South America)
Vancouver Island (Canada)
Victoria Island (Canada)

LARGE OCEANS AND SEAS OF THE WORLD
(*over 25,000 square miles*)

Arabian Sea
Aral'skoye More [Aral Sea]
  (Soviet Union)
Arctic Ocean
Atlantic Ocean
Baltic Sea (Europe)
Bering Sea (Asia-North America)
Black Sea (Europe-Asia)
Caribbean Sea (North
  America-South America)

Caspian Sea (Iran-Soviet Union)
Indian Ocean
Japan, Sea of (Asia)
Mediterranean Sea
  (Europe-Africa-Asia)
Mexico, Gulf of (North America)
North Sea (Europe)
Pacific Ocean
Red Sea (Africa-Asia)
Yellow Sea (China-Korea)

LARGE MOUNTAINS OF THE WORLD
(*above 10,000 feet*)

Aconcagua, Cerro (Argentina)
Annapurna (Nepal)
Antofalla, Volcán (Argentina)
Api (Nepal)
Ararat (Turkey)
Barú, Volcán (Panama)
Belukha, Gol'tsy (Soviet Union)
Blanc, Mont (France-Italy)
Blanca Peak (Colorado)
Bolívar (Venezuela)
Borah Peak (Idaho)
Cameroon Mountain (Cameroon)
Chimborazo (Ecuador)
Chirripó, Cerro (Costa Rica)
Citlaltépetl (Mexico)
Colima, Nevado de (Mexico)
Cook, Mount (New Zealand)
Cotopaxi (Ecuador)
Cristóbaol, Colón, Pico (Colombia)
Damāvand, Qolleh-ye (Iran)

Dhaulāgiri (Nepal)
Duarte, Pico (Dominican Republic)
Dychtau, Gora (Soviet Union)
Elbert, Mount (Colorado)
El'brus, Gora (Soviet Union)
Elgon, Mount (Kenya-Uganda)
eNjesuthi (South Africa)
Erciyeş Daği (Turkey)
Etna, Mount (Italy)
. Everest, Mount (China-Nepal)
Fairweather, Mount
  (Alaska-Canada)
Finsteraarhorn (Switzerland)
Foraker, Mount (Alaska)
Fuji-san (Japan)
Gannett Peak (Wyoming)
Gasherbrum (China-Pakistan)
Giluwe, Mount (Papua New Guinea)
Gongga Shan (China)
Grand Teton Mountain (Wyoming)

Grossglockner (Austria)
Gunnbjørn Field (Greenland)
Hadūr Shu'ayb (Yemen)
Haleakala Crater (Hawaii)
Hkakabo Razi (Burma)
Hood, Mount (Oregon)
Huascarán, Nevado (Perus)
Huila, Nevado de (Colombia)
Illampu, Nevado (Bolivia)
Illimani, Nevado (Bolivia)
Iztaccíhuatl (Mexico)
Jaya, Puncak (Indonesia)
Jungfrau (Switzerland)
K2 [Godwin Austen]
   (China-Pakistan)
Kāmet (China-India)
Kānchenjunga (India-Nepal)
Karisimbi, Volcan (Rwanda-Zaire)
Kenya, Mount (Kenya)
Kerinci, Gunung (Indonesia)
Kilimanjaro (Tanzania)
Kinabalu, Gunong (Malaysia)
Klyuchevskaya (Soviet Union)
Kommunizma, Pik (Soviet Union)
Koussi, Emi (Chad)
Kula Kangri (Bhutan)
Lassen Peak (California)
Llullaillaco, Volcán
   (Argentina-Chile)
Logan, Mount (Canada)
Longs Peak (Colorado)
Makālu (China-Nepal)
Margherita (Zaire-Uganda)
Markham, Mount (Antarctica)
Matterhorn (Italy-Switzerland)
Mauna Kea (Hawaii)
Mauna Loa (Hawaii)
McKinley, Mount (Alaska)
Meru, Mount (Tanzania)
Misti, Volcán (Peru)

Mulhacén (Spain)
Muztag (China)
Muztagata (China)
Namjagbarwa Feng (China)
Nanda Devi (India)
Nānga Parbat (Pakistan)
Ojos del Salado, Nevado
   (Argentina-Chile)
Pikes Peak (Colorado)
Pissis, Monte (Argentina)
Pobedy, Pik (China-Soviet Union)
Popocatépeti, Volcán (Mexico)
Rainier, Mount (Washington)
Ras Dashen Terara (Ethiopia)
Rinjani, Gunung (Indonesia)
Rosa, Monte (Italy-Switzerland)
St. Elias, Mount (United
   States-Canada)
Sajama, Nevado (Bolivia)
Sawdā', Qurnat as (Lebanon)
Semeru, Gunung (Indonesia)
Shastga, Mount (California)
Tajumulco (Guatemala)
Tirich Mīr (Pakistan)
Toubkal, Jebel (Morocco)
Trikora, Puncak (Indonesia)
Tupungato, Portezuelo de
   (Argentina-Chile)
Victoria, Mount (Papua New
   Guinea)
Vinson Massif (Antarctica)
Waddington, Mount (Canada)
Weisshorn (Switzerland)
Whitney, Mount (California)
Wilhelm, Mount (Papua New
   Guinea)
Wrangell, Mount (Alaska)
Xixabangma Feng [Gosainthan]
   (China)

LARGE RIVERS OF THE WORLD
(over 1,000 miles)

Aldan (Asia)
Amazonas-Ucayali (South America)
Amu Darya (Asia)
Amur (Asia)
Amur-Argun (Asia)
Araguaia (South America)
Arkansas (North America)
Brahmaputra (Asia)
Churchill (North America)
Colorado (North America)
Columbia (North America)
Congo (Africa)
Danube (Europe)
Dnepr [Dnieper] (Europe)
Don (Europe)
Euphrates (Asia)
Ganges (Asia)
Huang [Yellow] (Asia)
Indus (Asia)
Irrawaddy (Asia)
Juruá (South America)
Kama (Europe)
Kasai (Africa)
Kolyma (Asia)
Lena (Asia)
Limpopo (Africa)
Loire (Europe)
Mackenzie (North America)
Madeira (South America)
Marañón (South America)
Mekong (Asia)
Mississippi (North America)
Mississippi-Missouri (North
    America)
Missouri (North America)
Murray (Australia)

Negro (South America)
Niger (Africa)
Nile (Africa)
Ob'-Irtysh (Asia)
Orange (Africa)
Orinoco (South America)
Paraguay (South America)
Paraná (South America)
Peace (North America)
Pechora (Europe)
Pilcomayo (South America)
Plata-Paraná (South America)
Purús (South America)
Red (North America)
Rio Grande (North America)
Salween (Asia)
São Francisco (South America)
Saskatchewan-Bow (North
    America)
Snake (North America)
Sungari (Asia)
Syr Dar'ya (Asia)
Tarim (Asia)
Tigris (Asia)
Tocantins (South America)
Ucayali (South America)
Ural (Asia)
Uruguay (South America)
Verkhnyaya Tunguska (Asia)
Vilyuy (Asia)
Volga (Europe)
Xingu (South America)
Yangtze (Asia)
Yenisey (Asia)
Yukon (North America)
Zambezi (Africa)

PRINCIPAL LANGUAGES OF THE WORLD
(*by country*)

Afghanistan: Pushtu, Dari Persian, Uzbek (Turkic)
Albania: Albanian Tosk, Greek
Algeria: Arabic, Berber, French
Andorra: Catalan, Spanish, French
Angola: Portuguese, Bantu
Antigua and Barbuda: English
Argentina: Spanish, English, Italian, German, French
Australia: English, native languages
Austria: German
The Bahamas: English
Bahrain: Arabic, Persian
Bangladesh: Bengali, English
Barbados: English
Belgium: Flemish, French, German
Belize: English, Spanish, native dialects
Benin: French, local dialects
Bhutan: Dzongkha, Nepali, English
Bolivia: Spanish, Qucchua, Aymara
Botswana: English, Setswana
Brazil: Portuguese, English
Brunei Darussalam: Malay, English, Chinese
Bulgaria: Bulgarian, Turkish, Greek
Burkina Faso: French, Sudanic tribal dialects
Burma: Burmese
Burundi: French, Rundi
Cambodia: Khmer, French
Cameroon: English, French, African languages
Canada: English, French
Cape Verde: Portuguese, Crioulo
Central African Republic: French, local dialects
Chad: French, Arabic, numerous other languages
Chile: Spanish
China: Mandarin, Yue, Wu Minbei, Minnan, Xiang, Gan
Colombia: Spanish
Comoros: Shaafi Islam, French, Malagasy
Congo: French, Bantu dialects

Costa Rica: Spanish
Cuba: Spanish
Cyprus: Greek, Turkish, English
Czechoslovakia: Czech, Slovak
Denmark: Danish
Djibouti: French, Arabic, Somali, Saho-Afar, Arabic
Dominica: English, French patois
Dominican Republic: Spanish
Ecuador: Spanish, Quechuan, Jivaroan
Egypt: Arabic, English
El Salvador: Spanish, Nahuati
Equatorial Guinea: Spanish, Fang, English
Ethiopia: Amharic, Tigre, Galla, Arabic, English, other languages
Fiji: English, Fijian, Hindustani
Finland: Finnish, Swedish
France: French, regional dialects
Gabon: Fang, Bantu dialects
The Gambia: English, Mandinka, Wolof, local dialects
Germany: German
Ghana: English, numerous tribal languages
Greece: Greek, English, French
Grenada: English, French, African patois
Guatemala: Spanish, Indian dialects
Guinea: French, tribal languages
Guinea-Bissau: Portuguese, Criolo, tribal languages
Guyana: English, Amerindian dialects
Haiti: French, Creole
Honduras: Spanish, Amerindian dialects
Hungary: Hungarian (Magyar)
Iceland: Icelandic
India: Hindi, English, numerous other languages
Indonesia: Bahasa, Indonesian, Javanese, English, Dutch
Iran: Persian, Turk, Kurdish, Arabic, English, French
Iraq: Arabic, Kurdish, Assyrian, Armenian
Ireland: English, Irish Gaelic
Israel: Hebrew, Arabic, English, Yiddish
Italy: Italian
Ivory Coast: French, Dioula, tribal languages
Jamaica: English, Jamaican, Creole
Japan: Japanese
Jordan: Arabic, English

Kenya: Swahili, English
Kiribati: Gilberterese, English
Korea, Democratic People's Republic of (North Korea): Korean
Korea, Republic of (South Korea): Korean
Kuwait: Arabic, English, other languages
Laos: Lao, French
Lebanon: Arabic, French, Armenian
Lesotho: Sethoso, English
Liberia: English, tribal dialects
Libya: Arabic
Liechtenstein: German, Alemannic
Luxembourg: French, German, Luxembourgian
Madagascar: Malagasy, French
Malawi: English, Chichewa, Tombuka
Malaysia: Malay, English, Chinese, Indian languages
Maldives: Divehi
Mali: French, Bambara
Malta: Maltese, English
Mauritania: French, Hassanya Arabic, Toucouleur, Fula, Sarakole, Wolof
Mauritius: English, French, Creole
Mexico: Spanish
Monaco: French
Mongolia: Khalkha Mongol, Russian, Chinese
Morocco: Arabic, French, Spanish, Berber dialects
Mozambique: Portuguese, native languages
Nauru: Nauruan, English
Nepal: Nepali, other languages
The Netherlands: Dutch
New Zealand: English, Maori
Nicaragua: Spanish, English, Amerindian dialects
Niger: French, Hausa, Djerma
Nigeria: English, Hausa, Yoruba, Ibo
Norway: Norwegian, Lapp, Finnish
Oman: Arabic, English, Urdu, other languages
Pakistan: Urdu, English
Panama: Spanish, English
Papua New Guinea: English, Melanesian Pidgin, Police Motu, numerous other local languages
Paraguay: Spanish, Guarani
Peru: Spanish, Quechua, Aymara

Philippines: Filipino (Tagalog), English, other languages
Poland: Polish
Portugal: Portuguese
Qatar: Arabic, English
Rumania: Rumanian, Hungarian, German
Rwanda: French, Kingyarwandu, Swahili
Saint Christopher and Nevis: English
Saint Lucia: English, French patois
Saint Vincent and the Grenadines: English, French patois
San Marino: Italian
Sâi Tomé and Principe: Portuguese
Saudi Arabia: Arabic
Senegal: French, tribal languages
Seychelles: English, French, Creole
Sierra Leone: English, tribal languages
Singapore: Chinese, Malay, Tamil, English
Solomon Islands: English, pidgin, local dialects
Somalia: Somali, Arabic
South Africa: Afrikaans, English, Bantu languages
Spain: Spanish, Catalan, Galician, Basque
Sri Lanka: Sinhala, Tamil, English
Sudan: Arabic, tribal languages
Suriname: Dutch, Sranan, English, other languages
Swaziland: siSwati, English
Sweden: Swedish, Finnish
Switzerland: German, French, Italian, Romansch
Syria: Arabic, Kurdish, Armenian, French, English
Taiwan (Republic of China): Mandarin Chinese, Taiwanese, Hakka
Tanzania: Swahili, English
Thailand: Thai, local dialects
Togo: French, other languages
Tonga: Tongan, English
Trinidad and Tobago: English, Hindu, French, Spanish
Tunisia: Arabic, French
Turkey: Turkish, Kurdish, Arabic
Tuvalu: Tuvaluan, English
Uganda: English, Lugandan, Swahili
Union of Soviet Socialist Republics: Russian, local languages and
    dialects
United Arab Emirates: Arabic, Farsi, English, Hindi, Urdu
United Kingdom: English, Welsh, Scottish Gaelic

United States: English
Uruguay: Spanish
Vanuatu: English, French, Bislama
Vatican City: Italian, Latin
Venezuela: Spanish, local Amerindian dialects
Vietnam: Vietnamese, French, Chinese, English, Khmer, tribal dialects
Western Samoa: Samoan, English
Yemen Arab Republic (North Yemen): Arabic
Yemen, People's Democratic Republic of (South Yemen): Arabic
Yugoslavia: Serbo-Croatian, Macedonian, Slovenian, Albanian
Zaire: French, Bantu dialects
Zambia: English, Bantu dialects
Zimbabwe: English, Shona, Sindebele

CAPITALS OF THE WORLD

Afghanistan: Kabul
Albania: Tirana
Algeria: Algiers
Andorra: Andorra la Vella
Angola: Luanda
Antigua and Barbuda: St. John's
Argentina: Buenos Aires
Australia: Canberra
Austria: Vienna
The Bahamas: Nassau
Bahrain: Manama
Bangladesh: Dhaka
Barbados: Bridgetown
Belgium: Brussels
Belize: Belmopan
Benin: Porto-Novo
Bhutan: Thimphu
Bolivia: La Paz
Botswana: Gaborone
Brazil: Brasilia
Brunei Darussalam: Bandar Seri Begawan
Bulgaria: Sofia
Burkina Faso: Ouagadougou

Burma: Rangoon
Burundi: Bujumbura
Cambodia: Phnom Penh
Cameroon: Yaounde
Canada: Ottawa
Cape Verde: Praia
Central African Republic: Bangui
Chad: N'Djamena
Chile: Santiago
China: Beijing
Colombia: Bogota
Comoros: Moroni
Congo: Brazzaville
Costa Rica: San Jose
Cuba: Havana
Cyprus: Nicosia
Czechoslovakia: Prague
Denmark: Copenhagen
Djibouti: Djibouti
Dominica: Roseau
Dominican Republic: Santo Domingo
Ecuador: Quito
Egypt: Cairo

El Salvador: San Salvador
Equatorial Guinea: Malabo
Ethiopia: Addis Ababa
Fiji: Suva
Finland: Helsinki
France: Paris
Gabon: Libreville
The Gambia: Banjul
Germany: Bonn
Ghana: Accra
Greece: Athens
Grenada: St. George's
Guatemala: Guatemala
Guinea: Conakry
Guinea-Bissau: Bissau
Guyana: Georgetown
Haiti: Port-au-Prince
Honduras: Tegucigalpa
Hungary: Budapest
Iceland: Reykjavik
India: New Delhi
Indonesia: Jakarta
Iran: Teheran
Iraq: Baghdad
Ireland: Dublin
Israel: Jerusalem
Italy: Rome
Ivory Coast: Abidjan and Yamoussoukro
Jamaica: Kingston
Japan: Tokyo
Jordan: Amman
Kenya: Nairobi
Kiribati: Tarawa
Korea, Democratic People's Republic of (North Korea): P'yongyang
Korea, Republic of (South Korea): Seoul
Kuwait: Kuwait
Laos: Vientiane

Lebanon: Beirut
Lesotho: Maseru
Liberia: Monrovia
Libya: Tripoli
Liechtenstein: Vaduz
Luxembourg: Luxembourg
Madagascar: Antananarivo
Malawi: Lilongwe
Malaysia: Kuala Lumpur
Maldives: Male
Mali: Bamako
Malta: Valletta
Mauritania: Nouakchott
Mauritius: Port Louis
Mexico: Mexico City
Monaco: Monaco
Mongolia: Ulaanbaatar
Morocco: Rabat
Mozambique: Maputo
Nauru: No capital. Government agencies in Yaren District
Nepal: Kathmandu
The Netherlands: Amsterdam and The Hague
New Zealand: Wellington
Nicaragua: Managua
Niger: Niamey
Nigeria: Lagos
Norway: Oslo
Oman: Muscat
Pakistan: Islamabad
Panama: Panama
Papua New Guinea: Port Moresby
Paraguay: Asuncion
Peru: Lima
Philippines: Manila
Poland: Warsaw
Portugal: Lisbon
Qatar: Doha
Rumania: Bucharest

Rwanda: Kigali
Saint Christopher and Nevis: Basseterre and Charlestown
Saint Lucia: Castries
Saint Vincent and the Grenadines: Kingstown
San Marino: San Marino
São Tomé and Principe: São Tomé
Saudi Arabia: Riyadh
Senegal: Dakar
Seychelles: Victoria
Sierra Leone: Freetown
Singapore: Singapore
Solomon Islands: Honiara
Somalia: Mogadishu
South Africa: Pretoria and Cape Town
Spain: Madrid
Sri Lanka: Colombo
Sudan: Khartoum
Suriname: Paramaribo
Swaziland: Mbabane
Sweden: Stockholm·
Switzerland: Bern
Syria: Damascus
Taiwan (Republic of China): Taipei
Tanzania: Dar es Salaam
Thailand: Bangkok

Togo: Lomé
Tonga: Nuku'alofa
Trinidad and Tobago: Port-of-Spain
Tunisia: Tunis
Turkey: Ankara
Tuvalu: Funafuti
Uganda: Kampala
Union of Soviet Socialist Republics: Moscow
United Arab Emirates: Abu Dhabi
United Kingdom: London
United States: Washington, D.C.
Uruguay: Montevideo
Vanuatu: Port-Vila
Vatican City: Vatican City
Venezuela: Caracas
Vietnam: Hanoi
Western Samoa: Apia
Yemen Arab Republic (North Yemen): Sanaa
Yemen, People's Democratic Republic of (South Yemen): Yemen
Yugoslavia: Belgrade
Zaire: Kinshasa
Zambia: Lusaka
Zimbabwe: Harare

*[I]f you don't have the right words, you won't be able to think
what you want to think.*

—C. CARTER COLWELL AND JAMES H. KNOX
What's the Usage?
(Reston, Va.: Reston Publishing Company, 1973), p. 36.

Part XII

GLOSSARY

67 Glossary of Linguistics

67

Glossary of Linguistics

This glossary contains definitions of terms used by persons who are interested in or professionally involved in the study of languages and word usage. For a complete list of grammatical terms, see Chapters 24 and 33. Numerous other terms pertaining to language and word usage are defined in the various chapters of this book.

abstract term: A word or expression that designates a concept or idea (*freedom*).

accent: The stress, or emphasis, with which one pronounces a word (*ad-mit*).

alliteration: The repetition of the same usually initial consonant sound(s) or letter(s) in neighboring words (*pen* and *pen*cil).

assonance: Repetition of vowels without repetition of consonants (*stony* and *holy*).

biolinguistics: The study of language and communication as biologically induced, with an emphasis on genetics and neurophysiology.

clipped words: A short form of the actual word (*memo* for *memorandum*).

coinage: Creating a new, artificial word (*administrivia*).

colloquialism: An informal, conversational expression (*boss*).

concrete term: A word or expression that designates someone or something real that can be seen or sensed (*house*).

consonant: Any letter other than the vowels *a, e, i, o,* and *u.*

context: The setting or the portions of any written or spoken material that throw light on its meaning.

criticism: The evaluation of written or spoken material based on study and analysis applying recognized standards.

cursive writing: An informal, simplified, easy-to-use script or handwriting.

dead language: A language no longer accepted or used in spoken communication.

derivation: The creation of a new word (*transport*) from an existing word or base (*port*).

diacritic mark: An accent over, below, or through a character that indicates a different sound or emphasis (à).

epigraphy: The study of inscriptions, especially the deciphering of ancient inscriptions.

epithet: A word or phrase that accompanies or takes the place of a person or thing ("He was known by the epithet *The Terminator*").

etymology: The branch of linguistics that studies the origin and history of words.

gender: The classification of words according to sex: feminine (*mother*), masculine (*father*), common (*child*), or neuter (*table*).

grammar: The study of words and their use in sentences, including the rules that define the structure of a language.

hybrid language: A language with a vocabulary that has numerous borrowed words and expressions from other languages.

hybrid word: A word with elements taken from more than one language (*automobile,* borrowed *autos* from Greek and *mobilis* from Latin).

lexicology: The branch of linguistics that deals with the significance and application of words.

lexicon: The total vocabulary of a language, speaker, or subject.

linguistics: The study of all aspects of human speech or language.

malapropism: The use, sometimes humorous, of a word that sounds somewhat like the intended word but means something else (*derangement* for *arrangement*).

Middle English: The English language in use from the twelfth to the fifteenth century.

Modern English: The English language in use since the fifteenth century.

Old English: The English language in use from the seventh to the twelfth century.

onomatopoeia: The naming of something by vocally imitating the sound associated with it (*buzz*).

orthophony: Correct articulation or pronunciation.

paraphrase: A rewording or rephrasing of an exact quotation in other words.

pejoration: A change in the connotative status of a word for the worse (in some situations, *nice* has become a polite way of describing someone unattractive or dull).

penult: The next to the last syllable of a word (ep-i-*dem*-ic).

phoneme: The smallest unit of speech that distinguishes one utterance from another in a language or dialect (*g*ate/*h*ate).

phonetics: The system of speech sounds in a language or group of languages.

Pidgin English: Simplified speech used in communicating between people with different languages.

polysyllable: A word with more than one syllable.

prose: Ordinary language without the use of rhythm, meter, or any other characteristic of poetry.

redundancy: The use of unnecessary words; wordiness; repetition.

rhyme: The use of the same sound or syllable at the ends of words or lines (*drum*/*come*; elec-*tron*/neu-*tron*).

root: The basic element in a word to which prefixes, suffixes, and other parts are attached (*form:* con*form*ity).

semantics: The study of the meanings, changes, and relationships of words and expressions.

syllable: A unit of one or more letters in a word pronounced separately from any other syllable in the word (*dis-cov-er*).

syntax: The arrangement of words to show their relationships in a sentence.

tautology: Needless repetition of a word, an idea, or a statement.

tone language: A language in which pitch and tone are used to distinguish meanings of words or vowels that look or sound similar.

transliteration: Representing or spelling something using characters from another alphabet.

vernacular: The language or dialect native to a region or country rather than a literary, cultural, or foreign language.

vocabulary: The total collection of words and phrases in a given language or used by a given individual.

vowel: Any one of the letters *a, e, i, o,* or *u.*

vulgarism: A vulgar, crude, or obscene word or expression that primarily originates with or is used by illiterate persons.

Index

A

Abbreviations
    academic degrees, 298-302
    acronyms, 204
    capitalization of, 126, 207
    countries, 305-9
    French, 329-31
    general rules, 205
    German, 335-37
    Greek (modern), 340-41
    inappropriate use of, 205
    initialism, 204
    Italian, 345
    Latin, 348-53
    listing of common abbreviations,
        209-38
    numbers, 206
    for organizations, 267-97
    plurals, 160
    punctuation of, 207-8
    Russian, 357
    Spanish, 359-61
    spelling of, 206-7
    states, 303-4
    technical abbreviations, 239-66
    word division, 200
    words always abbreviated, 205-6
Abstract term, 482
Academic degrees, listing of abbreviations
        for, 298-302
Accent, 482

Acronyms, 204
Action words, 13-15
Active voice, 114-15, 116
    for emphasis, 11
Adjective, 116
Adjective pronouns, 93, 116
Adjectives, 93-94
    capitalization, 136-37
    comparative degree, 93, 100
    descriptive adjectives, 93, 94
    limiting adjectives, 93, 94
    predicate adjectives, 93
    relative adjectives, 93
    superlative degree, 93, 100
Adverbs, 94, 116
    position, for emphasis, 12
    relative adverbs, 94
Aircraft names, italics, 146-47
Alliteration, 482
Alphabet
    French, 328-29
    German, 334
    Greek (modern), 339-40
    Italian, 344
    Latin, 348
    Russian, 356
    Spanish, 359
Amino acids, 450
Antagonistic words/phrases, 51-52
Antecedent, 116
Appositive, 116
Article, 116

Arts, capitalization of terms related to, 127-28
Assonance, 482
Auxiliary verbs, 94, 116

B

Biolinguistics, 482
Birds
    of North America, 459-62
    state birds, 437-38
Birthstones, 435
Buzzwords
    nature of, 28
    terms to avoid, 29-30

C

Capitalization
    abbreviations, 126, 207
    acts/bills/codes/laws, 126-27
    adjectives, 136-37
    feast days, 133
    foreign names, 129
    geographical terms, 129-30
    government-related terms, 131-32
    historical terms, 132-33
    holidays, 133
    hyphenated words, 128
    legal terms, 134
    lists, 134-35
    military service, 135-36
    money, 136
    nouns, 136-37
    organizations, 137-38
    personification, 140
    planets, 140
    political terms, 131-32
    questions, series of, 142
    quotations, 141
    races, 138
    religion, 141-42
    resolutions, 142
    schools/colleges/department/courses, 128-29
    seasons, 133
    sport-related terms, 142-43

Capitalization *(cont'd)*
    titles (literature), 126
    titles (personal/professional), 138-40
    tribes, 138
    words related to arts, 127-28
Capitals, of world, 477-79
Centuries/decade, word vs. number symbol, 152
Chemical terms, word vs. symbol, 153
Cliches, 48-50
Clipped words, 482
Coinage, 482
Collective nouns, 99, 116
Colloquialism, 482
Common noun, 116
Comparative degree, 117
    adjectives, 93, 100
Comparison, 117
Complement, 117
Compound predicate, 117
Compound prepositions, 102
Compound sentence, 117
Compound subject, 117
Compound words
    hyphenated compounds, 192
    listing of common compounds, 194-97
    open compounds, 189-90
    solid compounds, 190-91
Concise statements, for emphasis, 11
Concrete term, 482
Conjunctions, 96, 117
    coordinate conjunctions, 96, 105
    correlative conjunctions, 96, 105, 106
    subordinate conjunctions, 96, 105
Consonant, 482
Constellations, 449
Context, 482
Contractions, word division, 200
Coordinate conjunctions, 96, 105, 117
Correlative conjunctions, 96, 105, 106, 117
Countries, abbreviations for, 305-9
Criticism, 483
Cursive writing, 483

D

Dangling modifier, 117
Dashes, word division, 201

Days of week
  French, 333
  German, 333
  Greek (modern), 343
  Italian, 347
  Latin, 355
  Russian, 358
  Spanish, 363
Dead language, 483
Demonstrative pronouns, 93, 117
Dependent (subordinate) clause, 117
Derivative, 483
Descriptive adjectives, 93
Diacritical marks, 144, 483
Direct object, 117
Discriminatory language, 18
  word substitutes for, 18-22
Drugs
  nonprescription drugs, 452-53
  prescription drugs, 451-52

E

Emotional aspects
  negative words/phrases, 23-25
  words to feel good, 2-5
Emphasis, techniques for, 13-14
Epigraphy, 483
Epithet, 483
Etymology, 483
Euphemisms, 43-44
  nature of, 43
Exact quotes, quotation marks, 148-49
Expletive, 117

F

Feast days, capitalization, 133
Figures, plurals, 160
Flowers
  of months, 435
  of North America, 466-69
  state flowers, 435-37
Foreign alphabet. See Alphabet
Foreign currencies, 364-68
Foreign names, capitalization, 129

Foreign terms
  diacritical marks, 144
  Greek roots, 316-17
  italics, 146
  Latin roots, 317
  listing of, 318-23
  overused terms, 324-25
  unaccented words, 326-27
French
  abbreviations, 329-31
  alphabet, 328-29
  days of week, 333
  months, 333
  numbers, 331-33
  seasons, 333
  time, 333
Future perfect tense, 108
Future tense, 108

G

Gender, 483
Geographical terms, capitalization, 129-30
Geologic terms, 442-43
German
  abbreviations, 36-366
  alphabet, 334
  days of week, 333
  months, 339
  numbers, 337-38
  seasons, 333
  time, 333
Gerund, 117
Governmental references
  capitalization, 131-32
  word versus number symbol, 152
Grammar, 483
Grammatical terms, listing of, 116-20
Greek (modern)
  abbreviations, 340-41
  alphabet, 339-40
  days of week, 343
  months, 343
  numbers, 341-42
  seasons, 343
  time, 343-344
Greek roots, listing of, 316-17

H

Historical terms, capitalization, 132-33
Holidays, capitalization, 133
Homographs, 70-73
Homophones, 64-69
Hybrid language, 483
Hybrid word, 483
Hyphenation
    capitalization and hyphenated words,
       128
    compound words, 192
    prefixes and, 171

I

Idiomatic expressions, 121-24
Imperative mood, 95, 109, 117
Indefinite pronouns, 93, 117
Indicative mood, 95, 108, 118
Indirect object, 118
Infinitive, 118
Initialism, 204
Insects, of North America, 457-59
Intensifiers, overuse of, 26-27
Interjection, 118
Interjections, 96-97
Interrogative pronouns, 93, 118
Intransitive verb, 94, 118
Irony, quotation marks, 150
Irregular verbs, 118
    past participle, 110
    present participle, 110
Islands, largest in world, 469
Italian
    abbreviations, 345
    alphabet, 344
    days of week, 347
    months, 347
    numbers, 345-47
    seasons, 347
    time, 347
Italics
    aircraft names, 146-47
    for emphasis, 11, 145-46
    foreign terms, 146
    Latin names, 146, 147

Italics *(cont'd)*
    legal cases, 146
    ship names, 146-147
    titles (literature), 147
    words used as words, 145

J

Jargon
    nature of, 28
    terms to avoid, 29-30

L

Languages, of world, 473-77
Latin
    abbreviations, 348-53
    alphabet, 348
    days of week, 355
    italics for Latin words, 146, 147
    months, 355
    numbers, 353-55
    roots, listing of, 317
    seasons, 385
    time, 385
Legal cases, italics, 146
Legal terms, capitalization, 134
Letters
    plurals, 160
    word division, 198-99
Lexicology, 483
Lexicon, 483
Limiting adjectives, 93
Linguistics, 483
Lists, capitalization, 134-35

M

Malapropism, 483
Mammals, of North America, 455-57
Measurement terms, word versus symbol,
       152, 154
Meridians, U.S., 446-48
Metric terms, 453-54
Middle English, 483

Military service, capitalization, 135-36
Minerals, 450
Misplaced modifier, 74-75, 118
Misplaced words, 74-75
Misused words, most common, 76-89
Modifier, 118
Money
    capitalization, 136
    foreign, 364-68
    word versus symbol, 152, 153-54
Months
    French, 333
    German, 339
    Greek (modern), 343
    Italian, 347
    Latin, 355
    Russian, 358
    Spanish, 363
Mood, 118
    verbs, 95
        imperative mood, 95, 109
        indicative mood, 95, 108
        subjunctive mood, 95, 109
Mountains, largest in world, 470-71

N

Names, word division, 200
Nationality, nouns/adjectives denoting, 369-373
Negative words/phrases, 23-25
Neologisms, 54-57
    nature of, 54
Nominative case, 118
Nonprescription drugs, 452-53
Nonrestrictive clause, 118
Nouns, 92, 118
    capitalization, 136-37
    collective nouns, 99
    plural form/singular meaning, 98-99
    plurals
        irregular nouns, 156-57
        nouns ending in *ch, s, sh, ss, x, z,* 157
        nouns ending in *f, fe, ff,* 158
        nouns ending in *o,* 158
        nouns ending in *y,* 159

Nouns *(cont'd)*
    singular nouns, 156
Number, of verbs, 95
Numbers
    abbreviations, 206
    French, 331-33
    German, 337-38
    Greek (modern), 341-42
    Italian, 345-47
    Latin, 353-55
    Russian, 357
    Spanish, 361-62
    word division, 200-201
    words for
        beginning of sentence, 151
        centuries/decades, 152
        general rule, 151
        governmental references, 152
        measurement terms, 152
        money, 152
        time, 152

O

Objective case, 118
Oceans, 470
Old English, 483
Onomatopoeia, 483
Open compounds, 189-90
Organizations
    capitalization, 138
    listing of abbreviations for, 267-97
Orthophony, 484
Oxymorons, 61-62

P

Paraphrase, 484
Parks, national parks, 438-42
Participle, 118
Parts of speech
    adjectives, 93-94
    adverbs, 94
    conjunctions, 96
    interjections, 96-97
    nouns, 92

Parts of speech *(cont'd)*
   prepositions, 95-96
   pronouns, 93
   verbs, 94-95
Passive voice, 114-15, 118
Past participle, irregular verbs, 110
Past perfect tense, 108
Past tense, 107
Pejoration, 484
Penult, 484
Percentages, word vs. symbol, 154
Person, 118
   verbs, 95
Personal pronouns, 93, 119
Personification, capitalization, 140
Phoneme, 484
Phonetics, 484
Phrasal prepositions, 102, 119
Pidgin English, 484
Planets, 448
   capitalization, 140
Plurals
   abbreviations, 160
   compound terms, 157
   figures, 160
   irregular nouns, 156-57
   letters, 160
   nouns ending in *ch, s, sh, ss, x, z,* 157
   nouns ending in *f, fe, ff,* 158
   nouns ending in *o,* 158
   nouns ending in *y,* 159
   possessive case, 160-61
   singular nouns, 156
Political terms, capitalization, 131-32
Polysyllable, 484
Possessive case, 119
   forming, 160-61
   plurals, 160-61
Predicate, 119
Predicate adjectives, 93, 119
Prefixes
   general rules, 171
   listing of common prefixes, 172-75
   word division, 199
Prepositional phrase, 95, 119
Prepositions, 95-96, 119
   commonly misused prepositions, 103-4
   common prepositions, 101-2

Prepositions *(cont'd)*
   compound prepositions, 102
   participles used as, 95
   phrasal prepositions, 102
Prescription drugs, 451-52
Present participle, irregular verbs, 110
Present perfect tense, 107
Present tense, 107
Pretentious language, 45-47
Pronouns, 93, 119
   adjective pronouns, 93
   compound, for emphasis, 12
   demonstrative pronouns, 93
   indefinite pronouns, 93
   interrogative pronouns, 93
   personal pronouns, 93
   reflexive pronouns, 93
   relative pronouns, 93
Proofreader marks, 313-14
Proper noun, 119
Prose, 484
Punctuation
   abbreviations, 207-8
   for emphasis, 11

Q

Questions, series of, capitalization, 142
Quotation marks
   exact quotes, 148-49
   irony, 150
   slang, 150
   specialized terms, 149
   titles (literature), 149
   words used as words, 149-50
Quotations
   capitalization, 141
   listing of famous quotations, 376-432

R

Races, capitalization, 138
Redundancy, 484
Redundant words/phrases, 37-42
Reflexive (intensive) pronouns, 93, 119

Relative adjectives, 93, 119
Relative adverbs, 94, 119
Relative pronouns, 93, 119
Religion, capitalization, 141-42
Repetition, for emphasis, 11
Resolutions, capitalization, 142
Restrictive clause, 119
Rhyme, 484
Rivers, largest in world, 472
Root, 484
Russian
    abbreviations, 357
    alphabet, 356
    days of week, 358
    months, **358**
    numbers, 357
    seasons, 358
    time, 358

S

Schools/colleges/department/ courses,
    128-29
Scientific terms, listing of signs/symbols
    used, 310-13
Seas, 470
Seasons
    capitalization, 133
    French, 333
    German, 333
    Greek (modern), 343
    Italian, 347
    Latin, 355
    Russian, 358
    Spanish, 363
Semantics, 484
Ship names, italics, 146-147
Slang
    contemporary slang, 58-60
    nature of, 58
    quotation marks, 150
Solid compounds, 190-91
Spanish
    abbreviations, 359-61
    alphabet, 359
    days of week, 363
    months, 363

Spanish *(cont'd)*
    numbers, 361-62
    seasons, 363
    time, 363
Specialized terms, quotation marks, 149
Spelling
    abbreviations, 206-07
    combinations of *i* and *e*, 159
    commonly misspelled words, 162-70
    prefixes and, 171
    See also Suffixes, spelling.
Sports, 454-55
    capitalization of terms in, 142-43
Stars, brightest, 449-50
State birds, 437-38
State flowers, 435-37
States, abbreviations for, 303-4
Subject, 119
Subjunctive mood, 119
    verbs, 95, 109
Subordinate conjunctions, 96, 105, 119
Suffixes
    common suffixes, 185-88
    spelling
        doubling final consonant, 176-77
        not doubling final consonant,
          177-78
        words ending in *-action,* 181-82
        words ending in *-al,* 181
        words ending in *-ance, -ancy,*
         -ant, 183
        words ending in *-ar,* 182
        words ending in *-ary* and *-ery,* 183
        words ending in *-cede, -ceed,*
         -sede, 184
        words ending in *-ce* or *-ge,* 179-80
        words ending in *-ible,* 182
        words ending in *-ie,* 180
        words ending in *-ise, -ize, -yze,* 183
        words ending in silent *e,* 178-79
        words ending in *y,* 180-81
        word division, 199
Superlative degree, 93, 100, 119
Syllables, 484
    word division, 198
Symbols
    listing for scientific/technical terms,
        310-13

Symbols *(cont'd)*
 proofreader marks, 313-14
 words for
  beginning of sentence, 153
  chemical terms, 153
  measurement terms, 154
  money, 153-54
  percentages, 154
  tabular matter, 154
Synonyms, 6-8
Syntax, 484

T

Tabular matter, word versus symbol, 154
Tautology, 484
Technical terms
 abbreviations for, 239-66
 signs/symbols used, 310-13
Tense, 119
 See also Verbs.
Time
 French, 333
 German, 333
 Greek (modern), 343-344
 Italian, 347
 Latin, 355
 Russian, 358
 Spanish, 363
 word versus number symbol, 152
Titles (literature)
 capitalization, 126
 italics, 147
 quotation marks, 149
Titles (personal/professional),
  capitalization, 138-40
Tone language, 484
Transitional words/phrases, 9-10
Transitive verb, 94, 119
Transliteration, 484
Trees, of North America, 462-66
Tribes, capitalization, 138
Trite expression, 33-36

V

Vague words, 31-32

Verbal, 119
Verbs, 94-95, 119
 active voice, 114-15
 auxiliary verb, 94
 intransitive verb, 94
 irregular verbs, 110-13
 mood, 95
 number, 95
 passive voice, 114-15
 person, 95
 tenses
  future perfect tense, 108
  future tense, 108
  past perfect tense, 108
  past tense, 107
  present perfect tense, 107
  present tense, 107
 transitive verb, 94
Vernacular, 484
Vitamins, 450
Vocabulary, 484
Voice, 119
Vowel, 484
Vulgarism, 484

W

Word division
 abbreviations, 200
 contractions, 200
 dashes, uses of, 201
 double letters, 199-200, 201
 letters, 198-99
 names, 200
 numbers, 200-01
 prefixes, 199
 suffixes, 199
 syllables, 198
Word position, for emphasis, 11
Words
 numbers as
  beginning of sentence, 151
  centuries/decade, 152
  general rule, 151
  governmental references, 152
  measurement terms, 152
  money, 152
  time, 152

Words *(cont'd)*
    for symbols
        beginning of sentence, 153
        chemical terms, 153
        measurement terms, 154
        money, 153-54

Words *(cont'd)*
        percentages, 154
        tabular matter, 154
Words used as words
    italics, 145
    quotation marks, 149-50